Islam and Modern World

Islam
And
Modern World

Dilshad Hasan

Reference Press

4831/24, Ansari Road
Darya Ganj
New Delhi-110 002
Phone: 51563444
Fax: 51563334
E-mail: info@essessreference.com
url: http://www.essessreference.com

First Published 2005

ISBN: 81-88583-81-2

Rs.750/-

Published by:
Reference Press
4831/24, Ansari Road, Darya Ganj,
New Delhi-110 002.
Phone: 51563444
Fax: 51563334
E-mail: info@essessreference.com
url: http://www.essessreference.com

Printed in India at:
Mehra Offset Press, New Delhi

Contents

1

Basic Ideology

Heavenly Knowledge

Thanks to its undisputed authenticity, the text of the Quran holds a unique place among the books of Revelation, shared neither by the Old nor the New Testament. In the first two sections of this work, a review was made of the alterations undergone by the Old Testament and the Gospels before they were handed down to us in the form we know today. The same is not true for the Quran for the simple reason that it was written down at the time of the Prophet; we shall see how it came to be written, i.e. the process involved.

In this context, the differences separating the Quran from the Bible are in no way due to questions essentially concerned with date. Such questions are constantly put forward by certain people without regard to the circumstances prevailing at the time when the Judeo-Christian and the Quranic Revelations were written; they have an equal disregard for the circumstances surrounding the transmission of the Quran to the Prophet.

It is suggested that a Seventh century text had more likelihood of coming down to us unaltered than other texts that are as many as fifteen centuries older. This comment, although correct, does not constitute sufficient reason; it is made more to excuse the alterations made in the Judeo-Christian texts in the course of centuries than to underline the notion that the text of the Quran, which was more recent, had less to fear from being modified by man.

In the case of the Old Testament, the sheer number of authors who tell the same story, plus all the revisions carried out on the text of certain books from the pre-Christian era, constitute as many reasons for inaccuracy and contradiction. As for the Gospels, nobody can claim that they invariably contain faithful accounts of Jesus's words or a description of his actions strictly in keeping with reality. We have seen how successive versions of the texts showed a lack of definite authenticity and moreover that their authors were not eyewitnesses.

Also to be underlined is the distinction to be made between the Quran, a book of written Revelation, and the Hadiths, collections of statements concerning the actions and sayings of Muhammad. Some of the Prophet's companions started to write them down from the moment of his death. As an element of human error could have slipped in, the collection had to be resumed later and subjected to rigorous criticism so that the greatest credit is in practise given to documents that came along after Muhammad. Their authenticity varies, like that of the Gospels. Not a single Gospel was written down at the time of Jesus (they were all written long after his earthly mission had come to an end), and not a single collection of Hadiths was compiled during the time of the Prophet.

The situation is very different for the Quran. As the Revelation progressed, the Prophet and the believers following him recited the text by heart and it was also written down by the scribes in his following. It therefore starts off with two elements of authenticity that the Gospels do not possess. This continued up to the Prophet's death. At a time when not everybody could write, but everyone was able to recite, recitation afforded a considerable advantage because of the double-checking possible when the definitive text was compiled.

The Quranic Revelation was made by Archangel Jibbrail to Muhammad. It took place over a period of more than twenty years of the Prophet's life, beginning with the first verses of Sura 96, then resuming after a three-year break for a long period of twenty years up to the death of the Prophet in 632 A.D., i.e. ten years before Hegira and ten years after Hegira.

The following was the first Revelation —(96:1-5)

"Read: In the name of thy Lord who created,

Who created man from something which clings

Read ! Thy Lord is the most Noble

Who taught by the pen

Who taught man what he did not know."

Professor Hamidullah notes in the Introduction to his French translation of the Quran that one of the themes of this first Revelation was the 'praise of the pen as a means of human knowledge' which would 'explain the Prophet's concern for the preservation of the Quran in writing.'

Texts formally prove that long before the Prophet left Mecca for Medina (i.e. long before Hegira), the Quranic text so far revealed had been written down. We shall see how the Quran is authentic in this. We know that Muhammad and the believers who surrounded him were accustomed to reciting the revealed text from memory. It is therefore inconceivable for the Quran to refer to facts that did not square with reality because the latter could so easily be checked with people in the Prophet's following, by asking the authors of the transcription.

Four suras dating from a period prior to Hegira refer to the writing down of the Quran before the Prophet left Mecca in 622 A.D.

"By no means! Indeed it is a message of instruction

Therefore Whoever wills, should remember

On leaves held in honour

Exalted, purified

In the hands of scribes

Noble and pious."

Yusuf Ali, in the commentary to his translation, (1934), wrote that when the Revelation of this sura was made, forty-two or forty-five others had been written and were kept by Muslims in Mecca (out of a total of 114).

"Nay, this is a glorious reading

On a preserved tablet" —56: 21,22

> "This is a glorious reading
>
> In a book well kept
>
> Which none but the purified teach.
>
> This is a Revelation from the Lord of the Worlds."
>
> —25: 77-80

> "They said: Tales of the ancients which he has caused to be written and they are dictated to him morning and evening." —25: 5

Here we have a reference to the accusations made by the Prophet's enemies who treated him as an imposter. They spread the rumour that stories of antiquity were being dictated to him and he was writing them down or having them transcribed (the meaning of the word is debatable, but one must remember that Muhammad was illiterate). However this may be, the verse refers to this act of making a written record which is pointed out by Muhammad's enemies themselves.

A sura that came after Hegira makes one last mention of the leaves on which these divine instructions were written:

> "An (apostle) from God recites leaves
>
> Kept pure where are decrees right and straight."
>
> —98: 2-3

The Quran itself therefore provides indications as to the fact that it was set down in writing at the time of the Prophet. It is a known fact that there were several scribes in his following, the most famous of whom, Zaid Ibn Thabit, has left his name to posterity.

In the Preface to his French translation of the Quran (1971), Professor Hamidullah gives an excellent description of the conditions that prevailed when the text of the Quran was written, lasting up until the time of the Prophet's death:

> "The sources all agree in stating that whenever a fragment of the Quran was revealed, the Prophet called one of his literate companions and dictated it to him, indicating at the same time the exact position of the new fragment in the fabric of what had already been received.. . Descriptions note that Muhammad asked

> the scribe to reread to him what had been dictated so that he could correct any deficiencies. . . Another famous story tells how every year in the month of Ramadan, the Prophet would recite the whole of the Quran (so far revealed) to Jibbrail . . ., that in the Ramadan preceding Muhammad's death, Jibbrail had made him recite it twice ... It is known how since the Prophet's time, Muslims acquired the habit of keeping vigil during Ramadan, and of reciting the whole of the Quran in addition to the usual prayers expected of them. Several sources add that Muhammad's scribe Zaid was present at this final bringing-together of the texts. Elsewhere, numerous other personalities are mentioned as well."

Extremely diverse materials were used for this first record: parchment, leather, wooden tablets, camels' scapula, soft stone for inscriptions, etc.

At the same time however, Muhammad recommended that the faithful learn the Quran by heart. They did this for a part if not all of the text recited during prayers. Thus there were *Hafizun* who knew the whole of the Quran by heart and spread it abroad. The method of doubly preserving the text both in writing and by memorization proved to be extremely precious.

Not long after the Prophet's death (632), his successor Abu Bakr, the first Caliph of Islam, asked Muhammad's former head scribe, Zaid Ibn Thabit, to make a copy; this he did. On Umar's initiative (the future second Caliph), Zaid consulted all the information he could assemble at Medina: the witness of the *Hafizun,* copies of the Book written on various materials belonging to private individuals, all with the object of avoiding possible errors in transcription. Thus an extremely faithful copy of the Book was obtained.

The sources tell us that Caliph Umar, Abu Bakr's successor in 634, subsequently made a single volume *(mushaf)* that he preserved and gave on his death to his daughter Hafsa, the Prophet's widow.

The third Caliph of Islam, Uthman, who held the caliphate from

644 to 655, entrusted a commission of experts with the preparation of the great recension that bears his name. It checked the authenticity of the document produced under Abu Bakr which had remained in Hafsa's possession until that time. The commission consulted Muslims who knew the text by heart. The critical analysis of the authenticity of the text was carried out very rigorously. The agreement of the witnesses was deemed necessary before the slightest verse containing debatable material was retained. It is indeed known how some verses of the Quran correct others in the case of prescriptions: this may be readily explained when one remembers that the Prophet's period of apostolic activity stretched over twenty years (in round figures). The result is a text containing an order of suras that reflects the order followed by the Prophet in his complete recital of the Quran during Ramadan, as mentioned above.

One might perhaps ponder the motives that led the first three Caliphs, especially Uthman, to commission collections and recensions of the text. The reasons are in fact very simple: Islam's expansion in the very first decades following Muhammad's death was very rapid indeed and it happened among peoples whose native language was not Arabic. It was absolutely necessary to ensure the spread of a text that retained its original purity: Uthman's recension had this as its objective.

Uthman sent copies of the text of the recension to the centres of the Islamic Empire and that is why, according to Professor Hamidullah, copies attributed to Uthman exist in Tashkent and Istanbul. Apart from one or two possible mistakes in copying, the oldest documents known to the present day, that are to be found throughout the Islamic world, are identical; the same is true for documents preserved in Europe (there are fragments in the Bibliotheque National in Paris which, according to the experts, date from the Eighth and Ninth centuries A.D., i.e. the Second and Third Hegirian centuries). The numerous ancient texts that are known to be in existence all agree except for very minor variations which do not change the general meaning of the text at all. If the context sometimes allows more than one interpretation, it may well have to do with the fact that ancient writing was simpler than that of the present day.

The 114 suras were arranged in decreasing order of length; there were nevertheless exceptions. The chronological sequence of the Revelation was not followed. In the majority of cases however, this sequence is known. A large number of descriptions are mentioned at several points in the text, sometimes giving rise to repetitions. Very frequently a passage will add details to a description that appears elsewhere in an incomplete form. Everything connected with modern science are, like many subjects dealt with in the Quran, scattered throughout the book without any semblance of classification.

In contrast to the Old Testament, the Quran does not provide a unified description of the Creation. Instead of a continuous narration, there are passages scattered all over the Book which deal with certain aspects of the Creation and provide information on the successive events marking its development with varying degrees of detail. To gain a clear idea of how these events are presented, the fragments scattered throughout a large number of suras have to be brought together.

This dispersal throughout the Book of references to the same subject is not unique to the theme of the Creation. Many important subjects are treated in the same manner in the Quran: earthly or celestial phenomena, or problems concerning man that are of interest to scientists. For each of these themes, the same effort has been made here to bring all the verses together.

For many European commentators, the description of the Creation in the Quran is very similar to the one in the Bible and they are quite content to present the two descriptions side by side. I believe this concept is mistaken because there are very obvious differences. On subjects that are by no means unimportant from a scientific point of view. We find statements in the Quran whose equivalents we search for in vain in the Bible. The latter contains descriptions that have no equivalent in the Quran.

The obvious resemblances between the two texts are well known; among them is the fact that, at first glance, the number given to the successive stages of the Creation is identical: the six days in the Bible correspond to the six days in the Quran. In fact however, the problem is more complex than this and it is worth pausing to examine it.

There is absolutely no ambiguity whatsoever in the Biblical description of the Creation in six days followed by a day of rest, the sabbath, analogous with the days of the week. It has been shown how this mode of narration practiced by the priests of the Sixth century B.C. served the purpose of encouraging the people to observe the sabbath. All Jews were expected to rest on the sabbath as the Lord had done after he had laboured during the six days of the week.

The way the Bible interprets it, the word 'day' means the interval of time between two successive sunrises or sunsets for an inhabitant of the Earth. When defined in this way, the day is conditioned by the rotation of the Earth on its own axis. It is obvious that logically-speaking there can be no question of 'days' as defined just now, if the mechanism that causes them to appear—i.e. the existence of the Earth and its rotation around the Sun—has not already been fixed in the early stages of the Creation according to the Biblical description. This impossibility has already been emphasized in the first part of the present book.

When we refer to the majority of translations of the Quran, we read that—analogous with the Biblical description—the process of the Creation for the Islamic Revelation also took place over a period of six days. It is difficult to hold against the translators the fact that they have translated the Arabic word by its most common meaning. This is how it is usually expressed in translations so that in the Quran, verse 54, sura 7 reads as follows:

> "Your Lord is God Who created the heavens and the earth in six days."

There are very few translations and commentaries of the Quran that note how the word 'days' should really be taken to mean 'periods'. It has moreover been maintained that if the Quranic texts on the Creation divided its stages into 'days', it was with the deliberate intention of taking up beliefs held by all the Jews and Christians at the dawn of Islam and of avoiding a head-on confrontation with such a widely-held belief.

Without in any way wishing to reject this way of seeing it, one could perhaps examine the problem a little more closely and scrutinize in the Quran itself, and more generally in the language of the time, the possible meaning of the word that many translators themselves still continue to translate by the word 'day': *yaum,* plural *ayyam* in Arabic.

Its most common meaning is 'day' but it must be stressed that it tends more to mean the diurnal light than the length of time that lapses between one day's sunset and the next. The plural *ayyam* can mean, not just 'days', but also 'long length of time', an indefinite period of time (but always long). The meaning 'period of time' that the word contains is to be found elsewhere in the Quran. Hence the following:

> ". . . in a period of time *(yaum)* whereof the measure is a thousand years of your reckoning." —32:5

(It is to be noted that the Creation in six periods is precisely what the verse preceding verse 5 refers to).

> ". . . in a period of time *(yaum)* whereof the measure is 50,000 years." —70:4

The fact that the word *'yaum'* could mean a period of time that was quite different from the period that we mean by the word 'day' struck very early commentators who, of course, did not have the knowledge we possess today concerning the length of the stages in the formation of the Universe. In the Sixteenth century A.D. for example, Abu al Saud, who could not have had any idea of the day as it dawned astronomically in terms of the Earth's rotation, thought that for the Creation a division must be considered that was not into days as we usually understand the word, but into 'events' (in Arabic *nauba).*

Modern commentators have gone back to this interpretation. Yusuf Ali (1934), in his commentary on each of the verses that deals with the stages in the Creation, insists on the importance of taking the word, elsewhere interpreted as meaning 'days', to mean in reality 'very long Periods, or Ages, or Aeons'.

It is therefore possible to say that in the case of the Creation of the world, the Quran allows for long periods of time numbering six. It is obvious that modern science has not permitted man to establish the fact that the complicated stages in the process leading to the formation of the Universe numbered six, but it has clearly shown that long periods of time were involved compared to which 'days' as we conceive them would be ridiculous.

One of the longest passages of the Quran, which deals with the Creation, describes the latter by juxtaposing an account of earthly events and one of celestial events.

(God is speaking to the Prophet)

> "Say: Do you disbelieve Him Who created the earth in two periods? Do you ascribe equals to Him. He is the Lord of the Worlds.
>
> "He set in the (earth) mountains standing firm. He blessed it. He measured therein its sustenance in four periods, in due proportion, in accordance with the needs of those who ask for (sustenance or information?).
>
> "Moreover *(tumma)* He turned to heaven when it was smoke and said to it and to the earth: come willingly or unwillingly ! They said: we come in willing obedience.
>
> "Then He ordained them seven heavens in two periods, and He assigned to each heaven its mandate by Revelation. And We adorned the lower heaven with luminaries and provided it a guard. Such is the decree of the All Mighty, the Full of Knowledge."
>
> —41:9-12

These four verses of sura 41 contain several points to which we shall return: the initially gaseous state of celestial matter and the highly symbolic definition of the number of heavens as seven. We shall see the meaning behind this figure. Also of a symbolic nature is the dialogue between God on the one hand and the primordial sky and earth on the other: here however it is only to express the submission of the Heavens and Earth, once they were formed, to divine orders.

Critics have seen in this passage a contradiction with the statement of the six periods of the Creation. By adding the two periods of the formation of the Earth to the four periods of the spreading of its sustenance to the inhabitants, plus the two periods of the formation of the Heavens, we arrive at eight periods. This would then be in contradiction with the six periods mentioned above.

In fact however, this text, which leads man to reflect on divine Omnipotence, beginning with the Earth and ending with the Heavens, provides two sections that are expressed by the Arabic word *'tumma',* translated by 'moreover', but which also means 'furthermore' or 'then'. The sense of a 'sequence' may therefore be implied referring to a sequence of events or a series of man's reflections on the events mentioned here. It may equally be a simple reference to events juxtaposed without any intention of bringing in the notion of the one following the other. However this may be, the periods of the Creation of the Heavens may just as easily coincide with the two periods of the Earth's creation. A little later we shall examine how the basic process of the formation of the Universe is presented in the Quran and we shall see how it can be jointly applied to the Heavens and the Earth in keeping with modern ideas. We shall then realize how perfectly reasonable this way is conceiving the simultaneous nature of the events here described.

There does not appear to be any contradiction between the passage quoted here and the concept of the formation of the world in six stages that is to be found in other texts in the Quran.

In the two passages from the Quran quoted above, reference was made in one of the verses to the Creation of the Heavens and the Earth (sura 7, verse 54), and elsewhere to the Creation of the Earth and the Heavens (sura 41, verses 9 to 12). The Quran does not therefore appear to lay down a sequence for the Creation of the Heavens and the Earth.

The number of verses in which the Earth is mentioned first is quite small, e.g. sura 2, verse 29 and sura 20, verse 4, where a reference is made to "Him Who created the earth and the high heavens". The number of verses where the Heavens are mentioned before the Earth is, on the other hand, much larger: (sura 7, verse 54; sura 10, verse 3; sura 11, verse 7; sura 25, verse 59; sura 32, verse 4; sura 50, verse 38; sura 57, verse 4; sura 79, verses 27 to 33; sura 91, verses *5* to 10).

In actual fact, apart from sura 79, there is not a single passage in the Quran that lays down a definite sequence; a simple co-ordinating conjunction (iva) meaning 'and' links two terms, or the word *tumma* which, as has been seen in the above passage, can indicate either a simple juxtaposition or a sequence.

There appears to me to be only one passage in the Quran where a definite sequence is plainly established between different events in the Creation. It is contained in verses 27 to 33, sura 79:

> "Are you the harder to create or is it the heaven that (God) built? He raised its canopy and fashioned it with harmony. He made dark the night and he brought out the forenoon. And after that *(bada dalika)* He spread it out. Therefrom he drew out its water and its pasture. And the mountains He has fixed firmly. Goods for you and your cattle."

This list of earthly gifts from God to man, which is expressed in a language suited to farmers or nomads on the Arabian Peninsula, is preceded by an invitation to reflect on the creation of the heavens. The reference to the stage when God spreads out the earth and renders it arable is very precisely situated in time after the alternating of night and day has been achieved. Two groups are therefore referred to here, one of celestial phenomena, and the other of earthly phenomena articulated in time. The reference made here implies that the earth must necessarily have existed before being spread out and that it consequently existed when God created the Heavens. The idea of a concomitance therefore arises from the heavenly and earthly evolutions with the interlocking of the two phenomena. Hence, one must not look for any special significance in the reference in the Quranic text to the Creation of the Earth before the Heavens or the Heavens before the Earth: the position of the words does not influence the order in which the Creation took place, unless however it is specifically stated.

Creation of Worlds : The Quran presents in two verses a brief synthesis of the phenomena that constituted the basic process of the formation of the Universe:

> "Do not the Unbelievers see that the heavens and the earth were joined together, then We clove thorn as under and We got every living thing out of the water. Will they not then believe?" —(21 : 30)

God orders the Prophet to speak after inviting him to reflect on the subject of the earth's creation:

> "Moreover (God) turned to the Heaven when it was smoke and said to it and to the earth . . ."
>
> —(41 : 11)

There then follow the orders to submit, referred to earlier.

We shall come back to the aquatic origins of life and examine them along with other biological problems raised by the Quran. The important things to remember at present are the following:

(a) The statement of the existence of a gaseous mass with fine particles, for this is how the word 'smoke' *(dukan* in Arabic) is to be interpreted. Smoke is generally made up of a gaseous substratum, plus, in more or less stable suspension, fine particles that may belong to solid and even liquid states of matter at high or low temperature;

(b) The reference to a separation process *(fatq)* of a primary single mass whose elements were initially fused together *(raff).* It must be noted that in Arabic *'fatq'* is the action of breaking, diffusing, separating, and that *'ratq* is the action of fusing or binding together elements to make a homogenous whole.

This concept of the separation of a whole into several parts is noted in other passages of the Book with reference to multiple worlds. The first verse of the first sura in the Quran proclaims, after the opening invocation, the following: "In the name of God the Beneficent, the Merciful", "Praise be to God. Lord of the Worlds."

The terms 'worlds' reappears dozens of times in the Quran. The Heavens are referred to as multiple as well, not only on account of their plural form, but also because of their symbolic numerical quantity:

> This number is used 24 times throughout the Quran for various numerical quantities. It often carries the meaning of 'many' although we do not know exactly why this meaning of the figure was used. The Greeks and Romans also seem to have used the number 7 to mean an undefined idea of plurality. In the Quran,

the number 7 refers to the Heavens themselves *(samawat)*. It alone is understood to mean 'Heavens'. The 7 roads of the Heavens are mentioned once:

> "(God) is the One Who created for you all that is on the earth. Moreover He turned to the heaven and fashioned seven heavens with harmony. He is Full of Knowledge of all things." —(2:29)

> "And We have created above you seven paths: We have never been unmindful of the Creation." —(23:17)

> "(God) is the One Who created seven heavens one above another. Thou canst see no fault in the creation of the Beneficent. Turn the vision again! Canst thou see any rift?" —(67:3)

> "Did you see how God created seven heavens one above another and made the moon a light therein and made the sun a lamp?" —(71:15-16)

> "We have built above you seven strong (heavens) and placed a blazing lamp." —(78:12)

Here the blazing lamp is the Sun.

The commentators on the Quran are in agreement on all these verses: the number 7 means no more than plurality.

There are therefore many Heavens and Earths, and it comes as no small surprise to the reader of the Quran to find that earths such as our own may be found in the Universe, a fact that has not yet been verified by man in our time.

Verse 12 of sura 65 does however predict the following:

> "God is the One Who created seven heavens and of the earth *(ard)* a similar number. The Command descends among them so that you know that God has power over all things and comprehends all things in His knowledge."

Since 7 indicates an indefinite plurality (as we have seen), it is possible to conclude that the Quranic text clearly indicates the existence of more than one single Earth, our own Earth *(ard)*; there are others like it in the Universe.

Another observation which may surprise the Twentieth century reader of the Quran is the fact that verses refer to three groups of things created, i.e.

— things in the Heavens

— things on the Earth

— things between the Heavens and the Earth Here are several of these verses:

"To Him (God) belongs what is in the heavens, on earth, between them and beneath the soil."—(20:6)

". . . the One Who created the heavens, the earth and what is between them in six periods." —(25:59)

"God is the One Who created the heavens, the earth and what is between them in six periods." —(32:4)

"We created the heavens, the earth and what is between them in six periods, and no weariness touched us".

The reference in the Quran to 'what is between the Heavens and the Earth' is again to be found in the following verses: sura 21, verse 16; sura 44, verses 7 and 38; sura 78, verse 37; sura 15, verse 85; sura 46, verse 3; sura 43, verse 85.

This Creation outside the Heavens and outside the Earth, mentioned several times, is *a priori* difficult to imagine. To understand these verses, reference must be made to the most recent human observations on the existence of cosmic extragalactic material and one must indeed go back to ideas established by contemporary science on the formation of the Universe, starting with the simplest and proceeding to the most complex. These are the subjects of the following paragraph.

Before passing on to these purely scientific matters however, it is advisable to recapitulate the main points on which the Quran gives us information about the creation. According to the preceding quotations, they are as follows:

(1) Existence of six periods for the Creation in general.

(2) Interlocking of stages in the Creation of the Heavens and the Earth.

(3) Creation of the Universe out of an initially unique mass forming a block that subsequently split up.

(4) Plurality of the Heavens and of the Earths.

(5) Existence of an intermediary creation 'between the Heavens and the Earth'.

Galaxies and Sun : The Earth and planets rotating around the Sun constitute an organised world of dimensions which, to our human scale, appear quite colossal. The Earth is, after all, roughly 93 million miles from the Sun. This is a very great distance for a human being, but it is very small in comparison to the distance separating the Sun from the furthermost planet from it in the solar system (Pluto) ; in round numbers it is 40 times the distance from the Earth to the Sun, i.e. approximately 3,672 million miles away. This distance, when doubled, represents the largest dimension of our solar system. The Sun's light takes nearly 6 hours to reach Pluto, and yet the journey is made at the terrifying speed of over 186,000 miles per second. The light coming from stars on the very confines of the known celestial world therefore takes billions of years to reach us.

The Sun, of which we are a satellite like the other planets surrounding it, is itself an infinitesimally small element among a hundred billion stars that form a whole, called a galaxy. On a fine summer night, the whole of space seems to be filled with stars that make up what is known as the Milky Way. This group has extremely large dimensions. Whereas light could cross the solar system in units of one hour, it would require something like 90,000 years to go from one extreme to the other of the most compact group of stars that make up our galaxy.

The galaxy that we belong to however, even though it is so incredibly huge, is only a small part of the Heavens. There are giant agglomerates of stars similar to the Milky Way that lie outside our galaxy. They were discovered a little over fifty years ago, when astronomy was able to make use of an optical instrument as sophisticated as the one that made possible the construction of the Mount Wilson telescope in the United States. Thus a very large number indeed of isolated galaxies and masses of galaxies have been discovered that are so far away that it was necessary to institute a special unit of light-years, the 'parsec' (the distance light travels in 3.26 years at 186,000 miles per second).

What was there originally in the immensely large space the galaxies now occupy? Modern science can only answer this question as of a certain period in the evolution of the Universe; it cannot put into numbers the length of time that separates this period from us.

Since the earliest time it can provide us with, modern science has every reason to maintain that the Universe was formed of a gaseous mass principally composed of hydrogen and a certain amount of helium that was slowly rotating. This nebula subsequently split up into multiple fragments with very large dimensions and masses, so large indeed, that specialists in astrophysics are able to estimate their mass from 1 to 100 billion times the present mass of the Sun (the latter represents a mass that is over 300,000 times that of the Earth). These figures give an idea of the large size of the fragments of primary gaseous mass that were to give birth to the galaxies.

A new fragmentation was to form the stars. There then followed the intervention of a condensing process where gravitational forces came into play, (since these bodies were moving and rotating more and more quickly), along with pressures and the influence of magnetic fields and of radiations. The stars became shiny as they contracted and transformed the gravitational forces into thermal energy. Thermonuclear reactions came into play, and heavier atoms were formed by fusion at the expense of others that were lighter; this is how the transition was made from hydrogen to helium, then to carbon and oxygen, ending with metals and metalloids. Thus the stars have a life of their own and modern astronomy classifies them according to their present stage of evolution. The stars also have a death; in the final stage of their evolution, the violent implosion of certain stars has been observed so that they become veritable 'corpses'.

The planets, and in particular the Earth, originated in a separation process starting from an initial constituent that in the beginning was the primary nebula. A fact that has no longer been contested for over twenty-five years is that the Sun condensed inside the single nebula and that the planets did the same inside the surrounding nebular disc. One must stress—and this is of prime importance for the subject in hand—that there was no sequence in the formation of the celestial elements such as the Sun nor in the formation of an earthly element. There is an evolutionary parallelism with the identity of origin.

Here, science can give us information on the period during which the events just mentioned took place. Having estimated the age of our galaxy at roughly ten billion years, according to this hypothesis, the formation of the solar system took place a little over billion years later. The study of natural radio activity makes it possible to place the age of the Earth and the time the Sun was formed at 4.5 billion years ago, to within a present-day accuracy of 100 million years, according to some scientists' calculations. This accuracy is to be admired, since 100 million years may represent a long time to us but the ratio 'maximum error/total time-to-be-measured' is 0.1/4.5, i.e. 2.2%.

Specialists in astrophysics have therefore attained a high degree of knowledge concerning the general process involved in the formation of the solar system. It may be summarized as follows: condensation and contraction of a rotating gaseous mass, splitting up into fragments that leave the Sun and planets in their places, among them the Earth. The knowledge that science has gained on the primary nebula and the way it split up into an incommensurable quantity of stars grouped into galaxies leaves absolutely no doubt as to the legitimacy of a concept of the plurality of worlds. It does not however provide any kind of certainty concerning the existence in the Universe of anything that might, either closely or vaguely, resemble the Earth.

Many a World : In spite of the above, modern specialists in astrophysics consider it highly likely that planets similar to Earth are present in the Universe. As far as the solar system is concerned, nobody seriously entertains the possibility of finding general conditions similar to those on Earth on another planet in this system. We must therefore seek for them outside the solar system. The likelihood of their existing outside it is considered quite probable for the following reasons:

It is thought that in our galaxy half of the 100 billion stars must, like the Sun, have a planetary system. The fifty billion stars do indeed, like the Sun, rotate very slowly; a characteristic which suggests that they are surrounded by planets that are their satellites. These stars are so far away that the possible planets are unobservable, but their existence is thought to be highly probable on account of certain trajectory characteristics; a slight undulation of the star's trajectory indicates the presence of a companion planetary satellite. Thus the Barnard Star probably has at least one planetary companion with a mass greater than that of Jupiter and may even have two satellites. As P. Guerin writes: "All the evidence point to the fact that planetary systems are scattered in profusion all over the universe. The solar system and the Earth are not unique." And as a corollary: "Life, like the planets that harbour it, is scattered throughout the universe, in those places where the physicochemical conditions necessary for its flowering and development are to be found."

The basic process in the formation of the Universe therefore lay in the condensation of material in the primary nebula followed by its division into fragments that originally constituted galactic masses. The latter in their turn split up into stars that provided the sub-product of the process, i.e. the planets. These successive separations left among the groups of principle elements what one might perhaps call 'remains'. Their more scientific name is 'interstellar galactic material'. It has been described in various ways; there are bright nebulae that reflect the light received from other stars and are perhaps composed of 'dusts' or 'smokes', to use the terminology of experts in astrophysics, and then there are the dark nebulae that are less dense, consisting of interstellar material that is even more modest, known for its tendency to interfere with photometric measurements in astronomy. There can be no doubt about the existence of 'bridges' of material between the galaxies themselves. Although these gases may be very rarefied, the fact that they occupy such a colossal space, in view of the great distance separating the galaxies, could make them correspond to a mass possibly greater than the total mass of the galaxies in spite of the low density of the former. A. Boichot considers the presence of these intergalactic masses to be of prime importance which could "considerably alter ideas on the evolution of the Universe."

We must now go back to the basic ideas on the Creation of the Universe that were taken from the Quran and look at them in the light of modern scientific data.

We shall examine the five main points on which the Quran gives information about the Creation.

(1) The six periods of the Creation of the Heavens and the Earth covered, according to the Quran, the formation of the celestial bodies and the Earth, and the development of the latter until (with its 'sustenance') it became inhabitable by man. In the case of the Earth, the events described in the Qurah happened over four periods. One could perhaps see in them the four geological periods described by modern science, with man's appearance, as we already know, taking place in the quaternary era. This is purely a hypothesis since nobody has an answer to this question.

It must be noted however, that the formation of the heavenly bodies and the Earth, as explained in verses 9 to 12, sura 41 required two phases. If we take the Sun and its sub-product the earth as an example (the only one accessible to us), science informs us that their formation occurred by a process of condensation of the primary nebula and then their separation. This is exactly what the Quran expresses very clearly when it refers to the processes that produced a fusion and subsequent separation starting from a celestial 'smoke'. Hence there is complete correspondence between the facts of the Quran and the facts of science.

(2) Science showed the interlocking of the two stages in the formation of a star (like the Sun) and its satellite (like the Earth). This interconnection is surely very evident in the text of the Quran examined.

(3) The existence at an early stage of the Universe of the 'smoke' referred to in the Quran, meaning the predominately gaseous state of the material that composes it, obviously corresponds to the concept of the primary nebula put forward by modern science.

(4) The plurality of the heavens, expressed in the Quran by the number 7, whose meaning we have discussed, is

confirmed by modern science due to the observations experts in astrophysics have made on galactic systems and their very large number. On the other hand the plurality of earths that are similar to ours (from certain points of view at least) is an idea that arises in the text of the Quran but has not yet been demonstrated to be true by science; all the same, specialists consider this to be quite feasible.

(5) The existence of an intermediate creation between 'the Heavens' and 'the Earth' expressed in the Quran may be compared to the discovery of those bridges of material present outside organised astronomic systems.

Although not all the questions raised by the descriptions in the Quran have been completely confirmed by scientific data, there is in any case absolutely no opposition between the data in the Quran on the Creation and modern knowledge on the formation of the Universe. This fact is worth stressing for the Quranic Revelation, whereas it is very obvious indeed that the present-day text of the Old Testament provides data on the same events that are unacceptable from a scientific point of view. It is hardly surprising, since the description of the Creation in the Sacerdotal version of the Bible was written by priests at the time of the deportation to Babylon who had the legalist intentions already described and therefore compiled a description that fitted their theological views. The existence of such an enormous difference between the Biblical description and the data in the Quran concerning the creation is worth underlining once again on account of the totally gratuitous accusations leveled against Muhammad since the beginnings of Islam to the effect that he copied the Biblical descriptions. As far as the Creation is concerned, this accusation is totally unfounded. How could a man living fourteen hundred years ago have made corrections to the existing description to such an extent that he eliminated scientifically inaccurate material and, on his own initiative, made statements that science has been able to verify only in the present day? This hypothesis is completely untenable. The description of the Creation given in the Quran is quite different from the one in the Bible.

Indisputably, resemblances do exist between narrations dealing with other subjects, particularly religious history, in the Bible and in the Quran. It is moreover interesting to note from this point of view how nobody holds against Jesus the fact that he takes up the same sort of facts and Biblical teachings. This does not, of course, stop people in the West from accusing Muhammad (PBUH) of referring to such facts in his teaching with the suggestion that he is an imposter because he presents them as a Revelation. As for the proof that Muhammad (PBUH) reproduced in the Quran what he had been told or dictated by the rabbis, it has no more substance than the statement that a Christian monk gave him a sound religious education. One would do well to reread what R. Blachere in his book, *The Problem of Muhammad* (Le Probleme de Mahomet), has to say about this 'fable'.

A hint of a resemblance is also advanced between other statements in the Quran and beliefs that go back a very long way, probably much further in time than the Bible.

More generally speaking, the traces of certain cosmogenic myths have been sought in the Holy Scriptures; for example the belief held by the Polynesians in the existence of primeval waters that were covered in darkness until they separated when light appeared; thus Heaven and Earth were formed. This myth is compared to the description of the Creation in the Bible, where, there is undoubtedly a resemblance. It would however be superficial to then accuse the Bible of having copied this from the cosmogenic myth.

It is just as superficial to see the Quranic concept of the division of the primeval material constituting the Universe at its initial stage — a concept held by modern science — as one that comes from various cosmogenic myths in one form or another that express something resembling it.

It is worth analysing these mythical beliefs and descriptions more closely. Often an initial idea appears among them which is reasonable in itself, and is in some cases borne out by what we today know (or think we know) to be true, except that fantastic descriptions are attached to it in the myth. This is the case of the fairly widespread concept of the Heavens and the Earth originally being united then subsequently separated. When, as in Japan, the image of the egg plus an expression of chaos is attached to the above with the idea of a seed inside the egg (as for all eggs), the imaginative addition makes the concept lose all semblance of seriousness. In other countries, the idea of a plant is associated with it; the plant grows and in so doing raises up the sky and separates the Heavens from the Earth. Here again, the imaginative quality of the added detail lends the myth its very distinctive character. Nevertheless a common characteristic remains, i.e. the notion of a single mass at the beginning of the evolutionary process leading to the formation of the Universe which then divided to form the various 'worlds' that we know today.

The reason these cosmogenic myths are mentioned here is to underline the way they have been embroidered by man's imagination and to show the basic difference between them and the statements in the Quran on the same subject. The latter are free from any of the whimsical details accompanying such beliefs; on the contrary, they are distinguished by the sober quality of the words in which they are made and their agreement with scientific data.

Such statements in the Quran concerning the Creation, which appeared nearly fourteen centuries ago, obviously do not lend themselves to a human explanation.

Stars and the Holy Book : The Quran is full of reflections on the Heavens. In the preceding chapter on the Creation, we saw how the plurality of the Heavens and Earths was referred to, as well as what the Quran calls an intermediary creation 'between the Heavens and the Earth': modern science has verified the latter. The verses referring to the creation already contain a broad idea of what is to be found in the heavens, i.e. of everything outside the earth.

Apart from the verses that specifically describe the Creation, there are roughly another forty verses in the Quran which provide information on astronomy complementing what has already been given. Some of them are not much more than reflections on the glory of the Creator, the Organizer of all the stellar and planetary systems. These we know to be arranged according to balancing positions whose stability Newton explained in his law of the mutual attraction of bodies.

The first verses to be quoted here hardly furnish much material for scientific analysis: the aim is simply to draw attention to God's omnipotence. They must be mentioned however to give a realistic idea of the way the Quranic text described the organization of the Universe fourteen centuries ago.

These references constitute a new fact of divine Revelation. The organization of the world is treated in neither the Gospels nor the Old Testament (except for a few notions whose general inaccuracy we have already seen in the Biblical description of the Creation). The Quran however deals with this subject in depth. What it describes is important, but so is what it does not contain. It does not in fact provide an account of the theories prevalent at the time of the Revelation that deal with the organization of the celestial world, theories that science was later to show were inaccurate. An example of this will be given later. This negative consideration must however be pointed out.

The subject is man in general.

> "Do they not look at the sky above them, how We have built it and adorned it, and there are no rifts in it."
> —(50:16)
>
> "(God) created the heavens without any pillars that you can see..." —(31:10)
>
> "God is the One Who raised the heavens without any pillars that you can see, then He firmly established Himself on the throne and He subjected the sun and moon. . ." —(13:2)
>
> These two verses refute the belief that the vault of the heavens was held up by pillars, the only things preventing the former from crushing the earth.
>
> "the sky (God) raised it . . ." —(55:7)
>
> "(God) holds back the sky from falling on the earth unless by His leave . . ." —(22:65)

It is known how the remoteness of celestial masses at great distance and in proportion to the magnitude of their mass itself constitutes the foundation of their equilibrium. The more remote the masses are, the weaker the force that attracts one to the other is. The nearer they are, the stronger the attraction is that one has to the other: this is true for the Moon, which is near to the Earth (astronomically speaking) and exercises an influence by laws of attraction on the position occupied by the waters of the sea, hence the phenomenon of the tides. If two celestial bodies come too close to one another, collision is inevitable. The fact that they are subjected to an order is the *sine qua non* for the absence of disturbances.

The subjection of the Heavens to divine order is often referred to as well:

> God is speaking to the Prophet.
>
> "Say: Who is Lord of the seven heavens and Lord of the tremendous throne?" —(23:86)

We have already seen how by 'seven heavens' what is meant is not 7, but an indefinite number of heavens.

> "For you (God) subjected all that is in the heavens and on the earth, all from Him. Behold! In that are signs for people who reflect." —(45:13)
>
> "The sun and moon (are subjected) to calculations" —(55:5)
>
> " (God) appointed the night for rest and the sun and the moon for reckoning."
>
> "For you (God) subjected the sun and the moon, both diligently pursuing their courses. And for you He subjected the night and the day." —(14:33)

Here one verse completes another: the calculations referred to result in the regularity of the course described by the heavenly bodies in question, this is expressed by the word *daib,* the present participle of a verb whose original meaning was 'to work eagerly and assiduously at something'. Here it is given the meaning of 'to apply oneself to something with care in a perseverance and invariable manner, in accordance with set habits'.

God is speaking:

> "And for the moon We have appointed mansions till she returns like an old shriveled palm branch." —(36 : 39)

This is a reference to the curled form of the palm branch which, as it shrivels up, takes on the moon's crescent. This commentary will be completed later.

> "For you (God) subjected the night and the day, the sun and the moon; the stars are in subjection to His Command. Verily in this are signs for people who are wise." —(16:12)

The practical angle from which this perfect celestial order is seen is underlined on account of its value as an aid to man's travel on earth and by sea, and to his calculation of time. This comment becomes clear when one bears in mind the fact that the Quran was originally a preaching addressed to men who only understood the simple language of their everyday lives. This explains the presence of the following reflections:

> "(God) is the One Who has set out for you the stars, that you may guide yourselves by them through the darkness of the land and of the sea. We have detailed the Signs for people who know." —(16:97)

> "(God sets on the earth) landmarks and by the stars (men) guide themselves." —(16:16)

> "God is the One Who made the sun a shining glory and the moon a light and for her ordained mansions, so that you might know the number of years and the reckoning (of the time). God created this in truth. He explains the Signs in detail for people who know."

This calls for some comment. Whereas the Bible calls the Sun and Moon 'lights', and merely adds to one the adjective 'greater' and to the other 'lesser', the Quran ascribes differences other than that of dimension to each respectively. Agreed, this is nothing more than a verbal distinction, but how was one to communicate to men at this time without confusing them, while at the same time expressing the notion that the Sun and Moon were not absolutely identical 'lights'?

2

Contemporary Significance

Glory and Grandeur

Having dealt with the present state of Islam in the Islamic world, it is now necessary to turn to more specific problems caused by the advent of modernism within the mind of those Muslims of various Islamic lands who, while modernized, still concern themselves with Islam and its history. In contrast to traditional Islamic scholarship, where in all branches of the sciences terms are clearly defined and always used with a specific meaning in mind, there has appeared during the past century among a large number of modernized Muslims dealing with their own tradition a tendency toward ambiguity and the careless use of many important terms, a tendency which reflects a confused state of mind to say the least. Words and expressions have been used by many of them in such a way as to betray the state of cultural shock and often the sense of inferiority vis-a-vis the West from which they suffer.

Their writings reveal most of all a slavery of the mind to the norms and judgments of Western civilization. Moreover, these norms are usually hidden under the veil of an 'Islam' of which there often remains little more than a name and certain emotional attachments, an Islam which has become devoid of the intellectual and spiritual truth which stands at the heart of the Islamic revelation. In the present analysis, it is our aim to discuss three widely used expressions, namely 'decadence', 'deviation' and 'renaissance', which are employed often in reference to Islamic history and to the present-day Islamic world, and which reflect in a profound fashion the attitude of a certain type of modernized Muslim toward the whole of Islam as a religion and as an historical reality.

Meaning of Decadence : Let us begin with the term 'decadence', which appears very often in the writings of modern Muslim scholars, who continually refer to the condition of the Islamic world before the advent of modernism as one that could aptly be described as 'decadent'. This value judgement immediately raises the following question: "decadence with respect to what, or in respect to which norm?' There must be a norm by which something is measured and in relation to which it is judged to have decayed. Here, while some take the early centuries of Islam as a norm, most often it is the value-system adopted consciously or unconsciously from the modern West that provides, in a hidden and subtle manner, the norm and criterion for determining the state of decadence.

This can be best illustrated by the question of science understood in its current Western sense. Many modernized Muslims, like so many other Orientals, equate science with civilization and judge the value of any human society and its culture by whether or not it has produced science, disregarding completely the lessons of the history of science itself. Islamic civilization is then considered to have begun to decay when it ceased to produce outstanding scientists as the West understands the function of the scientist today. And even the date of this cessation of activity is taken by most Muslim writers from Western sources, where, until very recently, interest in all aspects of Islamic intellectual life has for the most part been limited to the period when Islam influenced the West. As a result, everything in Islam from philosophy to mathematics suddenly 'decays' mysteriously somewhere around the seventh/thirteenth century, exactly when the intellectual contact between Islam and the West came, for all practical purposes, to an end. Modern Muslim authors who hold this opinion do not even bother to do any research of their own or even to delve into the more recent and less-known research of those Western scholars who have shown how important Islamic astronomy was in the ninth fifteenth century or how actively Islamic medicine was pursued in Persia and India until the eighteenth century.

The result of this concept of decadence, which is based upon the modern Western criteria for 'civilization' in its worldly aspect rather than on the traditional Islamic perspective which looks upon the Medina community as the most perfect Islamic society—a society according to which all other Islamic 'societies' are judged—has been to atrophy the minds of young Muslims and make them lose confidence in themselves and in their own culture. Rather than depicting the decadence which did take place in the Islamic world as a gradual and normal process of 'aging' and of becoming ever farther removed in time from the celestial origin of the revelation, and without, moreover, emphasizing the very recent nature of this decadence, such authors present the fantastic and abhorrent theory that the Islamic world began to decay in the seventh/thirteenth century. They remain completely oblivious of the fact that if this had been the case it would have been impossible for Islam to continue to nurture a vast civilization and remain a living force to this day. They brush aside such masterpieces of art as the Shah Mosque of Isfahan, the Blue Mosque of Istanbul, or the Taj Mahal, or the literary masterpieces of a Jami or a Saib Tabrizi, or the metaphysical and theological syntheses of a Mulla Sadra or a Sheikh Ahmad Sirhindi, not to speak of the ever-living spiritual tradition of Islam contained within Sufism, which has continued to produce great saints to this day. Surely, had decadence, as envisaged by those modernized Muslim writers who have adopted completely Western norms of judgment, taken hold of the Islamic world at the early date so often posited by this group, there would have been no Islamic civilization left for such a group to 'revive' during the present century. Islamic civilization would have died out long ago and become only a subject of archaeological interest, as in fact so many orientalists would like to consider it.

Meaning of Deviation : As for the term 'deviation', it is in fact rarely used by modernists, and is seen only in the writings of the more orthodox Muslim writers who are still aware of the presence of a spiritual and religious norm by which to judge any human society including their own, for to speak of 'tradition' in the widest sense of the word al-din is also to speak of the possibility of deviation. In fact, in the place where this term should be used, namely in reference to modern Western civilization, which is itself a major deviation and anomaly, not to say 'monstrosity' to use the words of R. Guenon, the group of modern writers with whom we are concerned shy away from utilizing it, again precisely because they lack an objective norm with which to judge the temporal flux determining the specific conditions of time and space of any particular 'world', a norm which must of necessity transcend this flux. This is all the more startling since traditional Islamic sources provide all the material that is necessary to discover such a norm and to formulate such a critique in a language comprehensible to contemporary man.

When we come to the word 'renaissance, we find a profusion of the wildest uses of this term in nearly every context, ranging from art and literature to politics. The modernists never tire of speaking of nearly every form of activity in the Islamic world as a renaissance, whose Arabic translation, al-nahdah, has become such a prevalent word in contemporary Arabic literature. There is something insidious about the carefree use of this word, for it recalls the Renaissance in the West when the rebirth of certain elements of Graeco-Roman paganism, deadly from the spiritual point of view—not the positive elements of this ancient tradition which had already been integrated into Christianity by the Church Fathers, especially St. Augustine—dealt a staggering blow to Christian civilization and prevented it from reaching its natural period of flowering as a Christian civilization. One cannot but recall in connection with the Renaissance the coming to life once again in the West of the Promethean and Titanesque spirit which stands at the very antipode of Islam. What many Muslims today often take as renaissance is usually precisely the rebirth in one form or another of the very forces that Islam came to supplant, forces which are identified in the traditional Muslim imagery with the age of ignorance waji ullah.

That is not to say that a form of 'renaissance' in a particular domain is impossible, for the appearance of a great saint can cause a 'renaissance' of spirituality in a particular region of the Islamic world. A great master of Islamic art can revive a particular artistic form, or a powerful intellectual figure can cause the revival of some aspects of Islamic intellectual life, provided he is himself genuinely rooted in the Islamic intellectual tradition. But most of what is paraded as 'renaissance' today is nothing of the kind. How often has a directly anti-Islamic form of thought been hailed as the 'renaissance' of Islamic thought, or an activity directly opposed to the teachings of the Shariah as an Islamic social renaissance! Intellectual honesty would require us at least to avoid using the epithet 'Islamic', even if the term 'renaissance' must, for some reason, be employed. Here again, it is the lack of vision of the objective Islamic norms which causes many people entranced by the errors of the modern world to identify simply any change and activity in the Islamic world with an Islamic renaissance, in the same way that in the secular world of the West and its dependencies in other continents any change is equated with 'progress' and 'development', even if this change is in every way a debasement and diminution of the quality of human life.

In all these cases, the common error results from the loss of vision of the objective, transcendent and immutable Islamic principles which alone can enable one to judge from an Islamic point of view whether a particular form or activity or period of human society is decadent, deviated or resurgent with the characteristics of a true renaissance. Without the Absolute the relative can never be fully understood, and without the immutable one cannot gauge the direction of flow of that which changes. But because of a 'metaphysical myopia' combined with a blind submission to the follies of the modern West, which has lost its vision of the Immutable, the group of modernized Muslims under discussion possess neither the intellectual vision to perceive the immutable essences of things, their malakut in Quranic terminology, nor the binding faith to remain steadfast to the norm established by the prophetic tradition (Sunnah and Hadith). Since the first of these ways of reaching the immutable principles of things is of an intellectual and spiritual order, it is brushed aside by the modernists of the type in question without too much popular opposition, and their energy is then concentrated on the subversion of normal faith in the immutable structure of traditional Islam, an undertaking which, because of its clearly religious colour, is bound to arouse greater opposition among believing Muslims. But in both cases the ultimate motive is the same. It is to remove the only objective Islamic criteria according to which one could judge present day Islamic society and in fact the modern world in general.

The desire to remove these objective and God-given criteria becomes, therefcre, concentrated in the attempt to weaken, in the eyes of faithful Muslims, the trans-historical significance of the prophetic Sunnah and Hadith by subjecting them to the so-called method of 'historical criticism', according to which the absence of the record of something is usually equated with the non-existence of the thing itself. The Holy Prophet provides for Muslims, both individually and collectively, the perfect norm for their private and collective lives. As long as his Sunnah is respected and kept intact, there remains within the Islamic community a divinely appointed norm by which to judge human behaviour and, along with the Holy Book itself, the means to provide the basis for the collective life of human society as well as for the inner religious life of its members.

The attack against the integrity of the Hadith literature has as one of its major objectives, whether realized consciously or not, to remove the divinely ordained criterion for judging Muslims and therefore to leave the door open for men to follow the line of least resistance before modernism and to surrender to their passions or to the transient fashions of the day, however demonic they may be. All of this is done, moreover, in the name of an 'Islamic renaissance' and by criticizing as reactionary or decadent any group which refuses to imitate blindly the cheapest products of Western civilization. The ambiguous and often wishy-washy judgments of many of the modernists with respect to Islam, past and present, is inseparable from the attempt to blur the clear example and norm for human life provided by the Quran and the Sunnah. And, conversely, many orthodox Muslims who have sought to defend the integrity of Islam have found it necessary to emphasize over and over again the significance of the prophetic norm as contained in the Hadith and Sunnah, without which even the message of the Holy Quran would become, in many parts, incomprehensible to men.

It may now be asked, 'Once this criticism has been made of the prevalent use of such terms as renaissance, decadence and deviation, what can these terms really signify if we accept the full authority of the Quran and the Sunnah, as well as the gradual unfolding of the tradition in stages to our own day?' To this question one can give a precise answer, which, however, because of the difference in premisses and point of departure, will be very different from that given by the modernist group in question.

Meaning of Renaissance : Renaissance in the Islamic sense can only mean a rebirth, or literally renaissance, of Islamic principles and norms, and not just a rebirth of no matter what. Every sign of life is not a sign of spiritual life, and every activity that occurs among Muslim peoples is not necessarily an Islamic activity, especially during this age of the eclipse of so many aspects of the Truth. A renaissance in its Islamic sense would correspond to tajdid, or renewal, which in its traditional context is identified with the function of a renewer or mujaddid. Islamic history has been witness to many renaissances in the true sense of the word in the form of the activity of a mujaddid in one part or another of the Islamic world. But always such a mujaddid has been the embodiment par excellence of the principles of Islam, which he has sought to re-instate and apply to a particular situation. He thus differs profoundly from the 'reformer' in the modern sense, who is usually a 'deformer' because he is willing to sacrifice an aspect of the Islamic tradition for this or that contingent factor, most often made to appear irresistible by being called 'an inescapable and unavoidable condition of the times'. One wonders what would have happened to Islam during and after the Mongol invasion if such 'reformers' had appeared and had tried to make Islam conform to what were then surely the most irresistible 'conditions of the time', those connected with the victorious Mangols and their ways of life. A true Islamic renaissance is, then, not just the birth or rebirth of anything that happens to be fashionable at a particular moment of human history but the re-application of principles of a truly Islamic nature.

And here the primary condition for a genuine Islamic renaissance becomes clear. This condition in our day resides in independence from the influence of the West and from all that characterizes the modern West. A Muslim far away from the influences of modernism can possibly experience spiritual renewal while remaining oblivious to what is going on in the modern world. But a Muslim intellectual or religious leader who wishes to renew the intellectual and religious life of the Islamic world, now under such heavy pressure from the West and from modernism in general, cannot hope to bring about an Islamic renaissance on either the intellectual or the social level except through a profound criticism of modernism and of the modern world itself. To speak of an Islamic renaissance and at the same time to accept without any discrimination all that the modern world stands for is a pure chimera and the wildest of dreams, a dream which in the end cannot but turn into a nightmare. Today, truly Islamic activity, especially on the intellectual plane, cannot take place without a profoundly critical attitude towards the modern world, combined with a deep understanding of this world. Nor is the practice of giving opinion, or Ijtihad, possible in the field of Islamic law for a mind that has been transformed by the tenets of modernism. If, despite all the talk about an Islamic renaissance among Muslim modernists during the past century, no such thing has taken place—certainly not issuing from their quarter—it is precisely because they lack this absolutely necessary critical view and at the same time a profound knowledge of the modern world and the means to assess its transient values in the light of the eternal principles of Islam. It is certainly time for those who want to speak in the name of the Muslim intelligentsia and who wish to bring about a renaissance of Islam to stop speaking from a position of inferiority vis-a-vis the West and begin to apply the sword of metaphysical discrimination, contained in its purest form in the shahadah, to the modern world itself.

Within such a perspective, the meaning of decadence and deviation also becomes clear. Decadence is always a falling off from a perfect norm, but following a course that is still related to that norm, while deviation is a complete departure from that norm itself. Moreover, there are two forms of decadence, one passive and the other active: one which the civilizations of the East have undergone during the past few centuries, and the other which has been followed by the modern West during the same period and which, because of the active and dynamic quality of the West, became properly speaking a deviation. Many Orientals—Muslims as well as others—have mistaken this activity for true life precisely because they have seen it in contrast to the relative lack of dynamism and activity within the traditional Oriental world. Today, strangely enough, before the startled eyes of many modernized Easterners, this deviation of the West is turning into decadence of a form that is easily recognizable, even to them. It can, in fact, be said that the curve of Site of modern Western civilization, beginning with the termination of its spiritual normalcy during the Middle Ages, has gone from 'renaissance' to deviation to decadence, this last phase becoming ever more evident during the last two decades. As for that interpretation of Islam of the group of modernists just mentioned, the curve can be described as going from decay to 'renaissance' to deviation—a deviation which will surely be followed by another phase of decadence, but of a type different from that which the modernists sought to remedy to begin with. Fortunately, however, the totality of the Islamic tradition remains above this process.

There is only one way to escape the insidious chain of deviation leading to decadence. It is to remain faithful to the eternal and immutable principles of Islam, which stand above all becoming, and then to apply these principles to whatever situation Muslims are faced with, to whichever 'world' presents itself to them. To take any transient spatio-temporal set of conditions or 'world' as the criterion of the validity of Islamic principles and teachings is to reverse the natural order of things. It is to put the cart before the horse; it is to make the contingent the criterion of judgement for the eternal. Its result can only be an unfolding similar to the fatal course pursued by the West, the end of which is the impasse which modern civilization now faces and which threatens the very.existence of man on earth.

The Muslim 'intelligentsia' cannot do anything better than to benefit from the lessons that can be drawn from a deeper study of the stages in the history of the modern West which have brought it to its present crisis. If they wish to speak for Islam and to renew its life they must remember the extremely heavy responsibility they bear. It must be recalled that a true death is better than a false life, and that if one wishes to renew the life of the Islamic community it must be the renewal of a life whose roots are sunk deeply in the Divine. There is no way to avoid both decadence and deviation and to achieve a true renaissance but to re-apply the principles and truths contained in the Islamic revelation, which have always been valid and will always continue to be so. And in order to be able to apply these principles to the outside world it is first of all necessary to apply them to oneself. Man must become spiritually revivified before being able to revive the world about him. The greatest lesson that all true reformers today can learn from the numerous failures of even well-intentioned reformers in the modern world is that the real reform of the world begins with the reform of oneself. He who conquers himself conquers the world, and he in whom a renewal of the principles of Islam in their full amplitude has taken place has already taken the most fundamental step toward the 'renaissance' of Islam itself, for only he who has become resurrected in the Truth can resurrect and revive the world about him, whatever the extent of that 'world' might be according to the will of Heaven.

Islam in Practice

For nearly all of its fourteen centuries of history Islam has filled the whole of the 'living space' of that part of the cosmos called the Islamic world, leaving no vacuum to be filled by elements which could properly be called un-Islamic. The earthly manifestation of Islam was practically synonymous with the Islamic world, and everything in the Islamic world from the method of ploughing fields to composing poetry was inseparable from the spirit and form of Islam. It is only now, when, as a result of the encroachment of modernism, the homogeneity created by the Shariah on one level and Islamic art on the other has been partially destroyed, that it is possible to speak of Islam in the Islamic world as distinct from other elements of a completely non-Islamic and even anti-Islamic nature which have crept into this world to destroy in part its marvellous unity and homogeneity. It is true that in the traditional world of Islam there were also occasional forms of decadence in both art and thought of the type characteristic of the European Renaissance, but they were so peripheral and so much on the fringe and were, moreover, overwhelmed so rapidly by the spiritual presence of the tradition that they cannot in any way be compared in dimension with the spread of modernism in the Islamic world today. No matter how much effort certain Orientalists spend in seeking to resuscitate the rationalistic tendencies of an Ibn al-Rawandi or Muhammad bin Zakariyya al-Razi, or to display in art exhibitions certain naturalistic vases, frescoes and paintings of Umayyad, Ottoman, Mogul or Persian origin, they cannot hide the overwhelming evidence of the presence of the spiritual character of the Islamic tradition, a presence which obliterated all such transient phenomena in the Islamic world.

Broken Unity : The unity of the Islamic world, however, is now partially broken as never before, not only politically—which had occurred already during the Abbasid period—but even religiously and culturally, by the erosion caused by Westernization, a process which as well as introducing a totally foreign element into the Islamic world also reflects directly an alien world which itself suffers from the most glaring forms of disunity and contradiction. Numerous works have been written in the West with various degrees of success on modern movements in the Islamic world, but few have considered the effect of the inner contradictions and tensions of Western civilization itself upon the confusion caused in the Islamic world by present-day modernizing elements. It is enough to see the difference of perspective and approach existing today among philosophers, sociologists and educators of Muslim universities, reflecting the centres of learning in which they were trained in continental Europe or England or America, to realize how complicated the pattern of Westernization—which of course has been synonymous with modernization until now— actually is.

In addition to the historical accidents of colonization and Westernization, there is also another factor to consider which reflects the multifarious tendencies within Western civilization itself. Because the Islamic world has always been a unity, it has until now functioned as an organism in which each part has played a particular role. During the classical period of Islamic civilization, each part of the Islamic world was especially known for its mastery of a particular art or science, from sword-making to navigation, from astronomy to Kalam. On a more inward level, each of the Islamic peoples, such as the Arabs, Persians, Turks, Berbers and Black Africans, emphasized a particular devotional aspect of Islam and even a particular interpretation of the Shariah, while the Shariat rites as well as the pure metaphysics of *Tasawwuf* and the techniques for its realization provided the thread of unity through this diversity.

The spread of modernism has had the effect not only of sowing the seed of confusion in the minds of those who are affected by it and therefore loosening the hold of Islam upon them, but also of separating different parts of the Islamic world from each other more than ever before. There is much talk of easy communication today, but as a matter of fact, intellectually and culturally, there is less communication between various parts of the Islamic world today not only than during the period of the classical caliphate but even than after the Mongol invasion, when Moroccans worked along with Syrian astronomers in Maraghah under the leadership of Nasir al-Din al-Tusi. The various parts of the Islamic world, which for centuries complemented each other and functioned organically and harmoniously, are now left to themselves to recreate a totality from something which was always part of a greater whole and was continuously enriched by other parts of the whole.

As a result, when one studies the situation of Islam and Islamic culture in the Islamic world today, one sees a certain element of this totality better preserved in one land and another element in another land. In one part of darul-Islam, certain parts of the Shariah are performed impeccably and certain other parts relatively neglected. In one place the juridical sciences are still studied and taught in their fullness, and in another the theological ones or certain other traditional sciences. Some of the Muslim peoples have preserved the formal aspects of the Shariah more strictly, and others place more emphasis upon their inner content and are less observant concerning the exactness of the outward forms. Likewise, in the domain of the sacred art of Islam, some have preserved the most beautiful Quranic psalmody, others calligraphy and yet others architecture. Some continue to preserve the traditional dress but are more modernized in their minds and attitudes than others who have been forced to abandon their traditional dress but whose psyche and mind remain less affected by modernism.

Many historical factors, ethnic characteristics, internal social and political elements and the like have created a pattern in which, overlying the deeper layer which unifies the Islamic peoples and displays the unity and totality of Islam, one can observe a differentiated patchwork of modern ways of thinking and acting throughout various Islamic countries, reflecting both the confusion of the Western world and the complicated processes through which this confusion reached the Islamic world. In the periods when Islamic civilization was at its height, when its homogeneity reflected the varieties of Islam on all levels of human life, a perceptive Muslim could gain a vision of the totality of the Islamic order through contact with any of its great centres; but today, such an experience of Islam in its totality is not easy to come by, even for a Muslim acquainted with only a part of darul-Islam, not to speak of an outsider. For example, in the intellectual field, a person possessing the necessary intellectual and spiritual capabilities and living in Cairo or Damascus or Isfahan of the fourth eleventh century, or even of the eleventh/seventeenth century, would have been able to gain knowledge through traditional education of the hierarchy of the Islamic sciences extending from the supreme scientia sacra contained in Sufism to various traditional schools of philosophy and the natural sciences to theology and the various juridical sciences. Although not impossible today, the task of attaining such a knowledge is certainly much more difficult than before for a Muslim brought up in a traditional Madrasa, not to speak of one whose Westernized education has cut him off from many of the essentials of his own intellectual heritage. In fact, the spread of modernism in the Islamic world was facilitated precisely by this diminution in the knowledge of Islam's totality on the part of many Muslims. Yet it is precisely this total knowledge, not limited to a single level but embracing the whole, that is necessary if an intelligentsia capable of answering all the challenges that the Western world poses for Islam is to be formed.

Re-awakening of Interest : Strangely enough, one of the results of the shock received by certain Muslims in their encounter with the Western world has been a re-awakening of interest in the totality of Islam. In these cases, a 'rediscovery' of Islam, and even a kind of renewal of some people's vision of their own faith, has taken place, in such a way that such persons could, in a sense, be called jadid al-islam, (having just become Muslim) with all the positive qualities connected traditionally with this term. The impact of modernism upon the Islamic world, combined with a certain amount of decadence which set in some domains of life and thought beginning in the twelfth/eighteenth century, destroyed the homogeneity of that world and veiled the totality of the tradition even from Muslims. To understand the nature of the impact of modernism upon the Islamic world, and to prepare to combat its evils, requires on the part of the Muslim intelligentsia a rediscovery of the vision of the whole of their tradition and a stepping outside the boundary of their national and local experience to view the encounter of Islam and modernism in other parts of the Islamic world. For them as well as for the student studying Islam from the outside, the study of the parts cannot but help them to gain a knowledge of the whole.

It must be added, however, that the emphasis laid upon the necessity of studying Islam in each part of the Islamic world today in its confrontation with various forms of modernism must not lead to negligence of the traditional and unchanging aspects of Islamic life so often forgotten in the studies made by Western students as well as by modernistic Muslims. We have had occasion to mention in our previous writings on Islam the danger of the type of method used by most modern students of Islam grounded in such pseudo-sciences as modern sociology and the like or paralyzed by the historicism which grew out of nineteenth-century European philosophy. But it is necessary to repeat here that for a mentality trained to measure and to consider as significant only that which changes, the only noteworthy phenomenon in any part of the Islamic world becomes that which is related to some kind of rebellion against the existing traditional order. If there are a dozen traditional commentaries written upon the Quran they are considered as mere repetitions, but if there is one which breaks with the traditional canons, it is immediately hailed as a significant departure and made known through articles in various European languages. One can hardly emphasize enough how diabolical this propaganda on behalf of perverted tendencies or trivial mental exercises has been and how on the one hand it has led the Western reader to the wrong conclusion about the contemporary state of Islam, and on the other hand it has misled the Muslim in whom the power of faith (iman) has become weakened by the illusion that traditional Islam is something that belongs only to the past and that by identifying himself with modernistic theories and interpretations he is allying himself with forces that must of necessity prevail in the future.

In reality nothing could be farther from the truth. Despite serious encroachments upon the body of Islam by modernism and by the confusion caused within the mind and soul of certain Muslims caught between the pull of their tradition and Western ideologies and values, Islam remains very much a living tradition on both the exoteric and the esoteric levels. Were this not so it would hardly be possible to speak of applying the teachings of Islam to the problems faced by modern man. If nothing had been left of Islam save some kind of sentimental or apologetic modern interpretation, one could hardly expect it to provide an antidote for the maladies caused by modernism itself. But authentic and traditional Islam continues to live. It is there to be studied and rediscovered in its totality by turning both to the oral and written sources of the tradition as it has been lived and transmitted since its revelation, and to its present-day manifestations in the souls and lives of the Muslim peoples in various parts of the Islamic world under the different historical, political and social conditions imposed upon the once unified darul-Islam during the most recent period of Islamic history. Being more acquainted with the Arab and the Persian worlds, it is to these parts of the Islamic world that we turn in seeking to understand something of the state of Islam in the Islamic world today and in its confrontation with modernism. These countries form only a part of the Islamic world, but they continue to be of great importance and centrality because of the fundamental role they have played as the heart of darul-Islam since the foundation of Islamic civilization.

Arab World : The Arabs were chosen as the recipients and the first propagators of the Islamic revelation, and since the inception of Islamic civilization their destiny hag remained indissolubly bound with the earthly manifestations of Islam wherever these might be. The vast majority of Arabs are Muslims, and even the few among the Muslim Arabs who have recently rebelled against the faith are nevertheless influenced in many ways by Islam's norms and spirit. Their psychic and mental make-up has been moulded and structured for too long by Islam to allow its influence to be eradicated overnight. In the lives of those Arabs who consciously practise Islam and accept its teachings, and even of the few who have wandered away from its sacred mould, Islam remains the overwhelming reality, penetrating even now into practically every aspect of their individual and collective existence. But despite this indissoluble bond between Islam and the Arabs, events of the past century have caused the penetration of many foreign ideas, ranging from nationalism and secularism to socialism and Marxism, into the traditional universe of the Arabs, and have brought about some modifications in the understanding of the traditional pattern of religion among certain classes. These factors must, of course, be evaluated and considered in any appraisal of the situation of Islam in the contemporary Arab world, for they form the background of the complex and often bewildering scene observable today.

The first element to consider in studying present-day religious life among the Arabs is the shock received by all Muslims, and especially the Arabs, during the nineteenth century, from the domination of the European powers, a domination Which for Muslims posed a crisis of cosmic dimensions. For the first time in their history, except for the short episode of the Mongol invasion, Muslims experienced political humiliation at the hands of non-Muslims. The very promise of the Holy Quran to give Afusnms victory in the world provided they remained faithful to Islam seemed to have become negated by the experience of history itself. This shock, at once political, social and religious, was the source of a series of reactions of differing natures, ranging from the 'reform' movements, which sought to purify Islam, to various forms of Mahdism, which saw in the corruption of the times a confirmation of the teachings of the Quran about the latter days, and to out-and-out secularism, which, however, did not gain any notable followers until the present century.

Nature and the Shock : The unitary nature of Islam, combined with the nature of the political shock received from Western domination, has made political considerations a major aspect of the religious thought and writing of many contemporary Arabs. Strangely enough, this emphasis has been fortified in the twentieth century by the final political humiliation of the Arabs in Palestine at the hands of a movement which is itself inseparable from religion, despite its fiercely nationalistic and often secular character. The tragedy of Palestine, which for the Arabs was the final confirmation of the immorality of Western politics, emphasized at the same time for many of them the religious aspect of political activity and the pertinence of the political expression of religious sentiments even in the modern world. Palestine has become for the Arabs at once the supreme political issue and the tracing upon the canvas of history of the image of traditional accounts of eschatological events of the greatest religious importance relating to the city of Jerusalem.

The political preoccupations of the Arabs in the nineteenth century, combined with the development of a sense of frustration and also a sense of cultural weakness vis-a-vis the West, resulted finally in the attempt to adopt Western patterns of nationalism. The fire of Arab nationalism, first lit by a group of Western-educated Arabs mostly from Syria and also mostly Christian, soon transformed the political life of the Arab World. First of all it helped to break up the Ottoman Empire, then to bring independence to various Arab states, and finally to bring about the movement to seek to unify them, this last phase remaining still in the stage of trial and experiment. But even this force, which was originally of a purely Western and secularist origin, became gradually Muslimized as it penetrated the masses, to the extent that today Arabism, or 'uribah, is identified closely by the majority of the common people almost automatically with Islam. For a simple Arab in the street, any Muslim who knows a few verses of the Quran and can perform his prayers is considered somehow to be 'an Arab', for in his mind to be Arab and to be Muslim are the same. Even in educated circles in such countries as Egypt and Algeria, many people closely identify national and Islamic bonds and affiliations. Politics remains inseparable from religion and a great deal of the religious thinking of the Arabs has been devoted during the past century to political facets of Islam and the Arab World.

The attack of the West upon the Arab World, aside from its political effects, was also a direct attack against Islam as a religion. The Arab has remained conscious of the fact that ever since his political subjugation his religion and his culture have been the target of innumerable assaults, ranging from out-and-out slander by older missionaries and orientalists to much more subtle techniques of 'de Islamicizing' the minds of Muslim youth in Western-owned and directed educational institutions in the Arab World. Much of Muslim religious thought, therefore, took an apologetic turn from late in the nineteenth century, and gradually there came into being a certain type of Muslim religious thinker who had already unconsciously lost the intellectual battle to modernism and the West, and was now seeking only to defend his faith by showing that somehow every fashionable thought of the time had been Islamic before being adopted by the West. Even discoveries of modern science, which, of course, soon become stale and outmoded, were traced back to the Quran as if to show that the grandeur of the Quran resides in anticipating this or that discovery of physics or biology. The apologetic attitude became, because of the incessant attacks of the West, an almost ubiquitous aspect of the religious thought and writings of modernized Arabs, and to this day it remains, along with the political preoccupation mentioned above, of importance in a certain type of religious writing that is read widely by the modernized classes of society.

The attack made upon Islam hastened another tendency which had been inaugurated in the twelfth/eighteenth century in the heartland of the Arab World by Muhammad ibn Abd al-Wahhab and others to 'purify' Islam by returning to the sources of the religion and doing away with the later developments of the Islamic tradition, both intellectual and artistic. Had there not been the shock of Western domination, this movement would have probably developed along lines very different from those which it actually took. As it was, frustration in the face of complete domination by the West forced this movement to become more and more the rallying point for the well-known 'reformist' movement associated with the names of such men as 'Abd al-Rahman al-Kawakibi, Jamal al-Din al-Afghani (or Astarabadi) and Muhammad Abdur Rashid Rida, to the extent that, with Rashid Rida, the intellectual background of the reform of the Salfiyyah—as his school was called—was nearly the same as that of the Wahabis. In both cases there was, along with a positive emphasis upon the Shariah, an opposition to Sufism and the mystical life, to Islamic philosophy and to nearly the whole Islamic intellectual tradition. A 'rationalism' was developed which was combined with 'puritanism' and based upon a juristic and theological attitude which drew much from the writings of Ibn Taymiyyah and his students and which limited the vast horizons of Islamic intellectual life to a small portion of its traditional expanse. The effect of this type of religious thinking among the educated classes in the Arab World is still considerable, especially in the Arab Near East. The Maghrib of the Arab World, however, has been to some extent spared from this wave which swept over Egypt and Syria, not to speak of Wahabi Saudi Arabia, during the past century.

In opposition to this fundamentalist and puritanical tendency, there developed gradually among the Arabs from the beginning of this century another mode of thought, which preached various degrees of secularism and ranged from mild defences of Western civilization to the writings of Salamah Musa and the early Taha Pusayn, who preached the complete adoption of Western culture and a total break with the sacred ambience of traditional Islam. Of course at the very moment when such men began to defend

Western culture and secularism, others like Mustafa Sadiq al-Rafii, Mustafa Lutfi al-Manfaluti and Taqib Arsalan rose and violently attacked their writings. Nevertheless, views similar to those of the secularists have continued to be held by a certain number of influential men, and the present situation of Islam among certain classes of Arab society today cannot be understood without this background, although the present supporters of such a position are of a type somewhat different from the earlier secularists.

In addition to the tendencies and movements already mentioned, another reaction began among the Arabs, mostly after the Second World War, which has modified greatly the effect of these earlier movements. This new reaction was the disenchantment with the West and the realization of its moral bankruptcy, made so evident by the atrocities of the World War and later in the Palestine war and its aftermath. The blind admiration of the West espoused by so many of the 'leaders' of the previous generation gave way to doubt about the value of the civilization for whose sake the Arabs were asked to forsake their own religion and way of life. Some men, like Taha Hussain, even recanted openly in their later writings and expressed serious misgivings about Western civilization and its fruits. This awareness, which is still in the process of transforming the Arab image of the West, has a profound effect upon the role and function of religion among the Arabs, for it must be remembered that since the nineteenth century it has always been on the strength of arguments drawn from Western sources, and by appealing to the success of the West, that Arabs have been asked, and in fact are still being asked by certain purblind leaders of the blind, to abandon their own tradition.

Social and Economic Factors : In the Arab World today, besides the purely intellectual and mental factors expressed in currents of thought and affecting religion on its articulate plane, there are factors of a social and economic nature and elements dealing with everyday life that have as much—if not more—effect upon religious life as philosophical and theological ideas. In fact, today in the Islamic world in general and the Arab World in particular, Islam is being corroded more by the penetration of foreign modes of everyday living than by the scientific or agnostic philosophical ideas which have affected Christianity so greatly since the Renaissance. One of the best means of gauging the intensity of

Islamic religious life is to study the degree to which the Shariah, in its full meaning and embracing all of life, is applied in a particular ambience. In its formal and legalistic aspect, the Shariah is applied in varying degrees, from countries like Saudi Arabia and Kuwait, which use only Shariat law, to lands like Tunisia, where much of the law is derived from European codes. On the juristic level there is discernible a complex pattern which, for the most part, shows the attempt of most Arab governments to modify the teachings of the Shariah but to remain as much as possible within its injunctions and principles.

But the more difficult and profound problem is to study to what degree the mode of life, which was once dictated totally by the Shariah, has become secularized. Here one will discover that, surprisingly enough, even in countries where non-Shariat laws have been introduced, the concept of secular law or the secularization of life remains singularly alien to the mind of the vast majority of Arabs, save for a few who are thoroughly Westernized. But the encroachment of the kind of mundane and frivolous life which is characteristic of modern industrial societies is to be seen in larger Arab cities. The breaking of the injunctions of the Shariah concerning such questions as adultery or the use of alcoholic drinks is an ever more frequent phenomenon in big cities, even by people who consider themselves definitely Muslim and who would protest violently if classified otherwise, but who are generally unaware of the contradictions involved in their manner of living. The modernized Arab, like his Persian or Turkish counterpart, is drawn away from religion more through the temptation to create a sensuous and false 'paradise' around himself than by the attempt to play the role of the divinity like an agnostic Western philosopher. For Islam, the danger comes more from men so engulfed by the life of the senses and mundanity as to forget completely the sacred aspect of life taught by religion than from the type of rationalistic philosopher who in the Renaissance destroyed the unity of Christendom and weakened the hold of faith upon men. The Shariah continues to be respected as the concrete expression of God's Will, but more and more men in the big cities allow its hold upon their lives to be compromised by the penetration of completely un-Islamic modes of acting and living.

One of the important aspects of Islam in contemporary life

among the Arabs has been the appearance of movements which stand for the reestablishment of the full and complete reign of the Shariah over the everyday life of Muslims. These movements range from the Istiqlal party in Morocco, which has also definite political and social programmes, to the Ikhwan ul-Muslimin, the most important movement of this kind to appear during the past decade in the Arab World. The writings of the intellectual elite of this movement, such as Syed Qutb, are based most of all upon a renewed and vigorous application of the Shariah to the whole of human life. The persistence of the influence of this movement, even among the young, reveals a strong desire on the part of a significant portion of even the modernized classes for a moral revivification and renewal. The continuing appeal of men like Hassan al-Banna and Syed Qutb is due not so much to their intellectual analyses of various contemporary problems, analyses which are often oblivious of the true nature of some of the questions involved, as to their firm belief in the Shariah and to their own personal example of adherence to the Shariah. The existence of movements such as that of the Ikhwan, despite its naivety vis-a-vis the problems posed by the modern world, reveals the continuing hold of religion upon public life in its economic, social and political aspects, not to speak of the inner life of men.

As far as political life in the contemporary Arab World is concerned, its ever greater Islamicization, in spite of existing revolutionary tendencies which bring into power alien forms of government often with anti-Islamic ideologies, is truly amazing. The nationalist leaders are usually forced to come to terms more and more with the Islamic views of the masses, who keep a constant pressure upon them. And many of the leaders themselves combine leftist political tendencies with very strong Islamic convictions. One observes in the Arab World today not only traditional rulers who are devout Muslims or at least espouse the cause of Islam publicly, but also the most revolutionary governments which combine an extreme 'leftist' policy with a degree of adherence to the Shariah and the Islamic tradition which seems outwardly incongruent and amazes many a Western observer who has prepared a priori criteria, drawn from his own experience in the West, to study the Arab World. The European type of nationalism, therefore, which is by nature against the universalism of Islam, which did much to weaken Islam in the early phases of Arab nationalism, and which has produced anti-Islamic tendencies in many non-Arab Muslim countries, seems after several decades to converge paradoxically enough toward the Islamic ethos within many parts of the Arab World today, although it has done much to alienate Muslim people from each other and to dissect and divide the heritage of Islam, which belongs to all Muslim people by right.

Parallel with secularizing forces of every kind, one observes forces at play which seek to re-assert Islam in the social and political field. Furthermore, in recent years there have also become discernible tendencies which seek to achieve the same on the intellectual plane. The past few decades have witnessed the turning of the interest of many men of letters to religion and religious subjects, to the extent that some of the best known among them, such as 'Abbas Mahmud al-'Aqqad and Taha Hussain, not known in their earlier writings for their interest in religion, have written later in life several biographical studies of the Prophet and the Companions, or works on other specifically religious themes. This tendency complements the continuing flow of religious literature from the religious centres, especially al-Azhar, and by graduates of such centres. It also complements a small but growing number of writings by men in other walks of life who are deeply concerned with religion. One of the best known religious works to have appeared in the Arab World during the past decades, the City of Wrong, was written by Kamil Hussain, an Egyptian surgeon.

This revival of intellectual interest in Islam, which of course does not by any means please the modernized and secularized so-called 'intellectuals', usually of ultra-nationalistic or Marxist tendencies, is complemented by a renewal of interest in the whole tradition of Islamic thought, especially philosophy and Sufism. Traditional Islamic philosophy was revived in Egypt by Jamal-al-Din al-Afghani after centuries during which it had ceased to be taught in most Arab Madrasas and remained a living intellectual tradition only in Persia and adjacent areas. During this century, an avid study of Islamic philosophy has been carried out in the Arab World, and especially Egypt, by such men as Mustafa 'Abd al-Raziq, Ibrahim Madkur, 'Abd al-Rahman Badawi, Fuad al-Ahwani, Muhammad Abu Ridah, 'Uthman Amin and others. The efforts of such men must be seen not only as simple academic scholarship but also as an attempt to revive the intellectual heritage of Islam. Their work certainly possesses a religious significance and is related in this sense to the writings of men of letters and other classes of educated Arabs on religious subjects. The ever-growing interest in Islamic philosophy in the Arab World is related to the general desire for a new self-discovery on the part of the modern educated classes after the disillusionment with the West, which indeed becomes ever more intense with the rapid decline and, in fact, disintegration of modern Western society and culture as it has been known during the past few centuries.

Traditional Modes : It must be remembered that the intensity of religious life among the Arabs cannot be gauged at all by studying simply the various reactions of the Arabs to the modern world. One must also study the unchanged but ever-living traditional modes of religious life. Most Western scholars, who as already mentioned are trained by profession to study only change and who have made an a priori judgement that only that which changes is significant, have tended to neglect the permanent elements in the traditional religious life of Muslims in general and of the Arabs in particular, and have exaggerated the importance of the so-called 'reform' movement. In reality, today, the influence of the 'reformists' in the Arab World is far less than that of the traditional Muslim authorities both past and present. One would like to know, for example, which work of the modernist "reformers' compares in popularity with those of an al-Ghazzali. The heart of the religious life resides and will continue to reside in traditional forms and practices, in the inner being of individuals for whom Islam means an approach to the Divine and a sanctification of human life, and not a mere assert with which to further particular worldly causes, whether they be political, social or economic.

To understand religion in the contemporary Arab World one must also understand the meaning of the still-continuing congregational prayers held in every city, of the countless pilgrims who continue to be attracted to the spiritual pole of Mecca, and of the millions who visit sanctuaries, from Mulay Idris in Morocco to Ras al-Hussain in Cairo and the Shiite sanctuaries of Najaf and Karbala. One must realize the vitality and the continuous subsistence of traditional religious teaching among both Sunnis and

Shiites. One must be aware of the continuity of the intellectual traditions of Islam among the 'ulama (religious scholars) and the traditional learned classes, and of the life of faith (iman) among the vast majority of the community, for whom prayer and devotion still constitute the celestial pattern into which human life is integrated. Any changes or reactions caused by the domination of the West and the political and cultural tragedies that have followed can only be understood in the light of the dominant presence of the still-living tradition of Islam. For every Arab, young or old, who speaks of secularism or socialism or Marxism there are many for whom no 'ism' can ever replace the all-embracing reality of Islam. To grasp the religious life of the Arabs in its fullness one must be aware pot only of the 'renovators', 'reformers' and rebels whose harm to the traditional order can hardly be over-emphasized, but also of the innumerable elements of permanence and continuity implied by the very notion of a living tradition and displayed fully by Islam in its manifestation among both Arabs and non-Arabs.

Also, in speaking of the religious life of contemporary Arabs it is not possible to overlook Sufism, which lies at the heart of the Islamic tradition and which has acted throughout Islamic history as the source for spiritual and religious regeneration, being the invisible origin of even external and social movements of a religious nature. Strangely enough, however, the majority of modern accounts of religion in the Arab World fail to take account of this basic element, and neglect the Sufi orders and their rejuvenation during the past century, with the sole exception of the Sanusiyyah Order, which has been studied more often precisely because of its puritanical and 'Wahabi' tendencies.

The fact is that during the nineteenth century, along with the gradual penetration of modernism and secularism into the Arab World and the rise of the modernist 'reformers' about whom so many studies exist in European languages, there occurred also a genuine renewal of life within several of the Sufi orders by great saints who were in fact 'renewers' (mujaddid) in the traditional meaning of the word, which is very different from 'reformer' (muslim) in its modern sense. The renewal of life of the Shadhiliyyah Order and the founding of certain new branches and orders such as the Yashrutiyyah, the Badawiyyah and the Medaniyyah, mostly in the Arab Middle East, and the Darqawiyyah in the Maghrib, marked a revival of an intense spiritual life that has affected the whole religious life of the community to this day.

During this century the same forces of inner renewal can be observed. The influence of the remarkable Algerian Darqawi master, Sheikh Ahmad al-'Alawi, who founded a new branch of the Shadhiliyyah Order, spread beyond the confines of the Maghrib and even the Arab World and is felt far and wide to this day. Anyone who has frequented a gathering of the Shadhiliyyah-'Alawiyyah Order in Damascus or Aleppo has become aware of the degree of influence of this master and the extent of his living grace (barakah) within branches of the order founded by his disciples in many Arab lands as far away from each other as Syria, the Yemen and Morocco.

In Egypt also, almost contemporary with Sheikh al-Alawi, another Shadhili master, Salma Hasan al-Radi, founded the Hamidiyyah branch of the order, which soon began to attract many into its fold. Its emphasis upon both the practice of the Shariah and spiritual discipline has made it one of the main spiritual forces in contemporary Egypt, attracting adepts from many walks of life, including the young in universities. Its current role in Egypt exemplifies the basic importance of Sufism in the contemporary religious life of many parts of the Arab World.

The events of the past two or three decades have caused major social and political strains in the Arab World and have accentuated many of the tendencies alluded to above as well as causing new ones to come into being. A sense of bewilderment combined with emotional irrationality has captivated the minds of certain men as a result of the extreme despair and unbelievable stress caused by the injustice brought upon the Arabs by the Palestine tragedy and its aftermath, including all the extremist forms of government that this event helped to bring into being. Also, an ever greater degree of destruction of the religious quality of life is to be observed in the bigger cities, especially among notable segments of the youth drawn to the frivolities and trivialities of modern life. Furthermore, out-and-out secularist and anti-Islamic political ideologies have gained power in certain regions of the Arab World.

But along with the growth of all these anti-traditional forces and tendencies one can notice a marked renewal of interest in religion, especially among the youth. It is enough to compare the number of young people who used to visit a place such as the tomb of Ibn Arab in Damascus or Ras al-Hussain in Cairo two decades ago with the number who are seen there now. Both Sufism and the Shariat practices of Islam have been attracting numerous people of late, not only from the traditional classes in the countryside but also from urban classes that only a generation ago showed little interest in religion. Along with the young Arabs studying in the West or in Western-oriented universities in the East who are becoming infatuated with various fashions of Western thought ranging from positivism to Marxism, there are those who are searching again for their own roots and looking within their own tradition for an answer to the dilemma of human existence in an inhuman world whose overt contradictions become more apparent every day. The rise of religious interest in the Arab World during the past decade or two is a phenomenon of central importance which can hardly be brushed aside as a momentary emotional reaction before the inevitable onslaught of complete secularism, as secularist historians would wish to do.

In reality, what has happened during this period is that on the one hand the blinding glitter of Western civilization has begun to fade and its innate faults and present difficulties have become more evident, and, on the other hand, the false gods for whose sake the modernized Arabs sought to brush Islam aside have failed them in the worst way imaginable. The defeat in the 1967 war and the humiliations before and after cannot possibly be blamed in any way upon traditional Islamic institutions. It is the failure of the modern ideologies whose adoption dates back to the nineteenth century that has now come into the open. For many an Arab, recent events have only strengthened their serious disillusionment with the programme of simply aping the West. Rather, they see recent tragedies as a divine punishment for their having forsaken Islam". They have come to view all these difficulties as trials which, according to the teachings of the Quran, the individual Muslim as well as Muslim society as a whole must pass through in this world. They have also come to realize that in order to return to Islam they must rediscover Islam in all its fullness, not in its atrophied and apologetic form as presented by so many of the modernist 'reformers' during the last centuries.

On the scholarly level also, a new class, small but of considerable significance, has come into being which is traditional and at the same time well acquainted with the West without being its slavish imitator. Both on the popular and the intellectual level the awareness of the necessity of taking religion seriously is to be discerned in many circles, whose members thus return to the living stream of the authentic Islamic tradition in both its Shariat and its Sufi aspects.

Today the Arab World stands at a most crucial stage of its history. There are still those who would like to secularize the Arab world and separate it from Islam as much as possible. But because Arabic was chosen as the vehicle of the Quranic revelation and the Arabs as the first propagators of Islam, the destiny of the Arabs remains inseparable from that of the whole Islamic world and in fact from the earthly manifestation of Islam itself. Moreover, the future well-being of the Arabs depends upon the degree to which they are able to remember their true identity and to remain faithful to the task which their identification with Islam upon the historical scene has placed upon their shoulders. Inasmuch as it is impossible for men to remove the imprint of the Divine upon the human order, Islam continues today as the most powerful and enduring motivating force within the Arab soul and mind, and an ever-present factor in Arab life in all its aspects. It is the source to which all things must of necessity return, even if they wander away momentarily, and it continues as an objective norm which moulds the lives of, and at the same time serves as the ideal for, the vast majority of Arabs, both individually and collectively. Islam remains a living reality without which it is impossible to understand the Arabs today. To speak of the Arabs is to speak of a people whose language is that of the Quran, and the fabric of whose soul has been woven over the ages from elements of the Quranic revelation in a manner that makes their contemporary history inseparable from Islam and the Islamic universe into which most Arabs still are born and in which they live and die.

Persian World : The situation of Islam in the Arab World differs from its situation in the rest of the Islamic world in that the Arab

Muslim, even if modernized, does not see in his pre-Islamic past anything but the 'age of ignorance' (al-jahliyyah), which he can hardly extol even in a modernistic and nationalistic milieu, and also in that the contemporary Arab Muslim cannot separate himself from his ethnic and linguistic attachment to the earthly vessel of the Quranic revelation. In contrast to this situation, the non-Arab Muslims have a distinct pre-Islamic past completely different from the background within which Islam was revealed, and do not share the ethnic and linguistic bonds with the earthly embodiment of the Quranic revelation, at least not to the same extent as the Arabs.

Historical Background : This distinction is particularly true of the Persians, who had a brilliant pre-Islamic civilization of great spiritual and artistic beauty, and played a major role in the very foundation of Islamic civilization. They and the Arabs (al-arab wal-ajam in traditional Islamic sources) together founded Islamic civilization and have influenced nearly every phase of its subsequent history. In fact, although Islamic thought and culture succeeded in freeing itself from becoming only 'Arabic' or 'Persian' during the Umayyad and Abbasid periods, both of these peoples left their indelible mark upon its historical deployment and development. The Persians, on the one hand, played a central role in building Islamic civilization and, on the other, were able to integrate within the universal perspective of Islam many elements of their pre-Islamic past, which thus became completely Islamicized. They therefore not only became thoroughly Islamic and have remained one of the most productive of Islamic peoples intellectually and artistically, but they were also able to preserve their own identity and remain distinctly Persian, creating a second cultural focus within the unity of Islamic civilization, which in its classical phase and almost up to modern times could be divided culturally into the Arabic and the Iranian zones. The situation of Islam in present-day Persia, and modernism's threat to the remarkable unity created between Persia's ancient past and Islam, cannot therefore be understood without reference to the historical background and an analysis of the forces and elements that were integrated to create the classical Islamic culture of Persia.

When we look at Persia today we see that it is one of the most overwhelmingly Muslim countries in the world. The life of the vast majority of Persians today is dominated and moulded completely by Islam, while, at the same time, the religious and cultural life of the country naturally reflects the long history of the Persian people. Because the Persians became thoroughly Islamicized and yet created a distinctly Persian Islamic culture related on a certain plane with their pre-Islamic past, to understand their present-day religious life—particularly in the form of Ithna 'Ashari or Twelve-Imam Shiism, which is dominant in Persia today—it is necessary to cast a brief glance at the religious history of the people who have lived on the Iranian plateau during the past three thousand years.

Persia has been both a centre from which major religious influences have radiated and a cross-roads at which the religious traditions of the Mediterranean world and Asia have met, resulting often in new currents of religious life. Having originally belonged to the same ethnic and linguistic stock as the Aryan conquerors of India, the early Iranians who settled on the plateau possessed a religion akin to that of the Vedas. From this early background there arose the reform of Zoroaster and the establishment of the specifically Iranian religion of Zoroastrianism. Although the dates of Zoroaster are still much debated, there is no doubt that in the fifth century OF his teachings became the official religion of the Persian empire. The sacred book of Zoroastrianism, the Avesta, is the most precious religious document of the early history of Persia as well as a basic source for the study of the Iranian languages. Zoroastrianism, with its firm belief in the angelic world, its accent upon the moral dimension of human existence, its emphasis upon the reality of the after-life and Last Judgment, and its stress upon the purity of the elements and the sacred character of human life, left an imprint both on the later religious life of Western Asia and on the general outlook of the Persians.

The positive qualities which this religion implanted in the souls of the Persians survived and became transmuted into the Islamic mould after Zoroastrianism itself had decayed and lost the spiritual struggle against the new forces of Islam. For example, the care that many devout Persians take in keeping their clothing, food and habitat clean in a ritual sense, sometimes even over-emphasizing this element of religion, is founded upon an old Zoroastrian teaching reinforced by the emphasis of Islam upon cleanliness. Whatever survived of Zoroastrianism in the Persian soul was, however, thoroughly Islamized and interpreted in the light of the unitary point of view of Islam.

From the matrix of Zoroastrianism, which is the stable and orthodox background of Iranian religions, there grew several religious movements which had world-wide repercussions and also shook the foundations of Zoroastrianism itself. With the fall of the Achaemenian Empire, Hellenistic influences spread throughout the domain of the Persian people. This cultural movement was combined with a religious one known as Mithraism (considered as a distinct religious movement and not general devotion to Mithra, which ante-dated Zoroastrianism itself) which itself contained important Hellenistic elements. The mystery cult of Mithra, which spread as far West as Germany and Scandinavia, was a synthesis of Zoroastrian, Hellenistic, Babylonian and Anatolian elements, as well as pre-Zoroastrian Persian religious practices. If, for the world at large, this religious movement meant the spread of Iranian religious elements, for Persia itself it implied perhaps more than anything else the establishment of a religious sanction for the syncretic cultural life through which the Persians were now passing as a result of the conquests of Alexander and the establishment of Seleucid rule.

During the Parthian period, Zoroastrianism and the proper Persian cultural tradition began to reassert themselves until, with the advent of the Sassanids, the religion of Zoroaster became once again the official state religion, remaining in this position until the fall of the Sassanid empire. Nevertheless, its authority did not go unchallenged even on the religious plane. In the third century AD, a second world-sweeping Iranian mystery religion, Manichaeism, came into being. Its founder, Mani, first found favour with the Sassanid ruler but was finally put to death through the opposition of the Zoroastrian priesthood. His cult nevertheless spread from China to France and in Persia itself gained many adherents. At once a socially revolutionary and a religiously mystical movement, it marked a major protest against established religious institutions. Although some of its cosmogonic and cosmological teachings found a place in certain forms of Islamic philosophy, for Persians of the later period Manichaeism has appeared as a rebellion against religious authority. It has never enjoyed the same status as Zoroastrianism, from which it came into being and against which it revolted.

The Sassanid period was also witness to other religious movements such as Mazdakism, a 'religious communism' known today mostly through what its enemies, both Zoroastrian and Christian, wrote against it. This movement, which was soon crushed, was again a protest against the Zoroastrian social order and foretold the collapse of this order which occurred with the coming of Islam. Also at this time there developed within Zoroastrianism the philosophico-religious school known as Zurvanism, which indicates a blend of Iranian religious thought with certain Greek philosophical ideas. Finally, it must be remembered that through rivalry with the Byzantines the Sassanids encouraged Oriental Christian sects, especially the Nestorians, these sects were given a free hand to establish schools and missions throughout the Sassanid empire, with the result that notable Christian communities came into existence in Persia and became an important minority religious community in the Islamic period. The Jews also had several centres in Persia from Achaemenian times, and continued to thrive under both Zoroastrian and Muslim rule. The tolerance toward minority religions shown by Cyrus the Great has been with few exceptions the rule in the religious history of Persia.

The major spiritual transformation in Persia came, strangely enough, not from one of the new members of the family of Iranian religions but from a religion of Abrahamic and Semitic background, namely Islam. Although the military defeat of the Sassanids before the Arab armies was a sudden and rapid process, the spiritual struggle between Islam and Zoroastrianism was a gradual one and did not really terminate until the fourth/tenth century. This fact itself indicates that the Persians accepted Islam, not through force, as is claimed by some modern historians, but because of an inner spiritual need. When the Persians regained their political independence from the caliphate there were still very sizeable Zoroastrian communities in Persia. But instead of showing any inclination to return to this tradition, the newly independent Persian rulers became themselves the champions of the spread of Islam, while insisting on the independence of the literary and cultural life of Persia. Most of the Muslim lands of Asia have, in fact, been Islamicized through the intermediary of the Persian form of Islam.

And to this day, when a Persian thinks of the domain of 'Persian culture' he sees before him nearly the whole of the Eastern lands of Islam, from the Western borders of the Iranian plateau to Western China, with Iraq as an intermediary realm where the Persian, Arabic and, later, Turkish elements met.

During early Islamic history Persia was dominated by the Sunni form of Islam. In fact it was from Khurasan that the theological defence of Sunnism was made during the tenth and eleventh centuries, by such masters of theology as al-Juwayni and al-Ghazzali, when many other lands of Islam were dominated by Shiism. Yet, certain centres in Persia such as Qum were from the beginning Shiite and the Persians in general had a particular reverence for the household of the Prophet of Islam from the earliest centuries of Islamic history. The figure of Salman al-Farisi, the Persian who in search of the ideal prophet journeyed all the way to Arabia to meet the Prophet and became so close to him as to be called 'one of the members of the household' (ahl-i bayt) of the Prophet, has the deepest significance for the religious consciousness of Islamic Persia. During the early centuries, therefore, Persia was at once a major centre of Sunni Islam, producing such scholars and theologians as al-Bukhari, al-Ghazzali and Fakhr al-Din al-Razi, and a land within which important centres of Shiism existed, where many of the greatest early Shiite theologians such as Ibn Babuyah and Kulayni were born and nurtured.

Before the Mongol invasion, a devastating material and social calamity for Persia, the forces of Ismailism were also strong in this land. Although the centre of their power was in the Yemen and later in Egypt, from the third ninth century onward, there were outstanding philosophers and theologians of this school in Persia, men like Abu Hatim al-Razi, Hamid al-Din al-Kirmani and Nasir-i Khusrau, who have left us so many doctrinal works on Ismailism. Moreover, with the 'resurrection of Alamut', Ismailism gained major political power in Persia and continued to exert political pressure until the destruction of Alamut by Hulagu.

Between the Mongol invasion and the establishment of the Safavids, Persia moved gradually toward Shiism through both social, political and purely religious factors marked by the activity of certain Sufi orders and several outstanding Shiite theologians. Yet, at the time of the establishment of the Safavids and the recognition of Shiism as the official state religion, most of Persia was still Sunni. The change, however, was made relatively rapidly and soon the country became predominantly Shiite, although noticeable Sunni elements have survived to this day in such areas as Khurasan and Kurdistan.

Persia was also from the beginning of Islamic history one of the lands in which Sufism, the esoteric and mystical dimension of Islam, spread rapidly and expressed itself in the most striking literary and artistic forms. Some of the greatest early Sufis, like al-Bastami and al-Hallaj were Persian, and later the direct influence of Sufism transformed Persian poetry into one of the most universal forms of literature. Both through the direct presence of Sufi orders and through the effect of Sufism upon Persian literature, music, architecture and other forms of art as well as certain social organizations, the spirit of Sufism has left an indelible mark upon many facets of the life of the Persians. It must be remembered, however, that being esoteric in character, Sufism has always preserved its inner teachings for those who have been qualified to follow the Sufi path. It is only the external manifestations of Sufism that have a general cultural and social bearing and are so noticeable a strand in the fabric of Persian life and culture.

It is in the light of this background that we must study the role of Islam in present-day Persia. Because of this long period during which the Persians have become Islamicized in the deepest sense possible, the world view of the Persian today is determined more than anything else by the teachings of Islam. Like other Muslims, the Persian is born, lives and dies with the verses of the Holy Quran echoing in his ears. He sees the world about him in the light of the conception of the Divine and His creation as delineated in the Holy Quran. There is, in fact, in spite of the secularist tendencies of the past fifty years, still no conception of a way of life in which religion is only one element among many or of a world view in which the religious factor is only one dimension. The total world view is religious, and even the apparent negation of religion by certain people has itself a religious significance.

Iran under Islam : The universe in which the Persian lives, like that of all Muslims, is one created and sustained by Allah, the Omnipotent and Omniscient Creator, Who is at once the Origin and End of all things, the First and the Last. His will reigns supreme over both the world of nature and the lives of men and their societies. He has knowledge of all things and His majesty causes all that is beside Him to melt into nothingness. Yet he has given man free will to pursue his own life and to choose the 'right path' (al-sirat al-mustaqim) of his own accord, without compulsion. The secret of man's life lies between these two logically contradictory assertions, of the absolute Omnipotence 'of Allah and of man's free will and responsibility before Him as the Supreme Judge.

Every Muslim is aware throughout his life of the ultimate significance of his actions beyond this world of change and corruption. The Persian Muslim, like his other brethren in faith, may, because of his own weakness, sometimes live a life that is mundane and even directly against various Divine injunctions, but he never doubts for one moment the presence of the Divine Command (al-amr) and his responsibility to follow it. As already stated for Muslims in general, so also for Persians it can be said that there are some who do not heed the voice of the Divine, but there is practically no one who doubts the presence of 'His voice'. That is why after a life of debauchery a man may become suddenly devout, and even in the midst of the most profane life remains aware of the presence of the transcendent dimension of life.

Inasmuch as the will of God is manifested in Islam in the form of a concrete and all-embracing law, the Shariah, the Persian is always aware of the religious character of all facets of life. Since the Shariah covers all aspects of human life, to the vast majority of Persians all laws which they encounter and all acts which they perform during their daily lives possess a sacred character even if non-Shariat laws have been promulgated in certain domains. Most Persians feel that they are performing a religious duty when they work to make a living, even if the particular work they perform is not itself of a traditional religious nature. By contrast, the small Western-educated classes that have been affected by the Western distinction between the religious and the secular often do not attach this religious significance to their daily work. For them the Shariah is identified with specific acts of worship which in fact they rarely perform. But they are a small minority. For most Persians, both the uneducated and the educated, the all-embracing nature of the Divine will which governs all facets of man's life through a sacred law is very much a reality and a permanent factor in their general world view.

The Divine will is also seen by Persian Muslims, as by other Muslims in general, in the world of nature, of which the phenomena, in conformity with the teachings of the Holy Quran, are considered as the 'signs of God'. There is no ultimate distinction between the Divine Law governing men and the laws governing nature, between religious and natural law as understood in the West. Nature is a complementary aspect of the religious reality that is revealed directly through revelation. It can therefore incite the deepest intellectual and contemplative response in the traditional Persian, who turns to it both as a source of enjoyment and as the background for the spiritual life. The very austerity of nature in Persia, the high mountains, the vast deserts, the green valleys hidden high in mountain ranges, evoke an awareness of the transcendent. The visible itself is but a veil for the invisible and the laws of the world of nature but a part of the universal law which of necessity governs all things.

The Persian is also keenly aware of the transient nature of things, a point so often emphasized in Islam. He lives with the reality of death and a realization of the instability of all that surrounds him. For him the angelic world, the hierarchy of spiritual beings that stands above the world of material forms, is a constant reality, one that is emphasized in both the ancient religions of Iran and in Islam. If this world is impermanent and transient, there stands beyond it the permanent and luminous world of angelic substances.

The awareness of the transient nature of this world is combined with a great joy in life and its beauties which reflect the beauty of the higher orders of existence. Few people are given as much to the enjoyment of life's pleasures and beauties as the Persians, but this attitude is always compensated for by the realization that a moment once gone never returns and all that is physical and sensual has an ephemeral character about it. These two attitudes are often reflected even in the distinctly religious activity of chanting the Holy Quran, during which people weep and are carried beyond worldly cares, but which is frequently held in the most beautiful gardens where the best refreshments are served and the voice of the reciter possesses the finest musical quality. At their most spiritual level, these two attitudes are to be found in all Persian Sufi poetry: here one is constantly reminded that the Infinite reflects an aspect of Its beauty at each moment, but because of Its Infinity Its theophanies (tajalliyat) never repeat themselves.

There is also an element of tragedy which characterizes the Persian and which is seen fully in the ethos of Shiism. This is not the humanistic tragedy of the later Greeks, a rebellion of man against the gods, associated with the Promethean mentality so characteristic of the decadent period of Greek culture and post-mediaeval Europe, but is a spiritual quality based on man's submission to God and yet his separation from Him. The tragic and sad element (huzn), which does not at all negate the aspect of joy (farah) in life, is always of a religious character and a basis for contemplation. It is most directly reflected in classical Persian music, where the apparently sad quality is in reality a nostalgia for the Divine. It is a tragedy based on the realization that the human condition contains an apparent contradiction. Man is in desperate need to realize the Divine and to become aware of his own spiritual nature. Yet this realization is made well-nigh impossible by the distance that separates him from the Divine and by his need to await Divine assistance to accomplish this end.

Closely connected with this point of view is the concept of the intermediary and intercessor before God, and the expectation of a future saviour, both so important to Shiism; man is in need of an intermediary between himself and God. Even after the descent of a revelation, the role of the intermediary must continue. Therefore, after the Prophet of Islam there must be Imams who act as intermediaries between men of later generations, and God. There must also be a future saviour, the Mahdi, who will redeem the world from its state of corruption. From the Shiite point of view, he too is an Imam, in fact the twelfth Imam of Shiism, but an Imam who, although living and present, is in occultation (ghaybah) and will not reveal himself until a future moment known only to God. The very expectation of his appearance (intizar) is a religious virtue. The ideals of appealing to saints and Imams and of patiently awaiting one who will in the future eradicate injustice and corruption and therefore end the hardships of present-day life are constant elements of the Persian religious outlook.

As far as religious institutions and organizations are concerned, the most important centre in the life of the Persians, as in that of other Muslims, is the mosque, whose size varies from the colossal Friday mosques of major cities to single rooms in small towns and villages. Its architecture also varies from ornate tiled mosques to mud structures whose walls are covered by whitewash. In all its forms, the mosque is the centre of both religious and social activity in the community. Its door being always open, it remains a calm sanctuary amid the turmoil of daily life, a place where people wander in to say their prayers as well as to consider a transaction or simply to relax with friends in the contemplative and peaceful atmosphere which the mosque creates. In the cities, in fact, the bigger mosques are nearly always situated in the bazaars and are an inseparable part of daily life.

The mosque is also used for congregational prayers, particularly those of Friday, as well as for special occasions of religious mourning or feasting or funerals. The Friday prayers, however, are less emphasized in Persia than in those Muslim lands where Sunni Islam predominates. This is because in the absence of the Mahdi the Friday prayers do not carry any political significance as they do in Sunni Islam, and their importance is not greatly emphasized by the '*ulama*'. Rather, the religious climate is such that the canonical prayers performed individually and often at home are considered as important as prayers at mosques, so that many who do not go regularly to mosques nevertheless do perform their prayers and other religious rites privately at home.

The role of the mosque differs both between the life of the country dweller and the city dweller, and between that of the traditional and the modern Persian. In the countryside, the imam of the mosque often acts as the teacher for elementary education, especially early religious education, and he is the arbitrator in most disputes. After daily prayers, people usually gather about him to pose questions about problems which would otherwise have to be taken to court. In the smaller cities, these customs are retained to a certain degree, but in larger cities both functions, elementary education and judging cases, are performed outside the mosque, although in the second case the arbitrator is himself usually a religious authority. The larger mosques in big cities also perform an educational service on a higher level, in that they are usually affiliated with a religious school or madrasa in which more advanced religious education is carried out.

As for the modern educated classes, particularly those who have been educated in the West, as a rule they do not go to mosques except on special occasions. Many of them do make pilgrimages or participate in the mourning of Muharram or funeral rites, all of which are usually connected with mosques, but they rarely attend their local mosques for daily prayers. Although there are notable exceptions, one can say that in this aspect of religious life they are sharply distinguished from the rest of Persian society.

The madrasa system, which has its roots in the early centuries of Islamic history, is the means whereby the intellectual aspect of the religious tradition is kept alive. In these schools, which are endowed and usually connected with a major mosque, students who have undergone an early religious education continue their studies. They are fully supported by the madrasa, receiving accommodation on the premises as well as board and other expenses. There is no pressure on them to finish their studies in a certain period as in modern universities, nor are any specific degrees conferred upon them. Some stay in a madrasa for their whole life and, if competent, become teachers in their turn. The students mostly choose the field of the transmitted (naq) sciences, studying law, the principles of jurisprudence, Quranic exegesis, hadith, etc. Some, however, choose the intellectual (aqli) sciences, and pursue logic, Islamic philosophy, theology, etc.

The largest madrasa system today, which is in Qum, has over six thousand students, and there are other major centres in Mashhad, Tehran, Isfahan and several other cities. Moreover, besides the official lessons taught in the madrasa, classes are often held in the homes of individual professors and masters, often in more advanced phases of study. These classes are particularly important in the field of traditional Islamic philosophy or theosophy (hikmati) as well as in gnosis (irfan). In these private circles, many who do not belong to the Madrasas also participate, including often some who have had a modern, rather than a purely traditional, education. One could even say that most of the teaching of the Islamic intellectual sciences in Persia today is performed outside formal institutions and in private circles.

Shrines, or tombs of the Shiite Imams, their descendants and Sufi saints, play a major role in the life of all classes of Persians. They consist usually of a mausoleum and a mosque, often with a madrasa and a library attached, and are supported by endowments and donations. Of those within Persia itself, the most important is that of the eighth Imam, 'All al-Rida, in Mashhad, which is visited by hundreds of thousands of people every month. It has a vast complex of mosques and courtyards around the central mausoleum, as well as dispensaries, hospitals, a major library, a museum, a madrasa, etc. Over a thousand people are fed at each meal free of charge and there is no time of the year when the shrine is not completely filled with throngs of the faithful from not only all corners of Persia itself but also the Arab World and the Indo-Pakistani sub-continent. Next to Mashhad, the holy city of Qum is the most important, inasmuch as it is the site of the tomb of Imam Rida's sister, Hadrat-i Masumah, and the seat of the most influential Shiite mujtahids. It too, is frequented by many pilgrims throughout the year. The tombs of Hadrat-i 'Abd al-'Azim near Tehran in Rayy, Shah Chiragh in Shiraz and cih Nimatallah Wall, the famous Sufi, near Kirman, are all shrine institutions of prime importance. Other shrines are located on tops of mountains in difficult locations, in awesome sites of nature connected with the traditional sense of sacred geography. There is no city or town without a site of pilgrimage and a saint to whom the people turn in their moments of trial as well as in moments of thankfulness. All of these shrines play a fundamental role in daily religious life, inasmuch as people turn to these saints as intermediaries between them and God and ask through them what they wish to ask of God. There is hardly anyone in Persia, even the most modern, for whom the power of the grace or barakah of these shrines has ceased to exist.

The Sufi centres, called khanaqah in Persian, are also major focuses of religious life, although Sufism itself transcends the exoteric dimension of religion and is concerned with the esoteric teachings of Islam. The khanaqah is usually either the home of a living Sufi master or the tomb of a dead one which has become the centre of the order. In either case, it is a complex of buildings in which the fuqara', or dervishes, meet for their sessions of spiritual practice and where there are rooms for travelling dervishes as well as cells for those who make spiritual retreats (khalwah). On special religious holidays such as the birthdays of the Prophet and 'All as well as during days of mourning, the khanaqahs open their doors to all who come to participate in the ceremonies held there. Even at other times the khanaqah acts as a pole of spiritual attraction for the community itself, even if those outside its organization are not completely aware of all that is taught within its walls to members of the order'.

The major Sufi orders in Persia today are the Nimatallahi, with many branches throughout the country; the Gunabadi (itself a branch of the Nimatallahi) centred in Khurasan; the Dhahabi with its major centre in Shiraz; the Qadiri, powerful mostly in Kurdistan and the Persian Gulf region; the Khaksar, popular especially among craftsmen; and the Naqshbandi, having its centre in Kurdistan. These orders, many of which have close contacts with branches in other Muslim lands, continue to influence the general structure of society and cultural life, in particular literature, music and calligraphy. The very presence of a living Gnostic path of spirituality also has its effect on intellectual pursuits, especially traditional Islamic philosophy, which for this very reason is not just a rational form of knowledge but a theosophy or hikmah, ultimately an aid to spiritual realization. But, of course, because of the nature of Sufism, the profoundest influence of its teachings remains confined within the circle of the spiritual elite.

The institution of religious endowment (waqf), which is one of the important Islamic institutions, is the means whereby the above-mentioned religious organizations as well as many others are in most cases supported. Usually cultivated lands, even pastures, wells, trees, etc., are given as endowment for a particular religious institution. A person is chosen to act as keeper and executor of the endowment, and under his direction the income is to be spent in accordance with the will of the founder. Today, a certain amount of organization has been given to this matter through the establishment of a department of waqf by the government. But the institution is far from being government-controlled, and in most cases it is still the person in charge of the endowment or his family who hold power in their hands.

Touch of Modernity : In traditional Persian society, as in other similar societies, every social institution possessed religious and spiritual significance. In modern times, although, as a result of the encroachment of secularism, some of these institutions no longer have a direct religious colouring, others have a religious connection even if they are not, strictly speaking, religious organizations. Of these the guilds (asnaf) are of great importance. Existing in all the bigger cities, the guilds draw members of a particular occupation such as bakers, bricklayers or carpet-weavers into an organization which still preserves in many fields its original connection with Sufi orders and the chivalrous brotherhoods or futuwasat. Most of the guilds have a particular reverence for 'All, the traditional patron saint of all Islamic guilds, and possess a strong feeling of fraternity'. Even labour organizations which resemble unions in the Western sense possess some of the characteristics of the guilds, and it is difficult in most cases to draw a line between the guild and the union.

In certain quarters, some social significance still pertains to the remnants of orders of chivalry centred around gymnasia called asar-khanah. Again closely connected with the name of All, these orders served traditionally to enhance the spirit of chivalry (jawanmardi) and to build up moral and spiritual character'. In their centres, bodily exercises are performed to the beating of a drum and the chanting of religious and epic verses. Traditional Persian cities, like other Muslim cities, have had local strong men who have kept the peace and protected the morals (namus) of their quarters of the city. Such types have usually been connected in Persia with the zw-khanah and still perform this function in many cities, although they stand in rather stark contrast to some of the Westernized youth in the modernized parts of Tehran who are devoid of the traditional virtues of chivalry inculcated by these orders.

Finally, mention must be made of certain recently founded organizations usually connected with bureaucratic professions and some which are affiliated to Sufi orders. There are also lodges of Freemasons which, in the Persian climate, have in a few cases gained a Muslim colouring, while some attempt has even been made to connect them to certain of the khanaqahs.' In a few cases, there has come into being a Persian version of an organization resembling these lodges but of a more directly religious character and attracting many from the modern educated classes. In all these cases, a religious element is present, though it varies from one organization, and even from one individual, to another.

Because of the all-embracing nature of the Sacred Law or Shariah, there is in reality no aspect of social life in Persia, as in the rest of the Muslim world, which is completely divorced from religious principles, even if modernism and older historical forces resuscitated as a result of the influence of modernism have removed certain aspects of social life from the direct jurisdiction of the Shariah. Those domains of social life in which the Shariah is still directly applied in Persia are personal law such as marriage, divorce, etc., as well as much of civil law. In this domain, even what was taken from European codes was taken with the approval of the 'ulama' and was integrated into the matrix of the Shariah through the practice of 'independent juridical opinion'. Moreover, those who practice law and administer it are nearly all either products of the madrasas or the law schools and theological faculties where they have been exposed to Islamic jurisprudence (fiqh).

It is rather in the domain of economic life that non-Shariat practices are most often seen. In the field of taxation, non-Islamic systems have been used from Umayyad times in addition to the Islamic religious tax which, in Sufism, consists of zakat and khwans. Many wealthy men, especially merchants in bazaars, do, however, continue to pay the religious taxes in addition to those demanded by the government. The religious tax is, in fact, a major source of support for centres of Shiite learning in such cities as Qum.

The religious spirit manifests itself in economic life not so much in specific norms as in attitudes. The Islamic view of the permitted (halal) and forbidden (haram), the condemnation of usury, of amassing wealth in gold and silver, of usurping the right of orphans, and many other injunctions, even if not practised by all, penetrate subtly into economic life. Also, the more philosophical attitude of uncertainty about what tomorrow will bring, distrust of purely human causation, the feeling of the impermanence of things, all play their role in fields of economic life where specific religious norms may seem to be absent.

As for political life, since Shiism in contrast to Sunnism does not accept the religious legitimacy of the institution of the caliphate and believes monarchy to be the best form of government in the absence of the Mahdi, the Persian monarchy possesses a positive religious aspect. Ever since the establishment of Shiism as the official state religion by the Safavids, the monarch has been considered from the religious point of view as the legitimate ruler who should govern with the consent of the 'religious scholars' or 'ulama', and whose duty it is to uphold the Shariah and to promulgate Islam. This view is explicitly mentioned in the present Persian constitution. The connection of the monarchy with the religious structure of Shiism in Persia has been a persistent element of Persian history during the past four centuries, and gives a religious tone to political life even if parliamentary government is not itself an institution of Islamic origin.

The confrontation between religious and modern secular norms is best seen in the present educational system in Persia. There are, in fact, two systems of education, one the madrasas which produce religious scholars, lawyers, imams of mosques, etc., and the other the modern educational system leading to university degrees in various fields. Here religion is taught as a subject among others in the elementary and secondary school curricula, but one does not find the pervasive religious character of all education that has always existed in traditional Islamic society. In the universities also, besides faculties of theology, subjects connected with religious philosophy, law etc., are taught in faculties of letters and law, but here again other subjects are left outside the religious sphere. There is a direct confrontation between religious and 'secular' disciplines of learning, a confrontation which did not exist in the traditional Islamic world view where every science, be it natural, mathematical or philosophical, possessed a traditional and sacred aspect and was never divorced from the total religious and intellectual life of Islam.

As far as philosophy is concerned, it is important to note that traditional Islamic philosophy is still very much alive in Persia. Secular European schools of philosophy are taught in universities but have had comparatively little effect upon the general intellectual life of the country. In fact the very presence of a living Islamic intellectual tradition has prevented facile and shallow modern interpretations of Islam in Persia such as are found in some other Muslim countries. Moreover, as mentioned before, even modern philosophical discussions, once translated into the Persian language, have had to take cognizance of the presence of the Islamic philosophical tradition.

In literature, architecture, the plastic arts, music, theatre, and other forms of artistic and cultural life, traditional forms which have a completely religious and spiritual basis subsist while modern forms have been introduced with varying degrees of 'success' among certain classes. In such cases as the theatre, where the traditional form consisted solely of passion plays, Western forms of theatre depicting problems of Western man have had little appeal to the vast majority of the population, their popularity remaining limited to the few, among Western-educated people located mostly in Tehran.

A few attempts have also been made to use Persian and Islamic themes and motifs. In the other arts, the traditional forms have sometimes been used in new contemporary settings, occasionally with success, but often with a result that falls far short of genuine traditional art forms. But by and large, the traditional religious forms of artistic and cultural expression subsist and in certain cases dominate, while the modernized minority in Persian society surrounds itself ever increasingly with various aspects of Western artistic expressions and forms.

The most important religious practices of Persians, like those of all Muslims in general, are the rites of prayers, fasting, pilgrimage and sacrifice, which are all slightly coloured by the secondary aspects that these rites have acquired against the background of Persian culture. Their essential element is that of the universal norms of Islam itself. The daily prayers, which most Shiites usually perform three times a day by connecting with a short pause those of noon and afternoon as well as those of evening and night, punctuate the rhythm of daily life. It would not be an exaggeration to say that the conception of time and the flow of life itself are determined by these canonical prayers, which are considered as the pillar of Islam. In addition the very devout perform supererogatory prayers (nawafil) and there are special prayers connected with hope, fear, expectation etc.

Fasting as a religious rite is connected particularly with the holy month of Ramadan, although, again, many devout people fast on different occasions throughout the year, especially the beginning, the middle and the end of the lunar Islamic month. During Ramadan the rhythm of life changes and there is a perceptible transformation of the most external aspects of daily life. Many of the modernized Persians do not fast, but on the whole the fast is observed throughout the country. During the holy month, days become calm and sombre and the evenings gay. Many more social calls are made to relatives during the evening, and at this time after the breaking of the fast religious and social life become completely intertwined.

The climax of the holy month comes during the nights of the 19th to the twenty first, the period during which the first Imam 'All was struck on the head while praying in the mosque at Kufa and died of the wounds two days later'. During these nights, all amusements and parties are halted and mourning is observed in both homes and mosques. The period culminates in the night of the zist, called the 'night of vigilance' (ihya'), during which mosques are thronged until the morning hours. People perform a hundred prostrations (rakah) of prayer and chant litanies and supplications (especially the famous Shiite prayer called Jawshan-i kabir) until the rising of the sun.

Pilgrimage, as already pointed out, plays a major role in Persian religious life. The obligatory pilgrimage is, of course, that made to Mecca (hajj), by virtue of which man crowns the religious performances of his life. Since making this pilgrimage requires financial means and the ability to provide for one's family in advance, those who make the hajj (who are called haji in its Persian pronounciation) are identified with a certain wealth and economic well-being. The haji is respected by all devout people, but, in the bazaar particularly, to be a haji also confers social and economic advantages. And since all hajis in the bazaar are not always beyond reproach in their dealings, some criticism of them can be sensed among the modernized classes. For many years, in fact, making the hajj had become rarer in the modern educated segment of Persian society. But this has changed completely in the last decade, and now the annual hajj caravan includes people from every walk of life.

The other places of pilgrimage, especially Najaf, Karbala, Samarra, al-Kazimayn in Iraq, and Mashhad and Qum in Persia, are also of the greatest significance in daily religious life. These centres, as well as the smaller sites connected with different saints, bring the barakah of the centre of Islam and of the Prophet to the outer territories. These centres are all echoes of the supreme centre where Heaven and earth meet. There is hardly a Persian who does not make at least a few pilgrimages to a tomb of some saint with the continuous hope of being able to visit the more 'central' ones whenever possible. Although some pilgrimages involve special hardship, the centres being located on mountain-tops or places with a bad climate, most pilgrimages combine religious asceticism with the enjoyment of God's bounties and the beauties of art and nature. For a large segment of the population, such a pilgrimage is the most enjoyable experience of the year, although it is also a time of the most intense purification, a period of prayer and asking for forgiveness that leaves its mark upon the person long after the pilgrimage has come to an end.

The hajj terminates with the feast of sacrifice ('id-ul- Adha or 'id-i qurban) commemorating the sacrifice of Ibrahim. During this day, not only in Mecca but throughout the Muslim world, sheep are sacrificed. Herds are marked with special colours and brought into the city before the occasion, and on the morning of the 'id the sacrifice is made, the meat being given to the poor and to neighbours. But besides this, sacrifice is made throughout the year. Firstly, all meat that is used for daily food is slaughtered ritually and sacrificed, and secondly, on almost any joyous occasion, such as the arrival of a traveller from a long journey, the birth of a child (particularly a son), the arrival of an honoured guest, and the building of a new house, sacrifices are made, usually of sheep but sometimes of other lawful animals, including, occasionally, camels'.

A religious practice that is particular to the Shiite world, especially Persia, is the raudoh, which was developed in its present form during the Safavid period. The roudoh (a word derived from the title of the work Rawdat al-shuhadd', meaning the 'Garden of

Martyrs') consists of sessions during which sermons are delivered combined with the chanting of verses of the Quran and religious poems, with special emphasis on the tragedy of Karbala. These sessions are held most of all during the two-month period of Muharram and Safar, revolving around the death of Hussain and its aftermath. Much religious and moral preaching to the public takes place on these occasions. The rawdah is held in mosques as well as in private homes. On the crucial dates of the ninth and tenth of Muharram on which the tragedy of Karbala itself occurred, there are even government-sponsored rawdah throughout the country, the sessions are marked by sobbing and wailing, particularly on the, part of women, as all discourse is brought back periodically to the theme of the death of the members of the household of the Prophet.

Religious practice also enters into daily life at the critical moments of birth, marriage and death as in other parts of the Islamic world and, in fact, in other religions. At the moment of birth there is the simple recitation of the 'testimony of Islam' or the Shahadah in the ear of the new-born child. In the case of boys, the rite of circumcision is perhaps even more directly connected with religious practices than birth itself. As for marriage, although it is a contract and not a sacramental act, nevertheless, since it is made valid by virtue of the Shariat, it is definitely a religious act. The verses binding the contract are usually read by one of the 'ulama' although any male Muslim can perform this and other functions of a priestly nature.

It is naturally at the moment of death that religious rites become most vividly remembered and seriously practised. The acts of washing the body and burial are all performed in accordance with Islamic law. Afterwards, a funeral service is held which men attend in a mosque, and another where women gather in the home of the deceased or of one of his or her relatives. Since to attend those services is a social duty and most men have many friends and relatives, attendance at funeral services in mosques is a regular event throughout one's life. The sermon delivered after the chanting of the Holy Quran is the best means available to religious authorities to reach the higher strata of society, especially those who hold political power in their hands. That is why a funeral service held for a member of the government or for a person of high reputation holds a special significance in the religio-political life of Persia. In fact, several political assassinations and attempts toward this end have been made on such occasions during the modern history of Persia.

There is also a practice called preparing sufrah, popular among women, at which a table is laid full of all kinds of food, to which friends and neighbours are invited. During the 'feast', a person specializing in performing the rawdah, called rawdah-khwan, chants the Quran and religious poems and preaches on religious, themes. The rest of the food is then given to the poor and some taken to each participant's home and given to friends and relatives, especially those who are ill, as an object possessing barakah (tabarruk). The sufrah, being especially for women, is usually connected with important events in the lives of women in the household of the Prophet such as Fatima and Zaynab. The whole process of preparing the table, which is done with the greatest care and the best taste, is considered as a religious labour, one in which, once again, denial of the world is combined with the enjoyment of God's bounty.

The sufrah, as well as pilgrimage and many other religious acts, is often performed as a result of a vow and solemn promise to God (nadhr) in return of which the person asks something of God. The practice of nadhr is very popular in all segments of Persian society, especially among women. Women make a vow to pay so much money to the poor or "set a sufrah if they bear a child or if their daughter finds a suitable mate". Students often vow to fast or perform a certain pilgrimage if they pass their examinations. Merchants in the bazaar make the nadhr to sacrifice so many sheep if their business transactions succeed. There is continuous 'religious barter', in which Persians, like other traditional people, ask of God something in exchange for which they perform acts pleasing to Him. One can hardly understand the psychology of the Persian and the tensions of hope and fear within him without understanding his attitude toward nadhr and the 'barter' he makes continuously with the Creator. Only the saintly man lives fully according to the will of God without asking anything in return. But this highest spiritual attitude does not in any way invalidate the general exoteric religious form of it.

Besides religious practices that have been sanctioned and

protected by the 'ulama', and represent the conscious, intellectual aspects of Islamic tradition there are many popular practices which are often combined with the most in tense religious fervour and enthusiasm. During the month of Muharram, long processions are organised by men who, dressed in black, celebrate the passion of Karbala by chanting religious poems and often beating themselves until they fall into a state of frenzy. Occasionally these practices are carried to extremes, some beating themselves with chains and even swords until they faint from loss of blood. Most processions, however, march through the streets of cities to the solemn rhythm of drum beats and the harmony of human voices choking with grief. In larger cities, the sight of thousands of men and boys marching behind religious emblems and symbols of the family of the Prophet is a most moving religious experience.

There is also the passion play (taziya), which, although developed into an aristocratic art in Safavid and Qajar times, is essentially a popular religious manifestation. It is not usually encouraged by the 'ulama', although they do not oppose it since it is a medium for profound religious expression. Varying from simple versions in the villages to elaborate ones in big cities, the tazia depicts the events that led to the martyrdom of Hussain at Karbala. The climax is usually performed at high noon on the day of 'Ashwa, the tenth of Muharram, when the third Shiite Imam, Hussain, died and was beheaded. In a city like Qum, where several thousand people participate in the performance of the drama and thousands more flock from the countryside to join the population of the city in observing the taziya, one sees one of the most overwhelming manifestations of religious life in Persia.

Finally, among popular religious phenomena one cannot overlook the interest in omens, magic and other occult arts. Islam, on the Shariat level, opposes the practice of magic, but that has not prevented people, especially women, from utilizing it often in combination with specifically Muslim practices. Furthermore, there is a complete traditional science of the 'magic-like' use of Quranic phrases, that is, the recitation of formulae for appropriate occasions. Although this science is itself far from being 'popular' in the usual sense, it has a widely extended field of application in daily life. There are also prayers (dud') connected with the names of Imams and Sufi saints which people carry about with them or recite on various occasions. Besides their purely religious aspect, practices of this kind have also acquired a kind of magical quality. The 'prayer writer' (dua-niwis), like the practitioner of geomancy (rammal), is a permanent fixture in the life of Persian women in both the city and the countryside. He combines strictly religious elements with all forms of fortune-telling and both occult and pseudo-occult sciences.

The rhythm of life in Persia is determined by a number of holidays, many Islamic, some derived from ancient Persia and a few celebrating modern national events. Both the Islamic and the ancient Persian dates have a wholly religious aspect. Even the ancient Zoroastrian naw-roz or 'New Year', which marks the Persian new year to this day, has acquired a completely Islamic colour. At the moment of the vernal equinox, people place the Quran on their tables along with the seven objects beginning with the letter 's' (the haft sin or seven s's) that have survived from Zoroastrian days. Prayers are also said and benedictions invoked upon the Prophet and his family.

As for the Islamic religious dates, the festivities of adha at the end of the hajj, Eid-ul-fitr at the end of Ramadan, the date of the birth of the Prophet, the birthday of All and 'Eid-i-ghadir, when according to Shiite belief, All was chosen by the Prophet as his successor, are widely celebrated as joyous occasions. Also of great importance is the date of birth of the Mahdi, when all cities are illuminated with countless lights.

The calendar is also dotted with tragic events, the most important being the loth of Muharram, the death of Hussain, the zist of Ramadan, the death of 'All, the 28th of Safar, the death of the Prophet and the second Imam Hassan, as well as the dates of the deaths of other Imams and of Fatima. All these dates mark an intensification of religious life and a transformation of many aspects of daily life. The tragic element in the Persian soul expresses itself at the highest levels during these occasions, which have the effect of cleansing the individual and society from the dross of neglecting their religious vocation.

There exist in Persia today a number of sects which are marked by their emphasis upon a certain aspect of Shiite teachings at the expense of other elements, and by their ensuing separation from the main community. Of these the Ismailis are perhaps the oldest, being the remnant of the much larger Ismaili community of early mediaeval times. In religious beliefs they are close to the Twelve-Imam Shiites except on the question of the Hidden Imam or Mahdi. Theologically, of particular interest are the Shaykhis, centred mostly in Kirman, and founded by Sheikh Ahmad Ahsai two centuries ago. They emphasize the role of tawil, or spiritual hermeneutics, and have a special reverence for the Imams. The 'Ali-Allahi and Ahl-i-Haqq have followers in Kurdistan, Mazandaran and some of the southern provinces. Some members of these sects even go to the extreme of believing in the divinity of 'All and also in re-incarnation.

The significance of these sects from the point of view of the general religious life of Persia is that most of them belittle the practice of the Shariah, and some do not even perform the daily prayers in the usual manner. In most cases they represent Sufi orders that have become politicized or have taken on an external social character resulting in the destruction, of the equilibrium which characterizes the orthodox Muslim community, Sunnite and Shiite alike. They are nevertheless Islamic sects in that they are still within the total matrix of the Islamic tradition. Such is not, however, the case with Babism and Bahaism, particularly the latter, which broke completely away from the structure of Islam and cannot in any way be considered as an Islamic movement or sect. The presence of Bahaism in Persia today, therefore, even if limited in its membership, has a role to play in the process of secularization and in the destruction of the religious unity of the country.

In conclusion it must be noted that the Persian psyche possesses an elasticity that makes the study of religion in Persia based on external forms alone difficult. From outward signs, one sees the superimposition of a modern, Westernized class, more or less torn away from religious practices, upon the traditional Persian society, nearly all aspects of whose life are dominated by the religious spirit. Even pre-Islamic norms have become, for those living in the matrix of the traditional Persian world, totally Muslimized. But even among the modernized who outwardly seem completely secularized there exist many traditional religious tendencies which in a people of less elastic mentality would not be conceivable. One often sees women who dress in the latest European fashions and try to act like Western women but who, at the same time, display a completely traditional religious attitude at moments of stress or sorrow or on religious occasions. Likewise, many men who present a rationalistic front indifferent to religion become totally transformed in holy places of pilgrimage or at moments of participation in religious ceremonies.

It can therefore be said that most of contemporary Persian life is still dominated in its universal principles as well as in its daily acts by the spirit and form of the Islamic revelation, which also integrated into its world view elements of older religions which were in conformity with its own principles. Moreover, whereas certain domains of life have drawn away from the orbit of traditional religious life as a result of the advent of modernism, even in these domains religious elements and attitudes persist. Of course in Persia, as in the Arab World, there are the few who have become torn away completely from Islam, at least outwardly, and who possess a world-view based upon imitation of various Western ideologies and who experience constantly that tension between East and West alluded to in earlier chapters concerning Muslims in general. But for the vast majority of Persians, the religious truths by which they have lived and died for centuries continue to dominate the horizon of their lives today, even if occasional clouds momentarily obscure the horizon from some eyes. The clouds, however, can never be permanent, and there is hardly anyone who during his lifetime does not gain some kind of vision of that horizon which has coordinated and oriented the lives of Persians, as of other Muslims, throughout the ages and continues as the most abiding reality today.

3

Natural Faith

The Sun is a shining glory *(diya')* and the Moon a light *(nur).* This translation would appear to be more correct than those given by others, where the two terms are inverted. In fact there is little difference in meaning since *diya'* belongs to a root *(dw')* which, according to Kazimirski's authoritative Arabic/French dictionary, means 'to be bright, to shine' (e.g. like a fire). The same author attributes to the substantive in question the meaning of 'light'.

The difference between Sun and Moon will be made clearer by further quotes from the Quran.

> "Blessed is the One Who placed the constellations in heaven and placed therein a lamp and a moon giving light." —(25:61)

> "Did you see how God created seven heavens one above another and made the moon a light therein and made the sun a lamp?" —(71:15-16)

> "We have built above you seven strong (heavens) and placed a blazing lamp." —(78:12-13)

The blazing lamp is quite obviously the Sun.

Here the moon is defined as a body that gives light *(munir)* from the same root as *nur* (the light applied to the Moon). The Sun however is compared to a torch *(siraj)* or a blazing *(wahhaj)* lamp.

A man of Muhammad's time could easily distinguish between the Sun, a blazing heavenly body well known to the inhabitants of the desert, and the Moon, the body of the cool of the night. The comparisons found in the Quran on this subject are therefore quite normal. What is interesting to note here is the sober quality of the comparisons, and the absence in the text of the Quran of any elements of comparison that might have prevailed at the time and which in our day would appear as phantasmagoria!.

It is known that the Sun is a star that generates intense heat and light by its internal combustions, and that the Moon, which does not give off light itself, and is an inert body (on its external layers at least) merely reflects the light received from the sun.

There is nothing in the text of the Quran that contradicts what we know today about these two celestial bodies.

As we know, the stars are heavenly bodies like the Sun. They are the scene of various physical phenomena of which the easiest to observe is their generation of light. They are heavenly bodies that produce their own light.

The word 'star' appears thirteen times in the Quran (*najm,* plural *nujum*) it comes from a root meaning to appear, to come into sight. The word designates a visible heavenly body without saying of what kind, i.e. either generator of light or mere reflector of light received. To make it clear that the object so designated is a star, a qualifying phrase is added as in the following sura:

> "By the sky- and the Night-Visitor, who will tell thee what the Night-Visitor is, the Star of piercing brightness."
>
> —(86:1-3)

The evening star is qualified in the Quran by the word *takib* meaning 'that which pierces through something' (here the night shadows). The same word is moreover used to designate shooting stars (sura 37, verse 10) : the latter are the result of combustion.

Solar Family : It is difficult to say whether these are referred to in the Quran with the same exact meaning that is given to the heavenly bodies in the present day.

The planets do not have their own light. They revolve around the Sun, Earth being one of them. While one may presume that others exist elsewhere, the only ones known are those in the solar system.

Five planets other than Earth were known to the ancients: Mercury, Venus, Mars, Jupiter and Saturn. Three have been discovered in recent times: Uranus, Neptune and Pluto.

The Quran would seem to designate these by the word *kaukab* (plural *kawakib*) without stating their number. Joseph's dream (sura 12) refers to eleven of them, but the description is, by definition, an imaginary one.

A good definition of the meaning of the word *kaukab* in the Quran seems to have been given in a very famous verse. The eminently spiritual nature of its deeper meaning stands forth, and is moreover the subject of much debate among experts in exegesis. It is nevertheless of great interest to offer an account of the comparison it contains on the subject of the word that would seem to designate a 'planet'.

Here is the text in question:

> "God is the light of the heavens and the earth. The similitude of His light is as if there were a niche and within it a luminary. The luminary is in a glass. The glass is as if it were a planet glittering like a pearl."
> —(24:35)

Here the subject is the projection of light onto a body that reflects it (glass) and gives it the glitter of a pearl, like a planet that is lit by the sun. This is the only explanatory detail referring to this word to be found in the Quran.

The word is quoted in other verses. In some of them it is difficult to distinguish which heavenly bodies are meant (sura 6, verse 76; sura 82, verses 1-2).

In one verse however, when seen in the light of modern science, it would seem very much that these can only be the heavenly bodies that we know to be planets. In sura 37, verse 6, we see the following:

> "We have indeed adorned the lowest heaven with an ornament, the planets."

Is it possible that the expression in the Quran 'lowest heaven' means the 'solar system'? It is known that among the celestial elements nearest to us, there are no other permanent elements apart from the planets: the Sun is the only star in the system that bears its name. It is difficult to see what other heavenly bodies could be meant if not the planets. The translation given would therefore seem to be correct and the Quran to refer to the existence of the planets as defined in modern times.

The Quran mentions the lowest heaven several times along with the heavenly bodies of which it is composed. The first among these would seem to be the planets, as we have just seen. When however the Quran associates material notions intelligible to us, enlightened as we are today by modern science, with statements of a purely spiritual nature, their meaning becomes obscure.

Thus the verse quoted could easily be understood, except that the following verse (7) of the same sura 37 speaks of a 'guard against every rebellious evil spirit', 'guard' again being referred to in sura 21, verse 32 and sura 41, verse 12, so that we are confronted by statements of quite a different kind.

What meaning can one attach moreover to the 'projectiles for the stoning of demons' that according to verse 5, sura 67 are situated in the lowest heaven? Do the 'luminaries' referred to in the same verse have something to do with the shooting stars mentioned above?

All these observations seem to lie outside the subject of this study. They have been mentioned here for the sake of completeness. At the present stage however, it would seem that scientific data are unable to cast any light on a subject that goes beyond human understanding.

Functioning of the System : The information the Quran provides on this subject mainly deals with the solar system. References are however made to phenomena that go beyond the solar system itself: they have been discovered in recent times.

There are two very important verses on the orbits of the Sun and Moon:

> "(God is) the One Who created the night, the day, the sun and the moon. Each one is travelling in an orbit with its own motion." —(21:33)

> "The sun must not catch up the moon, nor does the night outstrip the day. Each one is travelling in an orbit with its own motion." —(36:40)

Here an essential fact is clearly stated: the existence of the Sun's and Moon's orbits, plus a reference is made to the travelling of these bodies in space with their own motion.

A negative fact also emerges from a reading of these verses: it is shown that the Sun moves in an orbit, but no indication is given as to what this orbit might be in relation to the Earth. At the time of the Quranic Revelation, it was thought that the Sun moved while the Earth stood still. This was the system of geocentrism that had held sway since the time of Ptolemy, Second century B.C., and was to continue to do so until Copernicus in the Sixteenth century A.D. Although people supported this concept at the time of Muhammad, it does not appear anywhere in the Quran, either here or elsewhere.

The Arabic word *falak* has here been translated by the word 'orbit'; many French translators of the Quran attach to it the meaning of a 'sphere'. This is indeed its initial sense. Hamidullah translates it by the word 'orbit'.

The word caused concern to older translators of the Quran who were unable to imagine the circular course of the Moon and the Sun and therefore retained images of their course through space that were either more or less correct, or hopelessly wrong. Sir Hamzah Boubekeur in his translation of the Quran cites the diversity of interpretations given to it: "A sort of axle, like an iron rod, that a mill turns around; a celestial sphere, orbit, sign of the zodiac, speed, wave . . .", but he adds the following observation made by Tabari, the famous Tenth century commentator: "It is our duty to keep silent when we do not know." (XVII, 15). This shows just how incapable men were of understanding this concept of the Sun's and Moon's orbit. It is obvious that if the word had expressed an astronomical concept common in Muhammad's day, it would not have been so difficult to interpret these verses. A new concept therefore existed in the Quran that was not to be explained until centuries later.

Today, the concept is widely spread that the Moon is a satellite of the Earth around which it revolves in periods of twenty-nine days. A correction must however be made to the absolutely circular form of its orbit, since modern astronomy ascribes a certain eccentricity to this, so that the distance between the Earth and the Moon (240,000 miles) is only the average distance.

We have seen above how the Quran underlined the usefulness of observing the Moon's movements in calculating time (sura 10, verse 5, quoted at the beginning of this chapter.)

This system has often been criticized for being archaic, impractical and unscientific in comparison to our system based on the Earth's rotation around the Sun, expressed today in the Julian calendar.

This criticism calls for the following two remarks:

(a) Nearly fourteen centuries ago, the Quran was directed at the inhabitants of the Arabian Peninsula who were used to the lunar calculation of time. It was advisable to address them in the only language they could understand and not to upset the habits they had of locating spatial and temporal reference-marks which were nevertheless quite efficient. It is known how well-versed men living in the desert are in the observation of the sky; they navigated according to the stars and told the time according to the phases of the Moon. Those were the simplest and most reliable means available to them.

(b) Apart from the specialists in this field, most people are unaware of the perfect correlation between the Julian and the lunar calendar: 235 lunar months correspond exactly to 19 Julian years of 86514 days. Then length of our year of 365 days is not perfect because it has to be rectified every four years (with a leap year). With the lunar calendar, the same phenomena occurs every 19 years (Julian). This is the Metonic cycle, named after the Greek astronomer Meton, who discovered this exact correlation between solar and lunar time in the Fifth century B.C.

It is more difficult to conceive of the Sun's orbit because we are so used to seeing our solar system organised around it. To understand the verse from the Quran, the position of the Sun in our galaxy must be considered, and we must therefore call on modern scientific ideas.

Our galaxy includes a very large number of stars spaced so as to form a disc that is denser at the centre than at the rim. The Sun occupies a position in it which is far removed from the centre of the disc. The galaxy revolves on its own axis which is its centre with the result that the Sun revolves around the same centre in a circular orbit. Modern astronomy has worked out the details of this. In 1917, Shapley estimated the distance between the Sun and the centre of our galaxy at 10 kiloparsecs i.e., in miles, circa the figure 2 followed by 17 zeros. To complete one revolution on its own axis, the galaxy and Sun take roughly 250 million years. The Sun travels at roughly 150 miles per second in the completion of this.

The above is the orbital movement of the Sun that was already referred to by the Quran fourteen centuries ago. The demonstration of the existence and details of this is one of the achievements of modern astronomy.

This concept does not appear in those translations of the Quran that have been made by men of letters. Since the latter know nothing about astronomy, they have translated the Arabic word that expresses this movement by one of the meanings the word has: 'to swim'. They have done this in both the French translations and the, otherwise remarkable, English translation by Yusuf Ali.

The Arabic word referring to a movement with a self-propelled motion is the verb *sabaha* (*yasbahuna* in the text of the two verses). All the senses of the verb imply a movement that is associated with a motion that comes from the body in question. If the movement takes place in water, it is 'to swim'; it is 'to move by the action of one's own legs' if it takes place on land. For a movement that occurs in space, it is difficult to see how else this meaning implied in the word could be rendered other than by employing its original sense. Thus there seems to have been no mistranslation, for the following reasons:

(a) The Moon completes its rotating motion on its own axis at the same time as it revolves around the Earth, i.e. 29 days (approx.), so that it always has the same side facing us.

(b) The Sun takes roughly 25 days to revolve on its own axis. There are certain differences in its rotation at its equator and poles, (we shall not go into them here) but as a whole, the Sun is animated by a rotating motion.

It appears therefore that a verbal nuance in the Quran refers to the Sun and Moon's own motion. These motions of the two celestial bodies are confirmed by the data of modern science, and it is inconceivable that a man living in the Seventh century A.D.—however knowledgeable he might have been in his day (and this was certainly not true in Muhammad's case)—could have imagined them.

This view is sometimes contested by examples from great thinkers of antiquity who indisputably predicted certain data that modern science has verified. They could hardly have relied on scientific deduction however; their method of procedure was more one of philosophical reasoning. Thus the case of the Pythagoreans is often advanced. In the Sixth century B.C., they defended the theory of the rotation of the Earth on its own axis and the movement of the planets around the Sun. This theory was to be confirmed by modern science. By comparing it with the case of the Pythagoreans, it is easy to put forward the hypothesis of Muhammad as being a brilliant thinker, who was supposed to have imagined all on his own what modern science was to discover centuries later. In so doing however, people quite simply forget to mention the other aspect of what these geniuses of philosophical reasoning produced, i.e. the colossal blunders that litter their work. It must be remembered for example, that the Pythagoreans also defended the theory whereby the Sun was fixed in space; they made it the centre of the world and only conceived of a celestial order that was centered on it. It is quite common in the works of the great philosophers of antiquity to find a mixture of valid and invalid ideas about the Universe. The brilliance of these human works comes from the advanced ideas they contain, but they should not make us overlook the mistaken concepts which have also been left to us. From a strictly scientific point of view, this is what distinguished them from the Quran. In the latter, many subjects are referred to that have a bearing on modern knowledge without one of them containing a statement that contradicts what has been established by present-day science.

At a time when it was held that the Earth was the centre of the world and that the Sun moved in relation to it, how could any one have failed to refer to the Sun's movement when talking of the sequence of night and day ? This is not however referred to in the Quran and the subject is dealt with as follows:

> "(God) covers the day with the night which is in haste to follow it . . ." —(7:54)
>
> "And a sign for them (human beings) is the night. We strip it of the day and they are in darkness." —(36:37)
>
> "Hast thou not seen how God merges the night into the day and merges the day into the night." —(31:29)
>
> ". . . He coils the night upon the day and He coils the day upon the night." —(39:5)

The first verse cited requires no comment. The second simply provides an image.

It is mainly the third and fourth verses quoted above that provide interesting material on the process of interpenetration and especially of winding the night upon the day and the day upon the night, (sura 39, verse 5).

'To coil' or 'to wind' seems, as in the French translation by R. Blachere, to be the best way of translating the Arabic verb *kawivara.* The original meaning of the verb is to 'coil' a turban around the head; the notion of coiling is preserved in all the other senses of the word.

What actually happens however in space? American astronauts have seen and photographed what happens from their spaceships, especially at a great distance from Earth, e.g. from the Moon. They saw how the Sun permanently lights up (except in the case of an eclipse) the half of the Earth's surface that is facing it, while the other half of the globe is in darkness. The Earth turns on its own axis and the lighting remains the same, so that an area in the form of a half-sphere makes one revolution around the Earth in twenty four hours while the other half-sphere, that has remained in darkness, makes the same revolution in the same time. This perpetual rotation of night and day is quite clearly described in the Quran. It is easy for the human understanding to grasp this notion nowadays because we have the idea of the Sun's (relative) immobility and the Earth's rotation. This process of perpetual coiling, including the interpenetration of one sector by another is expressed in the Quran just as if the concept of the Earth's roundness had already been conceived at the time—which was obviously not the case.

Further to the above reflections on the sequence of day and night, one must also mention, with a quotation of some verses from the Quran, the idea that there is more than one Orient and one Occident. This is of purely descriptive interest because these phenomena rely on the most commonplace observations. The idea is mentioned here with the aim of reproducing as faithfully as possible all that the Quran has to say on this subject.

The following are examples:

— In sura 70 verse 40, the expression 'Lord of Orients and Occidents'.

— In sura 55, verse 17, the expression 'Lord of the two Orients and the two Occidents'.

— In sura 43, verse 38, a reference to the 'distance between the two Orients', an image intended to express the immense size of the distance separating the two points.

Anyone who carefully watches the sunrise and sunset knows that the Sun rises at different points of the Orient and sets at different points of the Occident, according to season. Bearings taken on each of the horizons define the extreme limits that mark the two Orients and Occidents, and between these there are points marked off throughout the year. The phenomenon described here is rather commonplace, but what mainly deserves attention in this chapter are the other topics dealt with, where the description of astronomical phenomena referred to in the Quran is in keeping with modern data.

Having called modern concepts on the formation of the Universe to mind, reference was made to the evolution that took place, starting with primary nebula through to the formation of galaxies, stars and (for the solar system) the appearance of planets beginning with the Sun at a certain stage of its evolution. Modern data lead us to believe that in the solar system, and more generally in the Universe itself, this evolution is still continuing.

How can anybody who is aware of these ideas fail to make a comparison with certain statements found in the Quran in which the manifestations of divine Omnipotence are referred to.

The Quran reminds us several times that: "(God) subjected the sun and the moon: each one runs its course to an appointed term."

This sentence is to be found in sura 13, verse 2; sura 31, verse 29; sura 35, verse 13 and sura 39, verse 5.

In addition to this, the idea of a settled place is associated with the concept of a destination place in sura 36, verse 38: "The Sun runs its course to a settled place. This is the decree of the All Mighty, the Full of Knowledge."

'Settled place' is the translation of the word *mustaqarr* and there can be no doubt that the idea of an exact place is attached to it.

How do these statements fare when compared with data established by modern science?

The Quran gives an end to the Sun for its evolution and a destination place. It also provides the Moon with a settled place. To understand the possible meanings of these statements, we must remember what modern knowledge has to say about the evolution of the stars in general and the Sun in particular, and (by extension) the celestial bodies that automatically followed its movement through space, among them the Moon.

The Sun is a star that is roughly 4.5 billion years old, according to experts in astrophysics. It is possible to distinguish a stage in its evolution, as one can for all the stars. At present, the Sun is at an early stage, characterized by the transformation of hydrogen atoms into helium atoms. Theoretically, this present stage should last another 5½ billion years according to calculations that allow a total of 10 billion years for the duration of the primary stage in a star of this kind. It has already been shown, in the case of these other stars, that this stage gives way to a second period characterized by the completion of the transformation of hydrogen into helium, with the resulting expansion of its external layers and the cooling of the Sun. In the final stage, its light is greatly diminished and density considerably increased; this is to be observed in the type of star known as a 'white dwarf.

The above dates are only of interest in as far as they give a rough estimate of the time factor involved, what is worth remembering and is really the main point of the above, is the notion of an evolution. Modern data allow us to predict that, in a few billion years, the conditions prevailing in the solar system will not be the same as they are today. Like other stars whose transformations have been recorded until they reached their final stage, it is possible to predict an end to the Suri.

The second verse quoted above (sura 36, verse 38) referred to the Sun running its course towards a place of its own.

Modern astronomy has been able to locate it exactly and has even given it a name, the Solar Apex: the solar system is indeed evolving in space towards a point situated in the Constellation of Hercules (alpha lyrae) whose exact location is firmly established; it is moving at a speed already ascertained at something in the region of 12 miles per second.

All these astronomical data deserve to be mentioned in relation to the two verses from the Quran, since it is possible to state that they appear to agree perfectly with modern scientific data.

Great Universe : The expansion of the Universe is the most imposing discovery of modern science. Today it is a firmly established concept and the only debate centres around the way this is taking place.

It was first suggested by the general theory of relativity and is backed up by physics in the examination of the galactic spectrum; the regular movement towards the red section of their spectrum may be explained by the distancing of one galaxy from another.

Thus the size of the Universe is probably constantly increasing and this increase will become bigger the further away the galaxies are from us. The speeds at which these celestial bodies are moving may, in the course of this perpetual expansion, go from fractions of the speed of light to speeds faster than this.

The following verse of the Quran (sura 51, verse 47) where God is speaking, may perhaps be compared with modern ideas:

> "The heaven, We have built it with power. Verily. We are expanding it."
>
> 'Heaven' is the translation of the word '*sama*' and this is exactly the extraterrestrial world that is meant.
>
> 'We are expanding it' is the translation of the plural present participle *musiuna* of the verb *ausaa* meaning 'to make wider, more spacious, to extend, to expand'.

Some translators who were unable to grasp the meaning of the latter provide translations that appear to me to be mistaken, e.g. "we give generously" (R. Blachere). Others sense the meaning, but are afraid to commit themselves: Hamidullah in his translation of the Quran talks of the widening of the heavens and space, but he includes a question mark. Finally, there are those who arm themselves with authorized scientific opinion in their commentaries and give the meaning stated here. This is true in the case of the *Muntakab*, a book of commentaries edited by the Supreme Council for Islamic Affairs, Cairo. It refers to the expansion of the Universe in totally unambiguous terms.

From this point of view, three verses of the Quran should command our full attention. One expresses, without any trace of ambiguity, what man should and will achieve in this field. In the other two, God refers for the sake of the unbelievers in Mecca to the surprise they would have if they were able to raise themselves up to the Heavens; He alludes to a hypothesis which will not be realized for the latter.

(1) The first of these verses is sura 55, verse 33: "O assembly of Jinns and Men, if you can penetrate regions of the heavens and the earth, then penetrate them! You will not penetrate them save with a Power."

The translation given here needs some explanatory comment:

(a) The word 'if expresses in English a condition that is dependant upon a possibility and either an achievable or an unachievable hypothesis. Arabic is a language which is able to introduce a nuance into the condition which is much more explicit. There is one word to express the possibility another for the achievable hypothesis (in) and a third for the unachievable hypothesis expressed by the word (lau). The verse in question has it as an achievable hypothesis expressed by the word (in). The Quran therefore suggests the material possibility of a concrete realization. This subtle linguistic distinction formally rules out the purely mystic interpretation that some people have (quite wrongly) put on this verse.

(b) God is addressing the spirits (*jinn*) and human beings (*ins*), and not essentially allegorical figures.

(c) 'To penetrate' is the translation of the verb *nafada* followed by the preposition *min*. According to Kazimirski's dictionary, the phrase means 'to pass right through and come out on the other side of a body' (e.g. an arrow that comes out on the other side). It therefore suggests a deep penetration and emergence at the other end into the regions in question.

(d) The Power (sultan) these men will have to achieve this enterprise would seem to come from the All-Mighty.

There can be no doubt that this verse indicates the possibility men will one day achieve what we today call (perhaps rather improperly) 'the conquest of space'. One must note that the text of the Quran predicts not only penetration through the regions of the Heavens, but also the earth, i.e. the exploration of its depths.

(2) The other two verses are taken from sura 15, (verses 14 and 15). God is speaking of the unbelievers in Mecca, as the context of this passage in the sura shows:

> "Even if We opened unto them a gate to Heaven and they were to continue ascending therein, they would say: our sight is confused as in drunkenness. Nay, we are people bewitched."

The above expresses astonishment at a remarkable spectacle, different from anything man could imagine.

The conditional sentence is introduced here by the word *lau* which expresses a hypothesis that could never be realized as far as it concerned the people mentioned in these verses.

When talking of the conquest of space therefore, we have two passages in the text of the Quran: one of them refers to what will one day become a reality thanks to the powers of intelligence and ingenuity God will give to man, and the other describes an event that the unbelievers in Mecca will never witness, hence its character of a condition never to be realized. The event will however be seen by others, as intimated in the first verse quoted above. It describes the human reactions to the unexpected spectacle that travellers in space will see: their confused sight, as in drunkenness, the feeling of being bewitched.

This is exactly how astronauts have experienced this remarkable adventure since the first human spaceflight around the world in 1961. It is known in actual fact how once one is above the Earth's atmosphere, the Heavens no longer have the azure appearance we see from Earth, which results from phenomena of absorption of the Sun's light into the layers of the atmosphere. The human observer in space above the Earth's atmosphere sees a black sky and the Earth seems to be surrounded by a halo of bluish colour due to the same phenomena of absorption of light by the Earth's atmosphere. The Moon has no atmosphere, however, and therefore appears in its true colors against the black background of the sky. It is a completely new spectacle therefore that presents itself to men in space, and the photographs of this spectacle are well known to present-day man.

Here again, it is difficult not to be impressed, when comparing the text of the Quran to the data of modern science, by statements that simply cannot be ascribed to the thought of a man who lived more than fourteen centuries ago.

Our Planet : As in the case of the subjects already examined, the verses of the Quran dealing with the Earth are dispersed throughout the Book. It is difficult to classify them, and the scheme adopted here is a personal one.

To explain them more clearly, one might begin by singling out a certain number of verses that deal with more than one subject at a time. These verses are largely general in their application and constitute an invitation extended to men to reflect on divine Beneficence by pondering on the examples provided.

Other groups of verses may be singled out which deal with more specific subjects, as follows :

— the water cycle and the seas.

— the Earth's relief.

— the Earth's atmosphere.

Although these verses provide arguments intended to lead man to meditate on the Beneficence of God towards His creatures, here and there they contain statements that are interesting from the point of view of modern science. They are perhaps especially revealing by virtue of the fact that they do not express the varied beliefs concerning natural phenomena that were current at the time of the Quranic Revelation. These beliefs were later to be shown by scientific knowledge to be mistaken.

On the one hand, these verses express simple ideas readily understood by to those people to whom, for geographical reasons, the Quran was first directed : the inhabitants of Mecca and Medina, the Bedouins of the Arabian Peninsula. On the other hand, they contain reflections of a general nature from which a more cultivated public of any time and place may learn something instructive, once it starts to think about them: this is a mark of the Quran's universality.

As there is apparently no classification of such verses in the Quran, they are presented here in the numerical order of the suras:

> "(God) is the One who made the earth a couch for you and the heavens an edifice, and sent down water from the sky. He brought forth therewith fruits for your sustenance. Do not join equals with God when you know." —(2:22)

"Behold! In the creation of the heavens and the earth,

In the disparity of night and day:

> In the ship which runs upon the sea for the profit of mankind, —(2:164)

In the water which God sent down from the sky thereby reviving the earth after its death,

In the beasts of all kinds He scatters therein, In the change of the winds and the subjected clouds between the sky and earth,

> Here are Signs for people who are wise." —(13:3)
>
> "(God) is the One who spread out the earth and set therein mountains standing firm and rivers. For every fruit He placed two of a pair. He covers the day with the night. Verily in this there are Signs for people who reflect." —(13:3)

God is speaking:

> "The earth, We spread it out and set thereon mountains standing firm. We caused all kind of things to grow therein in due balance. Therein We have provided you and those you do not supply with means of subsistence and there is not a thing but its stores are with us. We do not send it down save in appointed measure." —(15:19-21)
>
> "(God is) the One Who has made for you the earth like a cradle and inserted roads into it for you. He sent water down from the sky and thereby We brought forth pairs of plants, each separate from the other. Eat! Pasture your cattle! Verily in this are Signs for people endued With intelligence." —(20:55-54)
>
> "He Who made the earth an abode and set rivers in its interstices and mountains standing firm. He placed a barrier between the two seas. Is there any divinity besides God? Nay, but most people do not know." —(27:61)

Here a reference is made to the general stability of the Earth's crust. It is known that at the early stages of the Earth's existence before its crust cooled down, the latter was unstable. The stability of the Earth's crust is not however strictly uniform, since there are zones where earthquakes intermittently occur. As to the barrier between the two seas, it is an image which signifies that the waters of the great rivers and the waters of the sea do not mix at the level of certain large estuaries.

> "(God is) the One Who made the earth docile to you. So walk upon its shoulders! Eat of His sustenance! Unto Him will be the Resurrection." —(67:15)
>
> "After that (God) spread the earth out. Therefrom He drew out its water and its pasture. And the mountains He has firmly fixed. Goods for you and for your cattle." —(79:30-33)

In many such verses, emphasis is laid upon the importance of water and the practical consequences of its presence in the earth's soil, i.e. the fertility of the soil. There can be no doubt that in desert countries, water is the most important element governing man's survival. The reference in the Quran however goes beyond this geographical detail. According to scientific knowledge the character the Earth has of a planet that is rich in water is unique to the solar system, and this is exactly what is highlighted in the Quran. Without water, the Earth would be a dead planet like the Moon. The Quran gives first place to water among the natural phenomena of the Earth that it refers to. The water cycle is described with remarkable accuracy in the Quran.

When the verses of the Quran concerning the role of water in man's existence are read in succession today, they all appear to us to express ideas that are quite obvious. The reason for this is simple: in our day and age, we all, to a lesser or greater extent, know about the water cycle in nature.

If however, we consider the various concepts the ancients had on this subject, it becomes clear that the data in the Quran do not embody the mythical concepts current at the time of the Revelation which had been developed more according to philosophical speculation than observed phenomena. Although it was empirically possible to acquire on a modest scale, the useful practical knowledge necessary for the improvement of the irrigation, the concepts held on the water cycle in general would hardly be acceptable today.

Thus it would have been easy to imagine that underground water could have come from the infiltration of precipitations in the soil. In ancient times however, this idea, held by Vitruvius Polio Marcus in Rome, 1st century B.C., was cited as an exception. For many centuries therefore (and the Quranic Revelation is situated during this period) man held totally inaccurate views on the water cycle.

Two specialists on this subject, G. Gastany and B. Blavoux, in their entry in the *Universalis Encyclopaedia* (Encyclopaedia Universalis) under the heading Hydrogeology (Hydrogeologie), give an edifying history of this problem.

"In the Seventh century B.C., Thales of Miletus held the theory whereby the waters of the oceans, under the effect of winds, were thrust towards the interior of the continents; so the water fell upon the earth and penetrated into the soil. Plato shared these views and thought that the return of the waters to the oceans was via a great abyss, the Tartarus'. This theory had many supporters until the Eighteenth century, one of whom was Descartes. Aristotle imagined that the water vapour from the soil condensed in cool mountain caverns and formed underground lakes that fed springs. He was followed by Seneca (1st Century A.D.) and many others, until 1877, among them O. Volger . . . The first clear 13 formulation of the water cycle must be attributed to Bernard Palissy in 1580: he claimed that underground water came from rainwater infiltrating into the soil. This theory was confirmed by E. Mariotte and P. Perrault in the Seventeenth century.

In the following passages from the Quran, there is no trace of the mistaken ideas that were current at the time of Muhammad (PBUH):

> "We sent down from the sky blessed water whereby We caused to grow gardens, grains for harvest, tall palm-trees with their spathes, piled one above the other—sustenance for (Our) servants. Therewith We gave (new) life to a dead land. So will be the emergence (from the tombs)." —(50:9-11)

> "We sent down water from the sky in measure and lodged it in the ground. And We certainly are able to withdraw it. Therewith for you We gave rise to gardens of palm-trees and vineyards where for you are abundant fruits and of them you eat." —(23:18-19)

> "We sent forth the winds that fecundate. We cause the water to descend from the sky. We provide you with the water—you (could) not be the guardians of its reserves." —(15:22)

There are two possible interpretations of this last verse. The fecundating winds may be taken to be the fertilizers of plants because they carry pollen. This may, however, be a figurative expression referring by analogy to the role the wind plays in the process whereby a non-rain carrying cloud is turned into one that produces a shower of rain. This role is often referred to, as in the following verses:

> "God is the One Who sends forth the winds which raised up the clouds. We drive them to a dead land. Therewith We revive the ground after its death. So will be the Resurrection." —(35:9)

It should be noted how the style is descriptive in the first part of the verse, then passes without transition to a declaration from God. Such sudden changes in the form of the narration are very frequent in the Quran.

> "God is the One Who sends forth the winds which raised up the clouds. He spreads them in the sky as He wills and breaks them into fragments. Then thou seest raindrops issuing from within them. He makes them reach such of His servants as He wills. And they are rejoicing." —(30:48)

> "(God) is the One Who sends forth the winds like heralds of His Mercy. When they have carried the heavy-laden clouds, We drive them to a dead land. Then We cause water to descend and thereby bring forth fruits of every kind. Thus We will bring forth the dead. Maybe you will remember." —(7:57)

> "(God) is the One Who sends forth the winds like heralds of His Mercy. We cause pure water to descend in order to revive a dead land with it and to supply with drink the multitude of cattle and human beings We have created." —(25:48-49)

> ". . . In the provision that God sends down from the sky and thereby He revives the ground after its death and in the change (of direction) of winds, there are Signs for people who are wise." —(45:5)

The provision made in this last verse is in the form of the water sent down from the sky, as the context shows. The accent is on the change of the winds that modify the rain cycle.

> "(God) sends water down from the sky so that the rivers flow according to their measure. The torrent bears away an increasing foam." —(13:17)

God commands the Prophet:

> "Say: Do you see if your water were to be lost in the ground, who then can supply you with gushing water?" —(67:30)

> "Hast thou not seen that God sent water down from the sky and led it through sources into the ground ? Then He caused sown fields of different colours to grow." —(39:21)

> "Therein We placed gardens of palm-trees and vineyards and We caused water springs to gush forth." —(36:34)

The importance of springs and the way they are fed by rain-water conducted into them is stressed in the last three verses. It is worth pausing to examine this fact and call to mind the predominance in the Middle Ages of views such as those held by Aristotle, according to whom springs were fed by underground lakes. In his entry on Hydrology (Hydrologie) in the *Universalis Encyclopaedia* (Encyclopaedia Universalis) M.R. Remenieras, a teacher at the French National School of Agronomy (Ecole nationale du Genie rural, des Eaux et Forets), describes the main stages of hydrology and refers to the magnificent irrigation works of the ancients, particularly in the Middle East. He notes however that an empirical outlook ruled over everything, since the ideas of the time proceeded from mistaken concepts. He continues as follows:

> "It was not until the Renaissance (between circa 1400 and 1600) that purely philosophical concepts gave way to research based on the objective observation of hydrologic phenomena. Leonardo da Vinci (1452-1519) rebelled against Aristotle's statements. Bernard Palissy, in his wonderful discourse on the nature of waters and fountains both natural and artificial (Discours admirable de la nature des eaux et fontaines tant naturelles quartificielles (Paris, 1570)) gives a correct interpretation of the water cycle and especially of the way springs are fed by rainwater."

This last statement is surely exactly what is mentioned in verse 21, sura 39 describing the way rainwater is conducted into sources in the ground.

The subject of verse 43, sura 24 is rain and hail:

> "Hast thou not seen that God makes the clouds move gently, then joins them together, then makes them a heap. And thou seest raindrops issuing from within it. He sends down from the sky mountains of hail, He strikes therewith whom He wills and He turns it away from whom He wills. The flashing of its lightning almost snatches away the sight."

The following passage requires some comment:

> "Have you observed the water you drink? Do you bring it down from the rain clouds? Or do We? If it were Our will, We could make it salty. Then why are you not thankful?" —(56:68-70)

This reference to the fact that God could have made fresh water salty is a way of expressing divine Omnipotence. Another means of reminding us of the same Omnipotence is the challenge to man to make rain fall from the clouds. In modern times however, technology has surely made it possible to create rain artificially. Can one therefore oppose the statement in the Quran to man's ability to produce precipitations?

The answer is no, because it seems clear that one must take account of man's limitations in this field. M.A. Facy, an expert at the French Meteorological Office, wrote the following in the *Universalis Encyclopedia* (Encyclopedia Universalis) under the heading Precipitations (Precipitations) : "It will never be possible to make rain fall from a cloud that does not have the suitable characteristics of a rain cloud or one that has not yet reached the appropriate stage of evolution (maturity)". Man can never therefore hasten the precipitation process by technical means when the natural conditions for it are not present. If this were not the case, droughts would never occur in practice—which they obviously do. To have control over rain and fine weather still remains a dream therefore.

Man cannot wilfully break the established cycle that maintains the circulation of water in nature. This cycle may be outlined as follows, according to modern ideas on hydrology:

> The calories obtained from the Sun's rays cause the sea and those parts of the Earth's surface that are covered or soaked in water to evaporate. The water vapour that is given off rises into the atmosphere and, by condensation, forms into clouds. The winds then intervene and move the clouds thus formed over varying distances. The clouds can then either disperse without producing rain, or combine their mass with others to create even greater condensation, or they can fragment and produce rain at some stages in their evolution. When rain reaches the sea (70% of the Earth's surface is covered by seas), the cycle is soon repeated. When rain falls on the land, it may be absorbed by vegetation and thus aid the latter's growth; the vegetation in its turn gives off water and thus returns some water to the atmosphere. The rest, to a lesser or greater extent, infiltrates into the soil, whence it is either conducted through channels into the sea, or comes back to the Earth's surface network through springs or resurgences.

When one compares the modern data of hydrology to what is contained in the numerous verses of the Quran quoted in this paragraph, one has to admit that there is a remarkable degree of agreement between them.

Whereas the above verses from the Quran have provided material for comparison between modern knowledge about the water cycle in nature, this is not the case for the seas. There is not a single statement in the Quran dealing with the seas which could be used for comparison with scientific data per se. This does not diminish the necessity of pointing out however that none of the statements in the Quran on the seas refers to the beliefs, myths or superstitions prevalent at the time of its Revelation.

A certain number of verses deal with the seas and navigation. As subjects for reflection, they provide indications of divine omnipotence that arise from the facts of common observation. The following verses are examples of this:

> "(God) has made the ship subject to you, so that it runs upon the sea at His Command." —(14:32)
>
> " (God) is the One Who subjected the sea, so that you eat fresh meat from it and you extract from it ornaments which you wear. Thou seest the ships ploughing the waves, so that you seek of His Bounty. Maybe, you will be thankful." —(16:4)
>
> "Hast thou seen that the ship runs upon the sea by the Grace of God, in order to show you His Signs. Verily in this are Signs for all who are persevering and grateful." —(31:31)
>
> "His are the ships erected upon the sea like tokens." —(55:24)
>
> "A sign for them is that We bore their offspring in the loaded Ark. We have created for them similar (vessels) on which they ride. If We will, We drown them and there is no help and they will not be saved unless by Mercy from Us and as a gratification for a time." —(36:41-44)

The reference here is quite clearly to the vessel bearing man upon the sea, just as, long ago, Nuh and the other occupants of the vessel were carried in the Ark that enabled them to reach dry land.

Another observed fact concerning the sea stands out, because of its unusual nature, from the verses of the Quran devoted to it: three verses refer to certain characteristics shared by great rivers when they flow out into the ocean.

The phenomenon is well known and often seen whereby the immediate mixing of salty seawater and fresh river water does not occur. The Quran refers to this in the case of what is thought to be the estuary of the Tigris and Euphrates where they unite to form what one might call a 'sea' over 100 miles long, the Shatt Al Arab. At the inner parts of the gulf, the effect of the tides is to produce the welcome phenomenon of the reflux of fresh water to the interior of the dry land, thus ensuring adequate irrigation. To understand the text correctly, one has to know that the English word 'sea' conveys the general meaning of the Arabic word *bahr* which designates a large mass of water and is equally used for both the sea and the great rivers: the Nile, Tigris and Euphrates for example.

The following are the three verses that describe this phenomenon:

> "(God) is the One Who has let free the two seas, one is agreeable and sweet, the other salty and bitter. He placed a barrier between them, a partition that it is forbidden to pass." —(25:53)

> "The two seas are not alike. The water of one is agreeable, sweet, pleasant to drink. The other salty and bitter. You eat fresh meat from it and you extract from it ornaments which you wear." —(35:12)

> "He has loosed the two seas. They meet together. Between them there is a barrier which they do not transgress. Out of them come pearls and coral."
> —(55:19-20, 22)

In addition to the description of the main fact, these verses refer to what may be obtained from fresh water and seawater: fish, personal adornment, i.e. coral and pearls. With regard to the phenomenon whereby the river water does not mix with seawater at the estuary, one must understand that this is not peculiar to the Tigris and Euphrates; they are not mentioned by name in the text, but it is thought to refer to them. Rivers with a very large outflow, such as the Mississippi and the Yangtze, have the same peculiarity: the mixing of their fresh water with the salty water of the sea does not often occur until very far out at sea.

The constitution of the Earth is highly complex. Today, it is possible to imagine it very roughly as being formed of a deep layer, at very high temperature, and especially of a central area where rocks are still in fusion, and of a surface layer, the Earth's crust which is solid and cold. The crust is very thin; its thickness is estimated in units of miles or units of ten miles at the most. The Earth's radius is however slightly over 3,750 miles, so that its crust does not represent (on average) one hundredth of the sphere's radius. It is upon this skin, as it were, that all geological phenomena have taken place. At the origin of these phenomena are folds that were to form the mountain ranges; their formation is called 'orogenesis' in geology: the process is of considerable importance because with the development of a relief that was to constitute a mountain, the Earth's crust was driven in proportionately far down: this process ensures a foundation in the layer that underlies it.

The history of the distribution of the sea and land on the surface of the globe has only recently been established and is still very incomplete, even for the most recent and best known periods. It is likely that the oceans appeared and formed the hydrosphere circa half a billion years ago. The continents were probably a single mass at the end of the primary era, then subsequently broke apart. Some continents or parts of continents have moreover emerged through the formation of mountains in maritime zones (e.g. the North Atlantic continent and part of Europe).

According to modern ideas, the dominating factor in the formation of the land that emerged was the development of mountain ranges. The evolution of the land, from the primary to the quaternary era, is classed according to 'orogenic phases' that are themselves grouped into 'cycles' of the same name since the formation of all mountain reliefs had repercussions on the balance between the sea and the continents. It made some parts of the land disappear and others emerge, and for hundreds of millions of years it has altered the surface distribution of the continents and oceans: the former at present only occupying three tenths of the surface of this planet.

In this way it is possible to give a very rough outline of the transformations that has taken place over the last hundreds of millions of years.

When referring to the Earth's relief, the Quran only describes, as it were, the formation of the mountains. Seen from the present point of view, there is indeed little one can say about the verses that only express God's Beneficence to man with regard to the Earth's formation, as in the following verses:

> "For you God made the earth a carpet so that you travel along its roads and the paths of valleys."
> —(71:19-20)

> "The earth, We have spread it out. How excellently We did that." —(51:48)

The carpet which has been spread out is the Earth's crust, a solidified shell on which we can live, since the globe's substrata" are very hot, fluid and hostile to any form of life.

The statements in the Quran referring to the mountains and the references to their stability subsequent to the phenomenon of the folds are very important.

The context invites unbelievers to consider certain natural phenomena, among them:

> ". . . the mountains, how they have been pitched (like a tent). The Earth how it was made even."
> —(88:19-20)

The following verses give details about the way in which the mountains were anchored in the ground:

> "Have We not made the earth an expanse and the mountains stakes." —(78:6-7)

The stakes referred to are the ones used to anchor a tent in the ground (*autad*, plural of *watad*).

Modern geologists describe the folds in the Earth as giving foundations to the mountains, and their dimensions go roughly one mile to roughly 10 miles. The stability of the Earth's crust results from the phenomenon of these folds.

So it is not surprising to find reflections on the mountains in certain passages of the Quran, such as the following:

> "And the mountains (God) has fixed them firmly."
> —(79:32)

> "(God) has cast into the ground (mountains) standing firm, so that it does not shake with you." —(31:10)

The same phrase is repeated in sura 16, verse 15; and the same idea is expressed with hardly any change in sura 21, verse 31:

> "We have placed in the ground (mountains) standing firm so that it does not shake with them."

These verses express the idea that the way the mountains are laid out ensures stability and is in complete agreement with geological data.

In addition to certain statements specifically relating to the sky, examined in the preceding chapter, the Quran contains several passages dealing with the phenomena that occur in the atmosphere. As for the comparison between them and the data of modern science, it is to be noted here, as elsewhere, that there is absolutely no contradiction between today's modern scientific knowledge and the phenomena described.

A familiar feeling of discomfort experienced at high altitude, which increases the higher one climbs, is expressed in verse 125, sura 6:

> "Those whom God wills to guide, He opens their breasts to Islam. Those whom He wills lose their way, He makes their breasts narrow and constricted, as if they were climbing in the sky."

Some commentators have claimed that the notion of discomfort at high altitude was unknown to the Arabs of Muhammad's time. It appears that this was not true at all: the existence on the Arabian Peninsula of peaks rising over two miles high makes it extremely implausible that they should not have known of the difficulty of breathing at high altitude. Others have seen in this verse a prediction of the conquest of space, an opinion that appears to require categorical denial, at least for this passage.

Electricity in the atmosphere and the consequences of this, i.e. lightning and hail, are referred to in the following verses:

> "(God) is the One Who shows you the lightning, with fear and covetousness. He raised up the heavy clouds. The thunder glorifies His Praise and so do the angels for awe. He sends the thunderbolt and strikes with them who He wills while they are disputing about God. He is All Mighty in His Power." —(13:12-13)

In this verse there is the expression of an obvious correlation between the formation of heavy rain clouds or clouds containing hail and the occurrence of lightning: the former, the subject of covetousness on account of the benefit it represents and the latter, the subject of fear, because when it falls, it is at the will of the All-Mighty. The connection between the two phenomena is verified by present-day knowledge of electricity in the atmosphere.

The phenomenon of shadows and the fact that they move is very simply explained today. It forms the subject of the following observations:

> "Out of the things He created, God has given you shade . . ." —(16:81)

> "Have (the Unbelievers) not observed that for all the things God created, how their shadow shifts right and left, prostating themselves to God while they are full of humility." —(16:48)

> "Hast thou not seen how thy Lord has spread the shade. If He willed, He could have made it stationary. Moreover We made the sun its guide and We withdraw it towards Us easily." —(25:45-46)

Apart from the phrases dealing with the humility before God of all the things He created, including their shadow, and the fact that God can take back all manifestations of His Power, as He wills, the text of the Quran refers to the relationship between the Sun and the shadows. One must bear in mind at this point the fact that, in Muhammad's day, it was believed that the way a shadow moved was governed by the movement of the sun from east to west. This principle was applied in the case of the sun dial to measure the time between sunrise and sunset. In this instance, the Quran speaks of the phenomenon without referring to the explanation current at the time of the Revelation. It would have been readily accepted for many centuries by those who came after Muhammad. In the end however, it would have been shown to be inaccurate. The Quran only talks moreover of the function the sun has as an indicator of shadow. Evidently there is no contradiction between the way the Quran describes shadow and what we know of this phenomenon in modern times.

Life on Earth : Numerous verses describing the origins of life have been assembled in this chapter, along with certain aspects of the vegetable kingdom and general or specific topics relating to the animal kingdom. The grouping of verses scattered throughout the Book afford a general view of the data the Quran contains on these subjects.

In the case of the subject of this and the following chapter, the examination of the Quranic text has sometimes been particularly delicate on account of certain difficulties inherent in the vocabulary. These have only been overcome through the fact that scientific data which have a bearing on the subject have been taken into consideration. It is particularly so in the case of living beings, i.e. animal, vegetable and human, where a confrontation with the teachings of science is shown to be indispensable in the search for the meaning of certain statements on these topics contained in the Quran.

It will become clear that numerous translations of these passages in the Quran, made by men of letters, must be deemed inaccurate by the scientist. The same holds true for commentaries made by those who do not possess the scientific knowledge necessary for an understanding of the text.

This question has always preoccupied man, both for himself and for the living things around him. It will be examined here from a general point of view. The case of man, whose appearance on Earth and reproduction processes are the subject of lengthy exposes, will be dealt with in the next chapter.

When the Quran describes the origins of life on a very broad basis, it is extremely concise. It does so in a verse that also mentions the process of the formation of the Universe, already quoted and commented on:

> "Do not the Unbelievers see that the heavens and the earth were joined together, then We clove them as under and We got every living thing out of the water. Will they then not believe?" —(21:30)

The notion of 'getting something out of something' does not give rise to any doubts. The phrase can equally mean that every living thing was made of water (as its essential component) or that every living thing originated in water. The two possible meanings are strictly in accordance with scientific data. Life is in fact of aquatic origin and water is the major component of all living cells. Without water, life is not possible. When the possibility of life on another planet is discussed, the first question is always: does it contain a sufficient quantity of water to support life?

Modern data lead us to think that the oldest living being must have belonged to the vegetable kingdom: algae have been found that date from the pre-Cambrian period, i.e. the time of the oldest known lands. Organisms belonging to the animal kingdom probably appeared slightly later: they too came from the sea.

What has been translated here by 'water' is the word ma' which means both water in the sky and water in the sea, plus any kind of liquid. In the first meaning, water is the element necessary to all vegetable life:

> "(God is the One Who) sent water down from the sky and thereby We brought forth pairs of plants each separate from the other." —(20:53)

This is the first reference to the notion of a pair in the vegetable kingdom. We shall return to this later.

In the second meaning, a liquid without any further indication of what kind, the word is used in its indeterminate form to designate what is at the basis of the formation of all animal life:

> "God created every animal from water." —(24:45)

We shall see further on how this word may also be applied to seminal fluid.

Whether it deals therefore with the origins of life in general, or the element that gives birth to plants in the soil, or the seed of animals, all the statements contained in the Quran on the origin of life are strictly in accordance with modern scientific data. None of the myths on the origins of life that abounded at the time the Quran appeared are mentioned in the text.

It is not possible to quote in their entirety all the numerous passages in the Quran in which divine Beneficence is referred to concerning the salutary effect of the rain which makes vegetation grow. Here are just three verses on this subject:

> "(God) is the One Who sends water down from the sky. For you this is a drink and out of it (grow) shrubs in which you let (cattle) graze freely. Therewith for you He makes sown fields, olives, palm-trees, vineyards and all kinds of fruit grow." —(16:10-11)

> "(God) is the One Who sent water down from the sky. There—with We brought forth plants of all kinds and from them the verdure and We brought forth from it the clustered grains, and from the palm-tree its spathes with bunches of dates (hanging) low, the gardens of grapes, olives and pomegranates similar and different. Look at their fruit, when they bear it, and their ripening. Verily, in that there are Signs for people who believe." —(6:99)

> "We sent down from the sky blessed water whereby. We caused to grow gardens, grains for harvest, tall palm-trees with their spathes, piled one above the other—sustenance for (Our) servants. Therewith We give (new) life to a dead land. So will be the emergence (from the tombs)." —(50:9-11)

The Quran adds to these general data, others that refer to more specialized subjects:

> "The earth . . . We caused all kinds of things to grow therein in due balance." —(15:19)

On various food materials, the Quran says:

> "On the earth are adjacent parts; vineyards, sown fields, palm-trees, similar and not similar, watered with

> the same water. We make some of them more excellent than others to eat and verily in this are Signs for wise people." —(13:4)

It is interesting to note the existence of these verses because they show the sober quality of the terms used, and the absence of any description that might highlight the beliefs of the times, rather than fundamental truths. What particularly attracts our attention however, are the statements in the Quran concerning reproduction in the vegetable kingdom.

One must bear in mind that there are two methods of reproduction in the vegetable kingdom: one sexual, the other asexual. It is only the first which in fact deserves the term 'reproduction', because this defines a biological process whose purpose is the appearance of a new individual identical to the one that gave it birth.

Asexual reproduction is quite simply multiplication. It is the result of the fragmentation of an organism which has separated from the main plant and developed in such a way as to resemble the plant from which it came. It is considered by Guilliermond and Mangenot to be a 'special case of growth'. A very simple example of this is the cutting: a cutting taken from a plant is placed in suitably watered soil and regenerated by the growth of new roots. Some plants have organs specially designed for this, while others give off spores that behave like seeds, as it were, (it should be remembered that seeds are the results of a process of sexual reproduction).

Sexual reproduction in the vegetable kingdom is carried out by the coupling of the male and female parts of the generic formations united on the same plant or located on separate plants. This is the only form that is mentioned in the Quran:

> "(God is the One Who) sent water down from the sky and thereby We brought forth pairs of plants each separate from the other." —(20:53)

'One of a pair' is the translation of *zauj* (plural *azwaj*) whose original meaning is: 'that which, in the company of another, forms a pair'; the word is used just as readily for a married couple as for a pair of shoes.

> "Thou seest the grounds lifeless. When We send down water thereon it shakes and grows and puts forth every magnificent pair (of plants)." —(22:5)

> "We caused to grow (on the earth) every noble pair (of plants)." —31:10)

> "Of all fruits (God) placed (on the earth) two of a pair." —(13:3)

We know that fruit is the end-product of the reproduction process of superior plants which have the most highly developed and complex organization. The stage preceding fruit is the flower, which has male and female organs (stamens and ovules). The latter, once pollen has been carried to them, bear fruit which in turn matures and frees its seeds. All fruit therefore implies the existence of male and female organs. This is the meaning of the verse in the Quran.

It must be noted that for certain species, fruit can come from non-fertilized flowers (parthenocarpic fruit), eg., bananas, certain types of pineapple, fig, orange, and vine. They can nevertheless also come from plants that have definite sexual characteristics.

The culmination of the reproductive process comes with the germination of the seed once its outside casing is opened (sometimes it is compacted into a fruit-stone). This opening allows roots to emerge which draw from the soil all that is necessary for the plant's slowed-down life as a seed while it grows and produces a new plant.

A verse in the Quran refers to this process of germination:

> "Verily, God splits the grain and the fruit-stone." —(6:95)

The Quran often restates the existence of these components of a pair in the vegetable kingdom and brings the notion of a couple into a more general context, without set limits:

> "Glory be to Him Who created the components of couples of every kind: of what the ground caused to grow, of themselves (human beings) and of what you do not know." —(36:36)

One could form many hypotheses concerning the meaning of, the 'things men did not know' in Muhammad's day. Today we can distinguish structures or coupled functions for them, going from the infinitesimally small to the infinitely large, in the living as well as the non-living world. The point is to remember these clearly expressed ideas and note, once again, that they are in perfect agreement with modern science.

There are several questions in the Quran concerning the animal kingdom which are the subject of comments that call for a confrontation with modern scientific knowledge. Here again, however, one would gain an incomplete view of all that the Quran contains on this subject if one were to leave out a passage such as the extract which follows. In this passage, the creation of certain elements in the animal kingdom is described with the purpose of making man reflect upon the divine Beneficence extended to him. It is quoted basically to provide an example of the way in which the Quran describes the harmonious adaptation of Creation to man's needs; it relates in particular the case of those people who live in a rural setting, since there is nothing that could be examined from a different point of view.

> "(God) created cattle for you and (you find) in them warmth, useful services and food, sense of beauty when you bring them home and when you take them to pasture. They bear your heavy loads to lands you could not reach except with great personal effort. Verily, your Lord is Compassionate and Merciful; (He created) horses, mules and donkeys for you to ride and for ornament. And He created what you do not know."
>
> —(16:5-8)

Alongside these general remarks, the Quran sets out certain data on highly diversified subjects:

— reproduction in the animal kingdom.

— references to the existence of animal communities.

— statements concerning bees, spiders and birds.

— remarks on the source of constituents of animal milk.

The reproduction in animals is very summarily dealt with in these verses:

> "(God) fashioned the two of a pair, the male and the female, from a small quantity of liquid when it is poured out." —(53:45-46)

The 'pair' is the same expression that we have already encountered in the verses which deal with reproduction in the vegetable kingdom. Here, the sexes are given. The detail which is absolutely remarkable is the precision with which it is stated that a small quantity of liquid is required for reproduction. The word itself signifying 'sperm' is used.

Mention is made of animal communities in holy Quran, in this manner:

> "There is no animal on earth, no bird which flies on wings, that (does not belong to) communities like you. We have not neglected anything in the Book (of Decrees). Then to their Lord they will be gathered." —(6:38)

There are several points in this verse which require comment. Firstly, it would seem that there is a description of what happens to animals after their death: Islam does not apparently, have any doctrine on this point. Then there is predestination in general which would seem to be mentioned here. It could be conceived as absolute predestination or relative, i.e. limited to structures and a functional organization that condition modes of behaviour: the animal acts upon various exterior impulses in terms of a particular conditioning.

Blachere states that an older commentator, such as *Qadi*, thought that this verse only referred to instinctive actions whereby animals worship God. Sheik Si Boubakeur Hamza, in the commentary to his translation of the Quran, speaks of "the instinct which, according to Divine Wisdom, pushes all beings to group together, so that they demand that the work of each member serve the whole group."

Animal behaviour has been closely investigated in recent decades, with the result that genuine animal communities' have been shown to exist. Of course, for a long time now the results of a group or community's work have been examined and this has led to the acceptance of a community organization. It has only been recently however, that the mechanisms which preside over this kind of organization have been discovered for certain species. The most studied and best known case is undoubtedly that of bees, to whose behaviour the name von Frisch is linked. Von Frisch, Lorenz and Tinbergen received the 1973 Nobel Prize for their work in this field.

When specialists on the nervous system wish to provide striking examples of the prodigious organization directing animal behaviour, possibly the animals referred to most frequently are bees, spiders and birds (especially migratory birds). Whatever the case, there is no doubt that these three groups constitute a model of highly evolved organization.

The fact that the text of the Quran refers to this exemplary trio in the animal kingdom is in absolute keeping with the exceptionally interesting character that each of these animals has from a scientific point of view.

In the Quran, bees are the subject of the longest commentary:

> "Thy Lord inspired the bees: Choose your dwelling in the hills, in the trees and in what (man) built. Eat of all fruit and follow the ways of your Lord in humility. From within their bodies comes a liquor of different colours where is a remedy for men." —(16:68-69)

It is difficult to know what exactly is meant by the order to follow the ways of the Lord in humility, unless it is to be seen in general terms. All that may be said, with regard to the knowledge that has been gained of their behaviour, is that here—as in each of the three animal cases mentioned as examples in the Quran—there is a remarkable nervous organization supporting their behaviour. It is known that the pattern of a bee's dance is a means of communication to other bees; in this way, bees are able to convey to their own species the direction and distance of flowers from which nectar is to be gathered. The famous experiment performed by von Frisch has shown the meaning of this insect's movement which is intended to transmit information between worker bees.

Spiders are mentioned in the Quran to stress the flimsiness of their dwelling which is the most fragile of all. They have a refuge that is as precarious, according to the Quran, as the dwelling of those who have chosen masters other than God.

"Those who choose masters other than God are like the spider when it takes for itself a dwelling. Verily, the flimsiest dwelling is the dwelling of the spider. If they but knew." —(29:41)

A spider's web is indeed constituted of silken threads secreted by the animal's glands and their calibre is infinitely fine. Its fragility cannot be imitated by man. Naturalists are intrigued by the extraordinary pattern of work recorded by the animal's nervous cells, which allows it to produce a geometrically perfect web.

Birds are frequently mentioned in the Quran. They appear in episodes in the life of Ibrahim, Joseph, David, Solomon and Jesus. These references do not however have any bearing on the subject in hand.

The verse concerning the existence of animal communities on the ground and bird communities in the sky has been noted above:

Two other verses highlight the birds' strict submission to God's Power :

"Do they not look at the birds subjected in the atmosphere of the sky? None can hold them up (in His Power) except God." —(16:79)

"Have they not looked at the birds above them spreading their wings out and folding them? None can hold them up (in His power) except the Beneficent." —(67:19)

The translation of one single word in each of these verses is a very delicate matter. The translation given here expresses the idea that God holds the birds up in His power. The Arabic verb in question is *amsaka*, whose original meaning is 'to put one's hand on, seize, hold, hold someone back.

An illuminating comparison can be made between these verses, which stress the extremely close dependence of the birds' behavior on divine order, to modern data showing the degree of perfection attained by certain species of bird with regard to the programming of their movements. It is only the existence of a migratory programme in the genetic code of birds that can account for the extremely long and complicated journeys which very young birds, without any prior experience and without any guide, are able to accomplish. This is in addition to their ability to return to their departure point on a prescribed date. Professor Hamburger in his book, *Power and Fragiliti* (La Puissance et la Fragilite), gives as an example the well-known case of the 'mutton-bird' that lives in the Pacific, with its journey of over 15,500 miles in the shape of the figure 8. It must be acknowledged that the highly complicated instructions for a journey of this kind simply have to be contained in the bird's nervous cells. They are most definitely programmed, but who is the programmer?

The source of the constituents of animal milk is defined in the Quran in strict accordance with the data of modern knowledge.

Holy Quran says:

> "Verily, in cattle there is a lesson for you. We give you to drink of what is inside their bodies, coming from a conjunction between the contents of the intestine and the blood, a milk pure and pleasant for those who drink it."
> —(16:66)

This interpretation is very close to the one given in the Muntakhab, 1973, edited by the Supreme Council for Islamic Affairs, Cairo, which relies for its support on modern physiology.

The notion of a 'primary origin' of the constituents of milk is expressed by the word *min* (in English 'from') and the idea of a conjunction by the word *baini*. The latter not only signifies 'among' but also 'between' in the other translations quoted. It is however also used to express the idea that two things or two people are brought together.

From a scientific point of view, physiological notions must be called upon to grasp the meaning of this verse.

The substances that ensure the general nutrition of the body come from chemical transformations which occur along the length of the digestive tract. These substances come from the contents of the intestine. On arrival in the intestine at the appropriate stage of chemical transformation, they pass through its wall and towards the systemic circulation. This passage is effected in two ways: either directly, by what are called the 'lymphatic vessels', or indirectly, by the portal circulation. This conducts them first to the liver, where they undergo alterations, and from here they then emerge to join the systemic circulation. In this way everything passes through the bloodstream.

The constituents of milk are secreted by the mammary glands. These are nourished, as it were, by the product of food digestion brought to them via the bloodstream. Blood therefore plays the role of collector and conductor of what has been extracted from food, and it brings nutrition to the mammary glands, the producers of milk, as it does to any other organ.

Here the initial process which sets everything else in motion is the bringing together of the contents of the intestine and blood at the level of the intestinal wall itself. This very precise concept is the result of the discoveries made in the chemistry and physiology of the digestive system. It was totally unknown at the time of the Prophet Muhammad and has been understood only in recent times. The discovery of the circulation of the blood, was made by Harvey roughly ten centuries after the Quranic Revelation.

I consider that the existence in the Quran of the verse referring to these concepts can have no human explanation on account of the period in which they were formulated.

From the moment ancient human writings enter into detail (however slight) on the subject of reproduction, they inevitably make statements that are inaccurate. In the Middle Ages—and even in more recent time—reproduction was surrounded by all sorts of myths and superstitions. How could it have been otherwise, considering the fact that to understand its complex mechanisms, man first had to possess a knowledge of anatomy, the discovery of the microscope had to be made, and the so-called basic sciences had to be founded which were to nurture physiology, embryology, obstetrics, etc.

The situation is quite different in the Quran. The Book mentions precise mechanisms in many places and describes clearly-defined stages in reproduction, without providing a single statement marred by inaccuracy. Everything in the Quran is explained in simple terms which are easily understandable to man and in strict accordance with what was to be discovered much later on.

Human reproduction is referred to in several dozen verses of the Quran, in various contexts. It is explained through statements which deal with one or more specific points. They must be assembled to give a general idea of the verses as a whole, and here, as for the other subjects already examined, the commentary is in this way made easier.

It is imperative to recall certain basic concepts which were unknown at the time of the Quranic Revelation and the centuries that followed.

Human reproduction is effected by a series of processes which we share in common with mammals. The starting point is the fertilization of an ovule which has detached itself from the ovary. It takes place in the Fallopian tubes half-way through the menstrual cycle. The fertilizing agent is the male sperm, or more exactly, the spermatozoon, a single fertilizing cell being all that is needed. To ensure fertilization therefore, an infinitely small quantity of spermatic liquid containing a large number of spermatozoons (tens of millions at a time) is required. This liquid is produced by the testicles and temporarily stored in a system of reservoirs and canals that finally lead into the urinary tract; other glands are situated along the latter which contribute their own additional secretions to the sperm itself.

The implantation of the egg fertilized by this process takes place at a precise spot in the female reproductive system: it descends into the uterus via a Fallopian tube and lodges in the body of the uterus where it soon literally implants itself by insertion into the thickness of the mucosa and of the muscle, once the placenta has been formed and with the aid of the latter. If the implantation of the fertilized egg takes place, for example, in the Fallopian tubes instead of in the uterus, pregnancy will be interrupted.

Once the embryo begins to be observable to the naked eye, it looks like a small mass of flesh at the centre of which the appearance of a human being is at first indistinguishable. It grows there in progressive stages which are very well known today; they lead to the bone structure, the muscles, the nervous system, the circulation, and the viscera, etc.

These notions will serve as the terms of reference against

which the statements in the Quran on reproduction are to be compared.

It is not easy to gain an idea of what the Quran contains on this subject. The first difficulty arises from the fact already mentioned, i.e. that the statements dealing with this subject are scattered throughout the book. This is not however a major difficulty. What is more likely to mislead the inquiring reader is, once again, the problem of vocabulary.

In fact there are still many translations and commentaries in circulation today that can give a completely false idea of the Quranic Revelation on this subject to the scientist who reads them. The majority of translations describe, for example, man's formation from a 'blood clot' or an 'adhesion'. A statement of this kind is totally unacceptable to scientists specializing in this field. In the paragraph dealing with the implantation of the egg in the maternal uterus, we shall see the reasons why distinguished Arabists who lack a scientific background have made such blunders.

This observation implies how great the importance of an association between linguistic and scientific knowledge is when it comes to grasping the meaning of Quranic statements on reproduction.

The Quran sets out by stressing the successive transformations the embryo undergoes before reaching its destination in the maternal uterus.

> 'O Man! Who deceives you about your Lord the Noble, Who created you and fashioned you in due proportion and gave you any form He willed." —(82:6-8)
>
> "(God) fashioned you in (different) stages."
> —(71:14)

Along with this very general observation, the text of the Quran draws attention to several points concerning reproduction which might be listed as follows:

(1) fertilization is performed by only a very small volume of liquid.

(2) the constituents of the fertilizing liquid.

(3) the implantation of the fertilized egg.

(4) the evolution of the embryo.

The Quran repeats this concept eleven times using the following expression:

> "(God) fashioned man from a small quantity (of sperm.)." The Arabic word *nutfa* has been translated by the words 'small quantity (of sperm)' because we do not have the terms that are strictly appropriate. This word comes from a verb signifying 'to dribble, to trickle'; it is used to describe what remains at the bottom of a bucket that has been emptied out. It therefore indicates a very small quantity of liquid. Here it is sperm because the word is associated in another verse with the word sperm. —(16:4)
>
> "Was (man) not a small quantity of sperm which has been poured out?" —(75:37)

Here the Arabic word *mani* signifies sperm.

Another verse indicates that the small quantity in question is put in a 'firmly established lodging' (*qarar*) which obviously means the genital organs.

God is speaking:

> "Then We placed (man) as a small quantity (of sperm) in a safe lodging firmly established." —(23:13)

It must be added that the adjective which in this text refers to the 'firmly established lodging' *makin* is, I think, hardly translatable. It expresses the idea of a firmly established and respected place. However this may be, it refers to the spot where man grows in the maternal organism. It is important to stress the concept of a very small quantity of liquid needed in the fertilization process, which is strictly in agreement with what we know on this subject today.

The Quran describes the liquid enabling fertilization to take place in terms which it is interesting to examine:

(a) 'sperm', as has been stated precisely (sura 75, verse 37)

(b) 'a liquid poured out': "Man was fashioned from a liquid poured out" (sura 86, verse 6)

(c) 'a despised liquid' (sura 32, verse 8 and sura 77, verse 20)

The adjective 'despised' (*mahin*) would, it seems, be interpreted not so much on account of the nature of the liquid itself, as more the fact that it is emitted through the outlet of the urinary tract, using the channels that are employed for passing urine.

(d) 'Mixtures' or 'mingled liquids' (*amsaj*): "Verily, we fashioned man from a small quantity of mingled liquids" (sura 76, verse 2)

Many commentators, like professor Hamidullah, consider these liquids to be the male and female agents. The same view was shared by older commentators, who could not have had any idea of the physiology of fertilization, especially its biological conditions in the case of the woman. They thought that the word simply meant the unification of the two elements.

Modern authors however, like the commentator of the *Muntakhab* edited by the Supreme Council for Islamic Affairs, Cairo, have corrected this view and note here that the 'small quantity of sperm' is made up of various component parts. The commentator in the Muntakhab does not go into detail, but in my opinion it is a very judicious observation.

What are the component parts of sperm?

Spermatic liquid is formed by various secretions which come from the following glands:

(a) the testicles: the secretion of the male genital gland contains spermatozoons, which are elongated cells with a long flagellum; they are bathed in a sero-fluid liquid.

(b) the seminal vesicles: these organs are reservoirs of spermatozoons and are placed near the prostate gland; they also secrete their own liquid but it does not contain any fertilizing agents.

(c) the prostate gland: this secretes a liquid which gives the sperm its creamy texture and characteristic odour.

(d) the glands annexed to the urinary tract: Cooper's or Mery's glands secrete a stringy liquid and Littre's glands give off mucous.

These are the origins of the 'mingled liquids' which the Quran would appear to refer to.

There is, however, more to be said on this subject. When the Quran talks of a fertilizing liquid composed of different components, it also informs us that man's progeny will be maintained by something which may be extracted from this liquid. This is the meaning of verse 8, sura 32:

> "(God) made his progeny from the quintessence of a despised liquid."

The Arabic word, translated here by the word 'quintessence', is *sulala*. It signifies 'something which is extracted, the issue of something else, the best part of a thing'. In whatever way it is translated, it refers to a part of a whole.

Fertilization of the egg and reproduction are produced by a cell that is very elongated: its dimensions are measured in ten-thousandths of a millimeter. In normal conditions, only one single cell among several tens of millions produced by a man will actually penetrate the ovule; a large number of them are left behind and never complete the journey which leads from the vagina to the ovule, passing through the uterus and Fallopian tubes. It is therefore an infinitesimally small part of the extract from a liquid whose composition is highly complex which actually fulfills its function.

In consequence, it is difficult not to be struck by the agreement between the text of the Quran and the scientific knowledge we possess today of these phenomena.

Once the egg has been fertilized in the Fallopian tube it descends to lodge inside the uterus; this is called the 'implantation of the egg'. The Quran names the lodging of the fertilized egg womb:

> "We cause whom We will to rest in the womb for an appointed term." —(22:5)

The implantation of the egg in the uterus (womb) is the result of the development of villosities, veritable elongations of the egg, which, like roots in the soil, draw nourishment from the thickness of the uterus necessary to the egg's growth. These formations make the egg literally cling to the uterus. This is a discovery of modern times.

The act of clinging is described five different times in the Quran. Firstly in verses 1 and 2 of sura 96:

> "Read, in the name of thy Lord Who fashioned man from something which clings."

'Something which clings' is the translation of the word '*alaq*. It is the original meaning of the word. A meaning derived from it, 'blood clot', often figures in translation; it is a mistake against which one should guard: man has never passed through the stage of being a 'blood clot'. The same is true for another translation of this term, 'adhesion' which is equally inappropriate. The original sense of 'something which clings' corresponds exactly to today's firmly established reality.

This concept is recalled in four other verses which describe successive transformations from the small quantity of sperm through to the end:

> "We have fashioned you from . . . something which clings." —(22:5)
>
> "We have fashioned the small quantity (of sperm) into something which clings." —(23:14)
>
> "(God) fashioned you from a small quantity (of sperm), from something which clings." —(40:67)
>
> "Was (man) not a small quantity of sperm which has been poured out? After that he was something which clings; then God fashioned him in due proportion." —(75:37-38)

The organ which harbours the pregnancy is qualified in the Quran by a word which, as we have seen, is still used in Arabic to signify the uterus. In some suras, it is called a 'lodging firmly established' (sura 23, verse 13, quoted above and sura 77, verse 21).

The Quranic description of certain stages in the development of the embryo corresponds exactly to what we today know about it, and the Quran does not contain a single statement that is open to criticism from modern science.

After 'the thing which clings' (an expression which is well-founded, as we have seen) the Quran informs us that the embryo passes through the stage of 'chewed flesh', then osseous tissue appears and is clad in flesh (defined by a different word from the preceding which signifies 'intact flesh').

> "We fashioned the thing which clings into a chewed lump of flesh and We fashioned the chewed flesh into bones and We clothed the bones with intact flesh."
> —(23:14)

'Chewed flesh' is the translation of the word *mudga*; 'intact flesh' is *lahm*. This distinction needs to be stressed. The embryo is initially a small mass. At a certain stage in its development, it looks to the naked eye like chewed flesh. The bone structure develops inside this mass in what is called the mesenchyma. The bones that are formed are covered in muscle; the word *lahm* applies to them.

It is known how certain parts appear to be completely out of proportion during embryonic development with what is later to become the individual, while others remain in proportion.

This is surely the meaning of the word *mukallaq* which signifies 'shaped in proportion' as used in the following verse:

> "We fashioned . .. into something which clings . . . into a lump of flesh in proportion and out of proportion."
> —(5:22)

The Quran also describes the appearance of the senses and the viscera:

> "(God) appointed for you the sense of hearing, sight and the viscera." —(32:9)

It refers to the formation of the sexual organs:

> "(God) fashioned the two of a pair, the male and the female, from a small quantity (of sperm) when it is poured out." —(53:45-46)

The formation of the sexual organs is described in two sura of the Quran:

> "God created you from dust, then from a sperm-drop, then He made you pairs (the male and female)."
> —(35:11)

"And, (God) made of him a pair, the male and female."
—(75:39)

As has already been noted, all statements in the Quran must be compared with today's firmly established concepts: the agreement between them is very clear. It is however very important to compare them with the general beliefs on this subject that were held at the time of the Quranic Revelation in order to realize just how far people were in those days from having views on these problems similar to those expressed here in the Quran. There can be no doubt that they would have been unable to interpret the Revelation in the way we can today because we are helped by the data modern knowledge affords us. It was, in fact, only during the Nineteenth century that people had a slightly clearer view of this question.

Throughout the Middle Ages, the most diversified doctrines originated in unfounded myths and speculations: they persisted for several centuries after this period. The most fundamental stage in the history of embryology was Harvey's statement (1651) that "all life initially comes from an egg". At this time however, when nascent science had nevertheless benefited greatly (for the subject in hand) from the invention of the microscope, people were still talking about the respective roles of the egg and the spermatozoon. Buffon, the great naturalist, was one of those in favor of the egg theory, but Bonnet supported the theory of the seeds being 'packed together': the ovaries of Eve, the mother of the human race, were supposed to have contained the seeds of all human beings, packed together one inside the other. This hypothesis came into favor in the Eighteenth century.

More than a thousand years before our time, at a period when whimsical doctrines still prevailed, men had a knowledge of the Quran. The statements it contains express in simple terms truths of primordial importance which man has taken centuries to discover.

Our epoch believes that it has made manifold discoveries in all possible fields. It is thought that great innovations have been made in the field of sex education, and the knowledge of the facts of life which has been opened up to young people is regarded as an achievement of the modern world. Previous centuries were noted for their deliberate obscurity on this point and many people say that religion—without stating which religion—is the cause of it.

The information set out above is proof however that fourteen centuries ago theoretical questions (as it were) on human reproduction were brought to man's attention. This was done as far as was possible, taking into account the fact that the anatomical and physiological data needed for further explanations were lacking. One should also remember that, to be understood, it was necessary to use simple language suited to the level of comprehension of those who listened to the Preaching.

Practical considerations have not been silently ignored. There are many details in the Quran on the practical side of life in general, and the way man should behave in the many situations of his existence. His sex life is no exception.

Two verses in the Quran deal with sexual relations themselves. They are described in terms which unite the need for precision with that of decency. When translations and explanatory commentaries are consulted however, one is struck by the divergences between them. I have pondered for a long time on the translation of such verses, and am indebted to Doctor A. K. Giraud, Former Professor at the Faculty of Medicine, Beirut, for the following:

> "(Man) was fashioned from a liquid poured out. It issued (as a result) of the conjunction of the sexual area of the man and the sexual area of the woman."
>
> —(86:6-7)

The sexual area of the man is indicated in the text of the Quran by the world *sulb* (singular). The sexual areas of the woman are designated in the Quran by the word *taraib* (plural).

This is the translation which appears to be most satisfactory. It is different from the one that is often given by English and French translators, i.e. "(Man) has been created by a liquid poured out which issues from between the vertebral column and the bones of the breast." This would seem more to be an interpretation than a translation. It is hardly comprehensible.

The behavior of a man in his intimate relationships with his wife is stated explicitly.

There is the order concerning the menstruation period contained in following verses. God gives the following command to the Prophet:

> "They (the Believers) question thee concerning menstruation. Say: This is an evil. Keep away from women during menstruation and do not approach them until they are clean. When they have purified themselves, go to them, as God ordered it to you.
>
> "Verily, God loves the repentants and loves those who purified themselves.
>
> "Your wives are a tilth. Go to your tilth as you will. Do (some good act) for your souls beforehand."
>
> —(2:222-223)

The beginning of this passage is very clear in meaning: it formally forbids a man to have sexual contact with a woman who has her period. The second part describes the process of tilling which the sower performs before sowing the seed which is to germinate and produce a new plant. Through this image therefore, stress is indirectly laid on the importance of bearing in mind the final purpose of sexual contact, i.e. reproduction. The translation of the final phrase is by R. Blachere: it contains an order which seems to refer to the preliminaries before sexual contact.

The orders given here are of a very general kind. The problem of contraception has been raised with regard to these verses : neither here, nor anywhere else, is reference made to this subject.

Nor is provoked abortion referred to. The numerous passages quoted above on the successive transformations of the embryo make it quite clear, however, that man is considered to be constituted as of the stage described by the existence of 'something which clings. This being so, the absolute respect of the individual human being, which is referred to so often in the Quran, brings with it a total condemnation of provoked abortion. This attitude is today shared by all monotheistic religions.

Sexual relations are permitted at night during the Fast in the month of Ramadan. The verse concerning Ramadan is as follows:

> "Permitted to you, on the night of the fast, is to break chastity with your wives. They are a garment for you and you are a garment for them. So hold intercourse with them and seek what God has ordained for you."
> —(2:187)

In contrast to this, no exception to the rule is made for pilgrims in Mecca during the celebration days of the Pilgrimage.

> "For whom undertakes (the duty of) the Pilgrimage in its time, no wooing and no license." --(2:197)

This prohibition is formal, as is the fact that other activities are forbidden, e.g. hunting, fighting, etc.

Menstruation is again mentioned in the Quran in connection with divorce. The Book contains the following verse:

> "For your wives who despair of menstruation, if you doubt about them, their period of waiting will be three months. For those who never have their monthly periods and those who are pregnant their period will be until they lay down their burden." —(65:4)

The waiting period referred to here is the time between the announcement of the divorce and the time it comes into effect. Those women of whom it is said 'they despair of menstruation have reached the menopause. A precautionary period of three months is envisaged for them. Once this period is completed, divorced women who have reached the menopause may remarry.

For those who have not yet menstruated, the pregnancy period has to be awaited. For pregnant women, divorce only comes into effect once the child is born.

All these laws are in perfect agreement with physiological data. One can, furthermore, find in the Quran the same judicious legal provision in the texts dealing with widowhood.

Progressive Attitude

The Western world owes a deep debt to the Arabs in the realm of science. This does not consist in startling discoveries or revolutionary theories but in the scientific attitude that the Muslims developed:

"The ancient world was, we saw, pro-scientific. The astronomy and mathematics of the Greeks were a foreign importation never thoroughly acclimatized in Greek culture. The Greeks systematized, generalized and theorized, but the patient ways of investigation, the accumulation of positive knowledge, the minute methods of science, detailed and prolonged observation, experimental inquiry, were altogether alien to the Greek temperament. Only in Hellenistic Alexandria was any approach to scientific work conducted in the ancient classical world. What we call science arose in Europe as a result of a new spirit of inquiry, of new methods of investigation, of the methods of experiment, observation, measurement of the development of mathematics in a form unknown to the Greeks. That spirit and those methods were introduced into the European world by the Arabs.

Nature and History : Revelation is decidedly the most dependable source of human knowledge but its truth can be seen in nature and history and it is in tapping these sources of knowledge that the spirit of Islam is seen at its best. The Quran sees the signs of the ultimate Reality in the sun, the moon, the lengthening out of the shadows, the alternation of day and night, variety of human colour and tongues-in fact the whole of nature as revealed to the sense- perception of man. And the Muslim has been exhorted to see and reflect on the wide and varied manifestations of nature and not to pass by them as if he is blind and deaf. This appeals to the concrete and finite and its intellectual capture makes it possible for the intellect of man to realize its limits and then to pass beyond it for the ultimate limit is to be sought not in the direction of the stars, but in an infinite cosmic life and spirituality. This is an important point for the true appreciation of Islamic culture. Plato despised sense perception which in his view yielded mere opinion and no real knowledge. The Quran however regards hearing and seeing as valuable Divine gifts and declares them accountable to Allah for their activity in this world of his has led to the importance of observation and experiment in Islam, as opposed to the speculative approach of the Greeks.

The history of science has always been viewed under two aspects: either positively as the gradual unfolding of truth, the increase of light or negatively as the progressive triumph over error and superstition, the decrease of darkness. The modern scientist while assessing the contribution of the Muslim scientists gets a little importance. But he should turn his attention not so much to the startling discoveries but to the system of experimental inquiry which they evolved and nobody can deny the fact that every experimental discovery however humble was a step forward to the promotion of scientific knowledge. The Muslims fought successfully against the empiricism of the Greeks and paved the way for discovery, creative interpretation of new facts, experimentation, classification. From this point of view, the history of the Muslim is very fascinating. It is not possible to substantiate this statement with the account of the original contributions of the Muslim scientists. One who is interested in this subject may cast a glance on the famous book of George Sarton Introduction to the History of Science.

"It will suffice here to evoke a few glorious names without contemporary equivalents in the West Jabir ibn Haiyan, al Kindi, al Khwarizmi, al-Farghani, al-Razi, Thabit Ibn Qurra, al-Battani, Hunain Ibn Ishaq. al-Farabi. Ibrahim Ibn Sinan, al-Masudi, al-Tabri, Abul Wafa, Ali Ibn Abbas, Abul Qasim, Ibn al-Jazzar, al-Biruni, Ibn Sina, Ibn Yunus, al-Kashi, Ibn al-Haitham, Ali Ibn Isa al-Ghazzali, al-Zarqab, Umar Khayyam. A magnificent array of names which it would not be difficult to extend. If any one tells you that the Middle Ages were scientifically sterile, just quote these men to him, all of whom flourished within a relatively short period, between 750 to 1100.

The contribution of the Muslim Scientists may be divided under two heads: (a) Translations from the Greek works (b) Original discoveries.

"The rise of the Abbasids about 750 inaugurated the epoch of greatest power, splendour and prosperity of Islamic rule. At the very dawn stands the figure of a Muslim whose shadow lies a thwart the science of the Middle Ages in the orient as in the Occident."

In the time of the second Abbasid caliph al-Mansur, the task of translation of Greek wisdom was pursued with remarkable enthusiasm:

> "During the reign of Caliph Al-Mamun (813-33) the new learning reached its climax. The monarch created in Baghdad a regular school for translation. It was equipped with a library, one of the translators there was Hunayn Ibn Ishaq (809-77) a particularly gifted philosopher and physician of wide erudition, the dominating figure of this century of translators. We know from his own recently published Memoirist he translated practically the whole immense corpus of Galenic writings. Besides the translation of Greek works and their extracts, the translators made manuals of which one form, that of the 'pandects' is typical of the period of Arabic learning. These are recapitulations of the whole medicine, discussing the affections of the body systematically beginning at the head and working down to the feet."

Original Contributions : The Muslim scientists did not confine their activities of the translations of Greek works, but made their original contributions to the realm of science. The Muslims however could not content themselves with this approach of the Greeks as there was a fundamental difference between them. The Greeks as I have explained before, did not view the universe in terms of the infinite and their space and time had a static quality. Dynamism was thus abhorred in their thought:

> "The Muslim ideal was, it goes without saying, not visual beauty but God in His plenitude; that is God with all His manifestations, the stars and the heavens the earth and all nature. The Muslim ideal is thus infinite. But in dealing with the infinite as conceived by the Muslims, we cannot limit ourselves to space alone, but must equally consider time."

For the Muslims the universe is living and is a changing manifestation of God's creativeness. It is not a being but an eternal 'becoming'. With the Greeks beauty implied a static unity, the element of movement does not come into the question and the function of timers therefore completely ignored. Indeed, for Zeno and Plato time was unreal and for Heraclitus it is held within a circle. Since the Muslim scientists did not conceive the universe as a completed product which left the hand of its Maker ages ago but always looked upon it as a growing universe, time was therefore a matter of great importance for them.

"The first mathematical step from the Greek conception of a static universe to the Islamic one of a dynamic universe was made by al Khwarizmi (780-850) the founder of modern algebra. He enhanced the purely arithmetical character of numbers as finite magnitudes by demonstrating their possibilities as elements of infinite manipulations and investigations of properties and relations. In Greek mathematics, numbers could expand only by the laborious process of addition and multiplication. Khwarizmi's algebraic symbols for numbers contain within themselves the potentialities of the infinite. So we might say that the advance from arithmetic to algebra implies a step from being to 'becoming' from the static Greek universe to the living universe of Islam. The importance of Khwarizmi's algebra was recognized in the twelfth century by the West,—when Gerard of Cremona translated his theses into Latin. Until the sixteenth century this version was used in European universities as the principal mathematical text book. But Khawarizmi's influence reached far beyond the universities. We find it reflected in the mathematical works of Leonardo Fibonacci of Pisa, Master Jacob of Florence, and even of Leonardo da Vinci."

As in mathematics, so in medicine the Muslim advance beyond the Greeks has far deeper implications than those of a purely scientific character:

> "Through their medical investigations they not merely widened the horizons of medicine, but enlarged humanistic concepts generally. And once again they brought this about because of their overriding spiritual convictions. Thus it can hardly have been accidental that those researches should have led them to vistas that were inevitably beyond the reach of their Greek masters. It is regarded as symbolic that the most spectacular achievement of the mid-twentieth century

> is atomic fission and the nuclear bomb likewise it would not seem fortuitous that the early Muslim's medical endeavour should have led to a discovery that was quite as revolutionary though possibly more beneficent."

Sphere of Medical Science : The Muslim scientists made wonderful achievements in the sphere of medical science and here also their line of discovery was different from the one pursued by the Greeks. In the comparatively static world of the Greeks, man was regarded as a more or less self-contained entity. It was therefore thought that his illness was due to some factors for which his own self was primarily responsible. Such a doctrine or therapy, that in any way implied man's isolation from his fellowmen and the world at large was alien to the Muslims.

> "A philosophy of self-centredness under whatever disguise, would be both incomprehensible and reprehensible to the Muslim mind. That mind was incapable of viewing man, whether in health or in sickness as isolated from God, from fellowmen, and from the world around him. It was probably inevitable that the Muslims should have discovered that disease need not be born within the patient himself but may reach from outside, in other words, that they should have been the first to establish clearly the existence of contagion."

The Muslim doctors conducted research in such dreaded diseases as small-pox, cholera and bubonic plague. These diseases were common to non-Muslims also but the Muslims were the first to observe the contagious nature of such Ailments. This is not accidental, but it is perfectly in accordance with the Muslim's outlook on life which views human existence not in isolation from the rest of the universe but as an important link in the chain whose other links might be his fellow men an infected garment, air or water. Such an attitude manifested itself in different aspects:

(a) firstly it saved the Muslims from the frustration and the sense of loneliness which is very common in the man who believes that he is drifting in isolation as a self-propelled islet.

(b) It helped in finding the causes of disease outside man.

(c) Thirdly it taught the Muslim physicians not to rely on purely physical therapy, but also approach the spirit. Thus they seldom neglected the religious factor in treatment.

Amongst the Muslim physicians Hunayn Ibn Ishaq occupies a position of great importance because he headed the famous school of translators founded by Caliph Mamun at Baghdad. He also made valuable contributions of his own to the realm of medical science the most famous of which are his questions on medicine and treatise on the eye, considered to be the first systematic text book on opthalmology.

Advances in Medicine : Following in Hunayn's footsteps. Razi (known to the Latin West as Rhazes) (865-925) made great advances in medicine. He conducted research on smallpox and measles and recorded the results of his inquiries in books. It is said that his works on smallpox and measles were translated into Latin and later into various languages, including English, and were printed not less than forty times between the period 1498-1866.

The greatest medical work of Rhazes, and perhaps the most extensive written by a medical man, is, his al-itani i.e., 'Comprehensive Book', which includes indeed Greek, Syriac and early Arabic medical knowledge in their entirety. "The Hawi was translated into Latin under the auspices of Charles I of Anjou by the Sicilian Jewish physician Faraj Ibn Salim (Farrgut) of Cirgenti, who finished his enormous task in 1279. This greatest work of Rhazes was propagated in numerous manuscripts during the following centuries. It was repeatedly printed from 1486 onwards. By 1542 there had appeared 5 editions of this vast and costly work, besides many more of various parts of it. Its influence on European medicine was thus very considerable.

> "One of the most famous exponents of Muslim universalism and an eminent figure in Islamic learning was Ibn Sina, known in the West as Avicenna (980-1037). For a thousand years he has retained his original renown as one of the greatest thinkers and medical scholars in history. His most important medical works are the Qanun (Canon) and a treatise on Cardiac

> drugs. The Qanun fi-i-Tibb is an immense encyclopaedia of medicine. It contains some of the most illuminating thoughts pertaining to distinction of mediastinitis from pleurisy; contagious nature of phthisis; distribution of diseases by water and soil; careful description of skin troubles; of sexual diseases and perversions of nervous ailments."

Not only the principles of medical science were expounded by the Muslim physicians but they also created pharmacopoelo which but for the recent synthetic and Organotherapic preparations, is in use at the present day. The common drugs, such as "nux vomica, senna, rhubarb, aconite, gentian, myrrh, calomel, and the structure of our prescriptions belong to Arab medicine." A large number of hospitals were established by the Muslims which were not only divided into separate words but also had their own gardens in which herbs and other medicinal plants were cultivated. There were also medical schools attached to the big hospitals:

> "We have reason to believe that when during the crusades Europe at last began to establish hospitals, they were inspired to do so by the example set for them by the Arabs of the Near East .... The first hospital in Paris, Les Quinze—vingt was founded by Louis IX after his return from the crusade 1254-1260."

In Europe, throughout the early Middle Ages medicine was practised mainly by quacks. It was during this period that the Muslims had made wonderful progress in the medical craft. The profession of a doctor was highly esteemed and he was encouraged by the society to conduct his researches without any worry of livelihood. The results of their intellectual pursuits began to penetrate into Europe and the Western scholars began to turn eagerly towards Arabian science. Most of the Muslim doctors took keen interest in Chemistry. The very word alchemy (al-kimiya) is of Arab origin. The most famous name in Muslim alchemy is of Jabir Haiyan the alchemist Geber of Middle Ages who lived in Kufa in eighth century:

> "We find in his writings remarkably sound views on methods of chemical research, a theory on the geologic formation of metals (the six metals differ essentially

> because of different proportions of sulphur and mercury in them); preparation of various substances (e.g. basic lead carbonatic arsenic and antimony from their sulphides).

Jabir's work was further advanced by the great doctor Razi already spoken of who like the former, wrote on chemistry and alchemy and gave exact classifications of substances and of chemical process.

Abu Ali-al-Hassan ibn-al-Hassan ibn-al-Haitham (965-1039) was a renowned physicist and one of the greatest investigators of optics of all times. His master-piece Kitab al-Manzir, is regarded as the most valuable treatise on optics which had a great influence on the training of the later scientists of Western Europe.

"Ibn Haytham's writings reveal his fine development of the experimental faculty. His tables of corresponding angles of incidence and refraction of light passing from one medium to another show how closely he had approached discovering the law of constancy of ratio of sines, later attributed to shell. He accounted correctly for twilight as due to atmospheric refraction, estimating the sun's depression to be 19' below the horizon, at the commencement of the phenomenon in the mornings or at its termination in the evenings."

The Muslims made wonderful achievements in astronomy, geography, agriculture and botany:

> "A great deal of geographical as well as historical and scientific knowledge is contained in the thirty volume Meadows of Gold and Mines of Gems by one of the leading Muslim historians, the tenth century al Masudi. A more strictly geographical work is the dictionary Mujam al-buldan by al-Hamami (1179-1229). This is a veritable encyclopaedia that, in going for beyond the confines of geography, incorporates also a great deal of scientific lore."

Mariner's Compass : Mariner's compass was invented by Ibn Majid. This invention opened up the vast oceans and seas to the enterprising and adventurous voyagers. The Muslim mariners not only transversed the Indian, Atlantic and Pacific Ocean but also circumambulated the African continent. Sulaiman Al-Makri, a famous sailor travelled as far as Behring strait and embodied his valuable experiences in a number of books such Al-budat, Al-Mahriyyat fi-Zabt-i-Ulum il-Bahriyyaks. Allama Syed Sulaiman Nadvi in his famous book 'The Navigation of the Arabs' mentioned fifteen books compiled by Ibn Majid who has been rightly called the earliest writer of a nautical guide.

One feature of nature that invariably roused the curiosity of Muslim travellers in foreign countries was plant life:

> "They studied, collected and described plants that might serve some utilitarian purpose, whether in agriculture or in medicine. These excellent tendencies, without equivalent in Christendom, were continued during the first half of the thirteenth century by an admirable group of four botanists. One of these Ibn al-Baitar compiled the most elaborate Arabic work on the subject (botany), in fact the most important for the whole period extending from Dioscorides down to the sixteenth century. It was a true encyclopaedia on the subject incorporating the whole of Greek and Arabic experience."

Among last Eastern Muslims we may mention lion al-Suri-al Dimashqi's deliberate research on plants in the country surrounding Damascus and the mountains of Lebanon where he studied them at different stages of their growth, in the first half of the thirteenth century.

Human Anatomy : Abd al-Malik Ibn Quraib al-Asmai (739-831) was a pious Arab who wrote some valuable books on human anatomy. Al-Jawaliqi who flourished in the first half of the twelfth century and Abdal-Mumin who flourished in the second half of the thirteenth century in Egypt wrote treatises on horses. The greatest Zoologist amongst the Arabs was al-Damiri (1405) of Egypt whose book on animal life, Hayat-al Hayawan has been translated into English by A. S. G. Jayakar (London 1906,1908).

This is a very brief account of the Muslim's achievements in science. Even a cursory glance over them would convince one of the fact that the power which has transformed the modern world is the product of the direct infiltration of the Muslim's method of research and systematic inquiry into Europe. The Muslims opened the new fields of investigation and proceeded ahead with perseverance, courage, open-mindedness and practical wisdom :

> "The weight of venerable authority, for example that of Ptolemy, seldom intimidated them. They were always eager to put a theory to tests, and they never tired of experimentation. Though motivated and permeated by the spirit of their religion, they would not allow dogma as interpreted by the orthodox to stand in the way of their scientific research."

Without Islam : Is the world going to cease, and that any moment without notice? May be. The deadlier the bomb in the hands of man, the more unsafe is he who knows when this ungodly civilisation commits suicides.

In all history the peril is the greatest today. It all depends upon the decision of one and only one War Minister, wise or otherwise. It all depends upon the trigger-puffing of one and only one bomber, by intent or by accident, by move or by mistake. And whether or not the other party gets chance to retaliate, this planet will have been blown up, Jives and limbs shooting to the skies. And even if the crust of the earth persists, the hands of time will move back to a fifty thousand years in less than five minutes.

So far, what keeps this fatal move in check? Is it good conscience? Good judgement? Or, regard for international peace, justice and fraternity ?

Certainly not. The godless man has no such consideration, no such courtesy. He is self worshipper to the core. In his impulse he would have "fired the first shot" but for fear of retaliation. Thank Allah Almighty, there are more than one atomic powers, each in dread of the other.

And then there is the other danger, the internal white worm. Even if man is prudent enough not to plunge the world into the Third War, he is losing his flesh and blood through such slow but sure poisons as the exploitation of man by man and of nation by notion. Tyranny, crime, corruption, poverty, unemployment, ignorance, sex-anarchy, wealth-worship have made life very miserable. Material luxuries catering to no more than five senses are no substitute for the joy of heart, peace of mind, nobleness of spirit. In fact, divorced from any divine discipline, they have added to man's nervous tension and blood pressure, unbalanced his abilities and cut down his sense of safety and enjoyment

Man has conquered the moon, but has he conquered his worst enemy himself. The more he is in control of distance, of space, of nature, the more he is beset with problems, from domestic to diplomatic. He is entering the last quarter of the 20th century, the century which has so for given him such gifts as aeroplanes, cinema, radio, television, atomic and napalm, energies, flight to the moon. But with these have also come two world wars and a dozen other wars, the tragedies of Hiroshima, Vietnam, Palestine, Kashmir, These 81 years have produced by for the biggest number of crimes, divorces, unfathered and even unmothered children, sexual anarchy, suicides, economic depressions, revolutions, famines, floods, diseases and what not. Materially man is far more advanced in 1981 than in 188 1. But is he happier, healthier and safer than his great grandfather?

The man of today knows full well the dangers he is faced with, national and international. But can he save himself from the menacing perils of his own creation? However he is desperately taking so many kinds of steps to meet them, although to no success so far.

Can science save a nation, much less the world?

Knowledge is power. And science by its inventions and discoveries, has placed a vast potential in the hands of a man. But did it teach him how and why to use that power? Did it put any check, moral or material, on the use of that power?

It is a tragedy that science is not a science. It is not neutral. It is not complete. It is not impartial research. It chooses to discuss no more than one side of the pictures of the what and the how with the most unscientific bigotry and blindness, it refuses to discuss the who and the why, the Creator and His purpose of creation. Are we not justified to say that science is one-eyed and insists on remaining one-eyed ? Divorced from godliness, it is nothing but the power to seek pleasure at the cost of all values, moral and spiritual, including the pleasure of throwing bombs over the weak.

No doubt, these inventions and discoveries have made life easier, richer, speedier, more efficient, more powerful although less meaningful. The more man's inventions and discoveries, the more his worries, his lusts, his crimes, his sex-anarchies, his problems, his perils. Were science wedded to godliness, man would be the master not only of his world but also of his home.

Puffed with the powers of material science, man started believing in his own intellect without ever caring who made his mind, his physical machinery, his environments as they are and why. He set about in his own selfish material pursuit and refused to take command from the Divine Authority. He chose to keep a few religions but took good care to tailor them to suit his own social and political conveniences. He made his own goods, if at all, but cunningly made them careless and powerless enough not to interfere in his pursuit of wealth, sex and politics.

The so-called scientist never thought of recognising the Authority of the Creator of the universe, the Creator of man himself and of his vast abilities, the Creator of all laws and bodies of physics and chemistry, science and arts. He chose to plunge deep into the mysteries of the atom, of the land, of the water, of the air, of the fauna and flora but never for a moment thought to investigate whether or not the Creator of man was also the Commander of man in all sectors of his activity, whether or not he has given him a mission and a code to live for and live by, whether or not he meticulously watches every instant who obeys His laws and who does not with Reward or Punishment to follow of course.

The so-called scientist never cared to think in terms of the world eternal, the life to come with its Rewards and Punishments. He concentrated on his small transient material world alone to eat and drink and be merry. Intoxicated in his lust for unfettered power and unfettered freedom, he refused to recognise an all world or rather an all-world Authority, although unseen by the physical eyes. He chose to believe in the unseen electron but not in the unseen Maker and Master. He took to enmity against Islam for reasons selfish, sentimental or at best historical. The hot cold wars between

Islam and non-Islam are wars between discipline and lust between the seekers of the other world and the seekers of this world.

Let the true scientist be aware that materialism alone has signally failed to produce international goodwill and cooperation, love and benevolence, peace and justice, ease of mind and of conscience. Let him admit that with all its advance in scientific power, the life of today is much more wicked, much more fraudulent and much more selfish than it was a hundred years ago.

Triumphs of Technology : The inculcation of Islamic ideology is all the more important today. There is no doubt that the developing nations should try to catch up with the developed nations in their scientific and technical activities. But at the same time they should not allow the triumphs of technology to blind them to the demands of mind and soul. In this age of nuclear power and space travel when people are dazzled by the achievements of the unscientific science, it is necessary for everyone of us to maintain the balance between science and humanities so that man may not degenerate into a machine. Let the students of science know that whatever advancement they may attain in their knowledge of the laws of nature, they cannot put the knowledge into a constructive use without understanding the significance and purpose of their own life.

No doubt, the knowledge of science provides us with power—the power of instruments and the power of intellect. But how this power is to be used? It is here that Islam comes into play. Of course, we need a vast army of trained personnel to develop industry, to modernise agriculture, to harness rivers and to fight salinity, to extract minerals, to produce steel, to equip our defence with armaments. But what we need most is good soul and spirit. And good souls and spirits are given by Islam.

We are confident that if the nations of the world take to the mission and method of life as prescribed by Islam, not only will they reduce to the minimum such maladies as are eating into their body social and their body politic but also will save this planet for the conquest of other planets not by way of military aggression but by way of reaching them through the power of science and winning them through the power of Deen of Islam-fraternity, love, peace and justice. On the eve of the conquest of other worlds, it is up to this world to equip itself with a model universal system of life-as demonstrated by the Holy Prophet of Islam (peace and blessings of Allah be upon) and his immediate followers. Fortunately, history has a meticulous record.

Science Must Lead to Faith in God : Science works on laws and principles which remain unchanging throughout time and space. Had the laws of nature been changing, there would have been no science, no material progress of the human being. Who made those laws and why? For reasons of his own, the scientist doesn't choose to discuss who and why. He discusses what and how only. Had he chosen to dwell on who and why also he would have achieved Iman.

Even though we seem to have made big strides in research, discovery and invention, we are still in the dawn of the Age of Science. However every exploration, every new piece of information, every invention goes to show that the Universe of which this planet is only a tiny dot is made and worked on principles. Had there been no principles, no fast and permanent values, no eternal laws of nature to depend upon, there would have been no knowledge, no cause and effect and certainly no science.

The first and foremost reason why a true scientist cannot but believe in Allah is that the entire creation is built on and is run on the most perfect scientific principles. No doubt there are changes of atmosphere, of season, of life and death, of events, of people - but every change is based on unchanging principles. You can depend upon this fixed system. You can bank on this solid organisation. It was this full dependence, this hundred per cent banking upon, that made man anticipate, calculate, prepare and actually demonstrate his march to the moon.

In his progress towards the power of knowledge, in his observations, experiments and studies of the laws of nature, a scientist with an unbiased neutral brain must realise at each step that this Nature is a definite, planned, designed, pre-schemed, predestined and purposeful handicraft of the greatest Mechanic, Engineer, Architect, Planner, Artist and Scientist. In this machinery, every fibre counts, every cog calculates. Nothing in the least is immature, uncalculated, irresponsible, half-baked, insecure, unwise. Nothing is emotional, accidental, playful, by chance, by the way, by the mood. Each sector, each branch, each minute detail is the evidence of a master-planning, engineering, fitting and balance.

In his pursuit of science, even the beginner's brain cannot but take early deep-seated notice of the Master Maker and Master Designer, the All-Powerful Secret Brain that has done all the arithmetic, geometry, chemistry, physics, astronomy, mechanics, causation, balance, proportion and what not of the earth and of the space beyond, the Secret Hand that manifests itself in everything above, upon and below the sun, the Secret Being that exhibits its concern of science in anything and everything that is or is not the concern of a scientist. Can a scientist proceed a step without recognising the Authority of an All-Powerful Ruler who keeps the house in order, in working, in balance? Our Universe has no meaning; it can't have any meaning unless there is a Power that made it as it is, that runs it as it is the whole course of its life. You can't escape the inevitable conclusion.

Just as there cannot be a round square, there cannot be an atheist scientist. To call yourself a scientist, you must admit that there is a universal science. To call yourself a true and honest scientist, you must use brain and your instruments not only on the what and how but also on the who and why of this life and conditions of life.

Secondly, you will not deny that to be scientific, a law, a machinery or an organisation must have a definite defined purpose, use, aim and ambition. You will not deny that all laws of nature, taken separately or collectively, have a definite purpose and goal. They have been made for the benefit of life, particularly of the human being, the homo sapiens. The earth rotates on its axis approximately at one thousand miles an hour. If it rotated at one hundred miles an hour, our days and nights would be ten times longer. The long hot days would burn up all animal and vegetable life. The long cold night would freeze the survivors. Did you ever consider who made the earth rotate at a speed most suited to you?

Similarly, if the sun would have been a few thousand miles

nearer, you would roast black. If a few thousand miles farther, you would freeze solid. Could you have life even without all the intellects and enjoyments -unless there is a Power Who makes and unmakes in terms of none but your benefit?

The slant of the earth is tilted at an angle of 23 degrees. Why this slant and why exactly this angle? If there would have been no tilt, there would have been no change of season, no beauty in life, perhaps no life. If the moon would have been 25,000 miles farther, man would have been left high and dry without any tide at all, without any free transport of the big oceanic vessels to the inland ports. If the crust of the earth would have been only ten feet deeper, all carbon dioxide and oxygen would have been absorbed, leaving none for animal birth and growth.

Or take so simple a thing as the freezing of water. When water freezes, it gets lighter; the ice floats on top of the water. Why lighter, why not heavier? In all logic, it should sink beneath the liquid water. But for the All-Wise, All-Thoughtful, All-Caring. The floating makes the ice melt by the rays of the sun. It makes the water below the ice keep warm enough to support all animal and vegetable life there.

Who made it so and why? Who planted it that way? : Thirdly man has been given a brain, a scientific brain plus a scientific soul. No other animal can count up to five. No other animal can build up a history, a civilization, a politics and a science. No other animal can conceive of Allah in a way to worship Him out of free will. Man alone can conceive Him as the All-Scientific, All-Powerful, All Merciful, The Giver and The Forgiver, The Awarder and The Punisher through a scientific process of reasoning or a spiritual process of emotional feeling or both.

Nietzsche, the famous philosopher says:

> "There is more wisdom in the construction and working of the body and mind of a scientist than he can ever think of. There is more wisdom in the making of an ant than what all the libraries of the world can tell."

Dr. Alexix Carrol, Nobel Prize Winner in Philosophy, asserts emphatically that:

> "Science by worshipping the Maker of matter, and not matter exclusively, would restore to man the summit of his development in intelligence, in moral science, in virility.

Who could have said but Einstein:

> "No doubt Moses was a better leader of humanity than Machiavelli"?

Prof. Eddington asks :

> "Matter is matter. But what about the education, training and confidence of the scientist."

> The Maker and Master has given you not only a brain but also a soul. Why?

Who and Why : Of the six forms of question- what, why, how, when, where and who-the Western science has chosen to concern itself with What, How, Where and When. For political purposes, it has kept the Who and Why beyond its jurisdiction. It does not want to share its power of knowledge with the less fortunate brethren it aims to exploit. It therefore does not want to mix science with morality. It does not want to reach Islam.

Modern science is very good at answering how this is made, how can we control it, how does a cell become fertilised, what makes an aeroplane fly, how far away are the stars. But if you ask who made it that way and why, he shrinks back to his eggshell. Every scientist knows of Newton's Law of Gravity, but no scientist has ever cared to explore why it behaves so and who is the Agency that makes it behave so.

Unless the Who and the Why are enquired into, science at its best is only biased, partial, incomplete, political, motivated, fractional, incomplete and misleading. It is inexact, insecure and undependable. It is a political science.

4

Role of Islam

Pre-Islamic Era

It is generally agreed that the sixth century of the Christian era, represented the darkest phase in the history of our race. Humanity had reached the edge of the precipice, towards which it had been tragically proceeding for centuries, and there appeared to be no agency or power in the whole world which could come to its rescue and save it from crashing into the abyss of destruction.

In his melancholy progress from God-forgetfulness to self-forgetting, man had lost his moorings. He had grown indifferent to his destiny. The teachings of the prophets had been forgotten; the lamps that they had kindled had either been put out by the storms of moral anarchy or the light they shed had become so feeble that it could illumine the hearts of but a few men, most of whom had sought refuge in passivity and resignation. Having been vanquished in the battle between spiritualism and materialism, they had shut themselves up in monasteries or gone into wilderness. Such of them as were still left in the whirlpool of life had aligned themselves with the ruling classes of their lands. They helped them in the satisfaction of their sensual desires and in the maintenance of unjust political and economic systems and cooperated with them in reaping unlawful benefits out of the wealth of the people.

The Romans and the Persians, who enjoyed the monopoly of leadership in the West and the East, respectively, had sunk to a state of complete moral depravity. They wallowed in the inveterate vices of their corrupt and decaying civilizations. Their empires had become storehouses of confusion and mischief. The governing classes, drunk with power, indulged in reckless debauchery and sensuality. The middle classes, as is their wont, took the greatest pride in aping the modes and manners of the rich. As for the common people, they lived in grinding poverty. They filled their bellies like lower creatures and toiled and sweated like cattle so that others might live in voluptuous luxury. Not unoften would they solace themselves with narcotics and cheap entertainments, or fall blindfolded upon carnal pleasures whenever the curse of their lives afforded them a breathing moment.

Great religions became playthings in the hands of debased ecclesiastics who corrupted and twisted them beyond recognition, so much so that if it were possible for their founders to return to the physical life, they could not have recognized them.

In consequence of the moral debasement of the great centres of civilization and general disorder and unrest, people everywhere got entangled in their internal problems. They had no message to offer to the world. The world had become hollow from within; its life-springs had dried up. It possessed neither the light of religious guidance for their personal conduct, nor any abiding and rational principles for running a state.

Christianity : Christianity had never possessed a comprehensive or elaborate code which could provide the framework of a civilization or the basis of a polity. Consisting mainly of the barest outlines of the teachings of Christ, it did little more than to reflect dimly the simple creed of monotheism. But even this distinction was retained by it only till it had not fallen under the baneful influence of St. Paul. After that the flickering flame of the Divine Truth was utterly extinguished. St. Paul had brought with him all the old pagan rites and customs and introduced them into Christianity. Later on, during the reign of Constantine, the very roots of the Christian faith were destroyed.

Thus, by the fourth century, Christianity had become a curious mixture of Greek mythology, Roman idolatry, Egyptian Neo-Plutonism and Monasticism, in which the pure and simple teachings of Christ had been lost like a drop of sweet water in the ocean. It had been reduced to a hopeless mess of meaningless doctrines and empty rituals which could neither elevate the spirit, nor illumine the intellect, nor move the emotions. Instead of opening fresh avenues for the display of cultural energies this great religion had become a stumbling-block in the path of human progress. Centuries of morbid disintegration had pushed the faith of Jesus into the lap of Paganism. Sale, who translated the Holy Quran into English, has this to say of Christianity of the sixth century: "The worship of saints and images, in particular, was then arrived at such a scandalous pitch that it even surpassed whatever is now practised among the Romanists.

Roman Empire : Doctrinal divisions had turned Christendom into a seething cauldron of warring sects. Homes, schools and churches had been transformed into camps of war. The land was involved in a civil war. The main dispute was over the combination of the divine and the human natures in Jesus. The Melkite Christians of Syria held that he was both divine and human, while the Monophysites of Egypt insisted upon his being truly divine, the human part of his nature having lost itself in the divine as a drop of vinegar loses its identity in the ocean. The former view was, in a way, the official view of the Empire, and the Byzantine rulers did everything in their power to get it established as the united creed of the Eastern Empire. In the process they perpetrated brutal atrocities on their opponents, but the differences were not resolved. Both sides openly attacked each other as apostates and renegades, as if they belonged to two opposing religions Cruelties and persecutions of a most savage nature were witnessed during the ten years of the viceroyalty of Cyrus in Egypt (631-41 A. D.).

Social disruption had reached its highest peak in the Eastern Roman Empire. Taxes and other duties had multiplied manifold, though the people already were groaning under innumerable hardships. Over and above the taxes were the hardships of confiscations and monopolies. As a result of these causes there occurred widespread uprisings and rebellions. In the disturbances of 532 A.D., for example, as many as 30,000 persons were killed in the capital itself.

The people had become so hopelessly addicted to extravagance and lavishment that it was beyond their powers of self control to practise austerity, no matter how pressingly did their circumstances call for it. There was but one reigning passion: to amass wealth by every conceivable means, and then to squander it away on luxury and licentiousness.

The social horizon was extremely gloomy. The foundations of civilization were exposed to ruin and decay. Celibacy was preferred to matrimony, so that people could be free to indulge in debauchery to their hearts content. Justice was, according to Sale, publicly sold and corruption and breach of trust received all encouragement from the nation itself. Gibbon says that Rome, at about the close of the sixth century, had reached "the lowest period of her depression" and that "the lofty tree, under whose shade the nations of the world had reposed, was deprived of its leaves and branches, and the sapless trunk was left to wither on the ground."

Similarly, the Historians' History of the World says : "That it (Byzantine Empire) had nevertheless suffered very severely in the general decline caused by over-taxation, and by reduced commerce, neglected agriculture and diminished population, is attested by the magnificent ruins of cities which had already fallen to decay, and which never regained their ancient prosperity.

The nations of North-western Europe had not yet seen the dawn of civilization. They were steeped in the darkness of their abject states broken down by endless bloody tumults. Muslims and Arab Spain had not yet appeared on the stage of history to show them light nor had any historical calamity of such magnitude befallen them as could have jolted them into awakening. They were cut off from the broad stream of humanity and knew very little of the world around them. Religiously, these nations were between the newly-born Christianity and the old-time idolatry. In the words of H. G. Wells, "there was no sign of order or union" in Western Europe.

To sum up, "From the fifth to the tenth century Europe lay sunk in a night of barbarism which grew darker and darker. It was a barbarism far more awful and horrible than that of the primitive savage, for it was the decomposing body of what had once been a great civilization. The features and impress of that civilization were all but completely effaced. Where its development had been fullest, e.g., in Italy and Gaul, all was ruin, squalor, dissolution.'

Judaism : The Jews alone, of all religious communities, could boast of being still in possession of a large part of their spiritual inheritance. They were also the most efficient in the art of interpreting theological and scriptural terms and symbols. But they did not command a position in the fields of religion, culture or politics where they could influence others. On the other hand, they were destined always to live in subjection to other nations and ever to be exposed to injustice, oppression, chastisement, extradition, troubles and hardships. Political serfdom, oppression and anguish suffered indefinitely had produced in them a typical racial character. They were notorious all over the world for excessive pride of blood and greed. Meek and submissive in distress, they were tyrannical and mean when they had the upper hand. Hypocrisy, deceit, treachery, selfishness, cruelty and usuriousness had become the normal traits of their nature. In the Quran we find repeated references to the extent to which they had sunk into degradation in the sixth and the seventh centuries.

The mutual jealousy and hatred between the Christians and the Jews, which did not permit them to forego any opportunity of settling an old score was brought to its climax towards the close of the sixth century. In 610 A. D. the Jews of Antioch rebelled against the Christians, and Emperor Phocas sent his famous general Bonosus to put down the uprising, who set about his business with such enthusiasm that the whole of the Jewish population was wiped out. Thousands of Jews perished by the sword, while hundreds of them were drowned or burnt alive or thrown to the wild beasts. The Jews wreaked their revenge in 615 by instigating Khusrau Parvez to order a general massacre of the Syrian Christians when he overran that country. Then, in 630, Heradius wreaked such savage vengeance upon the Jews that in the Roman Empire those alone could save themselves who could take to flight or go into hiding.

Scene in Iran : Iran was Rome's co-equal in the governance and administration of the civilized world. Its moral foundations had never been sound. It was an old hotbed of vice and folly. Such conjugal arrangements as are considered criminal in other parts of the world were not unlawful or undesirable in the opinion of the Iranians, It is stated that Yazdegerd H, who ruled during the middle of the fifth century A. D., married his own daughter and afterwards killed her, arid that Bahram Chobin, in the sixth century, had marital relations with his sister. As Prof. Arthur Christensen has remarked, the Iranians found nothing repugnant in incestuous connections. The famous Chinese traveller Hiuen Tsang has stated that no relationships were excluded from conjugality in the Iranian law and society.

Partly as a reaction to unbounded immorality and perversion and partly under the impulsion of the supposed conflict between Light and Darkness that had been the favourite theme of Iranian philosophy from the earliest times, Mani appeared in the third century and preached his cult of celibacy as the panacea for all the ills from which humanity was suffering. Proceeding from the curious hypothesis that evil was the outcome of the conflux of Light and Darkness, he had declared that for the permanent victory of the former over the latter it was necessary that the human race voluntarily brought itself to an end by ceasing to procreate Mani was put to death, in 276 A. D., by Bahram as "a messenger of doom who should be liquidated before he liquidated mankind," but his teachings endured for a long time and its influence was still visible at the advent of Islam.

After two hundred years the innate licentiousness of the Iranian temperament once again revolted against the unnatural teachings of Mani and reasserted itself in the shape of the Mazdakite movement Mazdak advanced the view that since all human beings were descended from the same common parents, they have equal rights in the women and wealth of one another. This, he held, would put an end to all feuds and quarrels which generally arose on account of these two factors. Shahrastani says, "Mazdak proclaimed community of women, and made wealth and women freely and equally available to all men like fire, water and fodder." This movement was received with open arms by the young and the libertine sections of the society, and, to crown it all, the Iranian Emperor Qubad took it under his patronage and showed keen interest in its progress. Under royal encouragement the tenets of Mazdak spread like wild fire and the whole of Iran was thrown into an erotic crisis.

"Intemperate and pleasure loving persons, according to Tabari, jumped at the opportunity and became ardent Mazdakites". The common people were also caught in the tempest. So powerful did the movement become that everyone could walk into everyone else's house and take possession of his wife and property. The Mazdakites approached Qubad and threatened him with dethronement if he did not champion their cause. The Emperor yielded and, thenceforth, things quickly came to such a pass that neither parents could recognize their children, nor children their parents. No one had any right even over one's own property.

Tabari further writes: "Before Qubad had joined the movement, he was counted among the good rulers of Iran, but, after he had joined it, chaos and corruption swept over the land."

The Chosroes of Iran claimed, and were accepted by their people, to have Divine blood running in their veins and the Iranians also believed that there was Divinity in the very nature of their rulers. The people prostrated themselves before them, sang to the glory of their godhead and swore that they could do no wrong. It was disrespectful to utter the name of the Emperor or to sit down in his presence. The Iranians believed that the Emperor had a natural right over everyone, without anyone having any right over him. Whatever he granted to his subjects was purely of his sweet will.

The subjects were there to obey, and not to interfere in anything. The Divine Right of sovereignty being vested solely in the Kayani family, none but a Kayani could rule in Iran. This right was automatically transmitted from one generation to another. No one could dare encroach upon it. In case a male member of mature age was not available among the Kayinis to wear the Imperial crown, the crown was placed on the head of a minor, and if no male descendant was available, a woman was crowned. The dynastic line had to be preserved in all circumstance Tinis, after Sheruya, his seven-year-old son Ardasher was accepted as the emperor, and after Khusrau Parvez, his infant son Farrukhzaad was declared the emperor. Kisra's daughter, Boran, too, occupied the throne, and so did his other daughter, Azarmjdukht.' It did not occur to anyone to entrust the administration of the empire to an experienced general, a great nobleman or some other able and experienced person. As the people had no choice in the installation of an Imperial dynasty, the question of their selection of a particular ruler did not arise at all.

With the rulers the spiritual leaders, too, were regarded as superhuman, who enjoyed unlimited powers. Separative distinctions of class and profession were a permanent feature of Iranian life. Professor Arthur Christensen says: "There was an unbridgeable gap between the various classes of society. Common people were prohibited by law from purchasing the property of the privileged classes. It was a standing feature of the Sassani rule that no one should aspire for a rank higher than what he was entitled to by birth. No one could adopt a profession in which he had not been born. The Emperors of Iran did not employ the so-called low-born people in the state service. Social distinctions were rigidly enforced. Everyone had a fixed place in the society."

The Iranians were great believers in the purity of their blood and the superiority of their race. They considered themselves to be a sanctified lot, holier and nobler than the rest of humanity and gifted with unique natural abilities. They looked down upon the neighbouring peoples and called them by insulting and ridiculous nicknames.

Fire can neither educate nor inform. It can neither redeem the sinner, nor instruct its devotees in life's problems. The religion of the fire-worshippers was, therefore, but a conglomeration of certain rites and ceremonies to be performed at certain times and at certain places. Outside the temples, at home and in the market-places, and in other spheres of individual and collective life, the fire-worshippers were free to act as they pleased. There were no spiritual ideals, no ethical Do's and Don't's that could fit in with social or national life in Iran. The fire-worshippers had to have recourse to their own judgement or follow blindly the demands of expediency, as polytheists of all ages are known to have done.

The Zoroastrians of Iran were, as such, no better off than pagans and unbelievers in this respect. They were without the advantage of possessing a complete and self-contained religion which could be a source of moral awareness and which could furnish them with ideals that could hold good in all walks of life.

Buddhism : Because of assimilating the teachings of Brahmanism and adopting its gods and deities, Buddhism had, a long while ago, lost its individuality and the simplicity of its creed. Brahamnism had swallowed it up. In any case, the two religions had melted into each other after centuries of bitterness and conflict, and Buddhism had got converted into an idolatrous faith. Wherever the Buddhists went, they took the images of the Buddha with them and installed them there. The entire religious and cultural life of the Buddhists is over-shadowed by idolatry. Strangely enough, idol-worship was introduced into Buddhism when it was in full bloom of its power in India. Prof. Ishwar Topa observes that "the kingdom that was established under the patronage of Buddhism began to present a vast scene of idolatry. The atmosphere in the monasteries was changing and heretic innovations were being introduced one after another."

"Brahmanism", says Pandít Jawaharlal Nehru in his book *The Discovery of India,* "made of Buddha an 'avatar', a god, so did Buddhism. The Mahayana doctrine spread rapidly, but it lost in quality and distinctiveness what it gained in extent. The monastries became rich centres of vested interests and their discipline became lax. Magic and superstition crept into popular forms of worship. There was a progressive degeneration of Buddhism in India after the first millennium of its existence". Mrs. Rhys Davids thus describes its diseased state during that period: "Under the overpowering influence of these sickly imaginations the moral teachings of Gautama had been almost hid from view. The theories grew and flourished, each new step, each new hypothesis demanded another; until the whole sky was filled with forgeries of the brain, and the nobler and simpler lessons of the founder of the religion were smothered beneath the glittering mass of metaphysical subtleties."

Such being the position, the Buddhists in India, China and other countries of South-East Asia could scarcely be looked upon to play a significant role in the moral and spiritual rehabilitation of man, or the promotion of peace and stability in the world. The Chinese, in particular, were leading a sufficient-unto-themselves sort of life at the eastern end of the civilized world with their spiritual and cultural patrimony securely entombed in their breasts.

The other nations of Eastern and Central Asia (Mughals, Tartars,

Japanese, etc.) were oscillating between perverted Buddhism and barbaric Paganism. They were still in the transition stage of civilization, having only just begun to emerge from the Dark Ages. Most of them had yet to learn the rudiments of a civilized existence.

Scene in India : In India, the epoch opening with the sixth century was by all accounts the gloomiest in its long and chequered history. Once the cradle of great religions and mighty civilizations, it had now languished and absorbed all the features of social and moral degeneration that had overtaken the neighbouring lands, and to these it had added a few characteristics of its own, more prominent among which were (i) abundance of objects of worship, (ii) sexual wantonness and (iii) caste and other social distinctions.

In the sixth century A. D. idolatry had reached its lowest ebb in India. The Vedas give the number of Hindu gods as 33. During this period as many as 33 crore gods were worshipped among the Hindus. Almost everything that possessed any attractiveness or utility had been vested with divine attributes. Stones and minerals, trees and plants, rivers and mountains, animals and even organs of procreation were adored as gods. Thus, this ancient religion was turned into a heap of mythical traditions, beliefs and rites. Dr. Gustave le Bon says in his Civilizations de j'hsde.

The Hindu, of all people, stands most unavoidably in the need of visible objects for religious worship, and although at different times religious reformers have tried to prove monotheism in the Hindu faith, it has been an unavailing effort. From the Vedic Age to the present day, the Hindu has been worshipping all sorts of things. Whatever he cannot understand or control is worthy of being adored as divine in his eyes. All attempts of Brahmans and other Hindu reformers in the direction of monotheism or in limiting the number of gods to three have been utterly unsuccessful. The Hindus listened to them, and sometimes even accepted their teachings in principle, but in practice the three gods went on multiplying till they began to see a god in every article and phenomenon of nature.

Sculpture had attained its highest perfection in the seventh century A. D. The idols had caught the popular fancy so powerfully that even the Buddhist and Jain religions had to bow to them in the interests of self-preservation. An idea of the popularity and the profusion of idols during this epoch may be obtained from the following account of an important event in Harsha's reign supplied by Hiuen Tsang, who stayed in India from 630 to 644 A.D. :

> "Emperor Harsha held a religious assembly at Kannauj. First a full-size golden figure of the Buddha was installed on the top of a fifty-foot high pillar. Then a smaller statue was taken out in procession with great pomp and ceremony. Harsha himself held the canopy over its head, dressed as 'Sakr-devta', while his friend Kumara, the king of Assam, wielded the flapper to drive away the flies from it."

Of the members of the family and the courtiers of the Emperor, Hiuen Tsang says that "some of them were the followers of Siva; some had embraced Buddhism; some worshipped the sun; some worshipped Vishnu: everyone was free to choose any god or goddess for his devotions, or to worship all of them if he pleased."

Nowhere do obeisance subjects and sexual themes occupy such a conspicuous place in religion as they did in Ancient India. Extremely revolting and shameless accounts of the sexual misdeeds of gods and godesses by way of explaining the occurrence of important mythological events and the creation of things are found in the ancient Indian religious books. It requires no great strength of imagination to picture what indecent practices must have gone on in the name of religion. The worship of the 'lingum' (the sexual organ) of Siva was prevalent throughout the land. To quote Gustave le Bon once more:

> "The Hindus are deeply devoted to images and symbols......Their temples are full of these, chief among them being the 'lingums' and the 'yoni', as symbolising the generative power in nature. Even the pillars of Ashoka are regarded by lay Hindus as images of 'lingum'. All vertical and conical objects are held in veneration by them."

Some historians say that there was a religious sect in which naked women were worshipped by men and vice versa. A large number of temples had degenerated into cesspools of corruption with their priests conducting themselves as guardians of lust. The palaces of the kings and noblemen were seething with vice and immorality.

Parallel to this devotion to the flesh and sensuality, a strong movement of life-denial and self-mortification with a long routine of penances was also current in the country. Between these two the moral fabric of the society had been torn to shreds. While a tiny section of the population was subjecting itself to useless self-torture, the bulk indulged in vulgar self-indulgence.

Another glaring peculiarity of the religio-social structure of the India of olden days was the all-powerful caste system. Its foundations had been laid by the Aryans during the later stages of the Vedic Age with a view to protecting themselves against getting mixed up with the primitive races of the land. In the words of Gustave le Bon:

> "We have seen that, towards the close of the Vedic Age, occupations had started to become more or less hereditary, and the germ of the caste system had been sown. The Vedic Aryans were alive to the need of maintaining the purity of their race by not mixing with the conquered people, and when they advanced towards the east and subjugated vast population, this need became still more manifest and the law-givers had to pay due regard to it. The Aryans understood the problems of race well; they had come to realize that if a ruling minority did not take proper care of itself, it was rapidly assimilated with the servile population and deprived of its identity.'

The real credit, however, for evolving the caste-system into a rigid social frame and a law goes to Manu, who, in the heyday of Brahmanic civilization in India, three hundred years before the birth of Christ, formulated what is commonly known as the 'Manu Shastra' as the sacred law of Hindu society. Manu classified the entire Hindu population into four classes with reference to their birth, namely, (i) the Brahmans or the learned and the priestly class, (ii) the Kshatriyas or the fighting and ruling class, (iii) the Vaisyas or the trading and agricultural people, and (iv) the Shudras or the lowest caste people whose only business in life was to serve their superiors.

The Manu Shastra says:

> "The Lord created Brahman from His mouth, Kshatriya from His arms, Vaisya from His thighs and Shudra from His feet so that the world may prosper."

He assigned separate duties to each of them for its preservation.

For the Brahman he commanded "the study of the Vedas. The presentation of offerings to gods on his own behalf and on behalf of others, and the receiving of alms."

For the Kshatriya he commanded that "he should protect the people, give alms, offer oblations, read the Vedas and abstain from carnality."

For the Vaisya he commanded "the service of the cattle, the giving away of alms and oblations, the reading of the Vedas and trading and agriculture."

For the Shudra he commanded that "he should serve the above three."

This law gave to the Brahmans the distinction, superiority and sanctity which raised their status equal to that of the gods. Says the Manu's Shastra:

> "Anyone who is born a Brahman is the noblest creature on earth. He is the monarch of all the created things and his duty is to defend the Shastra."
>
> "Whatever is on the earth belongs to the Brahman, for he is the highest among all creatures. All things are for him."
>
> "A Brahman can acquire, by force, if necessary, the property of his Shudra slave. This will not at all be unlawful, because a slave can never own anything; whatever he has is his master's."
>
> "A Brahman who remembers the Rig Veda is absolutely sinless, though he may destroy all the three worlds or partake of food belonging to anybody."

> "However great be the king's need—he may even be dying of want — he must never levy any tax on the Brahmans, nor let a Brahman die of hunger in his kingdom.
>
> "In lieu of the sentence of death, the head of the Brahman shall be shaved, while persons of other castes shall be executed."

According to this Law, though higher in status than the Vaisya and the Shudra, the Kshatriya has no status in comparison with the Brahman. Says Manu:

> "A ten-year-old Brahman and a hundred-year-old Kshatriya are like a father and son unto each other, the Brahman being the father."

The Sudras in the Hindu society, according to this Law, were lower in status than animals and more degraded than the dog. Says Manu's Shastra:

> "Nothing can be more honourable for a Shudra than to serve the Brahman; nothing besides this can earn for him any reward."
>
> "A Shudra should never acquire property, even if he has the opportunity, for in so doing he causes pain to the Brahmans."
>
> "A Shudra who assaults a higher-caste man is liable to lose the limb with which the assault is made."
>
> "Should a Shudra try to sit at the same place with the 'twice-born', the king should get his buttocks branded with red-hot iron and banish him from the land."
>
> "If a Shudra touches a Brahman or abuses him, his tongue shall be pulled out from the root. If he claims that he can teach a Brahman, boiling oil shall be poured down his throat."
>
> "The atonement for killing a dog, a cat, a frog, a lizard, a crow, an owl and a Shudra is the same."

As compared with the Vedic Age, the position of women had considerably deteriorated during the Brahmanic Age. In the Law of Manu, according to Gustave le Bon, woman has been consistently shown as frail and referred to in disgraceful terms.

On the death of their husbands, women were condemned to a state of perpetual misery. They were not allowed to remarry. They lived as slave-maids of the brothers of their husbands, or their other descendants. A widow would often commit suicide. Dr. Gustave le Bon writes : "the immolation of widows on the funeral pyres of their husbands is not mentioned in the 'Shastra' but it appears that the practice had become quite common in India, for we find references to it in the accounts of the Greek chroniclers."

Scene in Arabia : The pre-Islamic Arabs possessed certain natural virtues that marked them out in their contemporary world. They were unrivalled in eloquence and in the skilful use of their language. Freedom and honour they valued above their lives. They were superb horsemen. They were ardent, bold, chivalrous, plain of speech, strong of memory, fraternizing, plain, hardy, firm of determination, truthful, loyal and trustworthy.

But centuries of isolation in the peninsula and a morbid insistence on the faith of their forefathers had severely undermined their moral and spiritual health. The sixth century A. D. found them plunged in depravity, perversion and dark idolatry and indulging in all the other characteristics of primitive life.

The belief in an over-ruling Providence had grown very feeble among them. It was confined to a select few, while the religion of the great mass of them was gross idolatry. The idols that had originally been introduced to serve as devotional mediums had got elevated to the status of Divinity. Homage was still paid to One Transcendent God, but only verbally; in their hearts a host of deities were throned, whose goodwill they sought to propitiate and displeasure to avert.

Each tribe, city, and locality had its own god. Al-Kalbi has stated that every household in Mecca had its own idol. When a Meccan started on a journey, his last act at home would be to invoke the blessings of the family deity, and the first thing he did on return was to pay reverence to it.

People used to vie with one another in collecting idols and constructing temples for them. Those who could afford neither, planted a slab of stone in front of the Kaaba and performed the ritual of circumambulation around it. Such stones were called Ansab. In the words of Abu Rija al-Utaridi, as reported in the *Sahih of al-Bukhari,* 'We worshipped stones. When we found a better stone than the one we had, we took it up and threw away the old one. Where no stones were available, we made a sand-mound, milked a goat over it and worshipped it." When a traveller halted at a place, he used to collect four stones, worship the most beautiful of them, and used the other three to rest his pot on for cooking.

Angels, stars, 'Jinns' (spirits) and all the rest of the objects of veneration found in polytheistic faiths were adored as divine beings by the Arabs. The Angels, they believed, were the daughters of God, whom they besought to intercede with Him on their behalf. 'Jinns' were regarded as the co-sharers of the Almighty in the practical control of the world.

Al-Kalbi says that Baitul Mal, a branch of the tribe of Khuzaah, worshipped the 'Jinns: and Said reports that the tribe of Himyan worshipped the sun; the tribe of Kinana adored the moon; the tribe of Tamim worshipped Al-dabaran; the Lakhm and the Juzam, Tay, Banil Qais and Banil Asad worshipped Jupiter, Canopus, the Dog-star and Mercury, respectively.

The social habits of the Arabs were quite outrageous. Drink was so common that even their literature stunk with it. The wealth of expressions contained in the Arabic language for the 'daughter of the vine' and the delicate variations of meaning these expressions convey, reveal how passionately the Arabs were in love with it. Banners were flown over liquor-shops. Gambling was a matter of pride with them. It was considered dishonourable to decline a gambling-bout. A Tabii theologian, Qatadah, has stated that often a gambler would stake his entire household on a single bet, and walk away in sorrow as he saw it pass into the hands of his rival. Such incidents would sometimes lead to bitter feuds.

Usury was most callously indulged in. Adultery was not considered much of a vice. A great interest was taken in the various attitudes and postures of sexual intercourse. Prostitution was rampant and brothels were frequently maintained

The lot of women was extremely lamentable in pre-Islamic Arabia. The right of inheritance was denied to them. Widowed and divorced women were not permitted to remarry. It was a common practice for the eldest son to take as wives his father's widows inherited as property with the rest of the estate. Discrimination was made against them even in the matter of food, men reserving certain dishes for themselves.

Daughters were buried alive at birth. Pride and poverty had introduced the abominable crime of female infanticide among all the Arab tribes. Haitham bin Adi tells us that one out of every ten men was guilty of it. Kind-hearted tribal chiefs often bought infant girls to save their lives. Shasaa says that before the dawn of Islam he had rescued as many as three hundred girls from the terrible fate by paying compensatory money to their fathers. Sometimes a young girl who had escaped being killed at birth or during childhood due to her father being away from home or some other reason would be treacherously taken to a lonely spot by her father and done to death. Several incidents of this nature were narrated from their past lives by the Companions after they had embraced Islam.

Tribal prejudice was very strong. The horizon of life was painfully limited by the narrow concepts of tribal organization. A maxim among them said "Stand by your brother, be he the oppressor or the oppressed "and they adhered to it to the very letter.

Everyone imagined that he came from the noblest stock. Some families thought it degrading to participate with others even in religious congregations. The Quraish, for example, kept their distance from the other pilgrims during some of the Hajj rites. They took the lead in performing the ritual of halting at 'Arafat', in order to avoid coming into contact with the rest of the pilgrims. There was, they thought, a class of born masters, another of born toilers and a third of the common people and the people of the street.'

In keeping with their primitive, desert environment, the Arabs had a very warlike temperament. War, in some respects, was with them a necessity, but, more than that, it was a fun. Their poets sang of war as a thing of joy. An Arab poet says:

If an enemy tribe we do not find,
We go to war with a friendly tribe.
And our lust for war is quenched.

Another poet says:

May a war break out among the tribes
When my colt is grown up for riding,
That I may get a chance to show
The worth of my colt and sword.

A most trivial incident could touch off a bitter inter-tribal war. The war, for instance, between the descendants of Wail, Bakr and Taghlib dragged on for full forty years. There were innumerable casualties in this war. An Arab chief, Muhaihil, has thus depicted the consequences of this war : " Both the tribes have been exterminated; mothers have become childless; children have become orphans; the flow of tears does not cease; the dead are not buried."

The whole peninsula was thus like a hornet's nest. One never knew when one would be looted or assassinated. People were kidnapped while travelling with caravans, in the presence of their companions. Even powerful kingdoms of the day needed strong escorts and guarantees of safe passage from tribal chiefs for their caravans and delegations to travel from one place to another.

R. V. C. Bodley has attempted a general survey of the world at the time of the advent of the Prophet in his book *The Messenger*. He says:

> "The Arabs did not command any respect in the sixth century world. As a matter of fact, no one counted very much. It was a moribund period when the great Empires of Eastern Europe and Western Asia had already been destroyed or were at the end of their imperial careers."
>
> "It was a world still dazed by the eloquence of Greece, by the grandeur of Persia, by the majesty of Rome, with nothing yet to take their places, not even, a religion."

"The Jews were wandering all over the world, with no central guidance. They were tolerated or persecuted according to circumstances. They had no country to call their own, and their future was as uncertain as it is today."

"Outside the sphere of influence of Pope Gregory the Great, the Christians were propounding all kinds of complicated interpretations of their once simple creed and were busy cutting one another's throat in the process."

"In Persia, a last flicker of empire-building remained. Jihusrau II was extending the frontiers of his domain. By inflicting defeat on Rome he had already occupied Cappadocia, Egypt and Syria. In 620 A.D. when Muhammad was about to emerge as a guide for humanity, he had sacked Jerusalem and stolen the Holy Cross and restored the might and grandeur of Darius. It looked almost like a new lease of life for the splendour of the Middle East. Yet the Byzantine Romans still had a little of their old vitality. When Khusrau brought his army to the walls of Constantinople, they made a final effort to survive."

"Further away in the east, the march of events was leaving few landmarks. India still consisted of many unimportant petty states which struggled mutually for political and military supremacy."

"The Chinese, as usual, were fighting among themselves. The Sui dynasty came into power to be replaced by the Tang which ruled for three centuries."

"In Japan, an Empress occupied the throne for the first time. Buddhism was beginning to take root and to influence Japanese Ideas and ideals."

"Europe was gradually merging into the Frankish Empire, which would eventually comprise France. Northern Italy, most of the countries east of the Rhine as far as the present Russo-Polish border. Clovis was dead and Dagobert, the last great Merovingian ruler, was soon to be crowned."

"Spain and England were unimportant petty States."

"Spain was under the control of Visigoths, who had lately been driven out of France which they had occupied as far in the north as Loire. They were persecuting the Jews, who would, consequently, do much to facilitate the Muslim invasion which was to follow a century later."

"The British Isles were divided into independent principalities. One hundred and fifty years had passed since the departure of the Romans, who had been replaced by an influx of Nordic people. England herself was made up of seven separate kingdoms."

Political Condition : In the pre-Islamic world, the common form of government was absolute monarchy, which was generally founded upon the popular belief in the innate sacredness and inviolable superiority of certain dynasties, as in Iran where the Sassanis believed they had a divine right to rule in succession.

On occasions, sovereignty was based on the grandeur of individual rulers. The Chinese, for instance, called their emperor the 'Son of the Heaven', for they believed that whatever there was the offspring of the marriage between the 'male' sky and the 'female' earth, and that the Emperor Khata was the first issue from that alliance. On this account their Emperor was taken to be the sole Father of his people, and as such he had the right to rule over them as he wished. "You alone are our benefactor," they said to him by way of formal acknowledgment of their allegiance. Under the spell of this concept, when Emperor Taitsung died, the Chinese were so overwhelmed with grief that many of them pierced their faces with needles, some cut their hair, and others bruised their ears by striking their heads against the coffin.

In some cases, sovereignty was considered to be the special prerogative of a particular group or a country. It was an article of faith with the Romans that they were the sovereign race and all other races had been created to be subservient to them. The other races were like the veins and arteries whose sole function was to carry the blood to and from the heart, which was Rome. The

Romans could override any law, violate any right and ravish any country. Community of religion or treaties of friendship with Rome were no protection against the high-handedness of the Romans.

The Roman dependencies had no legal status or administrative autonomy within the Empire. They were, so to say, like the animal, which gives milk and is used for transport, but receives, in turn, only as much of fodder as might keep its back strong and udder full. Says Briffault about the Roman Empire:

> "The intrinsic cause that doomed and condemned the Roman empire was not any growing corruption, but the corruption, the evil, the inadaptation to fact in its very origin and being. No system of human organization that is false in its very principle, in its very foundation, can save itself by any amount of cleverness and efficiency in the means by which that falsehood is carried out and maintained, by any amount of superficial adjustment and tinkering. It is doomed root and branch as long as the root remains what it was. The Roman Empire was, as we have seen, service for the enrichment of a small class of people by the exploitation of mankind. That business enterprise was carried out with all honesty, all the fairness and justice compatible with its very nature, and with admirable judgement and ability. But all those virtues could not save the fundamental falsehood, the fundamental wrong from its consequence."

Of the Roman rule in Egypt, Dr. Alfred Butler writes:

> "The whole machinery of rule in Egypt was directed to the sole purpose of wringing profit out of the ruled. There was no idea of governing for the advantage of the governed, of raising people in the social scale, of developing the moral or even the material resources of the country. It was an alien domination founded on force and making little pretence of sympathy with the subject race."

Their rule in Syria was no better, as a Syrian historian observe:

"The Roman rule over Syria was benevolent in the beginning. But when their Empire grew old and began to disintegrate, the Romans subjected the Syrians to the worst type of tyranny. As the Romans did not annex Syria directly to their Empire, the Syrians could never acquire the rights of citizenship in the Roman Empire, nor did their country ever gain the status of a Roman territory. The Syrians remained a stateless people.

"The taxes were so exorbitant that often people had to sell their children to pay them. Slavery and forced labour were common. The splendid buildings and manufacturings that were the pride of the Roman rulers were built by the toil of servile hands."

The seven hundred years of Roman rule in Syria made a dismal tale of pain, suffering and bloodshed. Before the Romans the Greeks had been in occupation of Syria for 369 years. Their regime, too, had been a dreadful curse for the Syrians. The insatiable greed of the Greeks had been laid bare by the inhuman methods they had employed in extorting money from the people.

The administrative and financial structure of Iran was neither just nor stable. It was subject to the ever-changing pattern of the needs and ambitions of the rulers. The author of Iran ba 'AM-Sasanian says:

"In the assessment and collection of taxes and levies those who realized them were guilty of extortion and misappropriation. It was not possible to make an estimate of income and expenditure at the beginning of the year, for the revenue varied from year to year.... The result often was that while a war was on, the coffers of the Empire were empty. In such circumstances it became necessary to impose extraordinary taxes, the chief target for which almost always were the rich Western provinces particularly Babylon."

A very meagre part of the Imperial revenue was spent on public welfare. The Emperors of Iran believed in amassing as much wealth for themselves as they could. When the treasure of Khusrau II was shifted to a new building in Madain (Ctesiphon) in 607-8 A. D., it included 468 million 'mithqals" of gold (worth about 375 million gold francs). By the thirteenth year of his reign, the accumulation of gold had reached 800 million 'mithqals'. His crown was made of 120 lbs (1½ maunds) of solid gold.

The distribution of wealth was grossly unjust. A few individuals were excessively rich, the rest of them were immersed in poverty and want. The reign of Naushirwan is famous in Iranian history for the justice and benevolence of his administration. The author of the *Iran ba 'Ahd-i-Sassanian* says:

> "In the land system of Naushirwan greater attention had been bestowed upon the interests of the Imperial Treasury than those of the people. The condition of the masses was as deplorable as ever. The Byzantine philosophers who had taken refuge in the Emperor's Court were soon disgusted with what they saw in Iran. Maybe, they were not intellectually detached enough to take an objective view of the customs and practices of an alien people like taking one's own daughter or sister into wedlock or leaving away the dead for the vultures to feed upon. They could not think with the mind of an ethnologist and were disappointed to find things different from what they had expected in the empire of a philosopher-king. But it was not its customs and practices alone that made them turn away from Iran. What really grieved them were the social divisions, the unconquerable distance between the high and the low, the rank misery of the poor and the heartless exploitation of the weak by the strong."

The division of society into castes and classes was not peculiar to Iran. In the Roman Empire the social classifications were no less severe. Says Robert Briffault:

> "When a social structure visibly threatens to topple down, rulers try to prevent it from falling by preventing it from moving. The whole Roman society was fixed in a system of castes; no one was to change his

avocation, the son must continue in the calling of his father."

In both the empires important jobs were reserved for prominent families which enjoyed great status and the confidence of the high officials.

The ever-increasing taxes had broken the back of the peasantry. Crushed and ruined, as also to save themselves from conscription—for they had no sympathy with the objects for which wars were fought — a large number of peasants had abandoned their fields and taken refuge in temples and monastries.

The condition of the peasants was really pitiable. They were tied down to their lands ; every kind of forced labour, every type of degrading service was taken from them.... 'large bodies of these poor peasants used to march on foot behind the army, as if they were doomed to eternal serfdom—they received no encouragement, salary, or wages of any kind. The relationship with the landlords was not very different from what obtained between the slaves and their masters."

A flood of licentiousness had swept over both Iran and Rome. Sensual enjoyment had become the chief objective in life. Both the nations seemed to be 'competing with each other in blind self-indulgence, luxury and extravagance. There was an amazing profusion of the voluptuous embellishments of life and the wares of pleasure and luxury among the ruling circles of either of them. Great ingenuity was displayed in these matters. A Parsi historian writes about Khusrau Parvez of Iran that he "possessed 12,000 women, 50,000 thoroughbred horses and countless palaces, huge amounts of cash and heaps of precious stones and other valuable articles. The grandeur of his court was unique in the world. In sheer splendour no rulers in history can beat the Iranian Emperors."

He also says that "tributes and presents used to pour in upon them from all the countries stretching from the Middle East to the Far East. A colossal amount of wealth was left behind by the Iranians when they were ejected from Iraq by the Muslims. It ranged from highly valuable remnants and large vessels of gold to high-class cosmetics and perfumes."

It is stated by Tabar that at the victory of Madain, the Arabs came upon several Iranian tents which were full of sealed wicker baskets. It was thought that they would be containing food, but when the baskets were opened, they were found to be packed with gold and silver vessels.

The Iranian emperors had a carpet, known as the 'Carpet of Spring', which was spread out when royal drinking parties were held in the autumn. "It was sixty yards square and could cover about an acre of ground. Its base was of gold in which costly stones and pearls had been set in such a way as to give the impression of a garden. It was divided into several beds of flowering plants and fruit-bearing trees, whose stems and branches were of gold, leaves of silk, buds of gold and silver and fruits of jewels. The border was studded with diamonds. A number of avenues and canals had also been cut in it with jewels. When the Sassanids sat in that ever-blooming garden and drank wine in the autumn, they presented to the world a spectacle it had never seen anywhere before."

Similarly, in Syria, the Roman rulers and their Syrian proteges set no limit to the lust of the flesh and its appeasement. Hadrat Hassan bin Thabit, who had spent some years of his pre-Islamic life in the company of rulers of Ghassan, has described the pomp and dazzling luxury of the Court of Jabala bin Aiham in the following words:

> "I saw ten slave-girls there, five of them were Romans, who sang on the harp, and the other five, who sang in the style of the people of Hira. They had been presented by an Arab chief, Ayas bin Qubaisa. Other musicians also used to come regularly from Mecca and other Arabian cities. When Jabala held his bacchanalian parties, jasmine, and other sweet-smelling flowers were spread on the floor, and sweet odoriferous substances like musk and amber were put up in gold containers. Musk of the purest variety was placed in silver salvers. 'Ud was burnt in winter. In the summer, the floor was cooled with ice and hot-weather garments were brought which Jabala and his friends used to throw over themselves. Furs and other valuable winter clothes were provided in the winter."

This unquenchable passion for amusement, this hideous excess of sensuality were by no means confined to the royalty and the aristocracy. The whole society, from the highest to the lowest, had degenerated into scandalous dissipation. Often a single individual spent on his dress what could clothe or feed a whole village. The distinguished and the high-born had to maintain fantastic standards of living, or they lost face in society. Shabi says that in Iran one's rank in one's tribe was reflected in one's headgear. The headgears of some tribal chiefs cost over one lakh of dirhams. Hurmuz, for instance, being one of those whose status was recognized on all hands, wore on his cap jewels that were worth a hundred thousand dirhams. The sole criterion of greatness in Iran was to belong to one of the seven high-grade families. Azadia, although he was the governor of Hira, was generally placed in the second order of nobility and, therefore, his headgear used to be worth fifty thousand dirhams. Rustam's headdress fetched a hundred thousand dirhams.

Frivolous amusement and ostentatious living had become a second nature with the Iranians. They could not get out of their extravagant habits even in grave emergencies. When Emperor Yazdgard of Iran had to flee his capital after the fall of Madain, he took with him a staggering revenue of 1,000 cooks, 1,000 musicians, 1,000 attendants of panthers and 1 ,000 falconers, and even this was not considered adequate by him.

When Hurmuzan came to Medina as a vanquished adversary and presented himself before Caliph 'Umar, he asked for a cup of water. But when the water came he refused to drink, as the cup in which it had been brought was coarse and ugly. He declared that he would prefer to die of thirst rather than drink from such a cup. Ultimately, another cup was procured for him under the order of the Caliph.

To keep themselves in a constant round of luxury, the rulers extorted money from their subjects with brutal unconcern. Their exactions became heavier day by day. According to the author of the Iran Baad-i-Sasanian. In Iran "in addition to the regular taxes, there was also the custom known as 'Ain', of extorting gifts from the people as on the occasion of 'Nauroz' and ' Mehrgan. The biggest sources of the royal income were, in our opinion, the crown estates and such other items of revenue as were considered to be the exclusive privilege of the crown, such as the gold mines of Armenia, whose entire output was the private income of the Emperor."

In Roman Syria "people had to surrender one-tenth of their income or produce, apart from paying the tax on principal stock. Then there was the capitation tax. The Romans had also many other important sources of revenue like the octroi, the commercial levy and the mines. Contracts were given for the collection of revenue from the wheat-growing areas and pastures. The contractors were called ashsharin. They had organised themselves into corporations and their agents realized much in excess of what was due. Sometimes they sold the tenants as slaves for non-payment of dues."

The population in both the Empires was split up into two sections. In the one section there were the rich and the privileged—the princes, the noblemen and the wealthy landlords and merchants— for whom life was a bed of roses. They rolled in wealth. They even adorned the shoes of their horses with jewels and hung brocade and silk on their walls. The other section comprised the common people— the artisans, the peasants, the labourers and the small traders. For them life was an unending series of hardships. Caught in an ever-tightening noose of taxes, imposts and exactions, they lived in abject poverty. To make their lives still more wretched, they had foolishly yielded to the temptation—a circumstance so common to the underdogs— of aping the customs and habits of those occupying the higher rungs of the social ladder. The result was that life for them was extremely bitter and their minds worried and confused. In fact, they were utterly devoid of real contentment and peace of mind.

Between the two, the nobler values of life and the precepts of the prophets had been thrown overboard. The ethical standards had become meaningless. The rich were too absorbed in their pleasures to pay heed to religion or the Hereafter. The peasants and the labourers were so crushed down by the worries of life that they could not afford to look beyond the humdrum of daily existence. Thus, material needs and interests had in, one way or the other, woven a web round everyone, and made him a prisoner.

Remarking upon the utter social and moral darkness that had come over the world during the epoch under review, Shah waliullah Dihlavi, in his outstanding work Hujjatullah-il-Baligha, says:

> "Centuries of undisputed mastery over large parts of the world, dissipation, irreligiousness and wholesale surrender to the devilish temptations had created among the Romans and the Iranians great fastidiousness of taste regarding comforts of life. They strove hard to outdo one other in the display of crude sensualism and luxury. Accomplished artists and craftsmen, who had collected in Rome and Iran from far and near, employed their skill to unite every refinement of convenience, elegance and splendour in the service of the rich. What improvements they introduced in the art of luxurious living gained currency immediately in society. A great value was set on the refinements of material existence. The standard of living had become so inflated that it was considered disgraceful for a nobleman to wear a cap or a waist-band worth less than a hundred thousand dirhams. One who did not possess stately mansions, sparkling fountains, gorgeous baths and shady groves and did not maintain an elegant suite of attendants and slaves received little notice in society. It is tiring to dwell further on this state of affairs. The reader can very well understand the situation in those Empires by studying the habits and manners of the rulers of their own country. Luxuries had enlarged themselves into necessities of life. A mortal sickness had come over civilization. It was a terrible affliction that had struck down both the high and the low. Everyone had slipped into a life of extravagance and folly, and in consequence, had involved himself in innumerable cares and worries. The worship of comfort called for a great deal of money, which could be acquired only by fleecing the common people, the peasants, the traders and the like. If the latter resisted the exactions, war was waged against them and they were punished; and if they yielded, they were brought into submission like dumb,

> driven cattle. They toiled day and night. Their woes gave them no respite to turn their minds to think of the good of the Hereafter. Often in a whole country not a single individual could be found with any real solicitude for religion."

In short, countries under the Roman or the Iranian domination were in a pathetic state. They were the lands of chaos and wretchedness.

Worldwide Gloom : There was, briefly, not a single nation in the whole world of the sixth century of the Christian era that could be called healthy in temperament, not a single society that was imbued with high ethical ideals, nor a single State that was based on principle of justice, equity and fairness, nor yet a leadership that possessed knowledge and wisdom, nor a religion that represented the pure teachings of the prophets of God. There was a universal lack of wholesome leadership. The Word of God had become corrupted. The few churches and monastries that still existed in the thick, encircling gloom could at best be likened unto the tiny glow of a worm in a dark rainy night. True knowledge and right action had become so rare, and moral teachers who could guide men along the sublime path of godliness so scarce, that Salman' of Persia, who had forsaken his home and the creed of his ancestors in quest of Truth, could, during the whole course of his journey from his native country to Syria, find only four persons who could provide the soothing balm of faith for his restless soul and who were living according to the way indicated by the Prophets.

The Holy Quran depicts this worldwide darkness and chaos in the following thought-provoking words:

> "Disintegration had appeared on the land and the sea because of (the need) that the hands of men had earned, that (God) might give them a taste of some of their deeds : in order that they might turn back (from evil)." (Al-Quran, XXX : 41)

Prayers Answered

As humanity lay gasping in the agonies of death, God raised up Prophet Muhammad (Peace be on him!) to resuscitate it and to deliver it from darkness into light. Says the Holy Quran:

> "A Book which we have revealed unto thee, in order that thou mightest lead mankind out of the depths of darkness into light— by the leave of their Lord—to the Way of (Him), the Exalted in Power, Worthy of all praise !" (Al-Quran XIV:1)

The Prophet broke the fetters of Ignorance and Superstition and invited men to a servitude that released them from every other form of bondage. He restored to them the legitimate comfort of life from which they had deprived themselves under false ethical and spiritual notions. The Book of Islam says:

> "For he commands them what is just and forbids them what is evil; he allows them as lawful what is good (and pure) and prohibits them from what is bad (and impure); he relieves them from their heavy burdens and releases them from the yokes that are Upon them." (Al-Quran, VII :157)

His advent gave to humanity a new life, a new light, a new faith, a new warmth a new Society and a new culture. It ushered in a new era in the human history marking the commencement of the real mission of Man Upon earth.

> "The blind and the seeing are not alike, nor are the depths of the darkness and the light; nor are the (chilly) shade and the (genial) heat of the sun; nor are alike those that are living and those that are dead." (Al-Quran, XXXV: 19-22)

Yawning between Islam and Ignorance there was a chasm as deep and wide as it could be. Yet, under the inspired leadership of the Prophet, the world jumped across it and passed from Ignorance to Islam with an alacrity that is without a parallel in history. In the following pages we shall see how this glorious miracle was accomplished.

It must have been clear from the preceding chapter that the world at the time of the Prophet's advent was like a house hit by a severe earthquake. All that was in it had turned topsy-turvy, creating a heap here and a heap there, while large spaces had been bereft of everything and made completely desolate.

In this confusion man had forgotten himself. He had lost self-respect to the extent that he was shamelessly prostrating himself before stones, trees and water—before all the helpless manifestations of nature. He could not comprehend even the simple everyday truths. His intellect was at a standstill. He had been so confused in the mind and his senses had become so perverted that he could not distinguish the real from the unreal and disputed about that which was obviously right and true.

Vice itself was looked upon as virtue. Wolves, so to say, were appointed to tend sheep; aggressors were allowed to act as arbitrators. The sinful and the wicked lived in peace and enjoyed plenty—the world belonged to them, while the righteous and the upright were condemned to privation and suffering. Cunning and deceit passed for wisdom and resourcefulness, while wisdom itself was considered foolishness.

Drinking, gambling, usury and plunder had become the order of the day. Daughters were killed at birth. God's wealth was the grime of the kings' palms, and human beings their bondsmen. The ecclesiastics had raised themselves to the position of Divinity. They waxed fat on the wealth of others whom they deliberately deceived and misled in order to gain their own ends.

The precious qualities which God had bestowed upon man were being wantonly misused. Courage and strength had become a means of cruelty and oppression, and wastefulness stood for generosity, arrogance passed for self-respect and artfulness for sagacity. The sole purpose of the intellect was taken to be to plan crimes and invent new ways of hideous debauchery and vulgar extravagance.

For long the most valuable of all materials, the human material, had been rotting. It had not had the good fortune to come to the notice of a master-craftsman who should have prepared from it the right mould of civilization. 'Where there should have been organised communities of men, there were untended flocks of human-cattle.'

Politics was unrestrained as a wild camel and power was like a naked sword in the hands of one who had lost his senses on account of heavy drinking and who was using it against himself and against everybody else.

Every section of that degenerate society, every aspect of that vicious civilization demanded the undivided attention of a reformer. An ordinary reformer, acting according to his own lights, without Prophetic Inspiration and Divine Guidance, might have concentrated all his energies on correcting a single social pathological condition and even then might not have succeeded. Human nature is a complicated affair, abounding in labyrinths and mysterious back-doors, and once it gets misguided or deflected from its natural course, it cannot be given a new lease of life by removing one defect only. It required a complete overhauling, a thorough reconditioning. If the plant of Godliness was to thrive on human soil, the entire undergrowth of ungodliness had first to be weeded out. There was no other way out.

The correction of a single moral defect of human society calls for the dedication of the whole life of a reformer. Sometimes large numbers of men spend their lifetimes in combating a moral fault or a social abuse without being rewarded with any measure of success. Take, for example, the evil of drinking. When this habit becomes widespread in a nation, its roots go deep into the collective sub-conscious, and a whole army of sensuous delights gets arrayed behind it. Can this evil be overcome by mere moral exhortation or by punitive legislation alone? No; only a fundamental psychological change, a radical change in the social and moral outlook of the society as a whole can eradicate it. Any other course will only drive it underground and make it more pernicious.

The Difference : Had the Prophet been a political leader, the ideal thing for him would have been to weld Arabia into one country and the Arab tribes into one nation, with himself at their head. Abu Jahl, 'Utba and all the rest of his relentless opponents would have readily accepted his leadership all over the country. They had already demonstrated their confidence in him by appointing him to arbitrate in Mecca's most dangerous dispute. 'Utba had definitely stated that if he so desired, the Quraish were willing to make him their king. After he had risen to power in Arabia, he could have led his splendid horsemen into Persia and Rome and brought these Empires under his heel. What a magnificent vista lay open to him! In case it was strategically unwise to fight with the Romans and the Iranians simultaneously, what was there to stop him from overrunning the neighbouring countries of Abyssinia and the Yemen?

But he had not been raised up to substitute one evil for another, to condemn an injustice at one place and condone it elsewhere. He had not been sent to erect the mansion of Arab glory upon the ruins of the hopes and yearnings of other nations, to emancipate men from the thraldom of the Romans and Iranians and to place them under subjugation to the descendants of 'Adrian and Qahtan.'

He was not a political leader. He was a preacher of the Divine World, a Warner and a Bearer of Glad Tidings. He was the "Lustrous Lamp." He had come to emancipate men from the worship of their fellow-men by calling them up to submit to the One and the Real Overlord, the Almighty God. He had come to rescue humanity from the dungeon of petty desires by working out its evolution in the boundless spaces of the heavens and the earth; and to deliver it from the tyranny of decayed religions to the bounteousness of Islam, to check evil and promote good deeds and to prohibit what was dirty and foul and to salification what was clean and wholesome.

He, therefore, did not address himself to any particular country or community. He made the whole human race his concern. It was only proper that he should begin his mission with Arabia, for being the darkest spot on earth during the darkest age of human history it deserved to receive the first rays of light. Besides this, the central place that Mecca occupied on the map of the then known world, together with its tradition of political freedom, made it an ideal base for a movement which stood for Liberty, Peace and Universal brotherhood. The Arabs also possessed certain inborn virtues that made them fit for being instrumental in spreading the teachings of Islam in the world.

The Prophet was not one of those reformers who content themselves with striving against a few moral abuses of their age and succeed in eradicating them for the time being, or depart from the world without having accomplished anything at all.'

The Holy Prophet applied the right key to the problem of human nature. It was the problem which had defied solution at the hands of all reformers before him. He began by entreating men to believe in God and to bring down all false gods from the pedestal of Divinity. "O people", he declared, "say, 'there is no god but One God' and you shall prosper."

This thunderous proclamation caused a stir in the ranks of paganism. In an instant paganism was up in arms against this simple human truth:

> "And the leaders among them (forthwith) said: 'Go forth and stick to your gods; for this is truly a thing designed (against you)." (Al-Quran, XXXVIII 7)

The ghastly deeds of crime and cruelty perpetrated upon the Muslims by the enemies of Truth are preserved in the pages of history. They show that Islam had found its mark. It had struck at the very root of unbelief. The citadel of Darkness had been stormed, and the beleaguered forces sailed forth to fight to the bitter end. But the Prophet wavered not. In the hurricane of hate and persecution he stood firm like a rock. He plainly told his uncle who had brought him up since his childhood, 'O my uncle, if they placed the sun on my right hand and the moon on my left to force me to renounce my work, verily I will not desist until God makes manifest His work or I perish in the effort."

For thirteen years he remained in Mecca, resolute and steadfast, insisting on belief in Divine Unity, Apostleship, Resurrection and the Last Judgment. His faith in his Mission was never shaken, not even for a moment. He did not compromise with untruth. He was convinced that the majestic message that had been vouchsafed to him alone held the answer to all the unsolved problems of humanity.

The whole of Arabia turned hostile to the Prophet. It needed the heart of a lion to accept his mission. It meant treading the path of fire; it meant walking into the jaws of death. Yet, some brave souls among the Quraish responded to the Divine Call. Theirs was not a hurried decision. They knew what they were doing. There were no worldly considerations to prompt them. They had deliberately shut upon themselves the doors to worldly comfort and luxury. They had heard the call to faith, and the world had shrivelled for them. Sleep had gone out of their eyes. Their soft beds had turned into beds of thorns. Truth had dawned upon them, and now there could be no running away from it. They knew it in their heart of hearts that there could be no peace for them until they had declared their faith in God and His Apostle. So they decided, once and for all, to go to the Prophet and accept the faith he preached. The Prophet lived in a part of their own town, only a few yards away. But the hatred of the Quraish had made the way to him so long and so perilous that to traverse it was like undertaking a long and hazardous journey. It was safer by far to take a trade caravan to Syria or the Yemen, eluding the barbarous highway-men, than to go to meet the Prophet in Mecca itself. Yet, they did go to him, took at his hand the oath of allegiance to God and His Apostle and pledged their lives to stand by him. They had run a tremendous risk. Severe hardships and unsparing trials were sure to visit them in the path they had taken. But they were prepared for the worst. They had heard the Quran which said:

> "Do not think that they will be left alone on saying, 'We believe', and that they will not be tested? We did test those before them, and God will certainly know those who are true from those who are false."
>
> (Al-Quran, XXIX: 2)

They had also heard the following Divine Commandment:

> "Or, do ye think that ye shall enter the Garden (of Bliss) without such (trials) as (came to) those who passed away before you? (While) they encountered suffering and adversity and were so shaken in spirit that even the Apostle and those who believed along with him cried out: 'When (will come) the help of God? 'Ah ! Verily, the help of God is (always) near (at hand)."
>
> (Al-Quran, II: 214)

At last, the dreaded happened. The Quraish emptied the quiver of their wrath at them. Not one arrow was left unused. But the believers remained steadfast. They said, "This is what God and His Apostle had promised; verily, the Word of God and his Apostle is true" and it reinforced them internally and strengthened them in their resolve. The more they were persecuted, the stronger did their determination grow. From this furnace of trial they emerged as pure as gold.

At the same time the Prophet had been supplying them with the spiritual fare of the Quran and looking after their religious education. He made them bow, five times a day, before the Creator and the Preserver of the Worlds with cleanliness of body, humility of heart and concentration of mind. Day by day, they were increasing in stature, morally and spiritually, and obtaining riddance from shallow earthly aspirations. Their love for the Lord of the World was ever on the increase. They were made of a stern stuff. War was their old hobby. Their history was full of bloody episodes like those of Basfis, and Dahis and Ghabra. The memory of the war of Fijar was still fresh in their minds. But the Prophet kept their warlike temperament under control. Their native arrogance had yielded before the sublimity of their Faith. The Prophet commanded them to "stay their hands and establish prayer", and they obeyed him. They had become like wax in his hands. Without a semblance of cowardice, they passively endured what no people in the world had ever endured. Not a single instance is recorded in the pages of history in which a Muslim raised his arm in the defence of his own person or resorted to retaliation or went back to his old days of Ignorance.

When the enmity of the Quraish exceeded all limits, God allowed the Muslims to migrate to Medina where Islam had already found its way.

In Medina, the Meccan and the Medinite Muslims fraternized with each other. There was nothing in common between them except the new Faith. Blood was still dripping from the swords of the Aus and the Khazraj—they had not yet removed from their clothes the stains of blood received in the battle of Buith. In circumstances like these Islam sowed the seeds of affection for one another in their hearts and brought about a fraternization that would not have been possible among real brothers at any price.

The ties that were established between the 'Ansar' and the 'Muhajirs' were even stronger than the ties of blood:

> This infant community, which consisted of the emigrants from Mecca and the Helpers from Medina, was the nucleus of a splendid Islamic Nation and the Commonwealth of Islam. It was born at a time when

> the world wavered precariously between life and death. Its birth tipped the scales in favour of life. To strengthen this community was indispensable for the survival of mankind; for this very reason when God laid stress on forging the brotherly bond between the 'Ansar' and 'Muhajirs', He gave the warning: "If you will not do so, there will be great corruption and mischief on the earth." (Al-Quran, VIII : 73)

The religious training of the Companions was continued in Medina under the eye of the Prophet who explained to them the real conception and purpose of religion and fostered among them the virtues of introspection and self-censorship, love of learning and anxiety for After-life. The Companions were seized by an over-mastering urge for self-effacement in the path of God. So easy had it become for them to turn their backs upon worldly attachments that in ten years they set forth more than a hundred times on jihad, twenty-seven times in the company of the Prophet himself.

The verses of the Quran, as revealed through the Prophet, brought into force numerous commands with regard to their personal conduct, possessions and families, which were quite new for them and by no means easy to observe, but they had become so accustomed to surrendering themselves unquestioningly to the Will of God, that they experienced no difficulty in complying with them. Once the Gordian knot of unbelief had been cut, it was easy to unfasten the other knots that bound them. Once the Prophet had opened their hearts to Islam, he did not have to struggle at each step to make them reject the Wrong and accept the Right. They had entered into the new faith heart and soul and submitted themselves without demur to what the Prophet decreed. They unhesitatingly confessed before the Prophet such crimes as were not known to anyone except themselves. If they committed any crime, they voluntarily submitted themselves for punishment. Many of them actually had the wine-cups in their hands when the Quranic injunction against the use of intoxicants was revealed, but the Word of God came between them and the cups. They threw away the cups at once and broke their wine-barrels so that the drains of Medina literally overflowed with their detestable contents.

Thus, when they had attained to the highest pinnacle of moral development and became proof against the inducements of Satan and of their own baser self, when they had learned to prefer the future good to the immediate good and had been transformed into lovers of the world Hereafter even while living in this world, when neither poverty could be a barrier in their path nor could riches make them vain, when they had become meek, yet unbending before power, and when they had come to be the dispensers of justice among men even though it might go against themselves, their own kith and kin, God made the whole world subservient to them and appointed them the Defenders of the Faith. The Prophet nominated them as his successors and went to join the Most High, happy in the triumphant fulfillment of his Mission and in the belief that he had left his charge in hands that would not falter.

Most Remarkable Revolution : The mighty revolution wrought by the Prophet among the Arabs which through them produced a new and lasting impression upon all the nations of the globe, was unique in all respects. It was a most extraordinary event in human history, yet there was nothing about it that could not be explained rationally. Let us study, not as Muslim enthusiasts but as students of human affairs, the character, the scope and the influence of this great Revolution upon the destinies of the human race.

During the pre-Islamic age people had generally taken to the worship of inanimate objects which could neither help them nor grant their petitions, and had, in fact, been created to serve their needs. Hence, there was no real moral enthusiasm, no genuine spirituality in their religions. The God of their conception was an artisan who had retired into a corner after finishing His job. They believed that He had bequeathed His kingdom to those whom He had adorned with the mantle of Divinity and now it was they who controlled the affairs of the universe. They lacked spiritual understanding of God. They did know of Him as the Creator of the universe, but it was akin to the knowledge of a historian who, when he is asked as to who built a certain building, replies that it was built by such-and-such a king, but the mention of the king's name neither inspires awe in his heart, nor makes any solemn impression on his mind. They had no intimate consciousness of the Divine attributes, and, consequently, their hearts did not bear the imprint of God's glory or love.

The Greeks had expounded what was largely a negative definition of God. It made no allowance of the positive virtues connected with His name like Benevolence, Compassion, Mercifulness and Omniscience. It did prove the First Cause, but divested it of knowledge-and will, and set forth such hypothetical premises and theories as were derogatory to Divine dignity. But no system of culture or faith has ever thrived on negative foundations. The Greek philosophers had, accordingly, ended up by destroying the spirit of religion and making it a rigmarole of empty ceremonies, sports and festivals.

The Muslims in general and the Arabs in particular rejected this vague and sickly religiousness and attained a Faith which was at once intense and profound and which permeated through every fibre of their existence. They pledged their Faith in God Who has Excellent Attributes, Who is the Most Exalted, the Most Magnificent and the faster of the Day of judgment. Says the Book of Islam:

> "God is He besides Whom there is no other god;— The Sovereign, the Holy One, the Source of Peace (and Perfection), the Guardian of Faith, the Preserver of Safety, the Exalted in Might, the Irresistible, the Supreme; Glory to God (High is He) above the partners they attribute to Him. He is the Creator, the Evolver, the Bestower of Forms and Colours. To Him belong the most beautiful names: Whatever is in the heavens and on earth, — both declare His Praises and Glory: and He is the Exalted in Might, the Wise."
>
> (Al-Quran, LIX : 23 ,24)

He is the God Who is the Creator and the Preserver of the universe, Who rewards with paradise and chastises with hell, Who swells or shrinks the subsistence of whomsoever He likes, Who is the Knower of all that is hidden in the heavens and the earth, and Who knows the stealth of the eyes and the secrets of the hearts, and is the embodiment of beauty and sublimity, strength and splendour and perfection and beneficence.

This solemn conviction produced a miraculous transformation

among the early followers of Islam. Whoever affirmed his faith in One Transcendent God and testified to 'La Ilaha Illallah' experienced a sudden change in himself. The inmost recesses of his soul were lit up with the sublime radiance of God-consciousness, the spirit and the flesh in him ceased to be the enemies of one another—he achieved equilibrium within himself—and extraordinary feats of courage, endurance and faith came to be performed by him.

This faith was a wonderful source of moral training. It generated among its followers an amazing strength of will, self-criticism and justice towards oneself. For, nothing can help to overcome the inducements of the self so successfully as a living faith in the Omnipresence of God.

If anyone ever succumbed to beastly urges and fell into error, even though unobserved, he would make a confession thereof straightaway before the Prophet and undergo the severest punishment willingly to save himself from Divine Displeasure. A number of incidents of this nature have been handed down to us by reliable historians, one of which is that of Maouz bin Malik Miami. One day he betook himself to the Holy Prophet and said, "O Prophet of God, I have been guilty of adultery, and I beg of you to cleanse me." The Prophet sent him away, but he returned the next day and repeated the confession. The Prophet again sent him back and inquired from his family whether he had lost balance of mind. The relatives of Maouz stated that, as far as they knew, there was nothing abnormal in his behaviour. When Maouz came for the third time, the Prophet again inquired about his mental condition, and his relatives returned the same answer. They would not think of telling a lie to save the life of a relative, be he a father, a brother or a husband. Maouz too, would not shrink back. He appeared before the Prophet and confessed his guilt for the fourth time. Then, at last, the Prophet ordered him to be stoned to death according to the Islamic Law.

A similar case was that of a woman named Ghamidiyah. She, too, had been guilty of adultery and wanted to be 'cleansed' so that she might not have to rise with the stain of sin on her on the Day of Reckoning. When she appeared before the Prophet again on the second day, having been sent back on the first, she earnestly said to him, "Why do you send me away like Maouz? I am pregnant too (and this proves my guilt beyond a shadow of doubt)." "Then go away now ", the Prophet replied. "Come after your child is born "She went back and waited, When the period of waiting was over and she was delivered of the child, she again came to the Holy Prophet, holding her baby in her arms. "Here is my child ", she said. But once more she had to return, for the Prophet had commanded her to go back and nurse the child till it was weaned. "Bring it to me," he said, "when it begins to feed otherwise than from the breast". When the child was weaned, Ghamidiyah reported back herself to the Prophet with her child, the child holding a piece of bread in its tiny hand in proof of the fact that it needed no longer, to be nursed from the breast. "Here I am, O Messenger of God " this strange woman declared, "Now I am free. My child is weaned." The Prophet placed the child under the care of a Muslim and ordered that the sentence of death by stoning be carried out on her. A pit was dug and she was buried in it up to her waist. Then she was stoned. As Khalid bin Walid hurled a stone at her and blood gushed forth from her body, some drops of it fell upon his skirt. Recoiling back from them, Alid uttered some uncomplimentary remarks about the woman, which the Holy Prophet heard. "No, Khalid, no" the Prophet admonished him, "By the Holy Being in Whose hand is my life, she has offered such penitence that if the octroi-official' did it, even he would be forgiven (by God)." After she was dead, funeral prayers were said over by the command of the Prophet and she was buried.

Virtues like honesty and trustworthiness developed in the early Muslims as the natural fruits of a sense of living belief in the Omnipresence of the Absolute God. Even when alone and unnoticed or in any other situation wherein they could easily transgress the bonds of religious conduct, the fear of God kept the Muslims under rigid control.

It is related in Tarikh-i-Tabari, that, after the victory of Madam, when the Muslims were collecting the booty, one of them brought something he had come upon and deposited it with the treasurer. It was so enormously valuable that those who saw it were astounded. They had not seen such a valuable treasure in their lives. They began to question him, "Are you sure, you have not held back a part of it ?" "By God", he replied, "had I wished I could have misappropriated the whole lot without any of you being the wiser." This straightforward reply made a deep impression on them and they felt that they were facing an extraordinary man. They begged him to disclose his name, but he declined. "I can't tell you my name," he said, "because you will then start praising me, while all praise is for Allah. I am well content with whatever He bestows as a reward ". When he departed, they sent a man after him to find out who he was. Then it was discovered that he was Amir, of the tribe of 'Abd-i-Qais.'

The belief in one God, the Sovereign Lord of the universe, had raised the heads of Muslims so high that now they could not be made to bend before anyone except the Almighty. Mirroring in their hearts, as they did, the glory of the Most Glorious, the glitter of worldly grandeur made no impression on them.

Abu Musa says that when he reached the court of the Negus along with other Muslim emigrants, he found that 'Amr bin al-As was sitting on the Emperor's right, 'Umara on his left and the priests were forming a double row in the front. 'Amr and 'Umara informed the Emperor that the Muslims were not wont to kneel before anyone. But the priests insisted that they should do so before the Emperor, upon which Hadrat Jafar unhesitatingly said, "We, Muslims, kneel before God alone and before no one else."

Rabi ul bin 'Amir was once sent by Hadrat Saad as his envoy to Rustam, the Commander-in-Chief of Iran. Rustam received him in a grand darbar hail which was decorated with magnificent carpets. The Commander-in-Chief, wearing a crown and robes which sparkled with gems, sat on a throne. Rabi, in contrast, was very poorly attired. He was almost in rags and was carrying a shield that was too small for him. His horse was also of a small breed, on which he rode straight towards Rustam, the pony trampling the costly carpets under its hoofs. On getting closer to the throne, he dismounted, tied the reins of the horse to a bolster and started to walk up to Rustam, still wearing his helmet and arms. The officers of the court demonstrated against it. They said that he should at least take off the helmet before going in the presence of the Commander-in-Chief. But Rabi ul retorted, "I have come at your request and not of my own accord. I am willing to go back if you do not want me". At this stage Rustam intervened and told his officers to let him come on as he was pleased. Rabi ul proceeded, leaning upon his lance, and piercing the carpets with it at each step. The people inquired about the object of his visit. He said, "We have been sent by Allah to deliver whom He pleases from the overlordship of His slaves (i.e., men) to His own overlordship, and from the narrow confines of his world to the boundlessness of the next and from the oppressiveness of other religions to the fairness and justice of Islam."

Rare Courage : The enthusiasm for After-life had endowed the Muslims with and almost superhuman courage. Worldly aims and interests having ceased to bear any significance in their eyes, they advanced towards the ultimate goal of paradise with the radiancy of a carrier-pigeon.

It is reported in the Sahih of al-Bukhari that as Hadrat Anas bin Nadhar was advancing upon the enemy at a critical moment in the battle of Uhud, he met Saad bin Muaz to whom he said, "By God, Saad, I can feel the sweet fragrance of Paradise coming from the direction of the Mount of Uhud." With these words he rushed into the heart of the battle. Saad says that when the dead body of Anas was recovered from the battlefield, there were more than eighty wounds on it. The infidels had literally cut him to pieces; as a result of this, his sister alone could recognize his corpse.

In the battle of Badr the Prophet was once urging the Muslims on to greater effort. When he was saying, "March forward to Paradise, the extensiveness of which is as the extensiveness of the heavens and the earth ", 'Umayr bin Hamam cried out, "O Prophet of God, is it really that much extensive ?" The Prophet replied, "Yes. Do you doubt it ?" "I doubt not," said 'Umayr, "I only wished that I attained it". "You will", the Prophet replied. 'Umayr had taken out some dates and begun to eat them. But the opening of the prospect of Paradise before his mind would not let him eat. Was it not foolish to waste one's time on such 'trifles', when heaven was beckoning him? He flung away the dates and jumped into the thick of the battle. His heart's desire was soon fulfilled.

Abu Bakr bin Abi Moora Ashari has narrated that on a certain field of battle his father was recounting how the Prophet had said that the gates of Paradise were under the shadow of the swords when a man, dressed in tatters, stepped forward and asked whether he himself had heard that from the Prophet. Abu Bakr's father replied that it was so. On hearing this, the man went back to his friends and took their leave. He unsheathed his sword, broke the sheath into pieces and took the field against the enemy. He was subsequently killed.

'Amr bin Jamuh, who was lame, had four sons. They used to accompany the Holy Prophet whenever he set out on Jihad. When the Prophet was leaving for Uhud, 'Amr also wanted to join, but his sons were opposed to it on account of his physical disability and old age. Finding them adamant, 'Amr sought the help of the Prophet. "My sons dissuade me from going with you", he said, "while it is my desire that I walk in Paradise with my impaired leg". The Prophet explained that the Jihad was not binding on him. At the same time, he did not like that 'Amr's Sons should stand in their father's way in the holy cause upon which he had set his heart. So he said to them, "Why don't you let him go? God may grant him martyrdom." The sons agreed and 'Amr went to join the holy war in which he was killed.'

Shaddad bin had says that in a journey a bedouin came to the Prophet and attached himself to his party after embracing Islam. The Prophet instructed a Companion to keep an eye on him. When the campaign of Khyber took place, the Prophet allotted a share in the booty to him also, but as he was not present — he was a cattle-lifter and used to slip away on his rounds when he got the chance—it was kept with a Companion who gave it to him on his return in the evening. The bedouin took the booty to the Prophet and inquired as to what it was. The Prophet told him that it was his share of the spoils, upon which he said, "But I did not join you for it," and pointing towards his throat he added, "I joined to be pierced by an arrow here". The Prophet replied, "God will fulfil your wish if you are true in your affair with Him". Then another battle took place in which he was killed. When his corpse was pointed out to the Prophet, he remarked," His affair with God was true; so God too made him true."

The unruly Arabs, who were so lawless in their ways, had surrendered themselves so absolutely to the guidance of the Faith that now it was not possible for them to infringe the Divine Law.

They had accepted the Sovereignty of God in its completest sense. In peace and in war, in joy and in sorrow, in every relationship of life, at each turn of affairs and in the minutest details of their concerns they looked on to His guidance and help and carried out His commands without the slightest demur.

They had known paganism. They had been born and brought up in it. They could, therefore, fully appreciate the value of Islam and understand that Islam meant the replacement of one mode of life by another, the passing over from the anarchy of desire to the rule of God. Till yesterday, they were at war with God; now they were His willing slaves. There could be no room for one's personal opinion after the Word of God had come. To disobey the Prophet, to hold a disputation with him, to take one's case to a court other than the one where the law of God was dispensed, to give priority to one's family tradition over Faith — these things were now out of the question. They had rejected paganism in toto and entered wholeheartedly into a new and fuller existence.

Once Fudhala bin 'Umayr bin Mulawwah made a plan to assassinate the Prophet during the Tawaf of Kaaba. As Fudhala drew near him, the Prophet inquired," Is it you, Fudhala? "Yes, it is I, O Prophet of God," replied Fudhala. "Tell me," the Prophet asked, "with what intention you had come." "There is nothing to tell," replied Fudhala, "I was only remembering God ". The Prophet smiled at this and placed his hand over Fudhala's heart. The peace of Fudhala's heart was restored. He, afterwards, used to say that as soon as the hand was lifted, the Prophet appeared to be so handsome to him as if God had not created anything in the world more beautiful than him. On his way back, Fudhala met his mistress who invited him to a chat, but he declined. He said that there could be no scope for such a thing after one had submitted to Islam.

True Knowledge : The prophets had imparted to man the true knowledge of God's existence and His attributes and actions. They had laid the foundations upon which man could erect the edifice of his own spiritual conduct without getting involved in fruitless metaphysical discussions on 'being' and 'knowing.' But man heeded not. Instead of being grateful for Divine guidance, he allowed the ship of his thought to drift on unchartered seas. He behaved like an explorer who, setting aside the geographical charts and maps, tries to scale every height, fathom every depth and measure every distance on his own initiative. The result of such endeavours can at best be a few sketchy notes and incomplete hints picked up here and there. So when the people tried to reach God with the help of reason alone and without the aid of the light the Prophet's teachings had furnished, the knowledge of God gathered by them consisted of little else besides random thoughts, conflicting theories and haphazard conclusions.

The Companions of Prophet Muhammad were twice blessed in this respect because by giving themselves up to his guidance they were spared the wild goose chase of speculative theology regarding the existence and nature of God and left free to devote their energies to more productive branches of learning. They served as the guardians of the Revealed Word. In consequence, they were able to retain the substance of faith while others only hugged its shadow.

The Islamic concept of God as the Creator, Nourisher and Sustainer of all people and nations and the universal scope of the ministry of Prophet Muhammad had demolished all barriers of blood, colour and geography between man and man and welded mankind into one family. In Islam all men formed, as it were, a single bouquet of humanity. They were the members of the same family, being the children of the same father, Adam. An Arab had no superiority over a non-Arab and he that was not an Arab had no superiority over an Arab. The most honoured one was he who was the most righteous.

The Prophet emphatically said, "O people, Verily God has removed from you the blemish of ignorance and the pride of birth. There are but two classes of men: those who are righteous and God-fearing and honourable in the eyes of God, and those who are wicked and sinful and dishonourable in His eyes."

Typical of his teachings was the advice he gave to Hadrat Abu Zarr: "Look here, you are neither greater than, nor superior to, anyone except, of course, in case you excel him in virtue."

Typical also was the affirmation he used to repeat to his Creator daily during the late night prayers: "I testify that all men are brothers".

Everything that tended to divide humanity into factions and groups was severely condemned by him. He said, "He who lives in factionalism is not one of us. He who dies in factionalism is not one of us. He who fights for factionalism is not one of us."

Once, in a battlefield, a Muhajir slapped an Ansari, upon which the Ansari cried out, "O Ansari" Following his example, the 'Muhajir', too shouted, "O Muhajirs," The Prophet at once checked them. "Leave these parochial slogans," he said, "these are filthy."

The Prophet had abolished the old tribal notion of kinship that demanded of one to stand by one's brother whether he was the oppressor or the oppressed. In his view, "helping a kinsman in an unjust cause was like trying to hold back by the tail a camel determined upon jumping into the well." He had succeeded in establishing a really classless society in which the high and the low, the rich and the poor, the white and the coloured were united into a single brotherhood. All sections of the people readily co-operated with one another and stood like one man in the hour of need. Women were the trusts of God in the hands of men; wives had their rights over their husbands, as the husbands had their rights over their wives.

Social Responsibility : The Muslims were charged with a strong sense of responsibility. Their minds had matured and they conducted themselves as responsible members of their families, their professions, their Faith and the entire human society.

They were the helpers of truth; they acted by mutual consultation; they obeyed the head of the State—the Caliph—wholeheartedly and overtly as well as covertly but only as long as he remained loyal to the Divine Commandments. "There is no loyalty unto the created which involves disloyalty unto the Creator", was an essential dictum of their polity. The revenues of the State, which till then filled the private purses of the rulers, were confided in God and spent as approved by Him. The position of the Caliph was like that of an orphan's guardian; he took from the public funds only what was needed for his sustenance in case he did not have an income of his own, otherwise he accepted no remuneration. The ownership of land, too, was vested in God, and they believed that they would be called upon to answer before Him for every inch of it held by them.

Centuries of ignorance and oppression had brought down the common folk to the level of animals, who mutely submitted to the many social wrongs to which they were subjected. In the righteous and democratic environment of Islam the civic sense of the people was aroused, and the Islamic society came to possess a social conscience. Social responsibility was hammered into human consciousness by Islam as a religious postulate.

The noble instinct of love, to whose credit lies many an outstanding achievement in history, had, before Islam been rendered dormant. It was lying in disgrace. Things had come to such a pass that it was now understood only in the context of the transient manifestations of beauty. For long, there had not appeared anyone who could, by the charm of his personality and the exquisiteness of his character, claim the unqualified devotion of his fellowmen and then divert it into the right channel. The world found such a man in Prophet Muhammad, in whom God had assembled all that was adorable in a human being.

Eyewitness accounts show that whoever came into the presence of the Holy Prophet all of a sudden was overawed, while those who came to know him better were bewitched. His admirers reported that they had not seen the like of him anywhere in the world. Hearts were drawn to him as if they had been waiting all the while only to be pulled by the magnetism of his personality. History cannot provide a single instance of anyone meeting with such love, obedience and respect as he inspired in his people.

We cite here some of the cases which illustrate the exceptional devotion of the Companions to the Prophet.

One day Hadrat Abu Bakr was assaulted by the enemies of the Faith at Mecca. 'Utba bin Rabia, in particular, beat him so severely that his face swelled till it became difficult to recognize him. He was carried home in a precarious condition by Bani Tamim. But so ardent was his love for the Prophet that the first thing he did on regaining consciousness towards the evening was to inquire about the Prophet's welfare, "How is the Prophet of God?" fell from his swollen lips. His attendants felt greatly piqued at it and they began to scold him for showing so much concern for one who, in their opinion, was the sole cause of his misfortune. But he persisted in his inquiry, and when his mother, Umm-ul-Khair, brought him nourishment, he refused to partake of it till he had received news about the Prophet. Umm-ul-Khair assured him that she knew nothing about his friend. He then asked her to go and inquire from Umm-i-jamal, the daughter of Khattab, but the latter was so terrified that she would not admit that she knew the Prophet. "I do not know who is Muhammad bin 'Abdullah or Abu Bakr," she declared, "but I am willing to accompany you to your son if you like." Umm-ul-khair replied that she would like nothing better, When Umm-i-Jamil came to Abu Bakr's house and saw his condition, she began to curse his assailants. She said, "I swear by God that the community that has done this is a community of shameless heathens. God will surely punish it for its sins." But Abu Bakr had no patience for such things. "Tell me," he cut her short, "how is the Prophet ?" Umm-i-Jamil cautioned him that his mother was listening. When Abu Bakr assured her that it was not necessary to observe secrecy in the presence of his mother, she disclosed that the Prophet was safe at the house of Ibn-i-Arqam. Abu Bakr, thereupon, declared that he would neither eat nor drink till he had joined the Prophet. They waited for the darkness of the night to deepen, and when it was safe enough for Abu Bakr to be taken out, he was conveyed to the Prophet by his mother and Umm-i-Jamil. It was then alone that he took his meal.

During the battle of Uhud, as the news went round that the Prophet had been seriously wounded, a woman whose brother, father and husband had been killed in the battle that very day, forgot her own sorrow and rushed to the battlefield shouting, "How is the Prophet?" People assured her that by the grace of God he was safe, but she refused to be comforted until she had actually seen him. She was taken to him. When she saw him, she said: "No calamity is a calamity if you are safe."

Hadrat Khubaib when mounted on the scaffold by his persecutors, was asked, "Don't you wish now that Muhammad were in your place?" He cried out, "I would not like to be released on the condition that he may be given even a pinprick."

On the battlefield of Uhud, the Prophet dispatched Zaid bin Thabit to convey his greetings to Saad bin Rabi' and inquire from him how he was feeling. Zaid made a long search among the killed and the wounded and then he came upon him just in the nick of time, for he was dying fast. He had received about seventy wounds. Zaid hastily communicated to him the Prophet's message. He replied, "Pay my respects to the Prophet, and tell him that I am smelling the sweet smells of Paradise, and to my community of Ansar do say that if anything happened to the Prophet while even one of them lived, they would not escape Divine wrath." Saying this he died.

On the battlefield of Uhud, again, there was an occasion when the Prophet's life was greatly impelled. Without a moment's hesitation, Abdul Dujana exposed his back to serve as a shield for him; arrows pierced his flesh but he did not flinch. The Prophet's wounds were sucked clean by Malik. The Prophet told him to spit out the blood, but he declined, saying, "By God, I am not going to spit it (on the ground)."

Abu Sufyan, when he came to Medina, went to meet his daughter, Umm-i-Habiba who was married to the Prophet. He was about to sit on the Prophet's bed when she came up and rolled it. Abil Sufyan was taken aback at this treatment and, sarcastically remarked, "Daughter, I could not understand whether I was not worthy of the bed or the bed was not worthy of me". "No", his daughter explained, "the thing is that it is the Prophet's bed and you are an unclean infidel."

The unique love and reverence shown to the Prophet by his followers is also apparent from the statement made by Urwa before his brethren Quraish on his return from Hudaibiyab. He said, "I have seen many monarchs. I have been in the courts of Caesar, khusrau and Negus. I can swear that I have not seen any king held in greater respect by his subjects than Muhammad is by his Companions. By God, when he gives an order, they all rush to carry it out, when he performs the wadu, they nearly come to blows in the scramble for. The water he has used for it; when he speaks, a hush overtakes them. So excessively do they revere him that they dare not raise their eyes in his presence to obtain a full view of him."

By reason of this unprecedented devotion to the Holy Prophet, the Companions never spared themselves in the service of the

Prophet. The declaration made by Saad bin Muaz on behalf of the Ansar just before the battle of Badr beautifully illustrates the boundless loyalty of these worthy Muslims.

"I declare unequivocally" it reads, "on behalf of the Ansar, that you may stay wherever you wish, establish or break relations with whomsoever you like, and take away from our possessions whatever it pleases you to take away and leave whatever it pleases you to leave. What you will take away will make us happier than what you will not. We shall not deviate from the path of loyalty, come what may. We shall follow you even if you march up to Burk Ghamdan, and were you to plunge your horse into the sea, by God, we, too, shall jump into it."

Such obedience did his word command among his people that when he proclaimed the social boycott of the three Muslims, who had held themselves back from the battle of Tabuk without a valid reason, the whole of Medina at once turned into a dead city for them. One of the defaulters, Kaab, himself gives the following account of the incident.

"The Prophet had prohibited social intercourse with us. People began to avoid our company; their entire attitude towards us was changed. The very earth seemed to have shrunk upon us. It was no longer the place we knew. When things became unbearable, I, one day, betook myself to Abil Qatadah's garden by jumping over its wall. Abil Qatadah was my cousin, my uncle's son, for whom I had the greatest affection. I greeted him, but he did not return my greeting. 'Then I asked him, 'Tell me, for the sake of God, don't you know that I love God and the Prophet?' He remained silent. I implored him in the name of God to answer my question, but again there was no reply. On being 'pressed by me for the third time for a reply, he said, 'God and the Prophet know better.' Tears welled up in my eyes at this answer and I jumped over the wall and came out of the garden."

Another incident in Kaab's life is worth mentioning here. While the Holy Prophet was enraged on some account, a messenger brought him the Prophet's order that he was to stay away from his wife. "Shall I divorce her?" asked Kaab. "No", the messenger replied, "only keep away from her." Kaab sent away his wife to her parents to await there the final settlement of the matter by the Almighty.

Right in the midst of his social boycott, Kaab received a letter from the ruler of Ghassan, which read as follows: "We have come to know that your Master has withdrawn his favours from you. God surely did not send you into the world to suffer disgrace and be left to rot. Come to us. We shall treat you with great honour."

Kaab did not vacillate. When he had read it, he said, "It is also a part of my trial," and threw it into the fire. That was the end of it.

The spirit of loyalty infused by the Prophet in his followers enabled them to overcome the most deep-rooted evils in their midst. A word from him was sufficient to enforce total prohibition. It is related by Abu Burda from his father who says. "We were having a drinking party. I rose up and left for the Prophet's place to pay my respects to him. On the way I learnt that the following verses had been revealed, announcing total abstinence:

> 'On ye who believe, intoxicants and gambling, (dedication of) stones, and (divination by) arrows, are an abomination,_ of Satan's handiwork; eschew such (abomination), that ye may prosper. Satan's plan is (but) to excite enmity and hatred among you with intoxicants and gambling, and hinder you from the remembrance of God and from prayer. Will ye not then abstain ?' (Al-Quran, V : 90-91)

I returned to my friends and recited the verses to them upto "Will ye not then abstain ?" Some of them were holding glasses in their hands which had been partly emptied. They stopped at once. The wine that had passed through the lips (but had not yet been swallowed) was spat out."

All the loyalties of family, friendship and tribe had faded before this loyalty. It is stated that the Prophet once summoned Abdullah, Son of Abdullah bin Obey, and spoke to him thus: "Do you know what your father says ?" Abdullah replied, "May my father and mother be a sacrifice unto you! O Prophet of God, what does he say?" "He says," said the Prophet, "that if I returned to Medina, he who was honourable would turn out him who was debased." On hearing this, Abdullah exclaimed, "He is right. You are honourable and he is debased. You come to Medina by all means. It is well known 'there that no son is more obedient to his father than I, but if it be the wish of God and His Prophet that I sever my father's head, I am ready to do so." The Prophet bade him not to do so.

On reaching Medina, Abdullah posted himself at the city-gate, sword in hand, to wait for his father's arrival. As soon as the son saw the father, the former roared: "Was it you who said that if the Prophet returned to Medina, he who was honourable would turn out him who was debased? You will soon learn who is honourable and who is debased. By God, you cannot live in Medina now without the permission of God and His Prophet."

Abdullah bin Obey was stunned when he heard these words from his son, and he began to wail. "Do you hear, O men of Khazraj, my son hinders me from returning to my home! But the son did not relent. "As surely as I believe in God ", he said, "you cannot enter Medina unless the Prophet allows you". People tried to intercede, but in vain. At last the Prophet was informed. He sent word to Abdullah to let his father come in. Then Abdullah yielded, saying, "Now that the Prophet's permission has come, he can enter."

New Men—A New Ummat : Thus it was that the most stupendous change in human history was brought about, The Prophet had uncovered rich treasures of human material that had been lying dormant under the mass of Ignorance since the beginning of creation and imparted to them the light of genius which was to hold the world spell-bound through ages to come. He had made into men what till then were mere herds of dumb driven cattle. He had aroused their innate possibilities; he had released the fountains of their real life and elevated them to be the standard-bearers of light and learning and Faith and culture in the world. Within a short span of time the desert of Arabia threw up mighty personalities whose names illuminate the ages of history to this day.

'Umar, who used to graze his father's camels rises all of a sudden to dazzle the world with the sublimity of his character and grandeur of his achievements. He humbles the might of Caesar and Chosroes and perfects the foundations of a dominion which spreads itself over the empires of both and is vastly superior to them in governance and organization. Nothing need be said of his high moral sense, justice and righteousness which have become proverbial.

And then there is Khalid, the son of Walid, an enterprising young Quraishite, who, having earned some renown in local feuds is held in esteem by the tribal war-lords, but enjoys no high distinction in the peninsula, for he has nothing great to his credit. But after embracing Islam he shines in the world as the Sword of Allah. This Sword falls upon Rome like lightning and leaves brilliant achievements to be recorded in history.

And then there is benevolent and trustworthy Abi Ubaidah, who commanded small detachments of the Muslims in the early wars. He assumed supreme command of the Islamic forces and ejected Heracius for ever from the fair land of Syria. Poor Heracius casts a parting glance at it and says, "Adieu, Syria, we shall not meet again."

This, again, is 'Amr bin al-'as, noted among the Quraish for his sagacity, who went all the way to Abyssinia to plead with the Negus for handing back the Muslim emigrants to their tormenters. He is now the conquerer of Egypt.

And this is Saad bin Abi Waqqas unknown to fame as a soldier before he had turned a Muslim. See him now as he captures the keys of Medina, annexes Iran and Iraq to the Islamic Dominion and goes down in history as the conqueror of 'Ajam."

This is Persian, the son of a village priest, who left his home and underwent all sorts of tribulations, exchanging one servility for another, till he reached Medina and embraced Islam. He has now returned to the country of his birth as its Governor. But this high honour makes no difference to the simplicity of his nature. He still lives in a modest cottage and is often seen carrying loads on his head.

There is Bilal the Abyssinian slave, who has acquired such eminence that even the Caliph 'Umar the Great, addresses him as his Master.

> Here is Zaid bin Harith commanding the Muslim army in the battle of Muta. The army includes men of the merit and valour of Jafar bin Abi Talib and Khalid bin Walid. His son leads another army which has in it such outstanding personages as Abu Bakr and Umar.

Here are Abu Zarr, Miqdad, Abu Darda, 'Ammar bin Yasir, Muaz bin Jabal and Ubaiy bin Kaab, The spring-breeze of Islam gives them a caress and they blossom up into renowned ascetics and profound scholars.

And here are 'Ali bin Abi Talib, 'Aishah, Abdullah bin Masud, Zaid bin Thabit and 'Abdullah bin 'Abbas, who have ascended to the highest pinnacle in the world of learning through sitting at the feet of the Prophet who had not been tutored by any mortal. They become fountainheads of knowledge and wisdom. The world is all ears to these "sons of the desert."

Never before, indeed, had a more harmonious body of men appeared on the stage of history. It was equipped with every requisite of success in both the worlds. It made out the blueprints of a culture and a Dominion which, within a remarkably short time, rose to hold sway over three large continents. It was a veritable mine of talent which sent forth what seemed to be an endless stream of men of quality and ability including wise rulers, honest administrators, impartial judges, prayerful leaders, pious army commanders and God-fearing scientists.

Owing to the peculiar mental upbringing of the Muslims and the ceaseless propagation of the Islamic ideals among them, the Islamic Commonwealth remained steadily supplied with earnest and God-fearing servants. The responsibilities of the government were vested in those who preferred the dissemination of Truth to the collection of revenue, and who possessed a correct understanding of the organic relationship between religion and life and knew how to coordinate the world of faith with the world of practical affairs in such a way as to make life full and righteous. Under the stewardship of these men the civilization of Islam unfolded itself in its full majesty and the blessings of the Faith sprang into life in a maimer never heard of before.

The Holy Prophet had applied the key of Apostleship to the lock of human personality and it opened up, laying before the world all the rich treasures with which God had endowed man. He had cut as under the mainsprings of ignorance and brought its power to dust. He had forced, with Divine power, the then benighted world to march on a new highway of life. He had inaugurated a fresh era in the annals of mankind. It was the Islamic era which will shine for ever in human history.

Spread of the New Faith

Once the Muslims were aroused, they quickly burst the bounds of Arabia and threw themselves zealously into the task of the fuller working out of human destiny. Their leadership held the guarantee of light and happiness for the world; it gave the promise of turning humanity into a single divinely-guided society. Some of the characteristics of Muslim leadership were :

> The Muslims had the unique advantage of being in possession of the Divine Book (the Quran) and the Sacred Law (the Shariat). They did not have to fall back on their own judgement on the vital questions of life, and were thus saved from the manifold difficulties and perils that are attendant upon such a course. The Divine Word had illumined all the avenues of life for them and had enabled them to progress towards a destination which they clearly envisaged. With them it was not to be a case of trial and error. Says the Holy Quran:
>
> "Can he who was dead, to whom We gave life and a Light whereby he can walk amongst men, be like him who is in the depths of darkness from which he can never come out?" (Al-Quran, VI: 122)

They were to judge among men on the basis of the Revealed Word; they were not to diverge from the dictates of justice and equity ; their view was not to be blurred by enmity, hatred or desire for revenge.

> "O ye who believe, stand out firmly for God as witnesses to fair dealing, and let not the hatred of others to you swerve to wrong and depart from justice. Be just; that is nearer to piety ; and fear God, for God is well acquainted with all that ye do." (Al-Quran, V : 8)

They had not by themselves leapt into power all of a sudden from the abysmal depth of degradation. The Quran had already beaten them into shape. They had been brought to a high level of nobility and purity by the Prophet through long years of unremitting care. The Prophet had conditioned them to a life of austerity and righteousness; he had instilled into their hearts the virtues of humility and courageous self-denial; he had purged them clean of greed and of striving after power, renown or wealth. It was laid down by him as a fundamental principle of Islamic polity that "We shall not assign an office under the government to anyone who makes a request for it, or shows his longing for it in any other way."

The Muslims were as far removed from falsehood, haughtiness and mischief as white is from black. The following words of the Quran had not in vain been grounded into them night and day:

> "That Home of the Hereafter We shall give to those who intend not high-handedness or mischief on earth; and the End is (best) for the righteous."
>
> (Al-Quran, XXVIII : 83)

Instead of aspiring for positions of authority and trust, they accepted them with great reluctance and when they did accept an official position they accepted it as a trust from God, to whom they would have to render full account of their sins of omission and commission on the Day of Judgment. Says the Holy Quran:

> "God doth command you to render back your trusts to those to whom they are due; and when ye judge between man and man, that ye judge with justice."
>
> (Al-Quran, IV : 58)
>
> It is He Who hath made you (His) vicegerents on the earth. He hath raised you in ranks, some above others; that He might try you in the gifts ye receive ; for thy Lord is quick in punishment; yet He is indeed oft-forgiving, Most Merciful." (Al-Quran, VI: 165)

Further, the Muslims were not the agents of any particular race or country; nor were they out to establish Arab Imperialism. Their mission was a universal mission of faith and freedom. They were happily free from all the sickly obsessions of colour and territorial nationality. All men were equal before them. The Quran had pointedly said:

> "O mankind, we created you from (a single pair of) a male and a female; and made you into nations and

> tribes, that ye may know each other (not that ye may despise each other). Verily the most honoured of you in the sight of God is (he who is) the most righteous of you. And God has full knowledge and is Well-Acquainted (with all things)." (Al-Quran, XLIX : 13)

Once the son of 'Amr bin-al-Aas, the Governor of Egypt, struck an Egyptian commoner with a whip. The matter was brought to the notice of Caliph 'Umar. The Caliph did not show the least regard for the high status of the offender's father, and ordered the Egyptian straightway to avenge himself for harm done to him. To the offender's father he administered this telling rebuke, "Why have you made them slaves while they were born free ?"

The Arabs were not stingy in making the benefits of Faith, culture and learning available to the non-Arabs. They did not care for the nationality or the family connections of the recipients when it came to the conferment of high honours and positions in the State. They were, as it were, a cloud of bliss that rained ungrudgingly over the entire world, and from which all peoples, everywhere freely profited according to their own capacity.

The Arabs allowed a free and equal partnership to all nations in the establishment of a new socio-political structure and in the advancement of mankind towards a fuller and richer moral ideal. There were no national divisions, no colour bars, no vested interests, no priesthood and no hereditary nobility in the Islamic Commonwealth. No special benefits were reserved for anyone. There was nothing to prevent the non-Arabs from surpassing the Arabs in the various fields of life. Even as Doctors of Fiqs and Hadith a number of non-Arabs attained to distinction for which the Muslims in general and the Arabs in particular feel proud. Ibn Khaldun writes: "It is an amazing fact of history that though their religion is of Arabian origin and the Law that the Prophet had brought had an Arab complexion, with a few exceptions, all eminent men of learning in the Muslim Milat, in the field of theological as well as secular sciences, are non-Arabs. Even those who are Arabs by birth are non-Arabs by education, language and scholarship." During the later centuries, too, the non-Arab Muslims continued to produce leaders, statesmen, saints and savants of exceptional merit. This would obviously not have been possible, had the Arabs been mean or prejudiced in sharing their opportunities with the people of other nationalities in the Islamic World.

Humanity has many sides—physical, emotional, social, moral, mental and spiritual. We cannot neglect any one of them for the benefit of another. Humanity cannot progress to its highest level unless every human instinct is brought into proper play. It would be futile to hope for the establishment of a healthy human society till an intellectual, material, moral and spiritual environment is created in which a man is enabled to develop his latent potentialities in harmony with Gods plan of creation. We learn from experience that this goal must remain a dream so long as the reins of civilization are not held by those who attach due importance to both the material and the spiritual yearnings of life, and can, together with having a high moral and spiritual sense, fitly appreciate the claims of flesh and blood upon man and the interrelationship between the individual and the society.

Any defect in the integration of the material and spiritual elements in the inner nature of a people should inevitably be displayed in its entire social outlook and organization. Thus, if a community which believes only in one side of life—material progress—and is unaware of its spiritual side and the transcendental realities like Resurrection and Futurity, acquires ascendancy over the world, civilization will manifest itself in material objects like brick, stone, paper, cloth, steel and lead; it will revolve round law-courts, battlefields, factories, ball rooms, hotels, clubs and theatres and flourish and grow rich there. But on the domestic plane, and in the domain of morality and the other spheres of human life there will be no demarcation between man and beast. In short, civilization will be like the corpulent body which may give the impression of well-being at first sight, but is, in reality, the victim of innumerable ailments.

Similarly, if a community which repudiates temporal interests and stands for the negation of the self, cherishing only the things of the spirit, comes into power, the natural potentialities of man will be stunted and civilization will wither away. Under its influence, people will renounce the world and become hermits. They will prefer celibacy to the matrimonial life, and the life of caves and forests to that of towns and cities. Self-torture will become the highest form of religious exercise, so that the hold of the body over the soul might weaken, and the spirit of man might be "purified." Death will gain superiority over life as through it mankind would be saved from the tumult of the 'world of matter' and gain access to the tranquility of the 'world of spirit' and complete their spiritual progress.

This philosophy of life being opposed to the natural scheme of things, whenever such a society comes into being, the spirit of man does not fail to react violently against it soon after the first flush of enthusiasm is over, and to avenge itself by rushing madly towards the other extreme of vulgar material enjoyment and debauchery.

Very few of the communities that had the privilege to act as torch-bearers of civilization during the various epochs of history could succeed in establishing a harmonious equilibrium between the temporal and the spiritual, between the body and the spirit or between the mind and the senses. Generally speaking, they were either crudely materialistic or plainly anchoretic in their mental and spiritual attitudes, and this kept mankind rocking most of the time between the two opposite ends of materialism and monasticism.

Uniqueness of the Companions : The Companions of the Holy Prophet were unique in the sense that religion, morality, social dynamism, politics, i. e. all the diverse requirements of a civilized society' were mirrored in the most beautiful colours in their lives. There was no schism, no corroding lack of integration in their souls. Due to it, they were ideally suited to operate as stewards of humanity. We, consequently, find that no period in the recorded history of the human race has been more auspicious for it in the true sense of the term than what is known among the Muslims as Khilafat-i-Rashida (i.e., the reign of the first four Caliphs). During this epoch, all the material, moral and spiritual resources of man were brought into use to make him an ideal citizen of an ideal State. The Government was judged by the yard-stick of morality, and the morals were judged by their utility to lift humanity in permanent values and establishing justice in human society. Though the Islamic Commonwealth was the richest and the most powerful State of its time, the popular heroes and ideal personalities in it used to be drawn from among those who possessed, not earthly glory, but purity and nobleness of character. There was no disparity between power and morality. Material advancement was not allowed to outrun moral progress. That is why in the Islamic World the incidence of crime was very low in spite of the abundance of wealth and the great heterogeneity of its population. To put it in a nutshell, this epoch was the most beautiful springtime mankind has to this day experienced.

All this was due to the moral strength of faith, excellence and the training of those who were at the helm of affairs in the Muslim State. In whatever capacity they served the State, they conducted themselves as the choicest perfect models of Islamic morality. Whether as administrators or petty officials or as soldiers or policemen, they performed their duties with exemplary modesty, justice and piety.

The sterling character and qualities of the Muslim soldiers were once praised by a Roman officer in these words : "At night you will find them prayerful; during the day you will find them fasting. They keep their promises, order good deeds, suppress evil and maintain complete equality among themselves."

Another testified thus: "They are horsemen by day and ascetics by night. They pay for what they eat in territories under their occupation. They are first to salute when they arrive at a place and are valiant fighters who just wipe out the enemy."

The third one said: "During the night it seems that they do not belong to this world and have no other business than to pray, and during the day, when one sees them mounted on their horses, one feels that they have been doing nothing else all their lives. They are great archers and great lancers, yet they are so devoutly religious and remember God so much and so often that one can hardly hear talk about anything else in their company."

It was because of this moral background of their training that when the fabulous Crown and the ' Carpet of Spring ' of the Chosroes of Iran fell into the hands of Muslim soldiers after the victory of Median, they promptly delivered them to their Commander, who dispatched them to the Caliph at Medina. When the latter saw those articles, he was filled with admiration for the high integrity of the soldiers who had handed them over to their leader intact and for those who had brought them safely all the way to Medina.

View of Life : Islam alone, of all religions, embraces life in all its aspects. It does not stand as a barrier between man and his legitimate desire to live. It does not regard man's earthly existence as a gloomy dale of sorrows or a punishment for some original or inherited sin. At the same time, it does not look upon this life as a fleeting opportunity for material satisfaction or a place for sensuous delight. Islam proclaims life to be a Divine gift so that man may attain nearness unto God and attain perfection by making full use of the possibilities of his body and spirit. It is an opportunity for action to make the best of oneself; there is not going to be another opportunity after it.

> "He Who created Death and Life, that He may try which of you is best in deed."
>
> (Al-Quran, LXVII : 2)

> "That which is on earth We have made but as a glittering show for it in order that We may test them—as to which of them are best in conduct."
>
> (Al-Quran, XVIII : 7)

The Companions of the Prophet considered this universe as the domain of God in which He had raised them in the first instance as human beings and then as Muslims to serve as His Vicegerents and the guardians of those who dwelt in it.

> "I will create a Vicegerent on earth."
>
> (Al-Quran, II : 30)

> "It is He Who hath created for you all things that are on the earth." (Al-Quran, 11:29)

> "We have honoured the sons of Adam; provided them with transport on land and sea; given them for sustenance things good and pure; and conferred on them special favours, above a great part of Our Creation." (Al-Quran, XVII: 70)

> "God has promised to those among you who believe and work righteous deeds, that He will, of a surety, grant them in the land, inheritance (of power), as He

> granted it to those before them; that He will establish in authority their religion —the one which He has chosen for them; and that He will change (their state), after the fear in which they (live), to one of security and peace; they will worship Me (alone) and not associate with Me." (Al-Quran, XXIV: 55)

God had granted mankind the right to enjoy the resources of the earth without being foolish, vain or wasteful.

> "Eat and drink : but waste not by excess, for God loveth not the wasters." (Al -Quran, VII : 31)

> "Say : who hath forbidden the beautiful gifts of God, which He hath produced for His servants, and the things, clean and pure, which He hath provided for sustenance? Say: they are, in the life of this world, for those who believe, (and) purely for them on the Day of Judgment." (Al-Quran, VII : 32)

The Muslims have been appointed shepherds of mankind. It is their religious duty to keep humanity on the straight path, to remove imperfections from human society, to defend the weak and to establish justice and peace on the earth.

Says the Holy Quran:

> "Ye are the best people raised up for mankind, enjoining what is right, forbidding what is wrong, and believing in God." (Al-Quran, III: 110)

> "O ye who believe, stand out firmly for justice and be the witnesses of God to fair dealing."
> (Al-Quran, IV:135)

Muhammad Asad has admirably summed up the Islamic conception of life as a well-balanced harmonious totality, which cannot be bifurcated into the physical and the spiritual. Says he:

> If Islam does not share the gloomy aspect of life as expressed by Christianity, it teaches us, none the less, not to attribute an exaggerated value to the earthly life as the modern Western civilization does. The Christian outlook is : The earthly life is a bad business. The modern West—as distinct from Christianity—adores

> life in exactly the same way as the glutton adores his food: he devours it, but has no respect for it. Islam, on the other hand, looks upon the earthly life with calmness and respect. It does not worship life, but regards it as a passing stage on our way to a higher existence. But just because it is a stage, and a necessary stage, too, man has no right to despise or even to underrate the value of his earthly life. Our travel through this world is a necessary, positive part in God's Plan. Human life, therefore, is of a tremendous value; but we must never forget that it is a purely instrumental value. In Islam there is no room for the materialistic optimism of the modern West which says: 'My kingdom is of this world alone,'—nor for the life-contempt of the Christian: 'My kingdom is not of this world.' Islam goes the middle way. The Quran teaches us to pray:
>
> 'Our Lord, give us the good in this world and the good in the Hereafter.' (Al-Quran, II : 201)

"Thus, the full appreciation of this world and its goods is in no way a handicap for our spiritual endeavours. Material prosperity is desirable, though it is not a goal in itself. The goal of all our practical activities always ought to be the creation and maintenance of such personal and social conditions as might be helpful for the development of moral stamina in men. In accordance with this principle, Islam leads man towards a consciousness of moral responsibility in everything he does, whether great or small. The well-known injunction of the gospel: 'Give Caesar that what belongs to Caesar, and give God that what belongs to God'—has no room in the theological structure of Islam, because Islam does not allow of a differentiation between the moral and the practical requirements of our existence. In everything there can be only one choice: the choice between Right and Wrong— and nothing in-between. Hence the intense insistence on action as an indispensable element of morality. Every individual Muslim has to regard himself as personally responsible for all happenings around him, and to strive for the establishment of Right and the abolition of Wrong at every time and in every direction.

The sanction for this attitude is to be found in the verse of the Quran:

> Ye are the best people raised up for mankind, enjoining what is right, forbidding what is wrong, and believing in God." (Al-Quran, III :110)

> "This is the moral justification of the aggressive activism of Islam, the justification of the early Islamic conquests and its so-called 'Imperialism'. For Islam is 'Imperialist', if we must use this term but this kind of Imperialism is not prompted by love of domination; it has nothing to do with economic or national selfishness, nothing with the greed to increase our own comforts at other people's cost, nor has it ever meant the coercion of non-believers into the belief of Islam. It has only meant, as it means today, the construction of a worldly frame for the best possible spiritual development of man. Moral knowledge, according to the teachings of Islam, automatically forces a moral responsibility upon man. A mere Platonic discernment between Right and Wrong, without the urge to promote the Right and to destroy the Wrong, is a gross immorality in itself. In Islam, morality lives and dies with the human endeavour to establish its victory upon earth."

The rise of the Muslim power and the coming of age of the Islamic civilization during the first century of the Hijra were events of unequalled significance in man's moral and social development. These events confronted the "World of Ignorance" with a crisis of an unprecedented magnitude. So far Islam was no more than a religious movement, but henceforth it emerged as a complete civilization, refined, progressive and full of life and energy.

Henceforth, there were two opposite systems in the world—one was a comprehensive, easy-to-understand, practical, revealed Faith, and the other a rigmarole of rigid formalism, conjecture, superstition and myth.

The superior society of Islamic ideology was envisaged and brought to life on solid spiritual foundations. The real emphasis in it was not on material prosperity but on the development of moral stamina in men and on the metaphysical orientation of life. The soul of man was, as such, free from contradictions within its framework. It was contented. There was no greed, no insatiate longing for worldly power or riches. The Government stood firmly for equity and held itself as much responsible for the moral and spiritual prosperity of its people as for the protection of their lives and property. Its governors and administrators were also the finest citizens of the Islamic State ; the most exalted ascetics were not unoften found among those who had the greatest opportunities of indulging in comfort and luxury of all kinds.

In contrast with the social soundness and spiritual vigour of the Islamic World were the avarice, confusion, and vulgarity of the "World of Ignorance," where everyone in authority seemed desperately resolved upon making hay while the sun shone.

Islam and Humanity : This being so, people had no hesitation in walking over from the realm of Ignorance to the Light of Islam. They stood to lose nothing, whereas there was everything to be gained. Islam offered to them the balm of belief, the sweetness of faith, membership of a democratic, cosmopolitan society—a society that really was without any kind of distinction—and the protection of powerful State. The expansion of the frontiers of Islam was, quite naturally, very rapid.

The effects of the growth of Islamic power were extremely far-reaching. The path of Godliness became easy to reverse. Till yesterday it was the most perilous thing to obey the commands of God; now it was the other way round. It was no longer necessary to preach the message of faith secretly:

> "Call to mind when ye were a small (band) despised through the land, and afraid that men might despoil and kidnap you; but He provided a safe asylum for you, strengthened you with His aid, and gave you good things for sustenance that ye might be grateful."
>
> (Al-Quran, VIII 26)

The people who had entered the fold of Islam could now exert themselves more effectively for the moral and spiritual revival of humanity. They could perform the duty of establishing Right and prohibiting Wrong with much greater success. The rejuvenating currents of Islam ran through the world, infusing men everywhere with a new life and an unparalleled enthusiasm for progress. The lost values of life had been discovered. Paganism became a sign of reaction, while it was considered progressive to be associated with Islam. Even nations that did not come directly under the influence of Islam, profoundly, though unconsciously, benefited by the freshness and vitality of the new creative impulses released by its impact on large parts of the world. Numerous aspects of their thought and culture bear evidence to the magic touch of Islam. All the reform movements that arose in their midst, owed their origin to Islamic influences.

A universal gift of Islam to humanity was the reestablishment of man's belief in the Unity of God. So uncompromisingly and so energetically did the Muslims espouse the doctrine of Monotheism that even the Trinitarians and the worshippers of idols had to offer apologies and excuses for their ideas on religion and for their modes of worship.

Islam and Christianity : Formerly, they used to be shocked at the mention of the idea of Divine Unity and exclaim:

> "Has he made the gods all into one God? Truly this is a wonderful thing !" (Al-Quran, XXXVIII : 5)

Now they took pains to explain that their beliefs and practices did not contravene the belief in the Oneness of God. There appeared a number of sects among Christians denying the Divinity of Jesus and explaining the doctrine of Trinity in a way so as to bring it within the orbit of Monotheistic teachings. The belief that the ecclesiastics acted as intermediaries between man and God was also criticised severely by Christian reformers and ultimately given up. A movement was started in Europe in the eighth century against the practice of making confessions before the priests. It was asserted that man should address himself directly to his Maker, without the aid of intercessors. In addition to this, a feeling of revulsion was created throughout Christendom, with the support of powerful Roman Emperors like Leo III, Constantine V and Leo IV, against paintings and statues in the churches. Emperor Leo III issued a decree in 726 A. D. prohibiting the adoration of the images. In 730 A. D. he proclaimed the arts of painting pan sculpture to be the remnants of Paganism. This new development in the very heart of the Graceo-Roman cultural zone was indisputably an echo of the message of Islam that had reached Europe through Spain. Claudius, one of the pioneers of the movement, had actually been born and brought up in Muslim Spain.' It was his custom to set fire to any image or painting that was found in his diocese. The Reformation itself, in spite of all its shortcomings, was inspired by Islam.

It was not, however, in the field of religion alone that Islam imparted a new glow of life to Europe. There is not a single department of European revival which is not indebted to Islamic thought. We will quote the following passages from Robert Briffault:

> "For although there is not a single aspect of European growth in which the decisive influence of Islamic civilization is not traceable, nowhere is it so clear and momentous as in the genesis of that power which constitutes the permanent distinctive force of the modern world and the supreme source of its victory—natural science and scientific spirit. "
>
> "Science is the most momentous contribution of Arab Civilization to the modern world. It was not science only which brought Europe back to life. Other and manifold influences from the civilization of Islam communicated its first glow to European life."

The contribution of Islamic civilization to the culture of the different peoples of India has also been of very great importance. Many progressive features in the socio-cultural structure of the different Indian communities, like respect for women and their rights, can be traced to the influence exercised upon them by Islam through various channels. It can safely be claimed that after the dawn of Islam no cultural or religious system in the world can honestly deny its indebtedness to Islam and the Muslims.

Several characteristics of the Muslim faith and civilization continued in operation even after the huge Islamic social structure had started to disintegrate, one of these being the belief in God. Islam had planted the idea of God so firmly in the minds of its followers that the vicissitudes of time could do no harm to it. The followers of Islam could indulge in immorality—as they wholeheartedly did during the period of their decline—but it was just not possible for them to shake off their belief in God. The moral sense of right and wrong, the faith in the Omnipresence of the Almighty, and the solicitude for the After-life would pinch their hearts in the midst of their follies, and, sometimes, it would do the trick and transform their lives in the twinkling of the eye. Not infrequently would it happen that people abandoned their wicked ways and took to a life of piety in response to a sudden call of the conscience. A simple heavenly warning would in a moment stir up princes to renounce their kingdoms and turn ascetics, while we see daily that warnings a thousand times more severe fail to make any impression if the hearts are frozen spiritually. Many a time, on hearing a Quranic verse like the following the people suddenly felt that they had awakened to a new life:

> "Has not the time arrived for the Believers that their hearts in all humility should engage in the remembrance of God and of the Truth which has been revealed (to them), and that they should not become like those to whom was given Revelation aforetime, but long ages passed over them and their hearts grew hard, for many among them are rebellious transgressors ?
>
> (Al-Quran, LVJI:16)

Such incidents were of common occurrence in the seminaries of religious leaders in Baghdad even when that city had slipped into moral stupor. It has been reported by Ibn Zubayr al-Andalusi that people used to weep during the sermons of Sheikh Raziuddin Qazwini and they swarmed around him to ask God for forgiveness of their sins.

During the sermons of Hafiz Ibn Jauzi, "people cried and fainted and had to be carried away. They would give their forelocks in his hands (as sign of submission), and he would caress their heads." According to his own estimate, about a lakh of persons repented at his hand. At the sermon assemblies of Sheikh Ismail, an Indian Traditionist of the 5th Century A.D., it is stated that thousands embraced Islam. Ibn Batuta has enumerated numerous incidents of a like nature in connection with the achievements of Muslim missionaries in India.

In the end it may be pointed out that the language of Islam had gained free currency in the languages of the world. Modes of expression that are peculiar to Islam were widely used by non-Muslims. Many non-Muslim scholars learnt the Quran by heart. Ibn Ishaq the Sabian, one of the most celebrated non-Muslim calligraphists and literateurs of his age, is reputed to have been in the habit of observing the Ramadan fasts.

People travelled in the Islamic world from one end to the other, across forests, mountains and rivers, in search of spiritual guides. The saints and the 'sufis' were the refuge of the world. Their dwelling—places were overcrowded with devotees and sparkled with life more than the palaces of the high dignitaries of the State. The sermon-assemblies of Sheikh 'Abdul Qadir Jilani inspired greater awe than the courts of the Abbasid Caliphs.

5

Relevance of Islam

Completion of the Job

We will not speak now of the grievous material losses the Eastern countries have suffered since the rise of the West. We will speak only of the real—the moral and spiritual—losses of mankind as a whole. In this regrettable development of history the greatest losers have been the followers of Islam. Their philosophy of life was radically opposed to the Western ideas and way of life. With the domination of the new barbarism, therefore, it was but natural that they should suffer the greatest loss.

There has always been something deeply spiritual in the Oriental character. From time immemorial a thousand thoughts have been assailing the mind of the Easterner. What is the end of this world? Is there a future life after death? Where should one look for guidance regarding the life to come? What is the secret of eternal happiness? The Easterner never failed to take note of these questions, not even on occasions of his deepest absorption in secular needs and interests. He gave them an unqualified priority in the manifold occupations of his life. During the whole course of his intellectual and cultural endeavours he kept himself steadily engaged in finding satisfactory solutions to them. His asceticism, his penances, his philosophy, his metaphysics, his mysticism were all directed towards it. Sometimes this quest took him along wrong paths. Sometimes he erred and stumbled. But he never shut his ears to the voice of his soul.

Questions pertaining to spiritual truths used to arise in Europe also before the Renaissance, but as the innate character of its civilization gradually unfolded itself and the West got lost in the adoration of its material achievements, they were disregarded. If one still hears of them there, it is only as problems of metaphysics. They do not occupy any place in practical life. The anxiety, the solicitude, the uneasiness which for thousands of years these questions evoked in the East is not at all felt there. And this is so, not because the soul of the West has become illumined with Divine truth or that peace has dawned upon it. The surroundings that the West has succeeded in creating for itself are not related to the Eternal and the Infinite; they have imprisoned man in the world of matter and the West has made him oblivious of his true self.

The fundamental psychological difference, therefore, between an Easterner of earlier times and a modern Westerner is that, while the former possessed a keen and quick spiritual instinct, the latter lost it in the process of his evolution. 'When a person loses any one of his senses, he loses the consciousness of all things the knowledge of which is dependent on it. One who loses the sense of hearing, for example, becomes insensitive to sound and the whole world of songs and sweet melodies is dead for him. Similarly, one who is devoid of the sense of religion is dead to all feelings and sensations that arise out of religious faith. Things like Futurity, Resurrection, Divine Pleasure and Salvation have no meaning for him.

Religious preachers have, in all ages, encountered the stiffest opposition from people who were devoid of religious feelings. Such people derided even the prophets of God. They listened to their soul-warming sermons and said:

> "There is nothing except our life on this earth, and never shall we be raised up again."
>
> (Al-Quran, VI: 291)

In the modern age there has appeared a class of people in every community whose material carvings and worldly occupations have ejected religion from the domain of practical calculations. The hearts of such people are adamant and their minds sealed against truths transcendental. However hard a religious preacher may try, he does not find an opening through which to reach the inner depths of their souls. Those who have had the occasion to preach among them would have come to appreciate the real significance of many a verse of the Quran like: "God hath set a seal on their hearts and their hearing, and over their eyes is a veil." (Al-Quran, II:7), and their difficulties in respect of them would have been removed. The Quranic truth 'The parable of those who reject faith is as if one were to shout like a goat-herd, to things that listen to nothing except calls and cries; deaf, dumb and blind, they are devoid of wisdom" (Al-Quran, II : 171), would have presented itself before them in flesh and blood.

Most of the evils of the modern age come from this indifference to religion. The propagation of religion was easier by far in the olden days of open and violent opposition than in the current atmosphere of quiet disinterestedness. One may put one's very heart into one's preaching, but when the innerselves of the listeners have become paralysed, they cannot be moved to realise the beauties of Divine Revelation.

We have already seen widespread longing for Truth during the days of Islamic ascendancy. It was customary then to undertake long and arduous journeys in the search for spiritual guides. These guides, who later on came to be known as 'Messiah' and 'Sufis', kept the spirit of God-seeking alive even after the World of Islam had fallen on evil days. Their abodes functioned as islands of celestial bliss in an ever-widening ocean of materialism. The presence of such men in any society is the standard by which we can judge the strength of religious consciousness in it. Among the Muslims, in particular, the way they turn towards the saints and sufis in their midst is a sure indication of the extent of their moral and spiritual awareness.

In former times, in nearly all important towns in the Islamic world, there were found men who were actually the beacons of spiritual light; Muslims were drawn to them from every nook and corner like moths. Our Sub-continent situated on the fringe of the Islamic world, has itself been a great centre of religious endeavour. Independent seats of spiritual power existed here side by side with powerful kingdoms throughout the course of Muslim rule. The spiritual settlement of Hadrat Nizamuddin Auliya', Ghiyathpur, offers an admirable illustration of it. Situated right within the capital city of Delhi, it maintained its independence through the reigns of eight powerful kings, from Ghiyasuddin Balban to Ghiyasuddin Tughlaq (664-725 A. H.). Votaries of Truth from Sanjar to Oudh used to make their way to it to seek spiritual guidance.

If we were to give an account of the religious establishments of the saints of all the sufi sects in India, and the manner in which people flocked to them from far and near, it would fill a whole volume. We will, therefore, confine our inquiry to the saints of only one sect, viz., the Naqshbandi sect.

To begin with, Sheikh Ahmad Sarhandi Mujaddid Alf-i-Thani (died 1034) had innumerable disciples. They were drawn from all parts of India and Afghanistan. Several influential nobles of the court of Jahangir were included among them.

The daily average of votaries staying at the Khanqah of his venerable ' Khalifah' Syed Adam (died 1053 A.H.) was about a thousand. They all took their meals at the Khanqah. A great throng followed Syed Adam Binnuri wherever he went. It is stated in the *Tazkira-i-Adamiyath* that ten thousand persons accompanied him when he went to Lahore in 1052 A.H. Seeing the boundless popularity of the saint, Emperor Shahjahan became so apprehensive that he thought of a plan to send him out of India. He sent to him a sum of money and then suggested to him that as the possession of money made the Hajj pilgrimage incumbent on a Muslim, he should now proceed to the Hijaz to perform the Hajj. The saint, thereupon, migrated from India.

Hadrat Mujaddid's eminent son, Hadrat Khwaja Mujaddid (died 1079 A.H.) had nine lakh disciples, who repented at his hand of them, seven thousand had the honour of being his 'Khalifahs'

The Khwaja's son, Sheikh Saifuddin Sarhandi, also had an overwhelming following. According to the author of Zail-al-Rashhat, about 1,400 persons dined with him daily at his Khanqah, each of whom was served with food of his own choice.

The rich were as enthusiastic in their loyalty to the spiritual leaders as the poor. It is said that noblemen used to cover the path with their scarfs and 'shawls' when Khwaja Muhammad Zubayr Sarhandi went to the mosque to say his prayers so that his feet might not fall on the bare ground. When he went out to visit the sick or on any other business, it used to be in right royal style with the carriages and palanquins of the wealthy lords bringing up the rear of the procession.'

This ardent devotion to the holy men was still very much in evidence among the Indian Muslims even during the suzerainty of the East India Company, till a little before the final overthrow of the Mughal Empire, in 1857. During the days of Shah Ghulam Ali (died 1240 A. H.), the 'Khalifa' of Mirza Mazhar Jan-i-Janan, the Mujaddidiya Khanqah of Delhi, was a mighty centre of attraction for pious Muslims from all over the Islamic world. Sir Syed Ahmad Khan says in the Asrarus Sanadid: "I have seen with my own eyes votaries from Turkey, Syria, Baghdad, Egypt, China and Ethiopia coming to the Khanqah and taking the bait at the Hadrat's hand, and considering it a rare good fortune to be of service to the establishment, not to mention the votaries from the adjoining areas of Hindustan, Punjab and Afghanistan who were continually swarming round the saint like bees. No less than five hundred destitute persons used to live in the Khanqah all of whom were fed and clothed by him."

Shah Rauf Ahmad Mujaddid has given the details of the places from which visitors to the Khanqah hailed on a single day— Jumada I 28, 1231 A. H.—which includes places like Samarkand, Bukhara, Ghazni, Tashkand, Kandhar, Kabul, Kashmir, Peshawar, Multan, Lahore, Sarhand, Amroha, Sambhal, Rampur, Bareilly, Lucknow, Jais, Bahraich, Gorakhpur, Azimabad, Dacca, Hyderabad and Poona." All this happened at a time when there were neither railways nor the other modern facilities of travel!

Just on the eve of the establishment of the British rule the majestic call of ' Run back to Allah' was raised by Syed Ahmad Shahid (died 1246 A. H.) and his glorious lieutenants, Shah Ismail Shahid (died 1246 A.H.) and Maulana Abdul Hay Burhanvi (died 1242 A.H.). The spectacular manner in which the cream of Muslim society in India rallied round the leader of this group ultimately to be mingled with the dust at Balakot (May, 1831), was a shining proof of the high sense of religious enthusiasm and courage the Indian Muslims were still capable of manifesting even at this stage of their decadence.

Unprecedented scenes of religious ardour were witnessed during Syed Sahib's tour of the Doab' and Oudh when he undertook to pull out the Muslims from the demoralization they had fallen into. In 1032 A. D., he set out for the Hajj, and a wave of great enthusiasm swept over the whole of Northern India. Religiously-minded Muslims came out in hundreds and thousands to meet him as his caravan advanced from place to place. They invited his party (that finally came to consist of 750 persons when they reached Calcutta) to their towns and villages and entertained them for days. It is said that Sheikh Ghulam 'Ali, harith of Allahabad, spent about twenty thousand rupees in entertaining the Syed Sahib and his companions for a fortnight—about a thousand rupees a day were spent by him on food alone. In many towns that fell along Syed Sahib's route, few persons were left who did not offer the baiat at his hand. His disciples in Allahabad, Mirzapur, Banaras, Ghazipur, Azimabad (Patna) and Calcutta must have run into lakhs. In Banaras the indoor patients of the Sadr Hospital sent a petition to him saying that since they were unable to move out, he might take the trouble to grace them with a visit so that they could take the bait. Syed Sahib went to the hospital and administered the vow to the patients

About a thousand persons became his disciples everyday during Syed Sahib's two-month stay in Calcutta. From morning till late at night a stream of men and women continued to pour in at the place where he was staying. When it became impossible for the baiat to be administered individually, it was arranged for the aspirants to collect in a large house where Syed Sahib went and initiated them into his fold. Seven or eight turbans were unrolled on the ground when he went there and the aspirants were told to hold them at different places, while one end of them was held by Syed Sahib himself. He then taught them the fundamental principles of Islam and read out the vow in a loud voice like the Adaan which they repeated and thus the ritual was completed. This was done seventeen or eighteen times every day.

For about twenty days, Syed Sahib delivered the sermons at Calcutta after the Fajr (morning) prayers. These sermons were attended by over two thousand doctors of theology, divines and noblemen and countless commoners. On Tuesdays and Fridays, Maulana 'Abdul Hay also addressed the congregation after the

Zuhr (mid-day) prayers, which lasted till the evening with a break for the 'Asr prayers. From ten to fifteen non-Muslims were converted daily to Islam.

An immediate effect of these reformatory endeavours was that the liquor business in that great city was suddenly brought to a standstill. The liquor merchants complained to the authorities that though they paid the taxes regularly, they had been forced to close down their business since the arrival in the city of a saint under whose influence more and more Muslims were being reformed daily and were taking the vow to abstain from the use of intoxicants. In fact they did not look at the liquor shops now.

On their way back from the Hajj, Syed Sahib and his companions stopped for a few days at Murshidabad with Diwan Ghulam Murtaza. The Diwan had it announced in the market that he would pay for any purchases made by his pilgrim guests and services rendered to them by the artisans. Syed Sahib protested that it was too much, but he replied, "It is a great honour for a Muslim that a 'Haji' should be his guest. I can never be proud enough of my good luck that so many Hajis' have graced me with a visit."

Finally, when Syed Sahib launched the Jihad, it called forth a marvellous response from the rank and file of the Muslim population. The ploughman forsook his plough, the merchant his shop, the servant his master, the nobleman his castle and the theologian his pulpit and they all rose like one man in the defence of God's Word.

We have dealt with these facts at some length to bring home to the reader how very susceptible to religious emotion the Muslims were even at a time when they had entered upon the gloomiest phase of their existence as a free people, and before the thunderbolt of Western Imperialism had come down upon them to shatter the fabric of their society.

Some traces of this earnestness lingered on for sometime among the Muslims during the early stages of the British rule, but they were diminishing fast.

The joy of faith had not yet deserted the hearts of Muslims. Religion was still valued by them as a vital factor in life. Apart from the educated and the enlightened, the common Muslims, too, had a share in their religious inheritance. There was hardly a Muslim hamlet that was without a moral teacher or a spiritual guide. If one cared to look at the India of thirty or forty years ago, one would find it illumined by a cluster of spiritual lights.

One by one, these lights went out. The British Government, of course, never demanded that the Madrasa and khanqahs should be closed down. Yet the inner urge that used to drag along votaries from Samarkand and Bukhara to Delhi had died down and the higher values of the mind and the spirit had been discarded by the people, and the Madrasa and khanqahs were utterly abandoned.

The new ideal of material advancement has completely taken hold of the modern mind.

In the present age of material progress there is great paucity of love for learning, nor is the love of religion much in evidence. The instinct of hunger has completely dominated human existence. Everywhere people now talk of problems concerning the flesh. Conversation on the problems relating to the spiritual or moral aspects of life is rarely to be heard in society.

Moral Degradation : Moral degradation had spread a great deal in India when the British arrived here. The age-old ideals of the Eastern and the Islamic ways of life had fallen into oblivion. But certain domestic and social virtues were still valued beyond all things by the people of the Indo-Pakistan sub-continent.

Family and social relations were based on extremely strong foundations. Filial love, parental affection, respect for the elders, affection for the young, marital fidelity, loyalty of servants, sincerity of friends,—under each of these headings authentic stories have been handed down to us which appear legendary when viewed in the context of the present-day conditions.

The Holy Prophet of Islam is reported to have said to a young man: "You and your possessions belong to your father". The dutifulness of the children to their parents was modelled after this command. It included respect for the friends and relatives of the parents as well. The love and regard for one's parents is to be continued even after their death as stressed by the Holy Prophet who is reported to have said, "The best of the good things to do is to do good to the friends of one's deceased father."

The parents on their side were living examples of loving care and self-sacrifice. They never hesitated to subordinate their own desires and interests to those of their children. Yet, when it was necessary to use the rod, they would turn their hearts into stones. It was below the dignity of a gentleman to show partiality for his child who was chastised by the teacher. Even illiterate parents would support the teacher on such occasions, though the teacher himself might have been to blame for being too severe. "The claim of the teacher is greater than that of the father" was a common saying among the parents.

Between the old and the young the relations were determined by the old Islamic maxim, "He who is not affectionate to those who are younger to him and respectful to the elders of the community is not one of us".

Constancy is a virtue of great merit in the Oriental pattern of morality. Astonishing instances of it were available even during the period of decadence. In the daily routine of life, in dress, manners and customs, people generally were consistent and unvarying. If they struck a friendship, they remained true to it to the last.

Wealth was not the sole criterion of respectability in the family or clan, neither was it a dominant factor in friendship. It was inconceivable that at family gatherings discrimination should be made among members of a family on the basis of wealth and if it ever chanced to be so, the whole family united against the offender, and sometimes broke off relations with him. A poor young man of noble birth did not feel embarrassed at facing a more prosperous cousin and the latter took great care to ensure that the former's indigence was not made known to anyone outside the family circle.

A gentleman used to hold his conscience above his life. He could not be persuaded to sell his honour at any price. During the official inquiry following the catastrophe of 1857, many a Muslim gentleman preferred mounting the gallows to bartering away his honour by feigning innocence while he had actually taken part in the uprising.

Honesty was highly valued both in private life and in cases where communal or national interests were at stake. Communal prejudice was unknown in India till then. The Muslims invariably acted upon the Quranic injunctions like the following:

> "O ye who believe, stand out firmly for justice, as witnesses to God, even as against yourselves, or (your) parents or (your) kin........."
>
> (Al-Quran, IV : 135)
>
> "And let not the hatred of any people make you swerve to wrong and depart from justice, be just; that is next to piety ; and fear God........." (Al-Quran, V : 8)
>
> "And when ye judge between mankind, (God doth command) that ye judge with justice."
>
> (Al-Quran, IV : 58)
>
> "Whatever ye say, speak justly, even if near relative is concerned. (Al-Quran, VI: 152)

Once, during the early days of the British administration, there arose in Kandhla, in the Muzaffarnagar District, a dispute between the Hindus and the Muslims over a plot of land which both of them claimed as their place of worship. The English Collector of the district privately inquired from the Muslims if they could name a Hindu in whose honesty they had full confidence so that the case might be decided on the basis of his evidence. The Muslims said that they knew of no such Hindu. The Collector then asked the Hindus whether there was a Muslim upon whose word they would be willing to let the decision of the dispute be made. The Hindus said that, grave as the matter was, there was a Muslim divine who had never uttered a falsehood and it could be hoped that he would not compromise his integrity over the issue in hand. The divine came from the family of Mufti Alam Bakhsh, who was a pupil of Shah 'Abdul 'Aziz and a Khalija of Syed Ahmad Shah. The Collector, thereupon, summoned him to his court, but he declined saying that he had sworn never to look at the face of an Englishman. The Collector said that he need not look at his face if he did not want to, but come he must, because the matter in dispute was serious and its settlement hung on whether he came or not. At last, the Maulana agreed. He came with his face covered with a mask and stood in the court, his back turned towards the Collector so that there could be no possibility of his vow being broken. The case was explained to him and he was asked to state whether he knew anything about the ownership of the plot. The Maulana declared that the plot in dispute belonged to the Hindus; the Muslims had nothing to do with it. The Collector decided accordingly. The Muslims lost the case, but Truth scored a magnificent victory. A number of Hindus embraced Islam on that very day at the hand of the Maulana.

Learning and wisdom were held sacrosanct in those days. Those who occupied a high place in the field of learning were not disposed to sell their intellectual wealth at any price because it was regarded by them as a precious gift and a sacred trust of God. To lend one's ability or knowledge, directly or indirectly, to serve the cause of injustice and unbelief was in their view tantamount to an open betrayal of religion.

Compare this intellectual loftiness with the prostitution of the intellect that is practised everywhere these days. The modern men of learning are ever open to be bought by the highest bidder. They have put themselves up or auction. If they are getting Rs. 100 per mensem in an Islamic institution and a Christian institution offers them Rs. 105 per mensem, they will at once go over to it. And if a Jewish State came forward and raised the bid by another Rs. 5, they would sell themselves to it with equal readiness. There is also no question of mental aptitude or preference. If the circumstances allow, a teacher will cheerfully join the Police or the Air Force for a nominal consideration. A Doctor of Philosophy will any day join a military or a political department where his academic attainments will be of little or no avail to him. A writer sees no difference between writing the biography of a national hero or of a scoundrel.

In the past, the ties that bound persons to one another were free from the taint of selfishness. They were forged in the hearts, with the consequence that often they acquired an emotional significance that was far beyond the scope of material explanation. The bond of affection that endured, for example, between the teacher and the pupil was so strong that the existing relations between the father and the son or the lover and the beloved pale into insignificance before it. It will be difficult for a modern man to believe that when the news of the death of Mufti Nizamuddin of Lucknow was received (which later turned out to be false), one of his pupils, Syed

Kamaluddin Azimuddin, died of the shock, while another, Syed Zarif Azimabadi, wept so much that his eyes were permanently damaged.'

In the West today ethical questions are confined to the considerations of practical utility alone. It is just the other way round in Islam with which the real goal is the inner progress of man. Material utility came to dominate Western thought and morals in the 17th century when its social philosophers propagated the view that all ethical principles that did not have a direct bearing on the material betterment of society were not deserving of serious attention. This view gradually gained in strength till it acquired a commanding hold on all fields of human activity. The virtues that had a purely ethical value were relegated to an obscure background of life and condemned to a mere theoretical existence, without the least power of influencing humanity.

In recent times, Western literature has exhibited a striking fondness for the word "nature". But the context in which it is used and the meanings that are sought to be conveyed through it show that it implies only animal nature. It stands for the world of flesh and shuts out the soul. Now, as the Western society is becoming more and more technological, even the animal warmth is vanishing from the nature of man and the individual is turning into a heap of inanimate matter.

"In the profound transformation the social life of the West is at present undergoing ", says Muhammad Asad, a European Muslim, "that new, utilitarian morality becomes daily more and more visible. All virtues having a direct bearing upon the material welfare of society, as, for example, technical efficiency, patriotism, nationalist group-sense, are being exalted and sometimes absurdly exaggerated in their value, while virtues which, until now, have been valued from a purely ethical point of view, as, for example, filial love or sexual fidelity, rapidly lose their importance because they do not confer a tangible, material benefit upon society. The age in which the insistence on strong family bonds was decisive for the well-being of the group or the clan is being superseded, in the modern West, by an age of collective organization under far wider headings. And in a society which is essentially technological and is being organised at a rapidly increasing pace, on purely mechanical lines, the behaviour of a son towards his father is of no great social importance, so long as those individuals behave within the limits of general decency imposed by the society on the intercourse of its members. Consequently, the European father daily loses more and more authority over his son, and the son loses respect for his father. Their mutual relations are being slowly over-ruled and—for all practical purposes—annihilated by the postulates of a mechanized society which has a tendency to abolish all privileges of one individual over another, and—in the logical development of this idea—also the privileges caused by family relationship; and the old relation between father and son is becoming obsolete."

Indian Muslim Rulers : In the Islamic Orient the conception of human progress and perfection was so high that in order to come up to it one had to cultivate such diverse qualities and merits as would seem opposed and contradictory to the lethargy and shortsightedness of the modern age. To take from the world of Islam only the Muslim rulers of India and their ministers and courtiers, one comes across among them such rare examples of human perfection as can scarcely be dreamt of today.

How extensive was the Empire of Sultan Shamsuddin Iltutmish is known to all students of Indian history. What, however, is not so generally known is that, despite the great responsibility of having to rule over such a vast Empire and to wage the numerous wars that he had to conduct, the Sultan was highly scrupulous in the discharge of his religious duties. When it was made known at the death of the august saint, Khwaja Qutbuddin Bakhtiyar Kaki, that he (the saint) had willed that his funeral prayers were to be led by him alone who had never in his life missed the 'sunnats" of the 'Asr (afternoon) prayer and the first ' takbir' of any congregational prayer, the Sultan reluctantly stepped forward and conducted the service. In like manner, Sultans Ghiyasuddin Balban, Nasiruddin Mahmud and Firoz Tughlaq were all prominent for their piety and religiousness.

The Sultans of Gujarat were particularly celebrated for the way they epitomized in themselves the splendid Islamic ideal of integrated material and spiritual progress. Maulvi Syed 'Abdul Hay has thrown light on the life and character of one of them, viz., Sultan Muzaffar Shah Halim, in the following words:

"After the death of Mahmud Shah, his son, Muzaffar Shah Halim, who was a worthy son of a worthy father, became the king. He had been a pupil of 'Allama Muhammad bin Muhammad al-Ijl. The Science of Hadith he had studied with 'Allama Jamaluddin bin Muhammad 'Umar Bahraq. He had learnt the Quran by heart in his youth, an age about which Sheikh Sadi has rightly said, "You know what happens in youth."

"Side by side with these intellectual attainments, God had endowed him with great piety and strength of purpose. Throughout his life he strictly followed the Sunnah of the Prophet, remained always with Wudu and offered his prayers' in congregation. He did not touch wine, was not unnecessarily hard on anyone, and never sullied his tongue with a foul word. Moreover, in this picture of piety there were gathered the highest qualities of a soldier and a statesman. When Mahmud Shah II of Malwa was deposed by his minister, Mandli Rae, and the rites of Islam began to be wantonly outraged there, his religious pride was stirred. Setting out with a powerful army, he covered the distance to Malwa with the utmost speed and besieged its fort. Mandli Rae, realising that he was no match for the besieging force, begged Rana Ṡanga to come to his aid. But before Rana Sanga could advance as far as Sarangpur, Muzaffar Shah sent a detachment of his valiant army to deal with him. Soon the fort of Malwa fell."

"The sum and substance of the story is that when Muzaffar Shah entered the fort and the chiefs of his escort beheld the great treasure the rulers of Malwa had amassed there and heard accounts of the richness of the land, they ventured to suggest in his presence that since 2,000 of their horsemen had been killed in the fighting, it would not be wise to restore the kingdom to a ruler who, owing to his incompetence, had lost it to his minister. As soon as Muzaffar Shah heard it, he cut short the round of inspection and came out of the fort, instructing Mahmud Shah not to allow any member of his party into the fort. The latter entreated him to rest in the fort for a few days more, but he firmly declined. On a later occasion, explaining the implications of his action Muzaffar Shah said, "I had waged that war simply to earn Divine approbation. When I heard the talk of the chiefs, I became apprehensive lest some unwholesome desire should crop up in my heart to ruin the sincerity of my act. I have not done any favour to Mahmud Shah. On the contrary, I am indebted to him, for it was through him that I got the opportunity of performing a noble deed."

When the hour of his death drew near, Muzaffar Shah, by way of public acknowledgment of boons conferred upon him by God, related to the courtiers and the divines who were assembled around his bed, "By the grace of God, in addition to knowing the Quran by heart, I have a full command over the points of law and precepts arising out of every verse of it, the occasion of its revelation and the method of its recitation. I remember by heart all the Traditions of the Prophet—their texts, references, the antecedents of their narrators and everything—about which I have received the certificate from my teacher, 'Allama Jamaluddin Muhammad bin 'Umar Bahraq. I possess such knowledge of Fiqh (Islamic Jurisprudence) that I hope to bear testimony to the veracity of the Prophet's words that 'Those for whom God makes a decision of virtue, are made by Him the jurists of His faith'. I have been engaged for some time in the purification of the soul after the system of the Sufis and aspire for their blessings on the strength of the principle that 'who so makes himself resemble a people becomes one of them'. I have read the Tafsir Muallim-ut-Tanz' once. I am now revising it and have gone through it half-way. I hope to finish it in heaven."

His condition deteriorated at the time of the Juma (Friday) prayers. He sent away his attendants to attend

> the prayers, while he himself offered the Zuhr prayers. After the prayers, he observed, "I have offered the Zuhr prayers in your midst; I hope to offer the 'Asr prayers in heaven." Then reciting the following prayer of Joseph, which was truly in keeping with his own condition, this saintly king passed away: "O my Lord, Thou hast given me (something) of sovereignty and hath taught me (something) of the interpretation of events—Creator of the heavens and the earth, Thou art my Protecting Friend in the world and the Hereafter. Make me die submissive (unto Thee), and join me to the righteous." (Al-Quran, XII : 101)

Likewise, the following account of the daily routine of Sher Shah Suri reveals an assiduousness for religion which an average man can hardly manage today, to speak nothing of an emperor of olden times who had set himself to complete the task of a century in five years:

> "Sher Shah got up when two-thirds of the night had passed, had his bath and offered the Nafil prayers. He used to finish the prerogative devotions before the Fajr prayers. Then he would look into the accounts of the various administrative departments and issue the necessary instructions so that he might not be disturbed by them during 'the day. After that, he would perform the Wadu for the Fajr prayers which he offered in congregation and remained at his devotions till the high functionaries of the Empire came to pay their respects to him. After the Ishraq prayers, the Emperor attended to the applications of the people and made to them grants of land, money and horses according to their needs. Then he heard the petitions and redressed grievances. Afterwards, he went out to inspect the troops and the arsenal and sanctioned the appointment of new recruits to the army after testing their ability. Then he inspected the Treasury. On returning from there, he met the grandees of the Empire and foreign emissaries. Then the reports of the provincial governors were presented to him. He listened

> to them and dictated orders. Then he sat down to the mid-day meal at which a number of 'ulama would be present. After the meal, he retired for two hours till the Zuhr prayers which he always offered in congregation. Then he recited the Quran. After it, he again occupied himself with the affairs of the Empire.
>
> "The emperor adhered strictly to his routine, whether he was in the Capital or out on a journey. He used to say that a great man was he who spent his time wisely."

The Empire of Aurangzeb stretched from Kabul and Kandhar to the Deccan and he used to look into everything connected with it personally. Yet, he was able to find time to offer the daily prayers at the earliest hour and in congregation, and the Friday prayers in the Jami' Masjid and to observe the Sunnats and the nawafil with scrupulous attention. He kept the fasts of Ramadan even in the hottest weather, and participated in the nightly Tarawih prayers and did the Aitkaf during the last ten days of the month. Apart from the Ramadan fasts, he fasted regularly on Mondays, Thursdays, Fridays and Saturdays. He took care never to be without Wudu and recited the Holy Quran and the other traditional prayers every morning. Notwithstanding the vexations and worries with which he was surrounded throughout his reign, he paid full attention to the spiritual lessons he took from Hadrat khwaja Saifuddin (the grandson of Hadrat Mujaddid Alf Thani, and with such success that the latter used to remark upon the progress made by him in his letters to his father, Hadrat Khwaja Masum. He listened, from day to day, to the Fatawa-i-Alamgiri, a Code of Laws, which theological doctors were compiling under his guidance and gave his own suggestions to them. He knew the Quran by heart and wrote the commentary of his own book Arbain in which he had collected forty Traditions of the Holy Prophet.

Among the ministers and courtiers of the Mughal Court there were such versatile men as 'Abdur Rahim Bairam Khan-i-Khanan, Saadullah Khan Allanil, Majduddin Muhammad bin Muhammad, Ikhtiyar Khan, Afzal Khan and 'Abdul 'Aziz Asaf Khan. Here we will give the life-sketches of only two of them.

Abdur Rahim Khan had read religious text-books with Maulana

Muhammad Amin Ajlan and Qadi Nizamuddin Badakhshan and the advanced books from 'Allama Saifullah Shirazi. Later, when he resided in Gujarat, he availed himself of the opportunity to sit at the feet of 'Allama Wajhuddin bin Nasrullah Gujarati. He also regularly held academic discussions with the scholars he always maintained in his retinue. The result was that he had become perfect in learning. On some subjects he was recognized as an authority. He was an accomplished linguist. 'Abdur Razzaq says in the Maathjy ul-Unara, that he enjoyed complete mastery over Arabic, Persian, Turkish and Hindi and could compose excellent poems in all the four languages.

Abdur Rahim Khan's passion for learning was so strong that he was often seen reading a book on horseback in the battlefield. He would also read while in the bath room. At the same time he was second to none as a soldier. The conquests of Gujarat, Sind and the Deccan speak volumes for his military prowess.

His manners were sublime. He was benevolent, forbearing and generous. Azad Bilgrami observes that if one were to pelt the riches given away by 'Abdur Rahim Khan in one pan of a balance and those by all the Safavid rulers (of Iran) in the other, the former would turn out to be the heavier.

So far as the religious and spiritual side of his life was concerned, it is enough to know that he was one of the few favoured ones who enjoyed the confidence of Hadrat Mujaddid Alf Thani and with whom the latter kept up a regular correspondence. The letters of the great Mujaddid show in what high esteem he held 'Abdur Rahim Khan.

The story of Asaf Khan presents another conspicuous example of composite excellence and versatility. His real name was 'Abdul 'Aziz. He received elementary education from his father, Hamid-ul-Mulk, and studied the 'Hadith and 'Fiqh' from Qadi Burhanuddin and ethics and philosophy from 'Abdul Fadhl Astrabadi. When his education was completed, he gained admission into the Imperial Court, rising to be a Minister in the reign of Bahadur Shah. When Mahmud Shah succeeded to the throne, he appointed Asaf Khan as the Prime Minister of the Empire. But neither position nor wealth could make any difference to his thirst for knowledge. He remained a scholar right up to the moment of his death.

Asaf Khan was once compelled, by political reasons, to migrate to Arabia where he lived for a number of years. The theological circles of Arabia were overwhelmed with wonder as they became aware of his intellectual and spiritual glory. Ibn Hajar Makki, the most distinguished Arab scholar of that time, was moved to write a book on him (which was perhaps the first to be written by a recognized Arab author in appreciation of an Indian Muslim). In it he paid glowing tributes to Asaf Khan's high learning and spiritual merit.

Asaf Khan's life in Arabia was genuinely that of an ascetic in spite of the pomp and splendour with which he was surrounded. It is worth mentioning that he recited ten Paras of the Quran every day in the Tahajjud prayers. We know from Ibn Hajar, "There was not a single occasion during the ten years he lived in Mecca on which he failed to offer his prayers in congregation at the Holy Mosque. His lodgings being by the side of the Malaf his activities were constantly under full view of the people. One almost never saw him except when he was engaged in prayer or meditation or study or religious discussion. Books of the highest standard were discussed at all hours in his presence in which the '*Ulama* of the Haram participated eagerly."

Ibn Hajaf goes on to say:

> "A peculiar glow had come over Mecca during Asaf Khan's stay. The learned and the wise considered it a privilege to converse with him. There was a great fostering of learning. Students hurried to Mecca from all sides. They took great trouble to think out literary problems so as to make them the vehicles for getting nearer to him. This was because the liberality with which he patronized learning and bestowed favours upon students had not been witnessed in Mecca for a long time. His name was blessed in the streets of Mecca in the same way in which the cries of Labbaik are raised during the Hajj days."

Asaf Khan was invited to Constantinople by the Sultan of Turkey. It has been narrated by a friend, who accompanied him that during this journey he did not even for once take advantage of the concessions granted by the Shariat to travellers. While in Egypt, the Governor, Khusrau Pasha, sent him a robe of honour through a special envoy. The envoy begged him to put on the robe if only for a minute, so that he could tell the Governor that Asaf Khan had worn it. The Governor would be very happy to know it. But Asaf Khan politely refused. The garment was made of silk and he could never prevail upon himself to wear it on any account.

We naturally do not mean to suggest that in former times every monarch was a Muzaffar Shah or an Aurangzeb or every minister or peer of the realm was an Abdur Rahim Khan or an Asaf Khan. What we want to impress is that the general quality of human material was much better in the past than it is now. Many of the things that were then considered essential for bringing the human personality to maturity have now been ruled out of existence under the devastating spell of Western ideals and inclinations.

Degeneration : Since religion was pursued in those days as a programme of life, worldly success was not allowed to thwart spiritual progress. With the levelling to the ground of the ethical ideals of Islam by Western convictions and aspirations, the human stuff has degenerated rapidly, mentally and morally, in the Muslim East. A few noteworthy exceptions like Mufti Sadruddin Khan, Nawab Qutbuddin Khan, Nawab Waziruddaula of Took, Nawab Kalb-i-Ali Khan of Rampur, Munshi Jainaluddin Khan, the Wazir of Bhopal, and Nawab Syed Siddiq Hassan Khan did, however, continue to appear occasionally during the period of transition, in whom the severe self-discipline of an ascetic, the love for learning of a scholar and the alertness of a soldier were combined with princely power and wealth. But the process of social disintegration, having once started, proved irresistible. Dazzled by the power and progress of the Western nations, Muslims began to imitate Western social and economic institution regardless of the consequences, although they were much inferior to their own and consisted of little more than the pursuit of material success with the ardour of an over-mastering urge. The prestige of religion was diminished. The teachings of the Prophet were forgotten. All those ideals of life, which truthfully displayed within themselves both the spiritual and the temporal aspects of life and did not subordinate the former to the latter, ceased to impress the minds of the great mass of Muslim society. Their place was taken by ideals far inferior to them. Life was assailed by frivolous desires and occupations to a degree that it had to eschew religious and spiritual carvings and activities. If one compared the daily occupations of the present-day Muslims with those of the aforementioned specimens of the old Islamic civilization, one would find it hard to believe that both professed the same ideology or that only a few generations actually separated one from the other.

Islamic Philosophy and Ideology

In the 6th century, when the world was hovering between life and death and there was no one to whom it could look for succour, the advent of Prophet Muhammad (Upon whom be peace!) gave humanity a fresh lease of life. He placed human welfare under the care of a community that was in possession of the Revealed Word and the Divine Law and in the light of these two did everything that was the symbol of purity and justice. This community had been blessed with the most harmoniously blended disposition and temperate outlook and had risen to the position of the trusteeship of mankind after going through rigorous moral training and attaining complete spiritual adjustment.

The emergence of this community marked a turning point in human history. It immediately arrested the progress of mankind towards its doom and made it safe, for centuries to come, against the moral and material hazards and calamities that were threatening to engulf it. Under its guidance humanity made a well-balanced advance towards its true goal, the various capabilities of man were called splendidly into play and an environment was created in which it was made possible for him to advance to the highest goal of progress in the shortest and the surest way.

Under the influence of this new community the lives of men, their minds and their morals were revolutionized. Unbelief and depravity of character were replaced by faith and virtuousness, false ethical values and wrong ideals gave place to high moral patterns. Politics was placed under the surveillance of ethics. In the system of Islamic civilization there was as unremitting a care for spiritual as for material prosperity. Economic development was matched with moral advancement; political expansion corresponded to spiritual uplift. A deep, inner unity of faith, an unswerving oneness of purpose, and peace and fellow-feeling had demolished all barriers between man and man in the World of Islam and made it into a society which, in spite of its being composed of diverse racial elements, was blissfully free from all social inhibitions, tensions and prejudices. The path of virtue that had been deserted for so long and had become so difficult to tread was now a smooth, even road on which people could walk in perfect freedom and security. Man's right to worship and obey God was restored. The call of religion developed great vigour that lifted millions of men from the depth of degradation to the greatest heights of glory. The spirit of man was aroused, and his genius was set to noble purposes. In short, the caravan of humanity was brought nearer to its destination and its vanguard did, indeed, arrive there.

But before the rest of the travellers could arrive at the journey's end, the caravan suddenly stopped and its leadership underwent a change. The old leader had to relinquish charge because he had not made adequate arrangements for the safety of the travellers. An unknown fellow-traveller assumed the reins of leadership at the point of dagger anti proceeded to take the caravan along a path that was tortuous and uneven and over which the nocturnal darkness prevailed even at high noon. He is engaged still in the same mad pursuit. The travellers stumble and fall headlong and groan, but the leader, in his arrogance and haste, presses heedlessly on.

European Nations : This, surely, is no figment of the mind, for, the Western nations, which succeeded the Muslims to the stewardship of the world, had, from the very beginning, been labouring under a serious disadvantage. They never had the good fortune to be possessed of an unpolluted source of Revealed Knowledge or an uncorrupted fund of Divine Wisdom. The insignificant part of the teachings of Jesus Christ that had reached them had got lost owing to distortions and interpolations. The Western nations tried to make up for the light of heavenly guidance with the learning of the Greeks and the Romans, and the entire Pagan legacy of Ancient Greece and Rome had fallen to their lot. They had received the worship of the perceptible, epicureanism, local patriotism and libertarianism from the Greeks and the bankruptcy of religious belief, racial pride, power-worship and imperialism from the Romans.

We have seen how what was left of the religious teachings of Jesus Christ was devoured by Roman paganism. What was still left was lost in the dogmatic quarrels of the clergy. This was followed by the epidemic of monasticism and then as a reaction to it the Christian world was immersed from one corner to the other in sensual enjoyment. The depravity and luxury of the ecclesiastics produced, in the European mind, a pronounced revulsion towards Christianity which was replaced in unthinking minds by religion in general. In the Middle Ages there occurred a bitter conflict between the Church and the State, which was succeeded by an even more violent clash between Christianity and science. The ghastly atrocities perpetrated by the Church officials during the course of this struggle sealed the fate of Christianity in the West, but succeeded in creating a distrust of religion is general. The Western intellectuals did the rest. They broke the remaining link with transcendental ethics. As a consequence, the West turned out and out materialistic, and power and wealth became the sole objects of its worship.

A further outcome of the peculiar development of the West was the growth of aggressive nationalism. For the preservation of national existence it became necessary to bear ill-will towards the rest of humanity. Europe, on the one hand, decided that the whole of the East was an opposite camp, and on the other, it divided itself into a number of watertight compartments on the illusory basis of national self-determination. The world was converted into a huge market place for the sale and purchase of the weaker nations.

The coupling of moral and religious depravity with a phenomenal progress in the scientific and industrial fields led to the creation of a striking disparity between power and ethics. Men learnt to fly in the air like birds and to swim in the water like fish, but they forgot how to walk straight on the earth. Indisciplined knowledge and unenlightened wisdom furnished every highwayman with a sword. Deadly weapons were placed in untrained hands which repeatedly plunged the world into horrible blood-baths. And now science has given the atomic and Hydrogen bombs to humanity as weapons for suicide.

Under the influence of these godless nations the sciences relating to inanimate matter made great progress while the human material was brought low in every respect. Religion was ostracized and secularized; moral enthusiasm was crushed under the weight of material carvings. The religious instinct of the Eastern peoples, too, which was the Pivot of their lives, was seriously impaired.

It is a tragic fact of modern life that there exists no community worth the name in Europe, Asia, Africa, or America genuinely opposed to the pagan philosophy of materialism. The nations like the Germans in Europe or the Japanese or Indians in Asia, and all becoming increasingly convinced of the merits of materialism. The ideological differences that one encounters in the modern world are mainly the off-shoots of an all-out struggle for political supremacy. They have no relation to moral or spiritual convictions. It is simply too much for the pride of a powerful nation that another should be in command of the international scene. No nation feels inclined to address itself to the moral regeneration of humanity should the opportunity ever come its way.

Communist Russia, though it gives the impression, at the lot that of being distinct from the rest of the Western countries, is the ripened fruit of the Western civilization. Its only distinction is that it has discarded the mask of hypocrisy and gone ahead to bring to their logical conclusion the social and ethical concepts the Western philosophers had been expounding for centuries.

The Communists were not satisfied with the speed with which the West was progressing towards the anti-religious and anti-spiritual ideals of its civilization. They accelerated the pace and attained the goal set before themselves by the Western nations and having done so, they are now trying to manoeuvre themselves into a position from which they can pull the rest of humanity to their side.

Asian Nations : The Eastern nations are by no means in a happy position. The same urges and ambitions that rule over the West are enshrined in their hearts, too. Their leaders have only one quarrel with the West: they do not want their nations to be exploited by Western nations. They aspire to be their own masters now. Apart from this, there is no fundamental difference in the mental attitudes of the Eastern and the Western nations. What the people of the East are opposed to is that the Western ideas and ideals should be pushed through their lands by the Westerners;

they want to be left free to do it themselves. They do not wish to give up the ideals of Western civilization. They only wish that they themselves should be the torch-bearers of that civilization. Further, many Eastern communities have their own traditions of paganism, together with which they are getting imbued with the pagan attitudes of the West. They are sure to bring the characteristics of both into play in the sphere of their own influence when they come into power.

What is to be regretted is that the traditional enemy of Paganism, the Muslim, too, has become its ally and is serving as its devoted camp-follower in many parts of the world. What better proof of the universal triumph of Paganism can there be than that Muslims should regard those countries as their friends and well-wishers who are the leaders of the Pagan movement in the present age? The modern Muslim has totally given up the idea of leadership; he has lost faith in himself. His whole mental attitude is being moulded by the under-currents of Paganism The Muslim states are exhibiting the same materialistic tendencies which are the hall-mark of the Western social system. The same enslavement to earthly longings is fast becoming the creed of the community the cornerstone of whose religious faith is the idea that the real life is the life to come. Its solicitude for After-life is declining day by day. It is subordinating its ethical principles to material expediency with a cheerful readiness that is really astonishing. In some respects the Muslims are actually out-doing the Western races in the glorification of material wealth.

Yet, it is here alone that one sees a ray of hope. With the solitary exception of the followers of Islam all the communities in the world have lost touch with their heritage of Divine guidance. The fight of the Apostolic teachings has departed from their hearts. The passage of time has severed their connections with the real origins of their spiritual inspiration. Past experience of religious reform movements among the various nations definitely precludes the possibility of a fundamental change being brought about in their outlook by re-projecting religion into their lives. Their primary ideals are rigidly opposed to a religious conception of life.

As against this the entire spiritual inheritance of the Muslims is preserved in its pristine purity. A full record of the life and

Traditions of the Holy Prophet and of the lives of his Companions, which holds the key to the understanding of the memorable rise of Islam, is still available to them without the least pollution. Moreover, a chain of religious redeemers and reformers has been continually operating among them, sustaining their spirits, nourishing their souls and guarding them against a relapse into ignorance.

The fact is that the Muslim mind, by the sheer nature of its ordering, is such that it can never be made to imbibe Pagan materialism, unless, of course, its very structure is destroyed and recast into a new form.

In an earlier chapter it has been pointed out that the Holy Prophet said of Muslims in the battle of Badr : "O God, if these (Believers) are destroyed, no one will be left on the earth to worship Thee". It is equally true of them today, because, if there is anyone who can stand up to the challenge of Paganism and offer to the world an alternative plan of life, it is they and they alone. The plan of Islam is an eternal plan. It will remain valid for all time to come. By virtue of their religion, the Muslims are the moral guardians of mankind and they will return to their duty when they will awake from sleep. That day will be a day of reckoning for the nations of the world. They certainly possess a spark which, if and when it blazes up, will burn down the whole structure of Ignorance.

'Allama Iqbal has used the medium of the presiding genius of the Order of Ignorance, the Devil himself, to give expression to this truth in his poem entitled, 'The Advisory Council of the Devil, 1936'. The evil spirits of the world are shown in it to have gathered together to ponder over the new challenges that are threatening their nefarious system. One adviser mentions Democracy as "the latest evil of the new world." Another mentions the name of Communism. He says :

> Stitch an awe this budding menace has struck,
>
> That the brooks, the hills and the yonder mountains shake.
>
> The world, my Lord is about to crumble.
>
> The world that depends upon Thy guidance alone.

The Devil allays their fears and explains to them the plans he has devised for meeting those threats. Then he speaks of what, in his opinion, is the real menace and says that though he has thought out the most appropriate line of campaign against it, too, its potentialities are so terrifying that he is constantly brooding over it. He goes on to say :

> If any fear attends me, it is from the people whose ashes yet the spark of Desire contain.
>
> Occasionally still, I see among them men who, with tears, perform the wudu in the early morning.
>
> He who knows the secrets of History knows
>
> That Communism is not morrow's menace, but Islam.
>
> That they from the Quran have departed, I know.
>
> And Capitalism is now the faith of the Believer;
>
> In the pitch-dark night that upon the East has fallen,

The wise-men of the Haram are without the light of faith, But from the exigencies of this age I fear the Law of the Prophet may reappear:

> Beware of the Law of the Prophet, a hundred times beware!
>
> The safeguarder of women's honour, the tester of men, the Maker of men,
>
> The voice of death for all forms of slavery.
>
> There is no distinction of the Ruler and the ruled in its domain.
>
> It purges wealth of foulness,
>
> And the rich the trustees of their goods it makes.
>
> Can a more radical thing than this there be-
>
> That the earth belongs to God, not to the kings ?
>
> The more this Law from the world's view is hidden the better. Luckily, the Muslim himself is devoid of faith.
>
> Let him in meticulous interpretations of the Book his energies waste.

And a helpless groper in the gloom of Theology be.

Satan then gives the following advice to his council :

Whose mighty 'takbirs' the spell of time and space can break,

May his night of decay no day-break see.

You keep him a stranger to the world of deed, I say,

That all his movements on the life's chess-board be frustrated.

For him such poetry and mysticism are, indeed, the best,

Which from his eyes life's broad spectacle conceal.

Every moment do the thought of their awakening tremble,

Me real purpose of whose faith is the supervision of the Universe.

The Message : The World of Islam can still give the message of faith and life to the disillusioned humanity. It is the message the Holy Prophet (Peace be on him!) had imparted to it about 1,400 years ago. It is a simple, dynamic, radiant message, a grander and more majestic message than which the world cannot hope to receive.

It is the same message which prompted the Muslims of Medina to come out of their homes and spread over the whole world; it is the same message which was so exquisitely summed up by a spokesman of the Muslims before the Emperor of Iran who had asked the followers of Islam as to what had brought them to his land: "We have been sent by Allah to deliver whom He pleaseth from the overlordship of His slaves to His Overlordship; and from the narrowness of this world to the boundlessness of the Hereafter; and from the oppression of other religions to the equity and fairness of Islam."

Not one word of this message can be altered even today, more than thirteen hundred years after it was first delivered. It is just as capable of moving the minds and filling the hearts of men in the 21st century as it was in the 6th.

Today, too, humanity is prostrated before false deities, sculptured and unsculptured, the worship of One Transcendent God is getting rare, the animal in man has got loose and the ecclesiastics, the rulers, the capitalists and the political leaders have lifted themselves to the dizzy heights of godhood.

The world with all its vastnesses has become more constricted, murky and suffocating toady than ever before. Being the devotee of material power the man of toady refuses to admit the existence of any other power. He has been captivated by his own material achievements. He finds himself deceived, and frustrated and is growing increasingly petty, exclusive, selfish and skeptical. Everyone believes that he alone has the right to live, the rest may go and hang themselves; who cares ? Politicians and national leaders have made life still more narrow and difficult by erecting artificial barriers in society. They have laid bold of the wells of life, and bound up the structures of economic and political forms with the wishes and necessities of the privileged classes. Lands which, in the past, were renowned for richness and fertility, have been rendered barren. Entire populations have been placed, like helpless children, under the trusteeship of aliens. The modern mode of life is forging constantly new fetters for the spirit of man, the levies and imposts are getting heavier day by day, peace is assailed from all sides, and mental stress, dissensions, riots and strikes have become the inevitable constituents of daily existence.

Toady, again, it is necessary to "deliver men from the oppression of other religions to the equity and fairness of Islam." Even in the 21st century there are religions abounding in superstitious beliefs and fantastic teachings, that tyrannize over their followers and drive them like deaf and dumb animals. Then there are the new-political and economic-religions like collectivism, nationalism and socialism that are a step ahead of the ancient pagan faiths in fanatical intolerance and coercion. The last two World Wars were the "gifts" of these very dogmas to humanity, beside which the sanguinary religious strifes of old Rome and the bitter conflicts between the Church and the intelligentsia of Europe in the Middle Ages recede into insignificance.

Toady, too, the Message of Islam is an open invitation to the worship of, and surrender to, One God and belief in the Apostleship of the prophets, particularly that of Prophet Muhammad (Upon whom be peace!) and in Resurrection and Final judgement. In return for submitting to this call the world will emerge from the darkness of Ignorance and the spirit of man will be set free. Man will rediscover his equilibrium and from the narrow confines of the world of matter he will come out into a world which, although enclosed within himself, stretches beyond time and space.

There never was a clearer appreciation of the need and the utility of this Message as now. The civilization of Ignorance has been publicly disgraced, its shame is being flagrantly exposed. People are disgusted with life; they are despaired of the intellectual and cultural leaders. Modern civilization is seriously ill. From all indications the psychological moment has arrived when a radical change in the leadership of human affairs is called for. So far, changes in leadership have only been in the nature of a change of personnel. There has been no major shift in thinking. It does not matter much to the ship of human destiny whether Britain is at the helm of affairs or America or Russia, because their moorings are basically the same and they are subject to identical intellectual impulses.

The only thing that can cure the world of its present ills and ailments is that its leadership should pass from the hands that are coloured with the blood of humanity to those that were destined to guide, humanity, i.e., from the hands of Britain, America and Russia to the hands of the followers of the Prophet Muhammad (Peace and blessings of God be upon Him).

New Renaissance : To attain this objective the World of Islam will have to find its spiritual roots. It will have to rededicate itself to Islam, There is absolutely no need of a new religion, a new Canonical Law or a new set of moral teachings for the Muslim. Like the sun, Islam was, is and will never be old. The Apostleship of Prophet Muhammad (Peace be on him!) is endowed with the quality of timelessness. No other Apostle of God is to be raised now. His religion is everlasting, his teachings are immortal. But the Muslims do require a renaissance of faith. One cannot face new hazards and meet new challenges with a dilapidated faith and unauthorized practices. A decaying building cannot stand through a flood. One must have a living, glowing and unbending faith in the cause one seeks to uphold. If the Islamic World aspires to inject a new enthusiasm and a new life into humanity, to give it the courage to resist and revert the torrents of materialism and religious disbelief, it will first have to produce that enthusiasm and that life in itself.

The Muslims will have to regenerate themselves internally. They cannot brave the onslaught of the ungodly West by imitating its empty cultural norms customs, and social concepts, for these things have no place in the growth and rise of nations. All cultural imitations are bound to make a people small. The Muslims can exert themselves only by means of that inner force, in respect of which the West is growing insolvent day after day.

The secret of a Muslim's strength lies in his faith in the Divine recompense and reward in the After-life. If the Muslim World, too, sets up the same worldly ideals before itself and gets caught in the same web of material desires as the West, the latter with its larger fund of material knowledge and power evidently has a prior claim to superiority.

History speaks of times when Muslims grew indifferent to the value of the inner force and the wells of spiritual vigour within them ran dry owing to distrait. Then arose, occasions calling for great feats of faith and the Muslims tried to draw upon that force, but to them dismay they learnt that it had deserted them long ago. It then dawned upon them that they had done themselves great injury by neglecting it, and they made frantic efforts to work it up artificially but it proved futile.

During such times there also occurred events in the course of which the honour of Wani seemed to he at its height and it was hoped that the entire Muslim World would be set ablaze with fury and Muslims would rush forth front every (quarter to defend their sacred rights but nothing happened beyond a ripple hue and a wavelet there. Under the surface everything remained (dead and motionless).

The major task before the Muslim leaders and thinkers toady is to rekindle the flame of faith in the hearts of Muslims. They should do in this respect all that the early preachers of Islam did, and at the same time avail themselves fully of all the opportunities the modern age has put into their hands.

The Quran and Umm Sumah can still re-vitalize the withered arteries of the Islamic World. Their study and influence still fire, one with the desire to smash the citadel of Ignorance. They have it rousing quality about them that can spur a slumbering people into a new life. Under their inspiration deadly struggles can once again ensue between belief and unbelief, faith and perfidy, the heart and the intellect. The world can once again be made to ring to the battle between the tranquillity of mind and the ease of body—a battle which all the prophets had to wage, and without which no vital change in the moral make-up of men can be brought about. There will then be born in every Muslim home high-souled men who will fully correspond to the description contained in the following verses of the Quran :

> "They were youths who believed in their Lord, and We advanced them in guidance. We gave strength to their hearts; behold, they stood up and said : 'Our Lord is the Lord of the heavens and of the earth; never shall we call upon any god other than Him; if we did, we should indeed have uttered an enormity.'
>
> (Al-Quran, XVIII : 13-14)

The world will then see again living specimens of the religious earnestness and sacrificial spirit of Bildi and 'Ammar, Khabbab and Khubaib, Suhaib and Musab bin 'Umayr and 'Uthman bin Mazun and Anas bin an-Nadhr; the gentle breeze of faith will once again Kiss the face of the earth and a new World quite different from the one we know will come into existence.

Today, the Muslim society is a victim of self-complacency and readiness to compromise with the circumstances. The perils which are so relentlessly closing in on it from all sides leave it unmoved. It is drifting and it does not know to what end. Its heart is without the warmth of desire.

There is a dire need of disturbing the complacency of this Community of the Faithful; it must be persuaded to care for human welfare more than for its own interests.

A Matured Nation : No matter how well provided with material resources a nation may be, it cannot hope to go far in the world without maturity of thought. It will always be playing in the hands of adventurers and exploiters.

Unfortunately the followers of Islam cannot distinguish between good and bad and will as willingly place their trust in a foe as in a friend. Often, indeed, it turns out to be easier for their enemies to win their confidence than for their well-wishers. The Holy Prophet (Upon whom be peace!) once said, "A Muslim is not bitten twice from the same hole." It is just the reverse of it now. 'The Muslims may be bitten from a hole, not once or twice, but a hundred times, yet will they put their finger into it again and again. The political awakening among them is almost nil. They are constantly acting so as to invite the foreigners and their own selfish leaders to exploit them.

On the contrary, the Western nations, in spite of all their moral and spiritual shortcomings, are characterized by keen political consciousness. No one can lead them by the nose where their own interests are involved. They choose their leaders with care. However glorious a leader's record might be, if they feel that he has done his job and a new man is called for, they will replace him without hesitation. That is why these nations are, on the whole, safe from the machinations of professional politicians and dishonest leaders. Their rulers know that an enlightened public opinion keeps a watchful eye on them.

The Muslim World cannot afford to lose time in catching up with the West in inculcating proper consciousness among its masses and educating them in the responsibilities of good citizenship. It goes without saying that mere education is no proof of consciousness in a community, though it is a necessary condition thereof. Deliberate and systematic steps will have to be taken in this direction. It is for Muslim leadership to realize that persons who cannot do their own thinking cannot constitute a reliable people, whatever enthusiasm they may show for a cause. There is no stability in their thoughts and emotions. They have a weakness for catch words; they are prone to think with their hearts rather than with their brain. Any slogan can lure them away, any juggler can fool them.

In spite of being a revealed religion, having its roots in Divine Revelation and Apostleship, Islam had worked out a typical consciousness among its people—a consciousness that was deeper; stronger and wider than what we mean by it toady. It had developed a frame of mind that was stoutly anti-Pagan and an understanding which, with all its breadth and flexibility, could not for a moment accommodate beliefs and notions which were inconsistent with its own basic pattern.

Take, for example, the following incident. Owing to the teachings of the Prophet (Peace be on him!) it had got fixed firmly in the minds of the Companions that injustice was an evil which was not to be permitted in any circumstances. They had given up their ancient family and tribal predilections, believing that there was no place for such things in Islam. Then one day they heard the Prophet (Peace be on him !) say:" Stand by your brother, be he the aggressor or the aggrieved." Had there been the slightest weakness in the development of their new understanding, they would have readily accepted the command in its apparent meaning, firstly, because of the background of their native traditions and, secondly, because they believed as a matter of faith that what the Holy Prophet (Peace be on him !) said was not out of his own volition but due to Divine inspiration. Their loyalty to the Prophet (Peace be on him!) was unmatched. Yet, they could not resist speaking out, " Helping the aggrieved is all right, O Prophet of God, but how can one help the aggressor?" The Prophet (Peace be on him !) explained that the way to help the aggressor was to restrain him from committing aggression. This gave them a new understanding and enlightenment. But until they had heard it, they were not disposed to accept even the advice of the Prophet (On whom be peace !) in spite of their implicit faith in him. This was because Islam had taught them to exercise their judgement and they learned how to use it.

Similarly, the Prophet once despatched an army under the command of a Companion and enjoined on it to remain obedient to its Commander. On the way it so happened that the Commander got upset with his men for some reason and had a big fire kindled. He ordered the soldiers to march into the fire. The soldiers refused. They said that they had embraced Islam to save themselves from fire and not to march into it. When the incident was reported to the Prophet (Peace be on him !), he commended the action of the soldiers and said that had they stepped into the fire, they would never have come out of it (meaning that they would have gone straight to hell).

The Companions did not hesitate even to challenge the Caliph publicly if they suspected him to be guilty of a wrong act. Once, as the mighty Caliph 'Umar arose to Mess a gathering Imams cut short by Aman who said that he would "neither listen to, nor obey" the Caliph unless he explained how he happened to be wearing a garment made of two pieces of cloth while to others he had allotted only one piece each. Hadrat 'Umar advised him to hold pewit and then called upon his son,, 'Abdullah. At the first instance there was no response. Hadrat 'Umar called again, "O 'Abdullah, the son of 'Umar!" This time 'Abdullah got up. Hadrat 'Umar said to him, "Tell them whether the Abdullah I am wearing is mine own or one borrrowed from you". 'Abdullah affirmed that it was his ('Abdullah's) and that he had lent it to his father for use. On hearing it, Salman said, "Proceed Amir-ul-Muminin, we will now listen to you."

This powerful awakening proved to be the strongest bulwark against the imperialistic ambitions of the Umayyads. It was not until the whole of the generation that had been brought up under the influence of the Prophet (Peace be on him !) had passed away that the Umayyads could have a sigh of relief.

Every movement has an intellectual background. No revolution can succeed unless minds of the people have been prepared for it. A study of the French Revolution will show how irresistible the masses can become, once their minds are aroused. The French Revolution was not the outcome of a sudden impulse. Its leaders, had patiently prepared the minds of Frenchmen much in advance. There was an army of intellectuals who had given a meaningful content to the popular urges that ultimately found expression in the three-word slogan of "Liberty, Equality and Fraternity." Though its leaders could not make the revolution beneficial for humanity, it proved to be a mighty force in human history because it had sprung from the minds of the people.

If the West is still alive and powerful, it is due to the stout political consciousness and the keen civic sense of its people. One hears but rarely of anyone there violating his allegiance to his country or subordinating national interests to personal considerations.

The leaders in the Muslim countries on the other hand, can a, day mortgage the destiny of their people and walk away with it. Their people will still swell their ranks and dance to their tunes. In a number of Muslim countries the conditions are extremely deplorable—the common man there leads a sub-human existence, the authority of God is brazenly violated and all sorts of shameful things are done, and it calls up no indignation and arouses no pain among the Muslims. This is so because the process of thinking among Muslims is stagnant and their social consciousness is almost dead.

It is essential for the revivification of Islam that conscious efforts should be made for the development of an enlightened and responsible public opinion in the Muslim countries. Without it all manifestations of religious enthusiasm or political fervour will be of little significance.

The famous book of fiction, the Arabian Nights, tells the story of an age when the State or the Empire was the lengthened shadow of one man—the King or the Caliph, who held sway over society like a huge tree that sends out enormous branches in all directions and robs the tiny plants growing under it of sunshine and air. The wheels of the nation's life moved for him alone, for him alone did the farmers till the soil, the traders ply their trade and the workmen work with their tools; for him alone did the authors write, the poets sing, the soldiers march into the battlefield, the mothers give birth to children, the earth open up its bowels and the seas dish out their treasures.

This exerted enormous influence on the Muslim social organization whether in Baghdad, Cairo or Damascus. The stories of the Arabian Nights and the literary masterpieces of "The Book of Aghani" are a living proof of the strength of this influence. But, for all that, the spirit of this age was diametrically opposed to the spirit of Islamic civilization. Islam had come to bring the structure of such a civilization to the ground. The Holy Prophet (Upon whom be peace!) had dubbed it as the "Age of Ignorance" and foretold the end of the reign of all imperial rulers.

This age has now forfeited its right to continue any more. The very idea of such an age is revolting to our mind. Who in the current context of things would like a state of society to exist in which a few individuals were permanently sick with indigestion due to over-eating, while the rest of them were permanently in the threat of death due to starvation ? Such a situation is illogical, unnatural and unjust. It should not have been tolerated even for a day. If it flourished in the past, it was because Islam had not yet acquired enough strength to expose its hypocrisy. As the Islamic movement spread and people learnt to distinguish clearly between right and wrong, they progressively emerged out of it. The age of the Arabian Nights has quit the stage of History for all time to come.

Islam can have nothing to do with egotism and self-conceit, individual or collective. Whether these sentiments take the form of family or sectarian pride, as in the Eastern and the Islamic countries, or of British Imperialism, American Capitalism or Russian Communism, as in the Western world, they are patently un-Islamic. These systems may succeed in putting off their doom for some time, but they are bound ultimately to go. The conscience of humanity cannot be cheated indefinitely. The future of the world is inseparably linked with the social justice of Islam.

The work of the regeneration of Islam, does not end here. If the Muslim World really wants to turn its way upwards and make Islam once again the instrument of realizing human destiny as has already happened, it cannot afford to ignore any more its educational, scientific and industrial development and the organization of its military strength. It must quickly make itself independent of the West and attain a position wherein it can work its natural resources, manufacture its weapons and feed and clothe its people without having to look to others for assistance. It must build up its economic and military strength so that it may not have to join this or that power bloc for security and protection.

So long as the Muslim countries continue depending on the West for economic and military aid, the West will not cease to suck their blood and keep them weak and disorganised. In the past, the Muslims were neglectful of their duty to themselves and to the rest of the world, and they were condemned to a long period of servitude and misery. The rule of the West was clamped down upon them, which proved to be the starting point of the degeneracy of man in modern times. If they do not pay immediate attention to their intellectual and economic rebirth, the period of their suffering will be extended and the world will be damned indefinitely.

The educational set-up of the Islamic World will have to be thoroughly over-hauled in the light of the Islamic ideals and precepts. To learn from the Western countries which are scientifically and technologically advanced is one thing, but the moment Muslims forget that their roots are in Islam, and become the intellectual camp-followers of others, their creative energies are damped. In former times the intellectual leadership of the Muslims was accepted all over the world. Their culture and learning had made their way into every sphere of human life all over the globe. For a long time the world continued to think in the Islamic way and draw inspiration from Islamic life. Arabic was the vehicle of learning in the Western world and every writer of note used this language to say what he had to say. Sometimes the original book was brought out in Arabic and a summary of it was produced in another language like Imam Ghazzali Kimiya-i-Saadaf. Though the educational system introduced by the Arabs was more Greek and Iranian in its essence than Islamic, and had a number of defects from the academic point of view, it had gained currency almost everywhere.

Then the time changed, and there dawned the epoch of Western ascendancy. It brought with it a new attitude towards learning, which was the product of Europe's own cultural experiences. The world began to follow the new structure. The Muslim countries, too, on account of their intellectual sluggishness succumbed to the illusion their salvation lay only in a slavish submission to the west and to its educational system.

Ground was thus prepared for not merely intellectual adoration but also for actual imitation of the Western civilization by the Muslim intelligentsia. Religious skepticism, self-conceit, discontent and all other characteristics of the modern Western mode of living began steadily to replace the cultural ideals of the rising generations of the Muslims. The spiritual civilization of Islam began systematically to be replaced by the material culture of Europe.

It is vital for the regaining of world-leadership for Islam now that the Muslim should re-establish their intellectual superiority over the West. For this the Islamic culture will, have to re-assert itself. Crusading endeavours will have to be made in all branches of learning. This, obviously, is not the work of a few individuals or associations. The Muslim states should take the task of intellectual regeneration seriously in hand. High-powered committees and institutions should immediately be set up for the purpose of evolving an educational structure that should fully conform to the spirit of the Quran and the Sunnah without overlooking the requirements of modern learning and scientific research. Muslim educationists and scientists ought to apply their own force of speculative reasoning to the empirical sciences so that they can save the coming generations of Muslims from developing a feeling of contempt for their own past and a despair for their future.

This is the way in which an Islamic revival can be brought about. This is the way in which the Muslims can spread the light of Islam to lands far away and save mankind from the stark ruin that is staring it in the face. Leadership is not an easy job. It calls for tremendous faith, labour and sacrifice.

Rate of Success

This is no secret, the history bears incontestable testimony to the fact that Islam gave unprecedented impetus to the intellectual development of the human race and that the early Muslims held high the torch of light and learning at a time when the whole world was immersed in ignorance and barbarity. The impression prevalent in the West that Islam is an unprogressive religion, antagonistic to science and civilization, is absolutely incorrect. Perhaps, no religion has been so greatly misrepresented and misinterpreted by prejudiced and uninformed critics as Islam. Far from adequately appreciating the glorious scientific achievements of the early Muslims and gratefully acknowledging the immense debt the world owes to them, the designing critics have shamelessly calumniated Islam by completely distorting historical facts and wilfully perverting established truths. Hopefully, it may be proved conclusively that Islam, far from retarding the progress of science, the chief factor of civilization, immensely furthered its cause. In fact, it was Islam that gave birth to modern science, inaugurated a scientific era in the world's history and made the early Muslims precursors of modern scientists and pioneers of modern civilization. The subsequent intellectual stagnation that came upon the Muslim world, giving rise to a false impression regarding Islamic influence, was entirely due to certain historical circumstances similar to those that prevailed in Europe during the Middle Ages, before the Renaissance and the Reformation. The Islamic faith and its teachings were in no way responsible for this social degeneration and political debacle.

It is now being realised that modern science owes its origin to Islam and modern progress is the outcome of the freedom of thought and spirit of enquiry prescribed for the Muslims by the Holy Quran, and not a product of Christianity which for a long time relentlessly proscribed all free thinking and liberal reasoning and even scientific researches on original lines, and horribly persecuted all those who indulged in these. The impression that it was Christianity that advanced science and civilisation is, therefore, as erroneous as the idea that Islam hampered their progress. In fact, there can be no comparison between Islam and Christianity as civilising forces. While the Muslims rose to a pinnacle of learning within a few centuries of the promulgation of Islam, the Christians remained steeped in ignorance for more than a thousand years.

After a careful study of the history of Islam, Canon Isaac Taylor came to the definite conclusion that "Islam has done more for civilisation than Christianity." If Europe's indebtedness to Islam for the extraordinary progress it has latterly made in science and civilisation were adequately known, it would have astounded the modern civilised world. "During the darkest period of European history writes Bosworth Smith, "the Arabs for five hundred years held up the torch of learning to humanity." Arthur Leonard has truly said, "Islam, in fact, has accomplished a great feat. It has left a mark on the pages of human history, which is so indelible that it can never be effaced............. only when the world grows wiser will that be acknowledged in full."

That the early Muslims very largely contributed to the cultural development of the world cannot but be admitted by all unprejudiced and fair-minded critics of Islamic history. It is nothing but religious prejudice and an overweening sense of racial superiority which have stood in the way of acknowledgement and appreciation by the West of the glorious achievements of the East. Draper is perfectly justified in deploring "the systematic manner in which the literature" of Europe has continued to put out of sight our scientific obligations to Muhamadans. Surely they cannot be much longer hidden. Injustice founded on religious rancour and national conceit cannot be perpetrated for ever.

Foundation of Physical Science : It is a historical fact that cannot be controverted that, before the advent of Islam, the cultivation of science was condemned as heresy. The reason for this is not far to seek. The bulk of mankind could not at that time think in the abstract, and they looked upon the elements of Nature, the subject-matter of science, as sacred objects, possessing supernatural powers. They made idols, symbolizing different elements, and worshipped them as gods and goddesses, either for protection from evil or for attainment of certain objects. Thus were the sun, the moon, the stars, air, water, animals, and even trees and stones, deified and adored. It was not unnatural that in such circumstances any deviation from the prevailing belief in their sanctity should have been branded as sacrilege, and any attempt at a critical examination of their potentiality, for good or evil, stigmatised as profanity. Thus all that was useful in the heavens and the earth remained altogether unexplored, and for thousands of years man did not realise the sublime utility of the forces of Nature. It was reserved for the untutored son of the desert to open man's eye to the wonderland of Nature by bringing down her elements from the high pedestal of divinity, on which they had been placed, to the position of servants of mankind.

Subservience of Natural Elements : *And He has made subservient to you the night and the day and the sun and moon and the stars are made subservient by His commandment; most surely there are signs in this for people to ponder......Al Quran.*

Thus were the gods of the pre-Islamic people reduced by one stroke to man's servants. For the first time in the history of the world the Holy Quran declared in unmistakable language that the main purpose for which all objects, from the mightiest sun to the most insignificant atom, were created, was to minister to man's needs. Everything in the universe being intended for his use, man has been commanded to investigate their intrinsic properties,—in other words, to cultivate every branch of science. Thus, by declaring man the lord of the universe and everything in it subservient to him, the Quran gave a tremendous impetus to the development of scientific research. In fact the foundation of modern science was thus laid by acquainting man with the real nature of the forces and laws of Nature and by teaching him how to harness them for human service. The initiation of the conquest of Nature leading to the utilisation of its forces for the gocd of humanity is, indeed, one of the greatest blessings Islam has conferred upon mankind.

The Quran clearly indicated the way in which to reduce Nature to human service by contemplation and observation of four kinds, viz., *Tafaqquh, Tadakkur, Tafakkur* and *Taaqqul.* By the first a correct idea of things and their different features can be arrived at, by the second the knowledge of how to utilise them properly can be acquired, the third teaches the ways by which things have come into existence, while the fourth gives the knowledge which enables man to make the right use of different things in everyday life. It was the meditations indicated by *Tafakkur* and *Taaqqul* that actuated different kinds of scientific research among the early Muslims. This is how the Quran placed in the hands of man the key to the treasure-house of Nature, and Divine Revelation came to show him the way to material progress. Everything in the universe having been intended for the use of man, it was a virtuous act for him to conduct research into the realms of Nature in order to discover the utility of its various components. Thus, the first principle of progress, — the utilisation of the forces of Nature for the needs of man —became an article of faith with the Muslims, and impelled them to engage in scientific research.

Nature's Exploration, God's Glorification : The Prophet of Islam went so far as to carry out explorations of the realms of Nature, the real glorification of God, and to place the acquisition of knowledge on an equal footing with His worship. Man was required to glorify God not by mere lip service, but by discovering and utilising the properties and potentialities of the things He created to meet the needs of His creatures. Realisation of the scattered bounties of God was to be the realisation of God Himself. A Muslim was to spiritualise, as it were, his whole material surroundings by seeing and feeling the evidence of God's power and love in every blade of grass and in every breath of air.

> *Truly, in the creation of the heavens and earth, and the alternation of night and day, there are signs for men of understanding, who remember Allah standing, sitting and while lying on their sides, and ponder over the creation of the heavens and earth (and say) our Lord, You have not created (all) this in vain. Glory be to You.*
> *Al-Quran*

Reason, the Test of Faith : Before the advent of Islam, learning was confined to the chosen few. The masses had to blindly accept whatever was placed before them as their religion and they were not permitted to use their intellect or judgment. In fact, before the promulgation of Islam, religion was synonymous with dogmas and doctrines, rites and rituals; and bigotry had placed an embargo on freedom of thought and enquiry. Whenever anyone conceived any new idea or propounded a new theory, he was condemned by his co-religionists as a heretic. Some of the most inhuman atrocities ever committed on men in search of truth were thus perpetrated in the name of religion. It was Islam that for the first time discountenanced all dogmatic teachings and made reason the test of faith. "The first thing created" says the Prophet of Islam, "was reason. God has not created anything better than reason." On another occasion the Prophet said, "Truly, a man may have performed prayers, fasts, charity and pilgrimages and all other good deeds, but he will not be rewarded save in proportion to the sense he employs." According to the Quran, "There is no piety in turning your face towards the East or the West." *Iman* (faith) means knowledge of a truth or principle with such conviction as to its truth as will incite one to live up to it. It does not signify belief that cannot be translated into action.

All this unmistakably demonstrates that Islam does not regard rituals and ceremonies as essentials of religion. In fact, mere dogmatic doctrines have no significance for a true Muslim, who has to observe his religion in every deed and action, in every thought and conception. He may indulge in free thought and free inquiry concerning everything that man's intelligence is capable of apprehending. To him, science, the aim of which is truth, is the greatest ally of true religion. "Islam stands almost alone," says Guizot in his *History of European Civilisation* "among the religions in discountenancing the reliance on tradition without argument. It demands that its votaries should undertake the investigation of the great work of their faith." Miracle has no place in Islam to which nature itself is a revelation of God, and its laws His eternal miracles, demonstrating His Majesty, His omnipotence and His benevolence. In fact, man knew nothing of God except through His work in Nature. Islam thus gave to scientific research a religious aspect unknown and unthought of before.

By thus putting an end to all conflicts between religion and science, and by making the first principle of scientific progress—the subservience of nature to man—an article of faith, Islam revolutionised the human mind, imparted immense energy and initiative to it and strongly impelled it to investigate the marvels of creation. Moreover, it immeasurably enlarged the scope of religion, which had till then been regarded only as a means of man's future salvation, but now, for the first time, came to be looked upon also as an effective factor in his material advancement. Every branch of learning conducive to human wealth and progress thus came within the purview of Islam, which harmonised the esoteric and exoteric sides of man's life. Thus modern progress had its origin in the spirit of free thought and investigation engendered by Islam.

Education made Compulsory : I have already stated what Islam did for two of the most important factors of modern culture and civilization. Let us now see what it did for another important factor, viz., the dissemination of knowledge. It is a historical fact that no messenger of God, from Nuh to Jesus, had done anything worth mentioning for the dissemination of knowledge, which was selfishly monopolised by a few priests and theologians, anxious to retain all power in their own hands. But the Prophet of Islam, though he himself did not know how to read and write, laid the greatest stress on the acquisition of knowledge and made it essentially incumbent upon all his followers, irrespective of sex, rank, colour and country. *Talabul-Ilm-e-Faridatun Ala Kulli Muslimin Wa Muslimatin:* "Seeking of knowledge is imperative for all Muslims, male and female." "He who has been gifted with knowledge", says the Quran, "has been gifted with an abounding blessing." Convinced that an ignorant person cannot adequately realise the greatness and goodness of God, the Prophet of Islam made acquisition of knowledge an essential of faith and did not approve of his followers being entirely absorbed in meditation upon God, "an hour's contemplation and study of His creation being better than a year's adoration." Muslims were particularly enjoined to be in constant search of knowledge "from the cradle to the grave," and they were told that "the ink of the scholar was holier than the blood of the martyr."

Thus in that dark age, when the world was enveloped in ignorance and illiteracy, Islam created an insatiable thirst for knowledge and caused a tremendous upheaval of science in realms hitherto altogether unexplored. Such an extraordinary outburst of intellectual activity was unparalleled in human history. Some undreamt of discoveries and inventions were made and these contributed immensely to the progress of civilisation and the welfare of mankind. There was hardly any science of which the Muslims did not make themselves masters. They created modern Chemistry, made most important discoveries in Astronomy, added much to the knowledge of Mathematics and Medicine and conducted very valuable research in Botany, Geology, Zoology and other branches of Natural Philosophy. The foundation of what is termed Physical Science was thus laid, and the gates of investigation into the marvels of creation were flung wide open.

The Muslims, by unravelling the mysteries of Nature and widening the scope of knowledge, introduced such blessings of comfort and happiness as were unknown in the world. It was the intellectual liberty and the spirit of scientific research inaugurated by them that brought about the European Renaissance and introduced into the modern world the arts and sciences which ennobled the heart, elevated the mind, thus making a major contribution to human happiness.

The height of scientific progress forecast by the Quran has not yet been fully attained. The world is full of materials that await man's exertion and ingenuity for their development and utilisation. There are millions of things in the realm of the seas and in the bowels of the earth and the ocean that have been created for man's use. All these have to be harnessed in order to meet the increased requirements of human society. The Quran repeatedly speaks of the subservience of the physical world and phenomena to man, whose duty it is to explore them for use.

Before the advent of Islam, the West, which nowadays claims all the credit for progress in science and civilisation, was steeped in ignorance and darkness. It was the intellectual liberty and scientific research inaugurated by the Muslims which brought about the Renaissance to which Europe owed its regeneration. Medieval Europe was a hotbed of religious fanaticism and social conservatism; and the intellectual stagnation which prevailed there is altogether beyond conception in modern times.

Persecution of Scientists in the West : In medieval Europe religion and science were thought to be quite irreconcilable to each other, and whoever ventured to express any opinion contrary to the prevailing sacerdotal belief was not merely branded as a heretic, but was relentlessly persecuted, inhumanly tortured and even mercilessly put to death. For his belief in the theory of evolution, Vanini's tongue was torn out of his mouth and he was burnt alive. Hypatia, the renowned commentator on Plato, had to pay the penalty for her intellectual audacity with her life. Copernicus tried to demonstrate that the earth revolves and not the heavens. Thereupon even Martin Luther denounced him as "an upstart astrologer," and Calvin most severely condemned him. He had, therefore, to end his life in disgrace. Bruno, who dared to advance the Copernican theory, was seized, imprisoned and at last put to death by a "fire made slow to increase the torture." Galileo, who supported the Copernican theory, was thrown into a dungeon, horribly tortured and forced to recant as follows: "I, Galileo, being in my seventieth year, being a prisoner on my knees before your Eminences, having before my eyes the Holy Gospel, abjure, curse and detest the error and the heresy of the movements of the Earth." Not content with mere recantation, the Holy Inquisition sent him into exile for the rest of his life. Thus many a devoted votary of science fell a victim to Christian fanaticism prevalent in the Middle Ages, and some famous libraries, containing the accumulated treasure of ages, were consigned to the flames.

All this conclusively proves that the credit given to Christianity, as a religion, for promoting the cause of science is nothing but a travesty of truth.

Western Civilization: Direct Offspring of Arab Civilization: It is an uncontroverted truth that modern progress in the West was not the outcome of Man's faith in Church dogmas. In fact, the West made no progress worth the name as it was in the iron grip of Christianity. This is borne out by the fact that centuries of domination of Spain, from them the utter darkness in which they were groping and the appalling ignorance in which they were immersed. The extraordinary progress made by the Christian countries during the last five hundred years is directly due to the teachings of Islam, which were promulgated six hundred years after Christianity. It was not till freedom of thought was advocated and the torch of learning was lighted by the Muslims in Spain that any progress in science and civilisation could be made in Europe, or any possibility could arise for the Renaissance and the Reformation to make their appearance in the Christian world. It was from Muslim Spain that a new life dawned upon the whole of Europe, giving birth to a new culture, which greatly stimulated the intellectual activity of its people. All that Christian Europe learnt of Greek and Hindu Philosophy and Science up to the Renaissance period emanated from the Saracenic culture of Spain.

After the conquest of Spain the Muslims established there several Universities which opened their doors to all students without distinction of creed, caste, colour or country; and also boarded and lodged them at public expense. Spain thus became the centre of European culture, and scholars from all parts of Christian Europe looked to her seats of learning. Rogers, Bacon and other pioneers of the Rationalist movements in Europe, all received their education in the Muslim University of Cordova. Even the great Emperor Charlemagne had to send his son to Spain to be educated by the Muslim teachers, for nowhere else in Europe was there any seat of learning worthy of the name.

Every branch of science was seriously investigated in Muslim Spain. Medicine achieved greater development through the discoveries of her doctors and surgeons than it had gained during all the centuries that had elapsed since the days of Galen. Astronomy, Chemistry, Geography, Natural History, all were studied at Cordova with great ardour; as for the graces of literature, there never was such a time when poetry became almost the common speech of everybody. "The taste for science and literature," writes Renan, "had by the 10th century established, in this privileged corner of the world, a toleration of which modern times hardly offer us an example. Christians, Jews and Muslims spoke the same tongue, sang the same songs, and participated in the same literary and scientific studies." All the barriers which separated the various peoples were effaced: all strove with one accord in the work of a common civilisation. The mosques of Cordova, where the students could be counted by the thousands, became the active centres of philosophical and scientific studies. "It must be owned" observes John Davenport, "that all the knowledge, whether of physics, astronomy, philosophy or mathematics, which flourished in Europe from the 10th century, was originally derived from the Arabian schools, and the Spanish Saracen may be looked upon as the father of European philosophy."

Some idea of the architectural beauty and grandeur introduced into Europe by the Muslims may be had from the Alhambra Court in the Crystal Palace in London. Stanley Lane-Pool in "The Moors in Spain" has aptly described all this; he says, "Beautiful as were the palaces and gardens of Cordova, her claims to admiration in higher matters were no less strong. The mind was as lovely as the body."

As rightly acknowledged by Gustav Diercks in his 'Europe's Debt to Islam,' there can be no denying that Europe is deeply in debt to Islam for all its scientific discoveries. In fact, it was Islam that produced scientists who anticipated Bacon, Newton, Kepler and other great scientists of Europe. But for the introduction into Europe by the Muslims of paper, gunpowder, the mariner's compass and such other instruments of progress, who knows that the condition of Europe in respect of science and civilisation would not still have been today what it was fourteen hundred years ago.

The industries developed by the Muslims during their rule in Spain were many and of far-reaching consequence. Shipbuilding, horticulture, tanyards, glassware, silver mines, cotton manufactures, silks, woollen carpets, iron and copper utensils and inlaid metal work were some of these. The Muslims gave Europe the mulberry tree, the maize, the sugarcane, the windmill and many such other items of industry. During the reign of the Spanish king, Al-Hakam, the irrigation systems were developed in Granada, Valencia and Arragon. In short, the art of war, industry, commerce and seamanship made unprecedented progress in Muslim Spain. It is a historical fact that 477 years before Columbus, the Arabs and the moors of Spain traded with the American continent.

Though the average westerner is under the impression that Europe's salvation was caused by the defeat of the Muslims at Tours (Poitiers), the real fact is that the world's progress was retarded for ages by this check on the advance of the Muslims in the West. Perhaps the darkest pages in the annals of history, dealing with the inquisition and such other disgraceful matters, would never have been written at all and Renaissance, which ushered in an era of civilisation in Europe, would have been accelerated by 700 years if the Muslims had won that battle and Islamised the whole of Europe. Anatole France who was above racial and religious prejudice, truly said in his *La Vie En Flour.* "The most tragic event in history is that of the Battle of Poitiers, when the science, the art and the civilisation of Arabia fell before the barbarism of the Franks."

It is indeed a most happy sign of the times that not only fair-minded individuals, whose illuminating observations have been quoted, but even a whole nation has at last realised that Europe's extraordinary progress in science and civilisation, which has given her a dominating position all the world over, is to be ascribed to the civilising force of Islam. As a mark of belated justice the Spanish Republic is arranging to establish an Arabic University at Madrid in order to commemorate what Islam achieved for science and civilisation during the Muslim occupation of Spain. It is hoped this will enlighten the world about the fact that the Muslims were the most zealous promoters and protectors of knowledge and culture for full one thousand years, during which other peoples were enshrouded in ignorance, bigotry and barbarism.

Intellectual Achievements of Early Muslims : It is now an undisputed fact that the early Muslims made incomparable contributions to the culture and civilizations of the world. Far from proscribing free thought and enquiry, or placing any ban upon the cultivation of science, as early and medieval Christianity had done, Islam gave it a tremendous impetus by making it a part of religion itself. A Muslim was enjoined to look upon the universe as an expression of God's attributes, and he had to explore it and utilise its objects for the service of mankind as an item of worship of their Creator. It was this religious stimulus to scientific research that particularly impelled the early Muslims to exert themselves so zealously for the advancement of science. A detailed account of their numerous scientific achievements would fill many volumes. The more the world advances in civilization, the more will their inestimable services to humanity be adequately realised and appreciated.

History bears witness to the fact that it was Islam that raised some of the most backward nations to the highest pinnacle of moral and material progress. Wherever the Muslims conquered a country, instead of slaughtering the vanquished, as was done by the Israelites of old, they gave them new life, inspired them with lofty ideals and raised them to a high level of civilization. Thus, indeed, were many savage tribes transformed into civilized people. To whatever land the Arabs migrated, they made it their home; they absorbed the culture of the conquered people and they did their best for the intellectual, moral and material improvement of the land of their adoption. The people to whom the later intellectual development of the Muslims was due were, for the most part, not Arabs but descendants of those who had adopted the faith of the conquerors. Wherever the banner of Islam was carried, remarkable centres of learning sprang up in no time and produced illustrious men in the fields of literature, arts, science and industry. Thus Damascus, Cordova, Granada, Baghdad and Cairo became, in turn, reputed centres of Muslim culture and held aloft the torch of light and learning, art and science in Asia, Europe and Africa, at a time when the West was sunk in ignorance and superstition.

Europe's indebtedness to Islam for her scientific progress is much greater than she cares to admit. She remained barren of all progress as long as she was under the heel of the Church. Even the intellectual development that had taken place among the Greeks and Romans disappeared under the persecutions of the Church. During the centuries of moral and intellectual stagnation in Europe, it was the Muslim who led the vanguard of intellectual progress in the world. There was a time when learning in Europe could be obtained only through the medium of the Arabic tongue. The very Renaissance, that awakened her from her long lethargy, was brought about by the impact of Islamic culture and learning. But for the conquest of Spain by the Muslims, who knows how long she would have remained in that savage condition. All her later achievements in the domain of science, art and learning owe their inspiration wholly and solely to the influences that emanated from Muslim Spain and penetrated the rest of the continent. All knowledge, whether of Astronomy, Mathematics, Physics or Philosophy, of which the Europeans later made themselves masters, was originally derived from the Saracenic schools. Besides, there has been hardly any reform—religious, social or political— from the time of Martin Luther to that of Lenin, which does not bear the stamp of Islamic influence. Draper has very truly said, "In whatever direction we look, we meet in various pursuits of peace and war, of letters and science, Saracenic vestiges."

Dr. Campbell, a reputed British scientist, in his book *Arabian Medicine* writes, "When Europe was lying torpid in the depth of intellectual obscurity and gloom in the dark ages, culture and civilization were spread in the Islamic States under the high patronage of the Caliphs of Baghdad and Cordova, and at a time, when the Barons and Ladies of Medieval Europe could not even sign their names, almost every adolescent boy and girl in Islam could read and write freely and with ease."

In his famous *History of Human Society*, Professor Frank Blackmore of the University of Kansas writes, "In every country that was conquered, the first duty of Islam was to build a mosque in which Allah would be worshipped and his Prophet honoured. Attached to this mosque was a school where people were taught to read and study the Quran. From this initial point they enlarged the study of science, literature and art, and, through the appreciation of these sublime things, they collected the treasures of art and learning wherever these could be found. From imitation they passed on to the great field of creation, and great advances were made to the sum of human knowledge. Schools were founded, great universities established, and libraries were built which laid the permanent foundations of knowledge."

The Muslims made phenomenal progress in Science in a

wonderfully short time. They visualised, thirteen centuries ago, many things which are being discovered today. They explored and exploited the potentialities of objects which had remained unknown and unthought of since the creation of the world. In fact, there was hardly any conceivable subject to which they did not give serious thought. They made most important discoveries in Chemistry, in Astronomy, in Mathematics, in Medicine. They specialised in History and Geography. They unearthed Alchemy and Algebra. They initiated and developed the study of Political Economy and Sociology, which till then had been unknown sciences. They carried out valuable research in Zoology, Geology and Botany. Muslim students, accompanied by artists, travelled far and wide to study various vegetations, which were minutely described by pen and brush. Alherin, a renowned botanist, travelled to and fro in India for forty years collecting materials for his studies. Besides, Muslims investigated and wrote on various other subjects such as navigation, agriculture, irrigation, gardening, statistics, chronology and topography. Even aviation, the latest achievement of Europe and an early wonder of the twentieth century, was not left untried. The first two martyrs among the conquerors of the air were Muslims. In the reign of Khalifa Al-Mamun, a scientist named Abul Qasim invented an aeroplane, but crashed when flying and was killed.

In the eighth century, the Abbaside Khalifas established the famous academy of Baghdad, where the works of the renowned mathematicians Euclid, Archimedes and Appollonius, of the astronomer Ptolemy, and of the naturalists, Hippocrates and Diomedes were translated. In this and other Muslim centres of learning, Greek culture was kept alive at a time when, outside Byzantium, it had no abiding place in the non-Muslim world. Many were the libraries, observatories and laboratories that were established by Muslim kings. In the library attached to Baitul-ul-Hikmat, the abode of learning, a remarkable university founded by Khalifa Harun-al-Rashid, there were many hundred thousand Sanskrit, Greek, Coptic, Chaldean, and Persian books besides those in Arabic. Khalifa Al-Hakim's library was so very extensive that its catalogue had to be prepared in forty large volumes.

Chemistry: Modern Chemistry, as Humboldt rightly says, was "admittedly the invention of the Muslims" whose achievements in this sphere were of unique interest. They conclusively proved the worthlessness of ancient chemistry. They found out the chemical affinities of mercury, lead, copper, silver and gold and knew the chemical processes of oxidation and calcination. A number of words such as alembic, alkali, etc., were derived from Arabic. Jabir bin Hayyana, known as Geber in the western world, wrote some five hundred treatises on chemistry. He discovered, for the first time, nitric acid, sulphuric acid, aqua regia, silver nitrate and several compounds. The Muslims were the first to teach the world distillation, filtration, crystallisation, etc. They knew how to change a liquid into vapour. It was in Muslim Spain that chemistry was first established in Europe, and would have reached its zenith there, had the Muslims not suffered the disastrous defeat at Poitiers. Jildaki was the last great Muslim chemist. He died in 1361 A.D.

Astronomy: The Muslims may be said to have written their names on heaven itself. They identified and classified a large number of stars in their observatories. They made wonderful discoveries concerning the movements of the Solar system and other astral bodies. They ascertained the size of the earth, the variation of the lunar latitudes and the precession of the equinoxes. Averroes (Ibn-i Rushd) discovered the sun-spot: Al-Hazan (Abul Hassan) discovered atmospheric reflection; Al-Maimun determined the obliquity of ecliptic; Ibn-i-Junus, Nasiruddin Tusi and Albani constructed astronomical tables of great value. Albani's tables were translated into Latin and formed the basis of astronomical study in Europe, where that science was introduced by the translation of the works of Muhammad Farghani. Abu Junus and Al-Batan were two of the greatest Muslim astronomers. It was the Muslims who first built observatories in Europe and invented the telescope, and compass, the pendulum and many other useful astronomical instruments. The most famous of the many observatories in the Muslim Empire was that at Marghana near Taurus, built in 1259 A.D.

Mathematics: Almost every branch of higher mathematics bears the impress of Muslim genius. Many were the improvements effected by the Muslims in this important subject. The Arabic numerals, the decimal system and the art of figures, which Europe got from the Muslims, gave a great impetus to learning. By means of these the Muslims led the world in Astronomy, Mechanics and Mathematics. Algebra, Statics, Conic Sections and other branches of applied Mathematics are amongst Muslim discoveries. In Geometry the Muslims were the first of all nations to translate Euclid and use his ideas. His work was not properly translated into any European language till the sixteenth century. The Muslims for the first time applied Algebra to Geometry. They discovered equations of the second degree, and developed the theory of quadratic equations and the binomial theorem. They invented spherical Trigonometry and, by introducing the use of Sine and Cosine, they made great contributions to the science of surveying and astronomy. The Muslims were the first to use instruments of precision for the measurement of time by the use of the pendulum and the measurement of heavenly bodies by the use of the astrolabe.

Medicine: The father of the present-day European medical science was Avicenna (Ibn-i-Sina), whose *Materia Medica* is still in vogue. Aven Zoor (Ibn-i-Zoor) was a great authority on pharmacy, which was an institution of Muslim invention. He and others carefully studied the effect on the body of drugs obtained from various parts of the world, and discovered many remedies. The Muslim doctors were the first to use anesthetics. Al-Bucasis of Cordova was an expert surgeon of world-wide reputation. There were renowned surgeons, opticians, dentists and specialists in female diseases. The science of optics owes much to Muslim research. Al-Hazan, who understood the weight of air, corrected the misconceptions of the Greeks as to the nature of vision and demonstrated, for the first time in history, that the rays of light come from the external object to the eye, and not from the eye itself, impinging on external things. He showed that the retina is the seat of vision, and proved that impressions made upon it were conveyed along the nerves to the brain. He discovered that the refraction of light varied with the density of the atmosphere and *vice versa.* In Baghdad, there were no less than 860 doctors of different classes, each class of whom made one particular branch of medicine their special study. Doctors as well as chemists had to pass an examination in order to obtain a license to practise. There were hospitals throughout the wide Muslim empire. All classes of people, irrespective of their creed, caste, colour and country, were freely admitted to these hospitals.

Geography and History: There are in Arabic many immortal works on Geography. The spherical shape of the globe was demonstrated by the Muslims at a time when the scientists of priest-ridden Europe emphatically asserted that it was flat. The great historical achievements of the Muslims are too well-known to require detailed mention. They produced several thousand books on history, ranging in magnitude from one to eighty volumes.

To sum up, for about one thousand years the Muslims made history; they held aloft the torch of light and learning and spread knowledge and culture throughout the world. But for-the vast intellectual heritage bequeathed by them to the people of the West, it would not have been possible for them to make the immense progress they have now made. The Muslims were in the vanguard of the world's advancement as long as they were true to Islam and faithfully followed the lofty injunctions of the Holy Quran. Their downfall began as they left the path of true Islam. Interestingly, there were orthodox Christians; in the iron grip of Christianity that they could make any appreciable advance in science and civilization. In one case the influence of a peaceful and progressive religion and in the other the effect of the disappearance of religious fervour and the presence of materialistic greed are clearly observable in the history of their respective notable achievements.

The pre-Islamic religions confined their operation to the moral aspect of human nature, and almost altogether ignored its worldly aspect. But Islam, in addition to morality, laid much stress on the practical aspect of man's everyday life. Under the inspiration of Islam, the chief mission of which is the service of humanity, the Muslims attended to such useful subjects as were calculated to contribute to the material welfare of mankind. Realising that man's material progress depends upon his mastery over nature, they devoted themselves to the development of useful sciences such as chemistry, astronomy, medicine, agriculture, irrigation, navigation, etc. Had the idea of man's capabilities to harness the forces of Nature to the service of humanity dawned on the human mind before the Holy Prophet of Islam taught it, the immense potentialites of Nature would have been utilised for the welfare of mankind long before the promulgation of Islam.

Most of the outstanding achievements of the people over

whom religion has little influence and who are guided more by the fear of man than by the fear of God, have been in the domain of arms, ammunition, explosives, poisons—of death and destruction rather than of peace and construction. Had their religion had sufficient influence over them, the followers of Christ, who enjoin the turning of one cheek if the other is smitten, would have never been so very eager for the invention of all sorts of death-dealing instruments.

After the enjoyment of power, wealth and supremacy for about a thousand years, the Muslims became enervated and luxury-loving, and a sort of blight overtook them. Spiritual stagnation and intellectual sterility soon followed as a natural consequence. This has more or less been the case with all other religious communities. The Muslims themselves, and not Islam, are entirely to blame for this regrettable check on their progress. A glance at the condition of the world before and after the promulgation of Islam would convince one of what it is capable of accomplishing. The decadence of the Muslims must not, therefore, be thought to stem from their religion. It would be a great injustice to Islam to judge it by the life led by its present-day followers. True Islam, which is life and light, is very different from what goes by its name today—a bundle of dead rites and meaningless rituals.

It is, however, gratifying to note that Muslims are at last realising that they have strayed from the essentials of their noble religion and are now engaged in controversies over mere trifles. I believe true Islam will again assert itself. Signs of Islamic renaissance are already visible all over the Muslim world. Movements pregnant with great potentialities are afoot in Turkey, Persia, Arabia, Egypt, and Afghanistan. It is hoped that, before long, Muslims will shake off the languor and lethargy that have come upon them, and will be able to take their rightful place in the progressive movements of the world.

Islam, which means peace and submission to the will of God, is not a new religion promulgated by the Prophet Muhammad, but the oldest religion based on the unity of God, proclaimed by Ibrahim, Moses, Jesus and all other Messengers whom the Lord was pleased to send at different times and in different climes for the reclamation of degraded and debased humanity. Islam simply claims to have purged that religion of adulteration and impurities which had crept into it in the course of time. It would, therefore, be a misnomer to call it Muhammadanism. A Muslim has to believe in all the Scriptures that were revealed from time to time, and he has to respect and revere all the Prophets who preceded his own. Universalism is thus the most distinctive feature of Islam, which is intended, not like other religions for a particular time or a particular country or a particular nation, but for all time, for all countries and for all peoples.

Some of the master minds of Europe and America, like the great poet Goethe, the great historian Gibbon, the great philosopher Carlyle, the great orator Ingersoll, the great socialist George Bernard Shaw, who is perhaps the greatest intellect of the present age, among others, were most profoundly impressed by the message of Islam, and all of them lauded the greatness of its Prophet. Although an atheist himself, and hardly any dogma of any religion has passed unscathed by his trenchant pen, Bernard Shaw thinks Islam is the only religion that can satisfy all intelligent people who want a religion to guide them spiritually, morally and socially. The strongest argument advanced by him to prove the universal acceptability of Islam is that it has the great power of absorbing every form of progress made by philosophy and science.

That Bernard Shaw is not beside the mark in his forecast regarding Islam's future may be judged by what Islam, which is now in its fifteenth century, has done. Its comparison with other religions in their fifteenth century may give an idea of what it is likely to be in its twenty first century. It is, in the opinion of unbiased judges, the only power that can effectively withstand the atheism, scepticism and materialism that are gradually getting a hold over the new world order.

Faith, as a Force

Religion is generally understood to mean the recognition of the existence of a supernatural ruling power, the creator and controller of the universe, who has given to man a spiritual nature which continues to exist after the death of the body, and of man's duty to be obedient to this power. As a concept of life, it is all-encompassing. Science, on the other hand, is the study of the perceptible world. Both are extremely broad-ranging subjects, and their respective spheres are in many aspects quite separate from each other. It is not intended here to go into the details of these two subjects, but to deal only with the clash — real, or unreal — which has taken place between science and religion on an academic level, and certain of its consequences. One of the reasons for this clash is the claim that scientific discoveries have proved religion baseless, and it is principally this point on which attention has been focused here.

The traditional conflict between science and religion made itself felt in the eighteenth and nineteenth centuries. It was during this period that, in the light of new scientific discoveries, many came to feel that there was no further call to believe in God. One of the most compelling reasons for believing in God, amongst others, was that without this belief, the universe was inexplicable. The antagonists of religion were quick to point out that we no longer required the 'God' hypothesis when there was no aspect of the universe which could not be explained quite easily by the findings of scientific research. To them, the idea of God was redundant and, therefore, baseless.

This claim was quite flimsy from the academic or logical point of view even at the time it was made, and now science itself has admitted, directly or indirectly, that it had no satisfactory ground for making such a claim.

Of what nature was this discovery of science which attempted to convince people that there was no further need for the concept of God? It was no more than the discovery that the universe is bound by certain laws. In ancient times, man had simply believed that all happenings in the world were directly attributable to God. But modern findings revealed that behind every event there was a cause which was discoverable by observation. For instance, Newton observed that all the stars and planets in the vastness of space are bound by certain immutable laws and move in strict accordance with those laws. Darwin's research showed that man had not come into existence through an act of special creation but had evolved, inconsonance with general material laws, from the lower species and had gradually developed into *homo sapiens*, i.e. man as we now know him. Similar observational studies showed that all events seemed to occur as part of a known system called the 'Law of Nature.' Significantly, this law of nature functioned with such effective regularity that it was considered entirely predictable.

These discoveries were taken to mean that the universe, which we had regarded as God's domain, was actually subservient to a set of material and physical laws. When these laws were applied, they yielded consistent results, and this further convinced members of the educated elite that they were right in embracing atheism. The German philosopher, Kant, declared: 'Give me matter and I shall demonstrate how the world is made out of matter.' Haeckel even went so far as to say that, given water, chemical elements and time, he would be able to create a man. Nietsche proclaimed with triumphant finality, 'God is dead.' Another belief had it that the creator and sustainer of this universe was not an alive, intelligent being possessing power; that the universe, from beginning to end, was material. All movements and all manifestations of the universe, whether related to life or to lifeless matter were nothing but blind material processes. The world discovered by science evinced no signs whatsoever of the hand of God — which is surely the basis of all religions. Then how could it be considered rational to believe in God?

All the heroes who had discovered the laws of nature were believers in God, but, ironically, when their research was brought before the public, it was thought that their discoveries had rendered meaningless the very existence of God. Since, in order to explain events, one had only to have recourse to the causes and laws of the material universe, there seemed to be no need to postulate the existence of a God who was extraneous to that universe. It was said, for example, that the rising and setting of the sun had not been properly understood until telescopes had been made and mathematics developed. The former ascription of these phenomena to the will and power of supernatural beings had been due merely to man's poor comprehension of these matters. And now that astronomy had proved that there was a universal system of gravitation which controlled the movements of the sun, moon and stars, there was no further need to believe in God. Gradually, all those happenings in nature, which were supposed in ancient times to have invisible superhuman forces at work behind them, were shown to be the results of the action and reaction of the forces of nature. It was as if, after the natural causes of events had been described in modern scientific terms, belief in God should automatically cease. Julian Huxley, in his book, *Man in the Modern World,* says:

> If the rainbow is generated by the refraction of the sun's rays on falling rain, it is not set in the sky as a sign by God. If the plague is inevitably generated by the Bacillus pestis and spread by rat-fleas, an outbreak of plague can no longer be looked on as sign of divine wrath. If animals and plants have slowly evolved through hundreds of millions of years, there is no room for a creator of animals and plants, except in a metaphorical sense totally different from that in which the word was originally and is normally used. If hysteria and insanity are the natural results of disordered minds, there is no place remaining in them for possession by devils.
>
> After presenting this piece of 'reasoning' with great conviction, he says that the ascription of such events 'to supernatural beings is merely due to man's ignorance combined with his passion for some sort of explanation.' He then sums up with: 'If events are due to natural causes, they are not due to supernatural causes' (pp. 18-19).

There is a serious weakness inherent in such arguments of the anti-religionists, which can be best understood through illustrations. Think of the railway engine speeding along the track. How do its wheels revolve? If we attempt to answer this question by studying the different parts of the engine and their movements, we shall arrive at the conclusion that the movement of the wheels is an extension of the functioning of the locomotive's mechanism. But would we be justified in believing that the reason for their movement is the engine and its various parts? Obviously, we would not. We should first have to consider the respective roles of the engineer who designed the engine and the engine driver who set it in motion. Without their instrumentality, the engine could neither exist, nor move. The engine and its parts are not then the final reality. The final reality is the mind which has brought the engine into existence, and runs it at will. A Christian scholar, Cecil Boyce Hamann, has aptly said: "Nature does not explain, she is herself in need of explanation." This is because, as he puts it, nature is a fact, not an explanation.

Let us consider, for example, how a chick comes into this world. In embryo, it develops inside the smooth, hard shell of an egg, then it emerges when the shell breaks up. How does it come about that the shell breaks up at the right moment and the fledgling, which is no more than a small lump of flesh, finds its way into the outer world? In the past, the obvious answer was: "It is the hand of God." But now, microscopic studies have shown that on the completion of twenty-one days, when the chick is ready to emerge, there appears on its beak a small, hard horn with which this 'lump of flesh' is able to break through the walls of its cell. The horn, having done its job, falls off a few days later. This observation, from the point of view of the anti-religionists, contradicts the old concept that it is God who brings the chick out of the shell, because the microscope has clearly shown that a 21-day law exists which is responsible for creating conditions which make it possible for the chick to emerge from the shell. This is a mere fallacy. What modern observation has done is to add a few more links to the chain of factors which lead up to an event. It does not tell us the real cause of the occurrence. It has just shifted the problem of the breaking up of the shell to the development of the horn. The breaking of the shell by the chick is simply an intermediate stage in the occurrence rather than its cause. Will the cause of the event be understood only when we learn what made the horn appear on the chick's beak? In other words, when we have traced the event back to its primary cause, the cause which 'knew' that the chick required some hard instrument to break through the shell and, therefore, in exactly twenty-one days, compelled a hard substance to appear on the beak in the form of a horn and to fall off after having discharged its function?

'How does the shell break?' was the question that faced man previously. Now, in the light of recent observations, instead of an answer, we have another question: 'How does the horn develop?' In the context of perceived phenomena, there is no difference in the nature of these two questions. At the most, questions of the type that lead us from one link to another in the chain of cause and effect demand an extension of the observation of facts, if they are to be answered at all. On this basis, they do not elicit any valid explanation.

The discoveries held by the atheists to be an explanation of nature and, as such, an alternative to God, can just as easily be thought of as being the way nature works. We can, quite rationally, say that God implements his will through these laws, only parts of which man, with his limited skills, has been able to discover. Let us suppose that religious-minded people, who believe that it is God who causes the ebb and flow of the tides, are confronted with the scientific explanation that the tides are actually caused by the gravitational pull of the moon and vary according to the geographical configuration of the seas and land surfaces. There would be no need for them to deny this explanation in order to uphold their belief in God's instrumentality. They could accept it without causing the slightest harm to their religious beliefs. It is true that tides do occur in consonance with geographical configuration and as a result of gravitational pull. But, after all, what are these things? They too are God's creations. It is through these phenomena that God acts. As John Wilson observed: This does not destroy my belief. It is still God (working through these things') who is responsible for the tides.'

Similarly, in the field of biology, the theory of evolution implies that biological processes no longer demand the existence of metaphysical realities. In other words, in order to understand the nature of life, we do not need to believe in a conscious God, modern studies having 'proved' that life automatically patterns itself along certain material lines: reproduction, variation and selective survival. That is, through reproduction, living creatures continue to be born, certain congenital variations go on developing, then after a long and complicated process of mutation, an altogether new species comes into being. Thus, according to the antagonists of religion, the application of Darwin's principle of natural selection in biology has made it not only possible but imperative to reject outright the concept of God's hand in life's development.

The supposition that the various species of living creatures have come into being through a gradual process of evolution has yet to be established as a fact, but even were we to give credence to this theory, it could still be said with equal conviction, that this is God's chosen way of creation, rather than its being the result of a blind, automatic force. Mechanical evolution can easily be proved to be a creational evolution. This being so, those anti-religionists who refer to science for support have no genuine basis on which to reject this argument of creational evolution.

This is far from being all that there is to the matter. The truth is that twentieth century science has lost its ability to convince. Today, Newton has been replaced by Einstein, and the theories of Planck and Heisenberg have overthrown those of Laplace. Now the anti-religionists, at least on an academic level, can no longer claim that science has arrived at the ultimate truth. Indeed, the theory of relativity and the quantum theory have led scientists to the conclusion that it is impossible in science to separate the observer from the observed. This means that we can see only certain external manifestations of reality; we cannot apprehend it in its essence. The revolution that has occurred in science in the twentieth century has itself proved the importance of religion from the scientific point of view.

In his book, *The Limitations of Science,* J.N. Sullivan states the case thus:

> What is called the modern "revolution" in science consists of the fact that the Newtonian outlook, which dominated the scientific world for nearly two hundred years, has been found insufficient. It is in process of being replaced by a different outlook, and, although the reconstruction is by no means complete, it is already apparent that the philosophical implications of the new outlook are very different from those of the old one. We are no longer taught that the scientific method of approach is the only valid method of acquiring knowledge about reality. Eminent men of science are insisting, with what seems a strange enthusiasm, on the fact that science gives us but a partial knowledge of reality.

This change in the scientific outlook seems to have taken place suddenly. It is not yet sixty years since Tyn-dall, in his

Belfahst Address, claimed that science alone was competent to deal with all man's major problems. But, in truth, so far as these remarks sprang from the conviction that the sole reality is 'matter and motion,' their foundations had already been undermined. The attempt to represent nature in terms of matter and motion was already breaking down. That attempt was at its most triumphant by the end of the eighteenth century, when Laplace was emboldened to affirm that a sufficiently great mathematician, given the distribution of the particles in the primitive nebula, could predict the whole future history of the world. The fundamental concepts isolated by Newton had proved themselves so adequate in the applications that had been made of them that they were regarded as the key to everything.

The first indication that the Newtonian concepts were not all-sufficient came when men tried to fashion a mechanical theory of light. This endeavour led to the creation of the ether, the most unsatisfactory and wasteful product of human ingenuity that science has to show. For generations this monster was elaborated. Miracles of mathematical ingenuity were performed in the attempt to account for the properties of light in terms of the Newtonian concepts. The difficulties became ever more heartbreaking until, after the publication of Maxwell's demonstration that light is an electromagnetic phenomenon, they seemed to become insuperable. For it had dawned on men of science that there was, after all, nothing sacrosanct about the Newtonian entities. After a certain amount of hesitation, and a few last desperate efforts to make electricity mechanical, electricity was added to the list of irreducible elements.

This may seem to have been a simple step to take, but it was, in reality, of profound significance. For the Newtonian concepts were all of a kind that one seemed to understand intimately. Thus the mass of a body was the quantity of matter in it. Force was a notion derived from our experience of muscular effort. Nevertheless, we supposed that we knew the nature of what we were talking about. But in the case of electricity its nature is precisely what we did not know. Attempts to represent it in familiar terms — as a condition of strain in the ether, or what not — had been given up. All that we knew about electricity was the way it affected our measuring instruments. The precise description of this behaviour gave us the mathematical specification of electricity and this, in truth, was all we knew about it. It is only now, in retrospect, that we can see how very significant a step this was. An entity had been admitted into physics of which we knew nothing but its mathematical structure.

Since then other entities have been admitted on the same terms, and it is found that they play precisely the same role in the formation of scientific theories as do the old entities. It has become evident that, so far as the science of physics is concerned, we do not require to know the nature of the entities we discuss, but only their mathematical structure. And, in truth, that is all we do know. It is now realized that this is all the scientific knowledge we have even of the familiar Newtonian entities. Our persuasion that we knew them in some exceptionally intimate manner was an illusion.

With this realization it is no long step to Eddington's position that a knowledge of mathematical structure is the only knowledge that the science of physics can give us. Leaving out all aesthetic, ethical, or spiritual aspects of our environment, we are faced with qualities such as massiveness, substantiality, extension, duration, which are supposed to belong to the domain of physics. In a sense they do belong; but physics is not in a position to handle them directly. The essence of their nature is inscrutable; we may use mental pictures to aid calculations, but no image in the mind can be a replica of that which is not in the mind. And so in its actual procedure physics studies not these inscrutable qualities, but pointer-readings which we can observe. The readings, it is true, reflect the fluctuations of the world-qualities; but our exact knowledge is of the readings, not of the qualities. The former have as much resemblance to the latter as a telephone number has to a subscriber:

> The fact that science is confined to a knowledge of structure is obviously of great "humanistic" importance. For it means that the problem of the nature of reality is not prejudged. We are no longer required to believe that our response to beauty, or the mystic's sense of communion with God, have no objective counterpart. It is perfectly possible that they are, what they have so often been taken to be, clues to the nature of reality.

> Thus, our various experiences are put on a more equal footing, as it were. Our religious aspirations, our perceptions of beauty, may not be the essentially illusory phenomena they were supposed to be. In this new scientific universe even mystics have a right to exist. (pp. 138-42).

Such explanations from scientific philosophers now abound. Morton White in his book *The Age of Analysis,* points out that 'the philosophically-minded scientists of the 20th century have started a new crusade, the names of Whitehead, Eddington and James Jeans are the most prominent among them.' He then bears out this notion of a 'crusade' with highly pertinent quotations from each of them:

> 'Nature is alive' (p. 84). Such was the interpretation of modern information by the English mathematician and philosopher, A.N. Whitehead (1861-1947).
>
> The stuff of the world is mind stuff (p. 134). So said the English astronomer, Sir Arthur Eddington (1882-1944), deriving this conclusion from his studies in science.
>
> The English mathematical physicist, Sir James Jeans (1877-1946), interprets modern research thus: The universe is a universe of thought' (p. 134).
>
> The views of the most perceptive scientists, can be summed up in J.W.N. Sullivan's words: 'The ultimate nature of the universe is mental' (p. 145).

The thoughts of these scholars clearly negate any material interpretation of the universe, their special virtue being that they have been advanced in the context of modern findings in the field of physics and mathematics. That the proponents of such ideas have had to make courageous, herculean efforts to overcome the materialistic outlook is aptly expressed by Morton White with reference to Whitehead: 'He is a heroic thinker who tries to beard the lions of Intellectualism, Materialism and Positivism in their own bristling den' (p. 84). Morton White may have said this only about Whitehead, but this applies to all the scientists mentioned above.

This philosophical question as to the final reality being mind or matter is actually concerned with the question of whether the universe has developed independently and spontaneously through some material process, or whether there is a non-material being who has created it at will. If we accepted the former proposition, it would be just like saying that, in the last analysis, a machine is simply a fortuitous compound of iron and petrol. That is to say, that the machine started off as iron and petrol, but owing to some blind, automatic process, it took on the form of a machine. All a pure accident! A machine, as we all know, is the product of an engineer's mind. That mind, quite distinct from the matter, existed before the machine. It conceived it, designed it, and brought it into being. The machine's existence was clearly consequent upon the exercise of mind and will.

In determining the nature of the mind, differences can be found among those who believe the mind to be the final reality, just as believers in God have diverse concepts of God. Even so, the conclusion arrived at by academic study that the final underlying reality of the universe is mind, testifies by its very nature to the truth of religion and amounts to a rejection of atheism. The truly significant change in modern science is not to be found in its increased powers to aid man's religion and science progress, but in the change in its metaphysical foundations.'

The best exposition of this viewpoint is to be found in *The Mysterious Universe,* by Sir James Jeans. By pure scientific argument, the writer has come to the conclusion that in the light of modern physics, 'The universe cannot admit of material representation, and the reason, I think, is that it has become a mere mental concept.'

> He later goes on to say that "if the universe is a universe of thought, then its creation must have been an act of thought" (pp. 133-34).

He holds that the modern concept which interprets matter in terms of waves of electrons is quite unconceivable to human thought, because these 'waves' could be only the 'waves of probabilities' without having any material existence. Such reasons have compelled Jeans to conclude that the substance of the universe is thought, not matter. Now where is this thought situated? His answer is that It exists in the mind of a great 'mathematical thinker? Because the structure of this thought that comes to our mind is a completely mathematical structure. The 'great Architect of the Universe thus begins to appear as a pure mathematician,'

Sir James Jeans then states the entire case with great precision: It seems at least safe to say that the river of knowledge has made a sharp bend in the last few years. Thirty years ago, we thought, or assumed, that we were heading towards an ultimate reality of a mechanical kind. It seemed to consist of fortuitous jumble of atoms, which was destined to perform meaningless dances for a time under the action of blind purposeless forces, and then fall back to form a dead world. Into this wholly mechanical world, through the play of the same blind forces, life had stumbled by accident. One tiny corner at least, and possibly several tiny corners of this universe of atoms had chanced to become conscious for a time, but was destined in the end, still under the action of blind mechanical forces, to be frozen out and again leave a lifeless world.

Today there is a wide measure of agreement, which on the physical side of science approaches almost to unanimity, that the stream of knowledge is heading towards a non-mechanical reality; the universe begins to look more like a great thought than like a great machine. Mind no longer appears as an accidental intruder into the realm of matter; we are beginning to suspect that we ought rather to hail it as the creator and governor of the realm of matter — not of course our individual minds, but the mind in which the atoms out of which our individual minds have grown exist as thoughts.

The new knowledge compels us to revise our hasty first impressions that we had stumbled into a universe which either did not concern itself with life or was actively hostile to life. The old dualism of mind and matter, which was mainly responsible for the supposed hostility, seems likely to disappear, not through matter becoming in any way more shadowy or insubstantial than heretofore, or through mind becoming resolved into a function of the working of matter, but through substantial matter resolving itself into a creation and manifestation of mind. We discover that the universe shows evidence of a designing or controlling power that has something in common with our own individual minds — not, so far as we have discovered, emotion, morality, or aesthetic appreciation, but the tendency to think in the way, which, for want of a better word, we describe as mathematical.

In spite of this complete about-face in science from the academic point of view, it is a fact that, in practice, there have been no noticeable changes in the attitudes of anti-religionists. On the contrary, they are engaged in seeking new arguments to support their theory. The reason for this is not to be found within any academic framework. No, the reason is to be traced, alas! to a biased mentality. How often have we seen educated people refuse to accept the truth when ample proofs have been offered to them, simply because of deeply-rooted preconceived ideas. It was just such a prejudiced attitude, in the seventeenth century, which had prevented Italian scholars from accepting Galileo's theory as an alternative to Aristotle's, although a ball thrown from the Leaning Tower had demonstrated quite conclusively that Galileo was right. Again, it was this bias which caused scholars at the end of the nineteenth century to ridicule Berlin Professor Max Planck when he gave a physical explanation of light,— the quantum theory, — which proved the Newtonian concept wrong. Planck's theory was not accepted for many years, but today it is considered one of the most important principles in physics.

There is a common belief that it is only laymen who are guilty of prejudice and not scientists; we should do well, therefore, to mark the words of A.V. Hills, himself a scientist: 'I should be the last to claim that we, scientific men, are less liable to prejudice than other educated men.

Sir James Jeans underscores this when he says, 'Our modern minds have, I think, a bias towards mechanical interpretation.'

Now, in a world where prejudice holds sway, how can we hope that a concept will be accepted only because it has been proved academically? The often-repeated experiences of history show that man has all along been governed by his emotions rather than by his intellect, in spite of the fact that academically and logically, reason occupies the higher position. More often than not, reason has played into the hands of emotion. It has seldom happened that it has gained a positive control over the emotions. Indeed, the intellect has always coined arguments to support the emotional and thus tried to prove that emotional attitudes were rational. Man finds it a psychological necessity to cling to his emotional being, even at the cost of remaining blind to reality. We must remember, therefore, that we are not dealing with machines, which ought to respond to the mere flicking of a switch. What we have to address ourselves to is man, and man accepts something only when he himself is willing to do so. If he is not, no argument, however sound it may be, will convince him. Arguments are not, sad to say, electric switches. That man, with all his capacity for reasoning, should so seldom, himself, be amenable to reasoning, is perhaps the greatest tragedy of human history.

Where Science Failed? : Modern scholars have come to the conclusion that we may have succeeded in making great discoveries about inanimate matter, but that we cannot be certain of having been successful in discovering the facts of man's nature and existence, for there exists a strange disparity between the sciences of inanimate matter and those of life. The sciences which concern themselves with the inanimate part of our world differ from the biological sciences in that the former are subject to definite laws whereas the latter are, to quote Dr. Alexis Carrel, inextricably lost 'in the midst of a magic forest whose countless trees unceasingly change their place and shape.' Unlike material phenomena, biological phenomena cannot be defined in terms of algebraic equations. The sciences of the material world are confined to description, a lower form of science altogether, because they do not unveil the ultimate nature of things, but only convey certain qualities such as weight and spatial dimensions. They do give us the power to predict future events, and often to determine at will their occurrence; in learning the secret of the constitution and properties of matter, we have gained the mastery of almost everything which exists on the surface of the earth — excepting ourselves. The science of living beings in general, and of the human individual in particular, has not made such spectacular progress. It still remains at the descriptive stage, while the elucidation of the real nature of living beings requires much more than mere description.

The Nobel prize winner, Dr. Alexis Carrel, who achieved unique fame in biological research at the Rockfeller Institute in New York, elaborates at some length in his book, *Man, the Unknown,* on what is meant by man:

> Man is an indivisible whole of extreme complexity. No simple representation of him can be obtained. There is no method capable of apprehending him simultaneously in his entirety, his parts, and his relations with the outer world. In order to analyze ourselves we are obliged to seek the help of various techniques and, therefore, to utilize several sciences. Naturally, all these sciences arrive at a different conception of their common object. They abstract only from man what is attainable by their special methods. And those abstractions, after they have been added together, are still less rich than the concrete fact. They leave behind them a residue too important to be neglected. Anatomy, chemistry, physiology, psychology, pedagogy, history, sociology, political economy do not exhaust their subject. Man, as known to the specialists, is far from being the concrete man, the real man. He is nothing but a schema, consisting of other schemata built up by the techniques of each science.

He is, at the same time, the corpse dissected by the anatomists, the consciousness observed by the psychologists and the great teachers of the spiritual life, and the personality which introspection shows to everyone as lying in the depth of himself. He is the chemical substance constituting the tissues and humours of the body. He is the amazing community of cells and nutrient fluids whose organic laws are studied by the physiologists. He is the compound of tissues and consciousness that hygienists and educators endeavour to lead to its optimum development while it extends into time. He is the homoaconomicus who must ceaselessly consume manufactured products in order that the machines, of which he is made a slave, may be kept at work. But he is also the poet, the hero, and the saint. He is not only the prodigiously complex being analyzed by our scientific techniques, but also the tendencies, the conjectures, the aspirations of humanity. Our conceptions of him are imbued with metaphysics. They are founded on so many and such imprecise data that the temptation is great to choose among them those which please us. Therefore, our idea of man varies according to our feelings and our beliefs. A materialist and a spiritualist accept the same definition of a crystal of sodium chloride; but they do not agree with one another upon that of the human being. A mechanistic physiologist and a vitalistic physiologist do not consider the organism in the same light. The living being of Jacques Loeb differs profoundly from that of Hans Driesch. Indeed, mankind has made a gigantic effort to know itself. Although we possess the treasure of the observations accumulated by the scientists, the philosophers, the poets, and the great mystics of all times, we have grasped only certain aspects of ourselves. We do not apprehend man as a whole. We know him as composed of distinct parts. And even these parts are created by our methods. Each one of us is made up of a procession of phantoms, in the midst of which strides an unknowable reality.

In fact, our ignorance is profound. Most of the questions put to themselves by those who study human beings remain without answer. Immense regions of our inner world are still unknown. How do the molecules of chemical substance associate in order to form the complex and temporary organs of the cell? How do the genes contained in the nucleus of a fertilized ovum determine the characteristics of the individual deriving from that ovum? How do cells organise themselves by their own efforts into societies, such as the tissues and the organs? Like the ants and the bees, they have advance knowledge of the part they are destined to play in the life of the community. And hidden mechanisms enable them to build up an organism both complex and simple. What is the nature of our duration, of psychological time, and of physiological time? We know that we are a compound of tissues, organs, fluids, and consciousness. But the relations between consciousness and cerebrum are still a mystery. We lack almost entirely a knowledge of the physiology of nervous cells. To what extent does will power modify the organism? How is the mind influenced by the state of the organs? In what manner can the organic and mental characteristics, which each individual inherits, be changed by the mode of life, the chemical substances contained in food, the climate, and the physiological and moral disciplines?

We are very far from knowing what relations exist between skeleton, muscles, and organs, and mental and spiritual activities. We are ignorant of the factors that bring about nervous equilibrium and resistance to fatigue and to diseases. We do not know how moral sense, judgement, and audacity could be augmented. What is the relative importance of intellectual, moral, and mystical activities? What is the significance of aesthetic and religious sense? What form of energy is responsible for telepathic communications? Without any doubt, certain physiological and mental factors determine happiness or misery, success or failure. But we do not know what they are. We cannot artificially give to any individual the aptitude for happiness. As yet we do not know what environment is the most favourable for the optimum development of civilized man. Is it possible to suppress struggle, effort, and suffering from our physiological and spiritual formation? How can we prevent the degeneration of man in modern civilization? Many other questions could be asked on subjects which are to us of the utmost interest. They would also remain unanswered. It is quite evident that the accomplishments of all the sciences having man as an object remain insufficient, and that our knowledge of ourselves is still most rudimentary.

This passage more than adequately demonstrates that we still have not formulated a true science of man. About the material part of human existence we are fairly well informed, but we are completely ignorant of who or what controls it. Life is still a mystery to us, and until it is unveiled, there can be no proper apprehension of what, in essence, it is. Alexis Carrel's book, *Man, the Unknown,* is an attempt to make scientific approach to its discovery.

Today man can split an atom; he can make icy lands habitable; he has walked on the moon and sent probes into outer space. Such instances of advanced technological progress give the impression that if man can learn so much about his material environment that he is able to exploit it at will, he should certainly be able to discover himself and, in the process, set right whatever ails him. But there are strong indications in our known world that man can never be understood in the same way that matter can.

Let us look at this entity, called man, on a purely physiological basis. He is composed of millions and millions of cells of protoplasm.

And what is protoplasm? We can say with certainty that it is a viscous, translucent, homogeneous, structureless substance endowed with contractility and a chemical composition allied to that of albumen: it is the physical basis of life and, clearly, we know a great deal about it as such. Yet we have to concede that we do not know why it should have this unique property of life, or how this came to be so. Moreover, it is a fact that the methods we employ to study the material world cannot be applied to protoplasm in any way which should elicit an answer to these awesome questions. All that is visible to us is a compound of certain things.

If we had the means and the resources, we should be able not only to destroy but also to create such compounds. Indeed, science has discovered the elements of which protoplasm is composed and the particular proportion of those elements have also been learnt. But it is in vain that we join together the two distinct forms of protoplasm, the nucleus and the cytoplasm, albeit in the correct proportions, for no protoplasm is thus formed which has the property of life. While other chemical compounds can be formed by combining their elements in the correct proportions, (e.g. one molecule of water is made up of one atom of oxygen and two atoms of hydrogen) the life-giving matter which is the main constituent of a human being's body can in no way be brought into existence by human agency. Our powers of creation extend only to inanimate matter, never to living entities.

This is the area in which we are the most helpless, and we have no option but to admit it. The greatest irony is that although all our physiological studies are concerned with the living man, the results they yield bear more relevance to this cadaver. Science has discovered both the elements which constitute protoplasm and their correct proportions, yet the particular order or arrangement which is responsible for the life-property of protoplasm has still to be revealed. The moment this arrangement disintegrates, the protoplasm is rendered lifeless. It is as if a particular arrangement was responsible for the existence of soul in the protoplasm. But the difficulty that confronts us is that so long as we keep this arrangement intact, the protoplasm cannot be chemically analysed. The moment we break it, life vanishes. Whenever protoplasm is subjected to chemical analysis, the soul has already left it. And this will always be the case. Science will always remain in the dark regarding the reality of life. But this is not the end of our problem. It goes much deeper than this.

Let us suppose someone sets out to unveil reality, thus disclosing to man the law of life, and, to this end, he begins the study of human settlements. After prolonged examination of different societies, he comes to the conclusion that, since society is composed of human beings, he had best concern himself with the individual, the better to understand the group. So he reduces his focus accordingly. His first preoccupation then is with psychology. But he soon realizes that no single philosophy emerges, because there are several schools of thought on the subject, all arriving at different conclusions. One school claims that the senses are central to all human actions while others say that all man's responses are reactions to impressions received consciously or unconsciously from the external world. Yet others say that it is sexual desires which provide the stimulus for all of man's actions. A different type of study shows that an unrecognized urge to realize a certain set of ideals keeps man active. Some schools of thought take consciousness to be a reality and explain the whole of man's being in relation to this; others hold that the mind and intellect, have no existence, and that there is no central power commanding the various parts of the body. Rather the parts which receive most attention are better developed and that is what makes it possible, for example, for one man to be highly skilled in dancing, another in archery and yet another in profound reflection. These differences in thinking in the field of psychology go to such extremes that one might be led to wonder if there was any such unified science as psychology.

On seeing this jungle of ideas, our inquirer thinks of studying another aspect of human existence — biology — in order to come to more cogent conclusions. But in this discipline he finds that man is treated as an amalgam of the metabolism, the respiratory system, the blood circulation, and so on. These systems are based on certain chemical changes and, judging from their action and reaction, it would appear that the different parts of the whole bodily system are sub-functions of the metabolism.

After deep reflection, he comes to the conclusion that since the existence of the human body and its development are related to chemical actions and reactions, the principles according to which chemical changes take place should first of all be properly understood, failing which no really satisfactory information about man could ever be discovered. So he engrosses himself in the study of physics and chemistry and, indeed, devotes the major part of his life to it. This branch of study leads him on to an investigation of the molecule and the atom, from which he proceeds to study the electrons and protons of which the atom is composed. The realization then comes to him that the whole universe is nothing but electric waves, and he becomes immersed in the study of the latest discoveries in nuclear science. He thus collects a huge mass of facts, but at the end of it all, he fails to arrive at any firm conclusions about the reality of man. He has become lost in a world which, in spite of being visible, has remained impenetrable. According to Dr. C.E.M. Joad, matter is something unreal which cannot be grasped. It is a part of the four dimensional space-time continuum, a network of electric waves, or a wave of probability which perished on being looked at; and it has even been considered an extension of the observer's consciousness instead of something solid and tangible.

This pathetic end to the quest for the secret of life in the material sciences shows that the secret of life is not discoverable by man. Now just as a sick man cannot treat his disease himself and is forced to consult a doctor, so a man who is in need of spiritual sustenance cannot provide this for himself without turning to God. The fact that he cannot discover the secret either of life or of his own nature is a sure indicator that he is in need of the God who created him in the form in which he exists. Just as God has created man in such a way that he needs oxygen and then has given him oxygen in abundance, He has made him yearn to know the secret of life and then sent His messengers to him so that all veils should fall from reality. And so the world went on.

6

Islam in New Age

Fundamental Faith

We have already exposed one aspect of the modernistic school of thought that they have made Western way of thinking and living a criterion of right and wrong. In this chapter, we are making some further submissions about the way of thinking and the method of argumentation of the modernists which are of fundamental importance to the subject under discussion. We intend to point out the reasons why all the efforts of our modern researchers have led them to the path of distortion in the name of "research".

Even a man with ordinary common sense knows that "Research" means "Search for Reality" and a researcher holds the position of a judge. It is his obligation that without forming any preconceived ideas and pre-drawn conclusions he should examine all the relevant matters thoroughly and impartially, consider all possible aspects of the problem with utmost honesty and add the weight of his judgement to the weightiest side of argument. On the contrary, if any one seeks and searches the arguments to support a preconceived idea or judgement he is certainly not the seeker of truth, nor his efforts in this direction deserve to be called a research work.

The duty of a researcher is not to collect arguments for a predetermined idea but to determine an idea in the light of arguments. He does not drag the arguments towards his judgement but the arguments drive him towards a judgement. But the process of working of our modernists is quite opposite. They believe that arguments are to serve a decision rather than the decision being dependent on arguments. This is what they think is the correct method of research and this what they teach as a methodology of research. They commonly make suggestions in their oral and written statements that:

> "We want to interpret the Quran and the Sunnah in a manner that it conforms to the needs of our time".

It is a clear admission to the fact that they want to bring the Quran and Sunnah to reconcile with their decisions and not make their decisions to correspond with the Quran and the Sunnah. That is they will first decide as to what are the needs of time and then in trying to find these arguments they will make such interpretations of the Quranic verses and prophetic traditions as to conform to their predetermined needs of the Time. This is what is termed as the "distortion of meaning". This way of argumentation can never be supported by any sensible person of the world. If the process of research is allowed to move in reverse direction then there will be no way left to protect the integrity of the truth. Because in this way every illogical claim can be supported by argument. Nothing in the world would then be devoid of argument, and as they say: "Everything can be proved by everything". Once it is decided that certain thing is to be proved through the Quran and Sunnah, and for this purpose you have decided to give new interpretation to the Quran and Sunnah, it would obviously mean that anything found supporting this idea would be presented as an argument no matter how weak and baseless it be and even the strongest argument against it would be thrown away being incompatible with present day life.

You probably know that the Christian missionaries, while preaching their religion in the Muslim world, always prove their beliefs through the Quran and traditions before common Muslims. For example, they say that the Quran has called Jesus as "Kalimatullah" (The word of Allah) which implies that he was Allah's attribute of "Kalam" (Speech) and the Bible of John also says the same. Also, the Quran said that Jesus was "Ruhullah" (The spirit of God) which implies that his relation with God was the same as that of Soul with body, and the same is said by Paul. They further say that the Quran said: "We supported Jesus with the holy spirit" and the same has been mentioned in the Bible that the holy Ghost was sent to Jesus in the form of a pigeon.

In this way they prove their concept of Trinity, and the tragedy is that they prove it through the Quran by virtue of its "new interpretation". As for the verses of the Quran which explicitly condemn the concept of Trinity, their "new interpretation" is that these verses condemn Trinity in the literal ' and real sense of the word, and even the Christians accept that there is only one God, and these three are only the components of one and not separate gods. Also according to their "new Interpretation" of Quran and its proclamation "Those who say Jesus son of Mary is god are Kafirs (unbelievers)" in fact meant to contradict the sect of monophacy. Where Quran has warned the Christians against the torment of Hell their "new Interpretation" is that this does not refer to Catholics but is meant for monophasics. The Quran says that Jesus was not crucified. The "new Interpretation is that Christians in general also believed that the third person of Trinity was not crucified and the Quran does not Contradict crucification of his body."

It can be seen how the magic of "new Interpretation" proved all Christians' beliefs to be in conformity with Islam. The question arises "What is the difference between your new Interpretation and that of the Christians?" If you have a right to make "new Interpretation" of the Quran and Sunnah in order to amend the established laws of Islam why the Christians should not have the same right? Under what rule or regulation can you reject the Christians' "new Interpretation"?

One may argue that our comparison of "new Interpretation" of modernists with the "new Interpretation" of Christians is exaggerated, but that is not true. The readers may go through their articles on the subject and the truth of our statement will become quite apparent.

We come across numerous interesting "new Interpretations" in the book named "Islam" written by the Director of Islamic Research, Dr. Fazlur Rahman. According to him only three daily Salahs were originally made obligatory, and two more were added in the last years of the Prophet's life. Hence their number has the possibility of accepting changes.

> "Anyhow, the fact that basically there were three daily Salahs is also supported by the incidence that there is one narration according to which Prophet (PBUH) has converted the four Salahs into two". Anyway it happened in the post-prophetic era that the number of Salahs without any alternative choice, was strictly fixed as five. In this way the fact that the number was basically three got swept away in the flood of traditions reported in support of the number of five". (Monthly "Fikr-o-Nazar, vol: 5, p.259)

This is the "new Interpretation". According to this, on one side "the flood of authentic prophetic traditions" which described the number of Salah as five from the very beginning of Islam is false and self-invented; on the other side the single narration describing the incidence of combining the two Salahs" has been considered by them as most reliable. Then again the term "combining two Salahs" has been taken to mean that the Prophet had converted four into two. This is the most interesting example of the expertise in the "new Interpretation" If you have read this narration you will definitely enjoy the fallacies of thought.' This is the way of argument about which somebody has said," you can prove everything by everything."

This is just one example that we have presented. If you go through the exegeses of these modernists you will come across many "master pieces" of their "new Interpretations" Wahy (Divine revelations) is interpreted as the Prophet's own words; Angels mean water, electricity etc.; Iblis (Satan) as the fantasy; Jinns as the savage tribes; mankind as the civilized people, Death is unconsciousness, disgrace or disbelief, life means honour and dignity, state of consciousness or embracing Islam etc.

If you keep the above exegetic points in view you will know that we have not exaggerated at all. Anyway, this was just a parenthesis. We wanted to impress that if we adopt the style of making arguments dependent on preconceived thoughts even Christianity can be proved from the Quran itself, and so can be Judaism, Socialism and Capitalism. Adopting the same style Dr. Perwez has proved Darwin's theory of evolution in his book "Iblis aur 'Adam" from the Quran. Also he has derived an economic system of socialist style from the Quranic phrase (Establish your prayers of worship). It is the same style of interpretations by which Mirza Ghulam Ahmad Qadyani had pleaded that by Damishq (Damascus) the Prophet had incant Qadiyan, the Mirza's headquarters.

Thus we see that the System of modernists is that they first fix some ideas themselves, label them as the exigencies of time and then impose the Quran and Hadith through their "new Interpretation" on them. This is the very first brick the angulation of which has resulted in the crookedness of entire structure of their views and thoughts, and this is the fundamental reason why their thoughts have entered the limits of 'distortion' overthrowing all principles, rules and regulations of research and knowledge.

Norms for Research : There are some rules and regulations for research in every art and science. You cannot reach the correct conclusion unless you follow them. In the present jurisprudence also "Interpretation of statutes" is a compulsory subject. It has definite rules and regulations and unless they are given due consideration no interpretation of any legal expert can be acceptable.

In the same manner, rather more reasonable and well organised are the detailed rules and regulations for interpretation (of Quran and Sunnah and Islamic law) that have been compiled after thorough research, devoted attention and minute observations. Hundreds of books are available on the subject and each rule has been thoroughly screened. Unless the Quran and Hadith are interpreted within the framework of these rules and regulations no reasonable person can accept diem, exactly as such explanations of present commentators cannot be accepted that do not conform to the principles of "Interpretation of statutes".

But our modernists do not bind themselves to any such rules in their interpretations and commentaries due to their stamped way of thinking. Thus they frequently defy the established rules of interpretation of the Quran and Sunnah. For example, the established rule of Islamic Jurisprudence that proverbial or allegoric meaning of any word or phrase of the Quran or Hadith would be adopted only when literal meaning is either impossible or have become obsolete in common use. This is perfectly a reasonable rule which can not be challenged through any intellectual argument, without it no definite conclusion can ever be derived from anything said by anybody. But this rule is profusely ignored by the modernists in their writings. Wherever they find a word in the Quran and Hadith clashing with their concepts they unhesitatingly give it allegoric and sometimes purely imaginative interpretation. "Son" has been interpreted as "grandson", staff turned into .'argument"; death as a state of "coma or disgrace", "Satan" as "fantasy or illusion "so much so that "Allah and Messenger" have been termed as "centre of the Ummah". These are just a few examples. If these absurdities are all compiled together a voluminous book can be prepared.

It can be said by the modernists that they do not agree with the rules and regulations fixed by the Islamic jurists and that is why they do not follow them. In that case they should have pointed out those rules and given some alternate principles better than the rules of the jurists. Then they should have used their formulated rules in their writings.

But we find that their interpretations are not supported by any principle at all. At one occasion they break a rule and oppose it, but at another occasion they derive their argument for their new interpretation. They reject any tradition that appears to contradict their views, no matter how authentic chain of reporters it has, but where a tradition appears to support their views, they ignore the clear verses of the Holy Quran on the basis of a tradition which is weak and without support of authentic narrators. A recent example is the statement of Dr. Fazlur Rahman in which he has said that the meat of an animal is lawful and permissible to eat even if it is slaughtered without the name of Allah pronounced on it, while the explicit injunction of Quran is this:

And eat not that (flesh) over which Allah's name has not been pronounced.

But since this was against the views of Dr. Fazlur Rahman, he based his arguments on a narration of Hadrat Aishah and on a saying of Imam Shafii which is perhaps the weakest argument of all his juristic inferences (as has been admitted by the scholars of my school of thought), while his own view about the application of a tradition is as follows:

> "If a tradition tells anything that is not in conformity with the apparent Quranic injunction I would attribute it to the specific historical era rather than to the Prophet himself'. (Monthly "Fikr-o-Nazar, p.515, vol.2)

Apart from the fact that his inference from Aishah's narration is highly misleading, Dr. Fazlur Rahman should not seek argument from this according to his own principle cited above. On what ground he attributed this tradition to the Holy Prophet (PBUH).

As far as Imam Shafii is concerned, the Doctor has commented about him as under:

> The enlightened views and quick understanding of Imam Shafii did create a mechanic system which undoubtedly led to stabilisation of social and religious structure of our mediaeval era, but due to it we have been deprived of modern thinking and creative intellect
> (Monthly "Fikr-o- Nazar", p. 3 0, vol. I)

If Imam Shafii had committed such a fundamental error bow can you quote him as authority on the validity of a religious precept? Does it not become apparent from the above examples that Dr. Fazlur Rahman and his co-workers have no set criterion for research in their mind. Not only that they have not taken into consideration any of the established rules of Jurisprudence, they do not even follow the rules framed by themselves?

There can be no other reason for this betrayal of their own principles that they form their own views and then seek arguments to support them. Obviously this method can not go along with rules and regulations, because with every new idea they have to frame new regulations. If they are requested in the name of God to let alone the "knowledge and research" and refrain from making the Quran and Sunnah a plaything as was done by the Jews and Christians in case of Torah and Injil, such persons are instantly labelled as "Obscurantists" and Ignorant of the exigencies of time". Their judgement about them is that they are blind to the new environment and have no knowledge of the modern demands. (Monthly "Fikr-o- p.731, vol.2)

We are conscious that in response to our sincere submissions, we shall also be rewarded with such titles but we are writing and continue to write the truth with a hope that there may be a heart in search of truth that may accept it. May be our suggestions can awake a sleeping conscience.

On Papacy : The million dollar questions : Who should be competent to interpret and explain the Quran and Sunnah (Prophetic traditions) and to deduce various injunctions for problems arising in new circumstances. What are the conditions and requirements necessary for this job? We find the answers to these questions in an authentic Tradition reported by Hadrat Ali in which he said:

> "I said, "O messenger of Allah! If we are confronted with a problem which has not been described in the Quran and Prophetic traditions, with no injunctions in favour or against it, what am I to do in such a situation?" He said: "Take advice of the jurists and faithful worshippers and do not employ your individual opinion".

The Holy Prophet (PBUH) has explicitly stated in this narration that two conditions must be fulfilled by a person who wants to deduce laws and injunctions from the Quran and Prophetic traditions. Firstly, he must be a jurist and secondly, he must be a devotee to worship. The importance of the first condition is obvious because objectives of the Quran and traditions can be well conceived only by those who possess vast and deep knowledge, who are fully aware of the rules laid down by the earlier jurists and who have spent their lives in understanding the intentions of divine laws. Similarly, the Prophet has made it a condition for him to be a devotee and faithful, that is, he must have devoted himself to the practices of these laws. Anyone who can not make distinction between permissibles and forbidden in practical life and whose every day practices are in contrast of these laws can not comprehend the intentions of Islam. Deduction of the laws is, in fact, the "Search for the Truth", and the Quran states that Allah bestows the faculty of cognizance of the truth to the one who confides in it in his practical life. It said:

> If you fear Allah He will give you the power of discrimination between truth and falsehood.

This verse has clearly stated that "Fear of Allah" is the primary condition for a sense of discrimination between right and wrong.

It is quite obvious from the above verse of the Quran and the Prophetic tradition that a religious and juristic solution can best be found by a person who is "jurist" and a "devotee" (or "Muttaqi" that is, the one who abstains from evil for fear of Allah).

Lately Mufti Muhammad Shafii, President, Darul-Ulum, Karachi had summarized the same thing in the following words.

"The method of solving the problems not mentioned in the Book and the traditions is the joint consultation of jurists and devoted scholars of Islam. Imposing the personal and individual opinion on the Muslims is forbidden."

But for reasons unknown our modernists are allergic to this way of thinking. The traditional knowledge of the Quran and the Sunnah is not considered by them as an essential requirement for interpretation of and deductions from the Quran and the Sunnah, nor do they think it necessary that such a person should necessarily be fearful of Allah and devoted worshipper. For some time they have been making loud suggestion to this effect.

"There should be no monopoly of religious scholars" on the interpretation of Quran and the Sunnah. No papacy should be allowed in Islam. No particular group, therefore, can be given the right of legislations. "The interpretation of the Quran and the Tradition is the right of all Muslims and not of the religious scholars alone" "Religious scholars cannot be given the power of veto in the affairs of Islam", etc.,

These are the suggestions that are expressed in almost all the writings of the modernists. As far as the instructions of the Quran and the Traditions are concerned we have already submitted that the greatest emphasis has been laid down on the fundamental requirement of knowledge and devotion for interpreting the religion. But it seems proper here to discuss real facts that are the source of these misunderstandings.

Their first suggestion is: " There is no Brahmanism or Papacy in Islam, hence the religious scholars cannot be given the exclusive rights of legislations".

Either they are totally ignorant of the real meaning of papacy and theocracy and their ills in them, or they are deliberately deceiving the simple people of the Ummah. Anyone having slightest sense of justice and the truth can understand that "knowledge" and "fearfulness of Allah" (Taqwa) is not limited to any race, colour, caste or creed which one cannot achieve through his efforts and resources. It is the name of "Eligibility and Qualification" of a specific objective which can be achieved by everyone at any time. If setting some qualifications for certain responsibilities is papacy, no section of life can be said to be devoid of it. The educational standard and moral character needed for the presidentship and ministership of a country would also be termed as "papacy". The condition of being an expert on legal affairs for a judge would also be another form of "papacy". The attainment of a law degree for legal advisor or advocate should be called papacy. The condition of having relevant academic degrees for teaching in a university, college or school should be removed. The limit of age, intellect and normal character fixed for qualifying as a candidate in elections, should all be cancelled as they are different forms of "papacy". But it is not so. How then the condition of 'knowledge' and "Taqwa" for interpreting the Quran and the Tradition be termed as papacy?

Anyone having a little knowledge of the term of "Papacy" and Brahmanism cannot overlook the differences between the religious scholars of Islam and the Popes and Brahmans.

(1) "Pope" and "Brahmans" are practically the titles of a specified class of colour, caste and creed. Anyone outside these jurisdictions cannot enter into their fold despite all eligibilities and efforts. That is why we find dacoits and robbers becoming "Popes" in the history of Christian church. Contrary to this, Religious scholars of Islam (*Ulama*) is an attribute for which there is no restriction of caste and creed. In the fourteen hundred years of the history of Islam we find religious scholars hi every colour or creed, even the slaves have emerged as great scholars of Islamic learnings and accepted as leaders of the Ummah. The cause of their dignified status had always remained their "Knowledge" and "Taqwa" rather than their parental background.

(2) The religion of which the Pope is claimed to be a spokesman is a religion which does not provide with guidance for the

most important aspects of life. That is why the word of Pope has become the word of God, and no one else can defy this. Thus he is no more an interpreter of law but a free and independent law-maker. Contrary to this, the injunctions of the Book (Quran) and the Sunnah (Prophetic traditions) are universal and the rules and regulations for their interpretation are prescribed and preserved in their original form. Any scholar saying anything against these rules and regulations will be rejected by other scholars on the ground of these principles. A number of such scholars is always present to check such misinterpretations.

(3) The process of law-making and interpretation of religion in papacy ultimately ends on one man. He alone has been regarded as the "Shepherd of the sheep of Maseeh" and the Deputy of the founder of the church. Contrary to this, "Religious scholars" of Islam is not the name of any person who is the head of an organisation, but anyone who has attained religious knowledge on true lines is a Religious scholar and a heir to the Holy Prophet. Hence no individual scholar has right to impose his personal views and whims on the entire Muslim Ummah.

In the presence of such an obvious difference between the role of the Pope and of the Islamic scholar any one applying the term Papacy to the services of the *Ulama* simply exhibits his loss of knowledge and common intellect.

The second demand of the modernists is that "there can be no monopoly of the *Ulama* on the Book and Traditions. Therefore, the right of their interpretation cannot be reserved for religious scholars alone".

Those under the charm of this propaganda are tirelessly repeating this slogan and do not stop for a while to think that thus they are making themselves similar to a person who had never seen a medical college but raises the objection as to why the treatment of diseases has been reserved for qualified doctors only or like a fool who criticises saying why the experts in law and jurisprudence alone have the right of the interpretation of law and why not others are allowed to do so?

No sensible or conscientious person can ever think on these hues. However, if one has such an imbecile approach he should know that any one has the right to perform all these duties , but to gain proficiency and eligibility for this you will have to spend years and years of hard work and labour, seeking the guidance from experts for practical experience, obtain degree and diplomas and other related experience, then, of course, you will be allowed to make interpretations.

The most sensitive and delicate work of interpreting the Quran and the Sunnah is said to require the same process how can it be termed as monopoly. Does it not require any one to get educated for it. Why the Quran and the Sunnah alone are considered to be as pitiable as to be treated by any individual at his own will? How one can be given right to interpret the Quran and the Sunnah while he has not spent even a few months in acquiring the relevant Knowledge.

They express their anger against the religious scholars all the day long as to why they alone should deserve the right to interpret the Quran and the Sunnah? But they never reflect on the amount of pain and labour they had undergone to acquire this right? How in the two hundred years of British rule in India they had remained the target of the British atrocities and aggression? With all the doors of livelihood closed on them by the British rule they preferred to live on meagre resources and devoted themselves to acquire this knowledge against all odds. They are still doing it despite the harassment from these modernists. How they glowed their eyes in front of the dim light of oil lamps of clay? And how they attempted to shape their lives in the mould of religion? If after all that, the Holy Prophet (PBUH) gives them the right to interpret the Quran and his Sunnah, and the Muslims place their trust in them why is this resented by them?

The eagerness of modernists for interpreting the Book and the Traditions is certainly commendable; but for this they should also undergo the physical and mental strain needed for it. They, too should spend some part of life in trodding the roads to knowledge of the Quran and learn the manners of living on that ground. If after that any one refuses to recognize them as interpreter of the Quran and the Traditions, then their complaint against the scholars would be justified.

Under the present circumstances their attitude is like what the poet said:

> Those who hold their life dear to them should not think of going to seek his beloved.

Your present state of mind has been well depicted by the poet of the East, Allama Iqbal, in this poem:

> The knowledge of others you gained is a mere correction as if you have glowed your face with foreign cosmetics.

You have given up your dignity so much that I cannot recognise you as yourself.

Your mind is chained by the thoughts of others and the succession of breaths in your throat has a foreign source.

The tongue is yours but the speech is borrowed from others and so are your wishes in your mind.

The canaries wish to sing their own songs, the cypresses wish to be clad with their own foliage.

You borrow the wine from others in your goblet. Even the cup you hold is not yours.

The Prophet is grieved, and the Creator asks "Am I not there?" But for you! Alas! Alas!

Under these circumstances how can the Muslim Ummah entrust you with the responsibility of interpreting the Quran and Sunnah, who, with all their shortcomings, have saved their ideological entity as Muslims.

As for the claim that Dr. Fazlur Rahman has published in the monthly "Fikr-o-Nazar" in these words:

> "In Islam the Muslim Ummah as a whole had been doing legislative work and it should still have the right to do so."

I wish they had further clarified what he meant by it. Does it mean that every individual of the Ummah should be allowed to become a legislator? Every illiterate and uncivilised person should be entrusted with legislation? Or, does it mean that the Ummah as a whole enjoys the fight to select some deserving, reliable and knowledgeable person from among them to be entrusted with this sacred job? In that case it will be a work of these selected people. Obviously even the very staunch believer in democracy does not take the term democracy to mean that every single individual can interfere with each and every affair of the state. In fact, they hold that every matter and problem is to be entrusted to the experts of that field and those who lack knowledge in that trade have to place their trust on these experts, and it is not termed as an infringement of the rights of democracy.

After this analysis of the rights of people one can easily conclude who, out of one hundred and twenty million people of Pakistan, are worthy of trust in the matter of interpretation and exegesis of the Quran and the Traditions? When any one of them really wants to understand the Quranic injunction or prophetic tradition would he seek the help of the Institute of Islamic Research or any other modernist institution or to those 'Obscurantist" scholars whom the modernists blame to have robbed the people of their democratic right? If the multitude of Muslims turn to these scholars without any compulsion, pressure or legal restrictions, place their trust on them and their conscience get satisfied with it where does the democratic right of people get hurt? Who have injured the beliefs of the Muslim Ummah with their interpolation, the *Ulama* or these modernists is known to all?

Their last and biggest objection is on the condition of "Taqwa" (Fear of Allah, Piety, Abstinence from evil doings). According to them "Taqwa" like "knowledge" is not essential for interpreting the Quran We do not understand what apprehension they have against it. According to them the complication in this regard is:

> "The condition of "Taqwa" is a condition that every scholar can reject the judgement of other scholar because everyone has his own standard for Taqwa". Nazis Nov.67, p.326)

We may be allowed to say that ignore for a while your individual apprehension and there will be no complication in this matter. The same 'Multitude' (Jamhur) whom they want to give the status of legislators is equally entitled to decide which of the scholars fulfils this condition of taqwa? Collectively the conscience of multitude of Muslims is never wrong. Their opinion is the will of Allah. Why should there be any hesitation in entrusting the job of interpretation of the Quran and traditions to a person whose Taqwa is accepted by the multitude?

It should be thoroughly understood that 'Taqwa' is not an ambiguous and unsettled term which can be given any meaning by anyone according to his individual liking. In Islam "Taqwa" is a legal phrase and countless religious injunctions depend on it. Whenever it is used in a legal sense it would mean "practising the permissibles, abstaining from major sins and not insisting on minor sins." In the phraseology of the Quran it is the opposite of "Fujur" (Apparent sins, Immorality). The Quran says:

> Then inspired it (with conscience of) its wickedness and its piety.

Hence anyone abstaining from "Fujur" is a man of Taqwa, and therefore the people shall have no difficulty in deciding about the piety and devotion (Taqwa) of a person. With this in view there one can easily conceive that there can be no complexity or difficulty arising from imposing the condition of knowledge and Taqwa for interpretation, explication or exegesis of the Quran and Prophetic tradition."

In the end we would again like to humbly request the modernists that the use of street slogans and propaganda weapon would neither render any service to the country or the nation nor can any problems be solved with them, nor would it leave any pleasant effect on any serious mind. In the hue and cry of their slogans at the most they can suppress the voice of truth for a short while. But that can only affect the ears, but not the hearts.

Struggle for Success

Religious scholars (*Ulama*) should behave according to the demands of time. This is a catchword we hear in a new style almost every day. Most of our secular minded leaders are repeating this suggestion off and on. And now we hear the echo of this suggestion even in our high level social gatherings whenever a religious subject comes under discussion. A group of people in our country is busy in surgical manoeuvres on the explicit injunctions of Islam and its established principles under the guise of modernism. They regard religious scholars as the biggest obstacle in their path. They consider that their success depends on baseless accusations and malicious propaganda against religious scholars in whichever way it is possible. For this, they have adopted the ambiguous phrase 'Demands of Time" as a hypnotiser for the modem minds, and make this a basis for their repeated appeals to the people and the government that religious scholars are the biggest obstacle in the way of progress and hence no attention should be paid to them and to what they say.

We leave them at the will of Allah from Whom no secrets of hearts are hidden. But there are some people who quite sincerely and seriously feel that religious scholars are unaware of the needs and demands of the modern age, and it is a result of this ignorance that they oppose every new thing. In these lines we wish to address this very group of people. But before this we humbly submit that if they are really well-wishers of Islam and Muslims they should give a cool thought to this matter and, for a little while, make their minds free from the grip of such hasty suggestions and try to understand what is meant by the "Demands of Time" and what is the best method of fulfilling it? With unbiased minds they should examine these allegations against the *Ulama*, the Islamic scholars.

The first thing to be defined is the phrase "Meeting the Demands of Time"? We feel that those who are so forcefully preaching the importance of demands of time themselves do not have a clear conception of these demands. They are simply making the ambiguous claims that religious scholars are opposed to the Demands of Time. But they never made it clear as to what those specific demands are which are opposed by the *Ulama*. If by the "Demands of Time" they mean that Muslims should endeavour to equip themselves with all the means of science and technology without which it is not possible to survive as a free nation in the world of today then indeed this is the greatest need and demand of this time. For God's sake tell us who is the single scholar who forbids this most important demand of time? Which of these scholars, and when, has issued any verdict (Fatwa) that progress in the fields of science and technology is forbidden, unlawful, meaningless or useless? Science has made amazing progress in the recent years and it is in progress. Even in our life-time we have seen that newer inventions are coming up every day. How many of them have been opposed by the religious scholars? Electricity, Telegraphy, Telephone, Teleprinter, Wireless Radio, Transistors, Tape Recorders, Cars, Heavy Motor Vehicles, Aeroplanes, Steamers, Trains, Tanks, Mortars, Fighter Planes, Bombers, Submarines, Warships, Rockets, Missiles, Radar, Industrial Machines, Factories, Tractors, Chemical Fertilizers, Insecticides and Pesticides, Surgical Instruments, X-ray & other Radiological Machines are in use with religious sanction of Islam. All sources of knowledge in Arts, Science, Commerce, Mathematics, Geography, Geology, Astronomy, Civics, and Politics are some examples of material progress. Which of these has ever been opposed by religious scholars or any obstacles been placed in their way?

The history of the past 55 years of our developing country is a witness to the fact that by the Grace of Allah our country has advanced by leaps and bounds in material and economic progress perfectly corresponding to the wishes of our righteous religious scholars and religious circles. Many of the great economic schemes have been completed during this period, large factories have been erected, vast network of roadways constructed, numerous canals dug out for irrigation, many dams were made, the old communication system was replaced with new inventions, many colleges and universities for various sciences and arts came into existence and barren land was cultivated. Only an insane person can feel unhappy about these advancements. Once again I ask our modernists to point out just one name of a religious scholar who ever opposed these achievements, or ever criticized production of expert scientists or educating people in engineering, or constructing roadways, factories, bridges, canals, river dams, using advanced technology in arms and ammunition for country's defence, or ever suggested that our army should not be trained in modern machine warfare, or that the latest telecommunication means should not be adopted, or education and training in modem arts and sciences should be stopped.

If none of the religious scholars has ever opposed it, there can be no other interpretation of this baseless accusations except malice and enmity against the righteous scholars of Islam. We know, Dot one but countless such scholars whose hopes and trust are centred around Ummah, and it is their greatest desire that side by side with its march in the straight path of Islam, they should progress by leaps and bounds in the material fields as well. That is why on the one hand they have been emphasizing on the Muslims that achievements of expertise of science and technology is an important component of our obligations, and if we fail to fulfil our obligations we shall be presented before Allah as an offender and on the other hand they are praying day and night for the prosperity and integrity of Pakistan which is best known by Allah, the All-knowing, All-aware.

We are, however, presenting below the excerpts from the writings of some of those religious scholars who are being blamed of opposing science and technology.

One of the most renowned of the religious scholars was Moulana Shabbir Ahmad Usmani. His selfless sacrifices can not be forgotten. In a conference at Dacca, in 1949, while explaining the policy of Pakistani scholars he declared in quite unequivocal terms:

> "No matter what treatment we meet from those in authority, we shall leave no stone unturned to make this new country safe and strong for the pleasure of Allah and supremacy of Islam and believers of Islam." (Presidential address Jamiat Ulama-e-Islam Conference, Dacca .10 February, 1949)

Further in the same speech he said,

> "We should not lag behind and show any laziness in the procurement of these material means and equipments to the last bit of our ability and competency, so that we may lower the morale of our enemy and show our supremacy on them, because this is in accordance with the Quranic injunction."

Continuing, he further said:

> "In my opinion the secret of all our success and

> prosperity lies in the four words namely, Patience and Perseverance, Fear of Allah and Purity, Unity of nation, and Numerical strength to the possible limits. In short, we must keep our relations with Allah in the right direction in our individual and collective life, so that we deserve His favour and assistance. And I pray that the entire Muslim nation should unite together and bring forth the Power that would subdue all evil forces".

The Grand Mufti Mufti Muhammad Shafii, President, Darul Ulum, has written in his treatise 'Jihad' as under:

> "Indeed, the Patience, the fear of Allah and total belief in and submission to Allah is the real and unconquerable strength of Muslims. Alongwith it, however, it is also essential that equipment of war and ammunition proper to the time and place should be acquired and stored. The Prophet (SA) always arranged for war exercises, and issued instructions to collect and acquire all those weapons that were in vogue anywhere in those days. It has been reported by Ibn-e-Katheir in his book "Al-Hidayah wan Nihayah" under the caption of Battle of Hunayn that two of the Prophets' companions could not take part in Jihad because they were in Damascus learning the techniques of manufacturing war weapons called 'Dhaba' and 'Dhabur' (The carriages that were used as Tanks in those days). Similarly, catapults were also manufactured there."

This incidence also proves that it is obligatory for the Muslims to make their countries self-sufficient in war weapons and technology and should not depend on others. Otherwise the Prophet could have purchased those carriages and catapults rather than sending his men to learn the techniques to manufacture them theirselves. We are bound to think it seriously how much our country is in need of all the equipment and weapons of war used in modern warfare so that we may not be lagging behind. We must put all our energy and resources to fulfil the aim that we become self- sufficient in the nearest possible future. ('Jihad' pp.53 to 56)"

In another of his books "Modern Weapons" the Grand.

Mufti has said:

> "......In short the industrial products and inventions, be they new or old, if related to mankind's economic prosperity, are all benefactions of Allah that have been bestowed on human beings. Man should be wise enough to take full benefits from them and be grateful to Almighty Allah." ('Alat- p. 15).

And Moulana Zafar Ahmad Usmani- Sheikh-ul-Hadith. Darul-Ulum-al- Islamiya, writes in one of his recent articles,

> "War weapons and technology against the enemy should be raised to the extent that the enemy is overawed with them .....our earlier Caliphs and Sultans religiously followed this rule. The companion Muawiyyah had prepared a fleet of 500 warships during the time of Hadrat Uthman (RA), the third Caliph. He used to supervise personally the collection of all defense equipments and never depended on others as we are today. The Muslim nations should join together to build up factories for ammunition and other weapons, and a continued process of research and inventions must be carried out. All these efforts are in conformity with Quranic injunction."
>
> (Monthly Al-Balagh, p.44 J.A 1387 (H)

Moulana Muhammad Yusuf Binouri, Sheikh-ul-Hadith Madrasa Arabiyah, New Town, writes:

> "There is no scarcity in the Islamic world, rather there is an abundance of natural resources, material reserves and wealth, but how great a tragedy it is that a major portion of their wealth is utilised by the enemies through deposits in foreign banks, or spent in extravagance, debauchery, undue luxuries, and immoralities. But defense stability, military training and ordnance factories are practically negligible, while the enemies of Islam are constructing airports, naval fleets, military cantonments and large ordnance factories. But the Islamic world is not only indulged in profane pursuits

> but has shown criminal negligence towards material progress."
>
> (Monthly Baiyyenat, R.S. 1387 (H), p. 4).

Moulana Abdul Haq, Sheikh-ul-Hadith of Darul-uloom Haqqania, has elaborated the same view in one of his speeches:

> "You have acquired only immorality and evil doings from Europe. They manufacture one plane in a minute and innumerable rockets and collect billions of dollars to save the Jews, and we remain asleep in our luxuries. If we ignore our collective problems the result can not be other than destruction."
>
> (Monthly Al-Haq, July 1967, p. 17)
>
> Moulana Shamsul Haq Afghani has written in one of his recent articles 'Taraqqi our Islam.
>
> (Islam and Progress)
>
> "Our deprivation from progress and our present decline is the result of our neglect towards Islam, otherwise Islam and Progress are inseparable. According to this verse it is obligatory on all Muslims that in all the modern equipments and instruments they should progress to the extent that they should be at least at par with Christian nations if not excel them. The Islamic world must use all its resources for this purpose."
>
> (Monthly 'Al-Haq', Sept 1967 p.22)

The above are the utterances of some high ranking and renowned religious scholars. These have come to our view just abruptly without any special efforts to find them. Those who had been reading the views of these scholars know it fully well that not only the religious scholars never opposed Science and Technology but they had always been inducing the Muslims to attain them. Despite this reality before their eyes there is a group of people who are beating their drums high and loud that the religious scholars are opposed to progress and advancement, they are allergic to Science and Technology, they give no importance to the demands of time, and discard every new thing.

Truth and Falsehood : The most clever advocate of "Falsehood" was Goebels, who spoke the Truth, when he said that if "falsehood" is spread with full force the world starts taking it as "truth". Our modernists have also been following Goebels' adage so much so that even some of the very learned and of balanced mind people regard this slogan as true while it is just a false blame, cunningly produced by propaganda machines of modern time.

If, however, these people consider music and dance, nudity and obscenity, profligacy and immodesty, co-education, free inter mixing of men and women, usury in banking and birth control as demands of time and means of progress, then indeed the religious scholars have openly opposed them, and they should have done so, they still do it and will continue doing it. We may be informed what logic and reason has ever claimed these things to be the demands of time? They must bring some logical argument to prove what relation material progress has with music and dances? Which is that progress that would stop without nudity and obscenity? What are the genuine obstacles in the way of promoting interest-free banking? How does coeducation and Free mixing of men and women help in science and technology?

The modernists may call music and dances, co-education and mixed gatherings, etc., as the demands of time, but in view of the circumstances we sincerely believe that the greatest need and demand of the present time is that the Islamic world should totally eradicate these things with full might and power. This is because, magnitude of the fatalities that has come to the forefront in the twentieth century was never witnessed before. The very Western intelligentsia itself is showing clear signs of extreme anxiety and restlessness on their premature but immoral and irrational social advancement. No literate person of the world can claim to be ignorant of this outcry that is echoing FROM the meeting chambers of Western thinkers as a result of social and moral ruin in their lives. The 'modernist' should, for God's sake, decide himself as to what really are the demands of time? Should it be that the Islamic world should march on the footsteps of the West and fall into the same abyss of moral degradation? Or should the Islamic world take lesson from the dreadful end of the West and save itself from this dangerous path forever?

Demands of Time ?: The group of people who consider these curses of Western civilization as demands of time and means of progress call themselves as "Modernists" but it is strange that in the field of thoughts and deeds they are preaching the same outdated ideologies of the West which have not given anything but burn scars all over the body. They know it very well how rapidly the Western style of thinking is changing about their old views, and what the latest studies of philosophy and science are proving about these subjects? Take for example the problem of population. A very substantial number of modern economists are against limiting the family size and birth control. Having been impressed by their latest arguments such economists are constantly increasing in number, but our "Modernists" are still embracing Malthus' outdated theory that has been thrown away by the march of time some two centuries ago. I do wish to quote here the views of Philosopher-Poet, Iqbal, who said:

> "Power of the West is not due to flutes and guitars, nor due to dances of veilless girls, nor due to the spell of their magical beauty, nor to their naked legs, nor to their trimmed hair styles. Their supremacy is not due to secularism, nor is their progress due to Latin script. Their power is due to science and technology. It is this fuel that is burning in their lamps. Wisdom does not lie in how your clothes are tailored, and the turban is no obstruction for science and technology".

The above is sufficient to show the nature of these accusations of our "Modernists" against the religious scholars of opposing the demands of time and Science and Technology? The question arises as to why the "Modernists" are so forcefully propagating this extremely irreasonable claim? As far as we can trace there is probably a psychological factor in action, if we rule out any specific motives behind it the fundamental error which misled these modernists is that they consider Islam analogous to Christianity and the Islamic world to the West. They had observed that at the time of revival of science and technology in the West the biggest obstacle was Christianity along with its scholars. As long as the supremacy of church prevailed in the West the whole of region was filled with ignorance and illiteracy. The Christian scholars tried to suppress every such attempt that was made to create scientific awareness among the people. People like John Hiss and Jerome were burnt alive in the city of Constance. The renowned scientist Galileo had to suffer calamities because he wanted to open new avenues in the field of science.

But gradually the awareness spread and several movements came out. These tortures could not stop them, and ultimately Martin Luther, John Calone and Zongli put up a struggle that defeated Popalism and these movements got their chance to flourish. Lately Ruso, Horonic and Reman with other modernists made further changes and innovations in the religion and brought it in conformity to the scientific researches of that time. The situation now is that Luther, Calone, Ruso and Horonic etc. have been titled as Reformers by the religious minded people of the West. They are regarded as national heroes and people of the new generation who have not yet become totally alien to religion regard them with a sense of honour and dignity that by making fundamental changes in Christian religion they freed the nation from the grip of Paplism which was the greatest obstacle in the way of their material progress.

Now, the modernists of Islam want to make similar amendments by considering Islam equal to Christianity and scholars of Islam parallel to popes and to themselves they regard Luthers and Rusos of the time. In this way they want to become the Reformers of Muslim nation by opposing and defaming the religious scholars. They aspire that some Henry VIII will soon appear and he will grace them by accepting their ideology and then officially implementing it for ever. Thus the coming generations will regard them in such high esteem as is the case of hero-worship with Luther and Ruso etc.

We may remark here that they are in great delusion and their dream is never going to come true. They are badly mistaken in considering Islam similar to Christianity and scholars of Islam to popes. The unnatural views of Christian religion which became common after the third century did not have adequate power to keep pace with time for all future days to come, and stand face to face with the latest scientific advancements. That was an era of dark ignorance and superstitions which could not stay in the light of knowledge. Hence science came as a great challenge and they were left with no other option than either to oppose science openly or by cutting and dipping their religion to bring it in conformity with the scientific knowledge. The popes initially adopted the first course and declared science as the forbidden tree. But Science was the real need of that time and they could not stop its progress merely by hollow claim and baseless charges against it. The result was that all their efforts faded to stop scientific advancement.

At this stage the modernists adopted the second course and started manipulating the religion and distorting its teachings in order that people may not mock and laugh at it. This was indeed a service to the Christianity, and if they had not done this favour Christianity would have been swept away by the torrent of Rationalism and no trace of it could be found today. The workmanship of Christian modernists helped the Christian religion to survive although its fundamental concepts were totally changed. At least its name and external structure is still existing. It is this favour of the modernists on Christianity that made them heroes of their nation and due to the major part of the Christian world holds them in high esteem.

But the case of Islam is totally different. It is a natural religion and it has come to exist till the Last Day. By virtue of this old and real interpretations it has the capability of marching forward with the researches of every era of time. Hence science has never been a danger to it nor will it ever be. Rather, we have observed that the latest inventions and researches of science generally make its beliefs and teachings more transparent. Hence it has no need either to oppose science and its progress nor to change its own concepts. That is why unlike the popes the religious scholars of Islam never opposed science, because they know the realities exposed by Islam will become more and more transparent with the advancement of science. Since the Muslim Ummah believes that Islam is the religion revealed by Allah it does not have to change at any time, and that is why this nation has always condemned and disregarded any attempts towards making any changes in its teachings.

To sum up, Islam is neither a spiritless religion like the Christianity to have any fear or danger from scientific and technological advancement, nor its religious scholars (*Ulama*) have ever opposed science and technology as the Popes had done, nor does need any Martin Luther, Ruso or Reman for its survival. That is why, in the history of this religion, all those who tried to amend, manipulate or modernize it, they got nothing but reproach and condemnation. In the history of this religion, the advocates of modernism have not been called Luther and Kalone, but the modernists of our history are remembered by the names of Musailma, Abdullah bin Saba, Abu Musa Mazdar, Hassan bin Saba, Karamat, Abul Fazl, Faizi and Kamal Ata-Turk. Even their children would feel ashamed of their lineage with these names.

The opponents of Luther and Kalone are mentioned with great disregard by the Christians. But the opponents of modernism in Islam, namely Abu Bakr Siddiq (RA), Ali bin Abi Talib (RA), Ahmad bin Hambal Mahmud Ghaznawi and Mujaddid Alf Thani are still living with their names, and as long as the human conscience is alive the names of these sacred personalities will continue to be taken with love and allegiance. It is a pity that our present day modernists have not been able to understand the great diversity between Islam and Christianity, and as a result of this grave misunderstanding they have been busy in abusing the scholars of Islam, calling them obscurantists, accusing them of ignorance for no reason. We earnestly request them with all the well-wishes and heart-felt sympathies that they revise their attitude with cool mind and balanced thoughts, otherwise the course adopted by them is in no way beneficial for Muslims, for the country and the Ummah and even for themselves.

I hope and pray that my humble submissions leave useful impression on them.

Relevance of Industrial Revolution : For millennia, the life is constantly on the move. Every new era is associated with new circumstances and fresh problems. But the great revolution which the world has experienced after the invention of Machine, has affected every sphere of life. It has opened the doors of research and observation for every art and science, and has created some new problems in every section of life. If we look into the teachings of religions other than Islam we find that they are not capable of absorbing the great revolution in them. The fountainhead of these teachings was human intellect rather than the Divine Revelation (Wahy), hence they had neither a full cognition of human nature nor was it based on the considerations of changing circumstances of time, nor did it have an insight on the possible future happenings.

The result is that most of the original teachings of those religions have died under the loads of machines. Now there exist only two possibilities before the followers of these religions. They have to say good bye to their religion if they want to keep pace with the march of time, and if their religion is more dear to them they have to turn away from the light of thought and cognition and make themselves an isolated group of people who do not belong to twentieth century. However, some people have designed an intermediary way to reshape and modify their religion in order to make it practicable for the present time. But, obviously he is the follower of his own whims and not his true religion. In this case he is deprived of the religion he followed before. But the matter of Islam is totally different. This is the only religion in the world whose guidance is ever fresh. No revolutions and circumstances make it old. It is fresh today and it will remain fresh as long as the world is existing.

The reason is obvious. Its percepts and injunctions are not the product of human brain which is unaware of the coming events. The source of its teachings is the divine revelations. The Being who made it the code of life for mankind is the One who is the Creator of mankind and the entire universe. He has full knowledge of the man's nature and his needs. He is fully aware of the changing circumstances and He knows what is going to happen when and where.

It is the miracle of His words that the rules and regulations laid down by Him in the Quran and those preached by His last messenger Muhammad (PBUH) encircle all problems arising till the last day. The world may turn to one side or the other, these teachings will continue to provide with. The principles and laws of Islam would always suffice for all times to come.

But it is a pity that a group of people in Islamic world known as 'Modernists" has been unable to get at this reality. That is why, in taking their lead from other religions, they have started a campaign of alterations and innovations in Islam. They have made it their duty to prove that every exhibit of industrial revolution is consistent with Islam. After every such alteration and innovation they present their only argument that Islamic Injunctions must change because the world has greatly changed after the industrial revolution bringing about revolutionary changes in thought and practice.

In this connection we wish to point out two types of changes that have occurred in every walk of life as a result of industrial revolution of Europe. Some of them were inevitable for the present advancements and without them it was not possible for Science and Technology to have attained the present standard. It was due to these that the world was benefited by the latest inventions, large factories came into being, bridges have been constructed, big dams and useful additions to human knowledge have been made. This aspect of industrial revolution is indeed commendable and it is imperative for the Islamic world to progress in this field. Islam does not Place any obstacle in this direction. Rather, it looks at this achievement of power with approbation.

But, at the same time, there are some changes that are not at all essential for industrial and material progress. The West has associated them to industrial revolution for no reason, and now realising this error is sighing with grief Obscenity and nudity, free mixing of man and woman, music and dances, interest and birth control are things that have nothing to do with material and industrial progress. Experience has proved that these things have served as an obstacle rather than assistance towards progress.

This is the evil from which the Islamic world has to save itself very diligently. Industrial revolution in the Islamic world has become a necessity, but it should be a revolution free of the profanities of Western civilization which have led them to the brink of total destruction. Unfortunately, our modernist group wants that we accept the industrial revolution of West as it is, and without an iota of change in it, and thus drown ourselves in their ideological and practical aberrances even before the Machine has taken roots in our society. That is why, instead of developing Science and Technology, this group is spending its energy in moulding Islam to bring it in conformity with Western civilisation. Supporting this new viewpoint the official spokesman of monthly 'Fikr-o-Nazar' of the Institute of Islamic Research, writes as wider:

> "The entire life style will be changed after the completion of fourth five-year plan. The rule of machine will prevail, and due to this family life will change, economy and social values will change. There will be changes in the relations between man and woman, and obviously, individual and collective thinking will be affected, and people will think more positively".
>
> (Fikr-o-Nazar p.733, vol. 2, p. 12)

It is obvious that such people do not want to make any distinction between the industrial revolution of the Islamic World and that of the West. Our humble submission is that the "rule of machine" in the industrial sphere is not negated, what we think highly venomous are the changes in the family life, economy and social values, relationship of man and woman and the thought of general people. These "changes" do not match with the temperament of Islamic ideologies. A study of Industrial Revolution of the West itself leads us to think that we shall have to abstain from these "changes" if we want to lead a peaceful life despite the sway of machine in our lives.

The philosopher-poet of Pakistan, Iqbal, bad a deep insight into the state of West, he said:

> Christianity (in Europe) is blackened with the smoke of machines
>
> and,
>
> The rule of machine is the death of soul. Instruments only crush the sense of tolerance.

It will not be proper to deduce from the above that he was allergic to machines and instruments or that he opposed the progress of Technology. What he means is that the evil which the West has imposed on them alongwith the machines are detestable and should be avoided.

Under the present circumstances proper line of action for us is that in the pursuit of Industrial revolution we may not blindly match on the path that has carried the West to the brink of total destruction.

The industrial revolution will give rise to many difficulties and new problems, which will be resolved under the Islamic guidance and this solution will be free from the defects of the Western thought. Rather, we should acquire science and technology with deep insight and open mind in a manner that Islamic values are not injured.

On the contrary, if alteration and innovation is carried out in Islam itself to fit it into the framework of Western civilization and, somehow or the other, it is moulded to meet the requirement of the modem time, what credit goes to Islam for this? In this manner any religion can be brought in conformity with the present time by twisting and distorting it. There are many who demonstrated such artistry in their religions. The credit of this goes to them and not to tile poor religion that became a plaything in their hands. We honestly feel that Islam cannot be matched with other religions. Treating Islam in this manner is by no means justified, and any such attempt will be an interpolation in religion and hence condemnable.

No doubt many injunctions of Islam are flexible enough to accept changes in varying circumstances, but there are certain prescribed rules which must be observed when applying these to new problems. It does not mean that every Islamic injunction can be dissolved in the readymade mixture of modern necessities. It may be understood that be Islamic injunctions prescribed by the Quinlan, the Sulinah and by the consensus of the Ummah are fixed and unalterable. They cannot be changed in any period. However, in the matters, which can be influenced by changes of time, the Holy Quran and Sunnah have provided us with some basic principles without giving specific commandment for a specific condition. These principles call be used as a basis for the deduction of new injunctions in every period. Had Islam permitted the people of every time to deduce Islamic injunctions according to their circumstances and in opposition to the unanimous decisions of the Muslim Ummah, it would have not provided us with so comprehensive and detailed commandments in every sphere of life.

Rather, it would have said, "Keep making your own commandments according to your circumstances." On the contrary, Islam has provided us with specific and elaborate precepts with divine wisdom in order that they were to be observed upto the end of time. In short, these Islamic injunctions are fixed and cannot be changed simply because time has changed. They are not only practicable upto the Day of Judgement but they, in fact, hold the key to real material progress of the Muslims.

There are injunctions which the Quran and traditions have themselves left to be decided by the time are alterable. They can be changed, and are being changed, according to the circumstances. But in the guise of this flexibility our modernists not only try to change those unanimously accepted injunctions that are being accepted as established for the last fourteen centuries but they desire to make amendments even in certain beliefs that are against the clear and explicit injunctions of the Quran and Sunnah, though not accepted by a single person of any significance.

In case we allow this attitude to be correct it would imply that no basic belief of Islam has been understood by any one in fourteen hundred years. It requires our serious thought if such a religion is worthy of being followed by any sensible person?

How funny it is that our modernists feel the change of time only when they want to give religious sanction to an activity or when they want to seek approval to a thought or practice of western ideology. On the contrary, when the change of time demands labour or some hard work they do not even think of it. For example, the modernists have made loud claims that usury and interest should be made permissible because time has changed but none of them ever demanded that the concessions in the Salah (Five daily prayers of Worship) and Fasting during journeys should be withdrawn because the change of time has made journey far more comfortable and easy than it was in olden days. They never insisted that these facilities should be withdrawn in modem time and they were meant only for the time foregone.

The hedonistic attitude of Modernism can be well conceived with this diversity of action. In fact all its arguments are designed for their pre-conceived ideas. Since their aim is to infuse Western ideologies in Islam and any situation where this may be achieved any trivial thing they find to use it as an argument, no matter how transient and superfluous it may be. While the same argument is simply ignored when it turns against their intentions. How I wish that our Modernists think over these submissions seriously and realistically and their able efforts are spent on some constructive service instead of distorting or innovating the Islamic guidance.

Reality at Stake

In our time, numerous judicial problems have indeed been created and in order to solve them it is essential that scholars of Islamic jurisprudence and those having insight in these matters make collective efforts through regular discussions, debates and research. There are many such problems facing the Muslim world which require that the scholars of Islam and experts of modern science hold joint discussions to solve them in the light of established principles of Islam. The importance and necessity of this splendid job is being felt in various circles of Islamic scholars and some efforts are also being made at some places but due to lack of resources these efforts have not so far been materialised into an organised collective forum.

This is not a matter of obstinacy or anybody's personal prejudice rather it concerns a problem on which depends the survival of Islamic thought and Islamic way of life. If it is not solved with solemnity and balanced thinking, the community will never be able to achieve the goal of unity. Hence the exigency of time demands that all concerned should think and ponder over this problem with a cool temperament disregarding sentimental pressures.

In our view the main cause of failure of this institution is that the people-in-authority could not differentiate between "Research" and "Distortion". They have taken the two words as analogous and thus found superfluous solutions to the problems not conforming to the ideology of Islam at all.

It was obligatory for the Islamic researchers of our time to acquire and explore the guideline of Islam provided about the problems being faced with the mankind in twentieth century. How can it be put into practice? How the practical difficulties in this way can be removed? It was their duty to have surveyed the Western civilization with a view of research and criticism rather than counterfeiting them. They should have discarded the things that clashed with the laws of Islam, and should have suggested alternate ways which conformed to Islamic laws and at the same time fulfilled the legitimate needs of time.

But the line of action of researches of the Institute of Islamic Research is quite in contradiction to this. On the one hand they pre-supposed that the thirteen hundred years old laws of Islam have now become worn out and outdated, and it is not possible to implement and comply with them unless some fundamental changes are made in them (They call these changes as "New interpretations"). And on the other hand it has rooted deep into their minds that ideological and practical expositions of Western civilization are all blessings and benedictions, and unless Muslims accept them in toto their survival in the present time is impossible.

The entire intellectual structure of Modernism has been constructed on the above two hypotheses As a result, the style of their working had been that any ideology or style of working from the West is first taken as granted to be cent per cent right and there is no way out for us in the present time than to accept it and adopt it. Their 'Research' is then wholly directed towards proving it to be in conformity with Islam, by reshaping and distorting Islamic teachings and even by changing the established commandments of Islam. They do not hesitate in denying the prophetic traditions, or write down a new dictionary to give new meanings to the verses of the Quran.

Research or Distortion : This is the very style for which the word "Distortion" should be used in place of 'Research". Our submission is that, if you believe that Islam is the natural religion, if you have faith that its principles and injunctions are not the product of any human brain but that of the All-knower Allah who is fully aware of all the needs of mankind for all times to come, if you are confident that the Islam proclaimed by Muhammad (PBUH) contains satisfactory solutions to all the problems and difficulties that may arise till the Last Day, then you must admit that the solution to the problems of twentieth century also lies in the same principles which were brought by the Holy Prophet Muhammad (PBUH) 1400 years ago.

This is, however, subject to the condition that you sincerely try to get rid of the inferiority complex which has made West as the standard of righteousness in your eyes. Once you get the courage to lift up the veil of deception of the West from your mind you will have the chance to understand the problems with full confidence. It is then that you will discover new ways of survival in the present time fulfilling all the needs and demands of time on the one hand and save you from the unholy ways of the West. If you follow this course you will be able to acquire the wealth of peace and tranquillity that has never been imagined by the West.

We may be excused if you find our tone unmannerly but if you have any claim to realism, be realistic in analysing your approach. While seeking the solution to your problems you have the fear of being called conservative or superstitious or uncivilized by the West. This complex does not allow you to give a serious thought to the true Islamic virtues. You are always anxious to give Islamic sanction to all those things that have a label of liberalism on them. May be that this kind of action brings you some good name in the Western circles, but this is never going to solve your problems nor will it give you the status of a living and free nation. It is not sensible.

We may seem to exaggerate about your mode of action but an honest and realistic self-analysis will testify to the truth of our claim.

You have observed that the West has based its entire banking system on "Interest". This is the system which is regarded as one of the prominent virtues of modern civilization. So, you started investing all your energy to make the interest permissible in trading system. You never bothered to ask yourself if the interest was really inevitable for the Banking system and why cannot this be run on the Principles of 'Mudaribah' provided by Islam and why the Islamic Principle of 'Mudaribah' cannot be adopted in Banking? At the cost of the opposition of the Muslim Ummah you have compound interests but you never cared to find out the principles of interest-free banking which assures us more equitable distribution of wealth.

The "Insurance" is regarded as a symbol of civilization in the West. You accepted it as it was and tried to give it Islamic sanction by making fabricated interpretations in the Quran and Sunnah. But you never knew that there was an easier and fairer way of making some minor changes in the prevailing insurance system and thus bring them in conformity with the established principles of Islam, making it more useful institution'

The Western countries have recently launched great campaigns to preach "Family Planning". You also followed them in propagating it. For this purpose you consumed your energies to misinterpret the laws of Islam in favour of family planning. But you never thought how China is surviving with its 700,000,000 population? According to Chu-en-lai every new child brings a message of prosperity. In the hue and cry of the Western world you looked at one mouth of a newly born child and felt uneasy to think from where to feed it? But you did not see the two hands of the child to work. The small country like Israel realised the importance of population and has been using all the means of increasing its population. The Westerner had said that population rise is dangerous far developing countries. You accepted this "sincere advice" and imposed birth control as a law, but you failed to see how Vietnam had humbled the big power like America and why the Western countries are scared of China? Americans had declared that in the East they would give financial aid only to those countries who would adopt the birth control. You took it as a sympathetic gesture from them but you did not try to argue why Israel gets the lion's share in aid inspite of being against the birth control?

You heard that polygamy is considered to be a crime in Western countries. In order to free yourself from this blame you made the excuse that Islam had allowed it only in some emergency conditions and now it is no more permissible. For this purpose you left no stone unturned in pulling and dragging the meanings of the verses of Holy Quran But did you ever try to investigate why the Westerners never feel the need of more than one wife? Thanks to Modern Civilization and the open practice of un-registered polygamy in every hotel, every night club and every park, there is no need of getting oneself involved in regular family life. The Westerners had publicised that polygamists are cruel to their wives. You started pleading that the fundamental conception of Islam is to stop such a tyranny and hence polygamy is forbidden in Islam. But you shut your eyes from the naked reality that there are innumerable people who are extremely cruel to their single wife. In fact the number of such people is greater. Hence this argument requires that single marriage also should be banned.

You observed that the Westerners consider Hijab (woman's veil) as a vice, so you started fabricating the established injunctions of Islam. But you never cared to think that by unveiling their women what disaster the West has brought to their homes? Did you ever care to know what is the cause of unabated grief of the serious thinkers of the West on this issue?

You came to know that co-education is practised in Western countries. You started advocating for it as an insignia of civilization, but never bothered to think of the reasons behind the dreadful scene of American culture presented by Kinsey Reports before the world?' Did you ever think who is responsible for ever increasing unlawful sexual relations in the young generation. What is the cause of ever decreasing standard of education?

You have read that many of the Westerners deity miracles and told them as superstition. Very obediently you also followed the example and tried to reject the miracles described by the Quran in detail. As a result of this you converted the entire Quran into a poetic and metaphorical book. But you never thought that those who had initially denied the miracles had also called the existence of God as the worst form of superstition. They had even mocked at prophethood and divine revelations. Further, you never paid any attention to the fact how rapidly the most recent researches of scientific knowledge are making miracles mote acceptable to human intellect.

Keeping all these facts in view, for God's sake, please tell us if there is any exaggeration in our assessment that you pay no heed to finding an Islamic and intellectual solution to these problems. On the contrary you are always looking for the Western ideologies. Whatever you receive from them as permissible you spend all your energy to prove it in conformity with Islam, with no concern to what damage you are causing to the Quran and Sunnah. When you notice any signs of dislike for something on the faces of Westerners you exhaust all your powers to declare it unlawful and prohibited in Islam even at the cost of giving away explicit injunctions of the Quran and Sunnah.

Further, it is noteworthy that so far you have taken into consideration only those problems which have been raised by the Westerners. You paid no heed to the multitude of genuine problems of our own society, and no attempt was made to solve these problems. A clear example of this is: You promptly noticed the injustice which the polygamist do to their wives even though such incidences are rare in our society, while the brutalities done by the monogamists are so common that hardly any family is devoid of it. You will find innumerable women who have no co-wives yet they are leading a miserable life due to inequity of their husbands. The plight of such women does not stir your heart, you feel no sympathy for their helplessness and make no attempt to free them from the cruel grip of their cruel husbands?

Your pen did not move for a single word against the evil customs of our society with reference to marriages, dowry, Mehr, living allowances, housing and inter family relations. You made no move against the defective, time consuming and outdated judiciary system, which has deprived society of justice. In matrimonial matters you could see only one thing, that is, polygamy which is practised hardly by 10% of people, and you consumed all your efforts in proving it as unlawful. The reason of your serious concern against polygamy is that it was initiated from the West and hence it sounded most important to you, while other problems being local, could not achieve your serious consideration.

Moreover, the problems that ever came to your attention, you tried to solve them by strange method. Inspite of investigating into the real causes of the problems you just took the easy way of finding temporary and easygoing solutions.

Due to ignorance from the teachings of Islam the common people have developed a practice of throwing three divorces to their wives on trivial matters. This practice is absolutely wrong and impermissible which is usually the cause of social disorder. It was essential that a wide publicity was made to educate people on gravity of this sin and its evil consequences. It was further necessary to decide if any legal punishment for such a sin can be imposed or not? Surprisingly, you brought out the solution to this problem that makes a mockery of the entire judicial system of Islam. Your solution was that "three" should be counted as one, thus giving free licence to men to give as many divorces as they could without being acknowledged as three. Is it not like a person being beaten by another, when the oppressed man calls you for help you tell him "Keep taking the punishment, we shall never accept that you had been beaten". Is this the way of freeing the oppressed from oppression?

You observed that sometimes an orphan grandson is left unprotected after the death of his paternal grandfather. Your solution to the problem is to cut a portion of legacy of his paternal uncles and give it to him. But you failed to conceive that if it be set into practice how would you solve the problem of orphan nephews? Why should they be deprived of a share in the heritage of their uncles? You also ignored the basic moral obligation that you cannot remove the distress of one person in the Robin Hood fashion. For removing the distress of such helpless persons Islamic Law provides adequate relief These methods are explained in "Kitab-un-Nafqat", "Kitab-ul-Wasiyyah" and "Kitab-uz-Zakah". If the rules laid down in them are implemented properly they would be of great help to the distressed.

The above observations if given due consideration, with no prejudices in mind, provide with the only conclusion that the Institute of Islamic Research and its co-workers are basically wrong in my very mode of thinking. As a result of it they have not only been unable to do any service to the country and the nation but in fact created disruption, uneasiness, confusion and anxiety throughout the country. How we wish that the authorities of this extremely important institute give serious, sincere and selfless thought as to how harmful and dangerous for national unity is the way adopted by them?

We have not made these submissions for supporting any group, but it is a sincere and devoted effort to incite them on giving a serious and sincere consideration to our deliberations.

The Reinterpretation : Some years ago, a convention of *Ulama* (Religious scholars) was held in Islamabad under the auspices of Ministry of Religious Affairs, Pakistan. In the open session of this convention the (then) president of Pakistan, Gen. Zia-ul Haq, was also present. One of the topics of this convention was "How to start the process of Ijtihad (reinterpretation) in the country". The extempore speech of the Editor of Al-Balagh given on this occasion has now been published in a booklet by transcribing it from tape-recorded speech which is reproduced below.

I conceive that the recommendations submitted by the four committees of this convention in this short time are promising and encouraging. When this programme was being announced yesterday it was not expected that such solid recommendations could be prepared in such a short time. But, on the whole, the recommendations prepared by all the four committees are very commendable and encouraging. Every person had to be a member of one of these committees therefore a member of certain committee did not get a chance to express his views before other committees. I, therefore, seek to express my views with regard to the problems that were discussed by the committees that did not have me as a member.

The committee dealt with the ways and means to enhance the speed of Islamization which is the real object of this convention has done a remarkable job. I fully endorse every word of the recommendations by this committee and also request that they should be given thorough consideration and be examined with all their intentions and spirits and immediate action should be taken.

Similarly the recommendations made by the Unity and Consonant committee are also very encouraging and in fact, if they can be put to practice they will play a very effective role in chooking the epidemics of disunity and disruption.

Just now I want to draw your attention about the third committee which have been formed in connection with the process of "Ijtihad", and its recommendations have been presented by Moulana Muhammad Malik Kandhalvi and Allama Syed Muhammad Razi Mujtahid. Since this gathering is, more or less, a representative gathering of *Ulama* (Religious scholars), I think the decisions taken here will have a far reaching effect. Hence I wish to state that contradicting misunderstandings are present about "Ijtihad" in our society at present. As a result at times we notice an extreme degree of inactivity and at other times equal degree of over-activity in this field..

In my opinion, and this is not my individual or exclusive opinion but it is derived from the Quran, Hadith and verdicts of jurists of Islam that "ijtihad" is like a double-edged sword. If it is properly understood, and used within its limitations of fulfilling the conditions laid down for it, this can be a source of great treasure of Islamic laws, and a matter of great pride for the nation. But, if it is allowed to be wrongly used by incapable persons it will result in creating false concepts and irreligious movements as we read in the books like Al-milal Wan-Nahl'. Those views and claims had their sway for sometime but now they exist only in the pages of ancient books.

The same Ijtihad can be used to find practical ways for the Muslim Ummah, and the same can lead to such ridiculous interpretations as were advanced in our country. The Quran said:

> And as the thief, man or woman, cut off the hands of both.

This Quranic verse was interpreted that 'thief man and thief woman" means "capitalists"; and "cut off their hands" signify "Nationalise their industries". This interpretation has not been made by a person of ordinary literary status, but by a person of our country who is supposed to be a renowned intellectual.

Similarly, in this country it has been expounded through Ijtihad that "interest" is not forbidden, and that intoxicants are also permissible. It is through the same type of Ijtihad that they tried every evil of Western civilization to make permissible; and it is through this that an endless chain of religious manipulations has been started.

It is in this context that I have called it a double-edged sword. If it is not used with necessary precautions and some one starts attempting it without having the required proficiency he would open the door to distorting the religion, and would lead to extreme degree of misleading conceptions.

Some people think that "Ijtihad" allows taking a decision through personal opinion in religious matters. This must be fully understood that this practice has never been regarded as "Ijtihad" in Islam. The one who considers it as "Ijtihad"' has in fact fallen into great error. The door of "Ijtihad" had been opened by the Holy Prophet (PBUH), and the Hadith reported by Maaz bin Jabal has made it clear. The Prophet asked Maaz "How will you decide on a thing not found in the Book of Allah?" He replied, "I will follow the Prophetic traditions (Sunnah). The Prophet then asked, 'what would you do if you find nothing in sunnah?" He replied, I will do "Ijtihad" with my personal opinion." It is quite apparent from this Hadith that there is no room for "Ijtihad" in matters explicated by the Quran and the Sunnah. If some one attempts Ijtihad in such matters it will not be called "Ijtihad" but fabrication or distortion.

If "Ijtihad" could be permitted in matters where explicit injunctions from the Quran and Hadith are present, there was no need for the advent of Prophets and Messengers. The purpose of Wahy (Divine Revelation) was that right way be shown to people through Wahy in matters, where man cannot make correct decision through his intellect. Had it been an open field for everyone to do as he or she thinks proper there was no need to follow the Quran or Prophetic traditions. It would have been sufficient to say that people should lead their lives according to their personal likings, opinions and reasoning as the time and circumstances demand. This misunderstanding must be removed about the application of Ijtihad, and whatever resolutions are passed must fully observe this point.

Sometimes, however, "Ijtihad" is not taken as a freedom of opinion to prevail over the Quran and tradition, but whenever the process of "Ijtihad" is discussed an impression is given that the Quran and traditions have been revealed to us for the first time and no work has been done in the field of interpretation and explanation for all these fourteen hundred years and that the meanings deduced by us through personal reasoning shall be "Ijtihad" that must be implemented.

This concept is sometimes deliberately propagated while the fact is that we are not living in a vacuum but we are living in an era which has the background of fourteen centuries of loudable efforts in the field of Quranic learning by renowned companions of the Prophet, their followers, religious scholars, jurists of Islam and devoted personalities of the Omamah. They have spent their lives in devotion to the cause of exegesis of the Quran and interpretation of the Prophetic traditions, and the sacrifices they have made for this cause are beyond our imagination. They had to go through the troubles of starvation and rough clothing and poorest means of sustenance for this noble cause and left behind a huge collection of this work. Now, throwing all this collection in a dust-bin and start making fresh interpretations through the agency of "Ijtihad" unsupported by the Quran and the Sunnah it will be an act of shameful self deception. It will mean that all the collections of the jurists be ignored and totally a Fiqh of Islam be prepared.

A sensible solution, however, that answers to new problems may be sought in the light of existing rules and principles derived from the Quran and traditions. This is the right application of "Ijtihad" in the right direction. Indeed countless problems may arise in every new period that are not defined by the Quran and the Prophetic traditions or no answer to these problems is provided by the available Fatawa (verdicts) of the jurists. Being within these limits and seeking the solutions to newer problems and understand the intentions of jurists and the intentions of the Shariah is called true "Ijtihad" and this is the "Ijtihad" whose doors have not been closed to anyone so far.

This is a sheer propaganda that the door of Ijtihad is closed. Nobody has ever closed it. This door has been opened by the Holy Prophet and shall remain open till the Last Day, and as long as this Ijtihad remains in capable hands nobody can close it. This is the type of Ijtihad that is needed in the present time. Countless problems have come up before us about which we find no explicit injunctions or there are practical difficulties in their implementations. The door of Ijtihad is open for solving these problems.

Here, I wish to point out that the topic of the committee has been phrased "How to start the process of Ijtihad in our country?" The sentence seems to claim that the process of Ijtihad has not been started out so far, and now it is being started Which was not in practice before. I wish to submit that this supposition is not correct. The required Ijtihad which the Muslim Ummah really needs is not a new thing. It was in practice before. If now an organised method is provided to it, it would be appreciable. But to think that the scholars of Islamic learning had not been doing this Ijtihad before is not correct. The true Ijtihad, that is needed, had been 'in process and shall continue to be in future.

What we said above was about the principles in this regard. The recommendation of the committee that has come before us is that a Board of the *Ulama* (The Religious scholars) be formed to carry out Ijtihad and present their opinions on new problems. In this connection, I may be allowed to point out an important Islamic practice. The history of fourteen hundred years of Islam reminds us that Islam did never form a supreme authoritative institution or clergy an institution whose opinion should be the last word depriving everyone of the right of criticism as is the case with Christianity. It is in Christianity that Pope is regarded as beyond all errors and infallible to everything.

The system in Islamic Ijtihad has been that no authoritative organisation with absolute powers was ever formed. The opinions of the *Ulama* carrying out Ijtihad are publicised and are open to free criticism by other *Ulama* and ultimately the decision about their being right or wrong is made only on the basis of the collective consensus of the Ummah to accept an Ijtihad or reject it. Hence, if the intention of creating a Board of Ijtihad is that its interpretations are imposed on the Muslims as the last word, and other *Ulama* are not allowed to express their opinion against it, then in my opinion this is not a right objective.

Another thing to be noted is that establishing an institution exclusively for Ijtihad at this time may have some practical problems and may call for some financial implications as well. Hence I propose that we have already got an institution by the name of "Council for Islamic Ideology" and another institution by the name of "Institute of Islamic Research", this responsibility may be entrusted to them. As has been proposed by the committee, a comprehensive list of the problems which need Ijtihad be prepared and handed over to these institutions. However, the officials of these institutions should not limit these considerations to themselves but they should invite other *Ulama* and scholars of the country to express their opinion before a decision is announced by the Council for Islamic Ideology.

It will reduce the financial burden on the one hand and on the other the duplication of work will be eliminated. Otherwise the new Board for Ijtihad in the presence of the Council of Islamic Ideology may give birth to new problems. If a difference arises between the two institutions a third committee or institution will be needed to remove it. Hence it will be better if the Council of Islamic Ideology or Institute of Islamic Research are entrusted the work of preparing a list of such problems and then call for the renowned, qualified jurists and devoted scholars of Islam for a joint session, and take guidance from them and then arrive at a unanimous conclusion.

It has been reported with authentic sources in the tradition of Majma-al-Zawaid by Hadrat Ali bin Abi Talib that the Prophet (PBUH) was asked "We may be faced with problems after you in which there may be neither a command nor prohibition from you. What should we do in a situation like this?" In quite a few words the Prophet provided us with the right way. He said, "Consult the jurists (Legal experts) and the devotees cognisant with religion, and do not impose individual opinion as if it was the collective view of the Ummah". He thus advised to call for people having two qualifications, that is, they are jurists and devoted to the cause of Islam, consult them and then reach a conclusion.

If the Council of Islamic Ideology and Institute of Islamic Research keep these principles in view and consult the *Ulama* when needed, then publish their opinion allowing open freedom of criticism to other *Ulama*. Anyone having opposing views be allowed to express himself. In this way the process of Ijtihad can continue in the same manner as it had been continuing over the last fourteen hundred years. In case we adopt self-conceived means and methods we cannot hope to make the desired progress.

In the end I wish to submit that any such institution if formed under the supervision of the State it is essential to take into consideration the fact that governments keep changing and rulers replaced. Hence it should be formed on the principles which keep them practicable under all circumstances. Thus the selection of the workers should be made on the basis of knowledge and devotion rather than on political grounds. If this factor is effectively incorporated in the basic terms of reference of such institutions, the process of Ijtihad will, by the Grace of Allah, be a source of blessing to us, and we shall be able to guard against the dangers which could be created by the wrong use of Ijtihad in our society.

With these reservation I endorse the recommendations of the committee."

Progressive Thoughts

A critical question :

> "Is the present day research about the moon, the sun and the planets in accordance with the Quran There, are some people who claim that there is no inconformity between science and the Quran and the Traditions, hence everything the science presents is correct, while others say that the views of science clash with the Quran. Kindly give your comprehensive view and opinion about it"

Answer : An elaborate answer of this question requires comprehensive article. However, I am presenting certain things by way of principles hoping that they will be helpful to remove your doubt in this matter.

1. First of all it must be understood that the purpose of science is to explore the fundamental forces which Allah

has created in this universe. If these forces are used for the welfare and well being of mankind it is not only permissible but desirable in Islam. Rather than raising obstacles in the way of such attempts Islam encourages them. In this connection Islam only demands that these forces should be used for the purpose that are permissible and useful in the eyes of Islam. In other words, science aims at discovering the hidden forces of universe but the correct use of these forces is told by religion which provides proper direction and better atmosphere for such attempts. Science and technology can be useful to mankind only if they are used on the principles laid down by Islam. Nobody would deny the fact that whereas science can be a means to the welfare and material progress of mankind, its wrongful and misdirected use can be disastrous for us. The example is before us. In recent years science has provided mankind with the means of comfort and ease, but at the same time its wrongful use has converted the whole world into the hell of turmoil and disturbance. It is the science that invented the high speed means of travel like the jet planes but at the same time the science is responsible of creating disastrous nuclear bombs, hence true benefits from it can be achieved only when it is used according to the principles laid down by Allah.

2. The second thing to understand is that scientific discoveries are of two kinds. Firstly those which pertain to human observation. Such discoveries are never in opposition to the Quran and the Traditions. In fact, they have helped to affirm the Quran and traditions in many things which were difficult for people to understand. For example, the tremendous speed of the "Buraq" (The heavenly horse) on which the Prophet travelled from Mecca to Jerusalem on the night of Ascension, was regarded as unimaginable by the so-called intellectuals of that time. But the science has today proved that the speed is a relative entity that cannot be bound to any limits.

Secondly, there are some views that are based on conjectures and presumptions due to lack of knowledge, rather than observation and certainty. The scientists have not reached any definite conclusions on these matters so far. Such findings sometimes are opposed to the explicit views of the Quran and the traditions. In such situations the most proper way is to maintain firm faith in them without making new interpretation to the Quran. The scientific researches that clash with them should be regarded as yet inconclusive due to lack of knowledge about them. The more scientific knowledge keeps growing the more it will help to expound the realities described by the Quran and the Traditions.

For example, the scientists think that the "sky" has no physical existence. Obviously this hypothesis is not based on observation and definite proof but on the assumption that they have not been able to get any trace of the existence of the sky hence they do not accept its existence. In other words this hypothesis is based on "non existence of knowledge" rather than "knowledge of non -existence". Hence we, the believers in the Quran and the Traditions, assert with full confidence that this hypothesis of the scientists is not correct. According to the Quran and Tradition the skies do exist but due to its lack of knowledge science has not been able to discover it. If scientific knowledge continues to increase it is quite possible that the scientists realize their mistake and they accept the existence of the ideas, just as they have accepted many other things which they had been denying earlier.

The problem is that the tendency of looking everything in its own perspective is gradually fading away from our minds. Whenever the importance of certain thing dominates our mind we find it difficult to remain within bounds. Undoubtedly, science and technology are Very useful and essential branch of learning, and in the present times they are an inevitable requirement for the Muslim (Ummah) to survive. It is not possible to attain their due place in the world today without science. But this certainly does not mean that any hypothesis proclaimed by a scientist based on conjectures and individual ideas should be accepted as true and given the status of Divine Revelation (Wahy) and the door of interpolations and alterations in the Quran and the Sunnah be opened, or doubts and suspicions be given air on this basis, particularly when it is often observed that scientific views and theories are changing every day.

3. It must be remembered that the case of Islam is quite different from that of Christianity. 'The latter did not have the very force and spirit to stand against newly arising needs and scientific discoveries of man. Hence, science threatened it as a great danger. Thus, in order to uphold the prestige of the church, it was essential for Christianity either to oppose scientific achievements or make amendments in the religion itself. In the beginning Roman Catholic church adopted the first course. Having full power and authority on the people, the scientists, like Galileo, had to face tremendous punishments. But when the authority of church was made to lose its grip they had no alternatives than to make new interpretations and fabricate the religion itself. Hence the scholars of modernism adopted this way.

It happened because the whole edifice of Christianity was erected on extremely unnatural and baseless grounds. Islam is a different religion. It is the natural religion and no sensible argument can challenge it. It is fully capable of fulfilling the needs of the time and to satisfy the demands of new circumstances without making any changes in the religion. Our belief is that the truth of Islam will flourish more and more with the advancement of science and scientific knowledge, provided that his point of view remains scientific in the real sense of the word and he does not give his conjectures the status of certainty and observation.

This is what the religious scholars of Islam think. It implies that everything must be looked in its true perspective. It will not be wise to cross the limits misled by sentimental slogans.

How strange it is that due to this moderate and absolutely reasonable attitude some people are constantly propagating that the scholars of Islam are opposed to science and technology and they do not like any progress in this field. We can only pray to Almighty Allah to bless them with common sense. Ameen!

Conquest of Space : In the last few years the historical achievements attained by American scientists in the field of space technology, particularly the incident of man's landing on the moon, has attracted the attention of the entire world. Undoubtedly, the amazing journey of Apollos in the space have presented a wonderful exposure of human intellect. The success achieved by them is extremely valuable and a historical marvel from the scientific point of view. They have indeed demonstrated the highest accuracy of mathematical calculations and technological implementation of the scientific ideas. They are able to make predictions of extraordinary circumstances.

The first time man has examined the moon from so near through these spacecrafts. If a century ago somebody claimed that man had reached the moon by flying in the space or that he had seen the earth rising from the horizon of the moon, it would have been considered a fabulous story of the Arabian Nights. It is a reality today.

Every phase of this journey, right from the "take off' of the spacecraft to its successful landing on the earth, is an extremely amazing feat for the common man. From the purely scientific point of view this journey is an achievement that can never be forgotten. But this is only one side of the picture. Taking in view the end result of this wonderful journey reminds us an incident that occurred at the time of Caliph Haroon-al-Rasheed.

It is stated that a certain person sought the permission of Caliph to present an astonishing performance in his court. When the permission granted he erected a needle upright on the floor and himself stood at some distance with a few needles in his hand. Then he took one of those needles in the other hand, aimed at the needle on the floor, and threw the needle in his hand toward it. People saw that this needle passed through the eye of the needle on the floor. He repeated this performance several times and never missed the target even once.

On seeing this astonishing feat the Caliph ordered, "Give him ten dinars, and punish him with ten lashes!" The courtiers asked for an explanation of this equally astonishing reward. The Caliph said, "He gets ten dinars for his accuracy of aim, truthfulness and ambition, as a reward. But he will get ten lashes as a punishment for spending his capabilities in a thing that is of no benefit to any one materially or spiritually."

This incident of the prudence and wit of Haroon-al- is fully applicable to the space-race of the present times. In fact one feels obliged to commend and praise the scientists on the remarkable feat of landing on the moon who have set unique records of their technical and intellectual skill and their courage and endurance. But when we see how much mental, financial and physical energy of mankind has been spent on this and what humanity received in return, this very achievement becomes an international crime.

Since there are several misunderstandings, perplexing the minds of the people we would discuss the matter in some detail.

There is a group of simple people who think that all these attempts to conquer moon and space are contradictory to the views of the Quran and the tradition and (God forbid) they are a challenge to the authority of God. So much so that, some people have been heard saying, purely out of love for Islam, that all the news about landing on the moon are fictions and they cannot be relied upon. But the fact is that if the scientists of America or Russia or any Other country reach the moon or mars or any other planet, it does not in any way clash with the Quran and the traditions, nor does it affect the supreme authority of God. There is not a single verse of the Quran or narration of the Prophet which denies the ascent of man to moon or Mars or any other planet.

On the contrary, if those travelling in the space keep their eyes open to realities they will find clear signs of the truth of the Quran and the traditions. They will observe with their naked eyes the realities of many Islamic concepts which are made more comprehensible through the progress of the scientific knowledge, and which were previously mocked at by the blind followers of Rationalism. For instance, the description of the incredible speed of the "Buraq" in the Holy Traditions, with reference to the Ascension, was regarded as fairy-tale by the so-called pioneers of rationalism. But the astronauts of today have circled around the world in less than an hour and thus proved that speed is something that can not be confined to any limits. So when the American scientists and astronauts can exhibit such an astonishing super speed through the limited powers of their mind why can't the unlimited power of the Cherisher and Sustainer (Allah) of this universe give even a higher speed, to any of His creatures.

In short, we have firm belief, and there is nothing to shake it, that man is bound to salute and acknowledge the realities of the Quran and the Sunnah with the ever increasing progress of science and technology, if, of course, he remains within the bounds and does not claim his calculations to be scientific observations. The religion brought by the Holy Prophet Muhammad (PBUH) is not like the religion of Christianity which should be frightened by the progress of science. This is the religion which is the most symmetrical with human nature. It had openly proclaimed fourteen centuries ago, that:

> "We shall soon show them Our signs in the horizons and within themselves, until it becomes clear to them that this is the Truth". (Ha Mim As Sajdah: 53)

Imam Razi has quoted earlier commentators to say that the signs in the "Horizons" means the wonders of skies, moon and stars and the elements. The phrase "We will show our signs" means that these wonders have no limits. Thus Allah will continue exhibiting new wonders in every era of time.

On the other side there is a group among the Muslims who are so much dazzled with the grandeur of science that they see nothing more valuable, more important and worth following than throwing rockets on the planets. The overawed tone and longing with which these people talk of this type of scientific advancement gives an impression that for them the most fortunate and exalted and benefactor of mankind is the nation that has performed this wondrous feat, and most deprived are those who have lagged behind in this "sacred" race.

The Same Mentality : You must have heard people saying— "the world has entrapped the moon and planets but the Muslims are still entangled in the problems of Salah, fasting, marriage and divorce"-. This expression actually depicts the same mentality that the Western nations, have surpassed all other nations in every walk of life by inventing the rockets and satellites, and hence the solution to all our problems must be sought by following the footsteps of the West.

In fact both these trends are dangerous. We have no hesitation in acknowledging that this is an amazing achievement, and from the scientific point of view, it is a great success of man. But the question arises whether this "achievement" was worth attempting in view of the price man had to pay for it? There are many who take pleasure out of the success of space explorations but very few know what quantity of wealth was spent in each of these space journeys? The expenses incurred on Apollo-8 were one trillion and twenty billion rupees (*Jang*, Karachi, 14 January 1969). This amount was equivalent to at least twenty annual budgets and six years of national income of Pakistan. In other words the amount spent by Pakistan in twenty years and the money earned by 100 million people of Pakistan in six years was spent on only one space journey. It is the amount spent only on the journey of the Appollo-8. The journey of Appolo- 10 must have cost far more money than the Appollo-8. It is equal to the money that could be spent by Pakistan in 80 years.

The question arises can it be the act of any one having slightest compassion for mankind to spend billion of trillions rupees in space journey in a world where people are massacred by hunger and poverty, where millions of people are begging for a loaf of bread, where countless people die for not being able to get the medicines required for their ailment, where about half the population remain deprived of education facilities? In America itself which has the "honour" of performing the "great achievement" a report was published in the same month in which one trillion and twenty billion rupees were spent on Apollo-8, that one out of every nine persons is destitute, and that:

> "Poverty is the greatest material problem of today"
> (Weekly "Time" New York, 24 January 1929, p29)

This huge expenditure on the useless probe of space in a country like America cannot be justified for a nation who claims to be sympathetic to mankind. It seems that Saadi had been addressing the astronauts of today when he said:

> You have well solved the problems of the earth That
> you are going to play with the heavens.

If a man from the East tries to show the other side of the picture of space-race, it may be said that lie is saying it due to his jealousy for Western advancement. Hence we present the comments of a renowned historian and thinker of the West itself on this subject. A very thoughtful article of distinguished historian and philosopher of England Dr. Arnold Tyne Bee has been published. We are presenting herewith a summary of its excerpts. After admitting the wondrous feat of space achievements he writes:

> "Even today 10% or 20% of American population comprises of indigent people. Looking at the world as a whole only one third of its increasing population is such as is getting proper food. Hence utilisation of the economic resources of mankind is in the foolish pursuits of erecting the Pyramids of Egypt or landing on the moon, which, in themselves, are included in the list of the crimes.
>
> "The world of today is involved in three wars. Individual strikes are getting frequent. Students are protesting everywhere and different ways of terrorism are being adopted. All this is happening under the disgraceful feeling that use of force is the only way to attract attention of people when one is offended."
>
> "People of Russia and America had been congratulating each other on their space achievements although the main cause of this "stupidity- had been their own rivalries. If these two political powers had not been in combat with each other on the small planet of Earth this "stupidity" would not have occurred."
>
> "From the very early days of history of human activities, the technical advancement and moral degradation of man are becoming inseparable. The history of our science and technology is indeed a wonderful "Tale of achievements" but the history of our mutual relations has been proved to be a story of grief and regrets on our failures. This is the moral "gap" which after 1945 A.D. has widened to the extent that it has opened a vast channel for disaster to enter."

In this atomic age, the priority must be given to save ourselves from the crime of wasting the lives of other human beings For, this, it is essential that a Supreme government should be formed on the universal level and all local governments be placed under it. But this is becoming even more difficult than landing on the moon because at present Nationalism has become as sacred as an idol. To part with a false deity need greater courage and bravery in this world than is needed by the astronauts.

"Next in the list of priority comes making effective arrangements to produce food for the population on this earth. We do not know the extent to which world population would have gone by the time the movement of' family planning gains popularity throughout the world However we do know that we should not waste a single moment to increase the supply of food. The fast moving technological progress should equally speed up the productivity in every field."

These are the two most important targets before mankind while space adventures can not be of any service to any of them.

Hence, the fact is that the conquest of space is an absolutely wasteful exercise, and by spending out energies in this direction we are intentionally imposing on ourselves huge economic liabilities. We cannot, and should not ignore our economic problems at a time when human race is heading fast toward starvation.

As to the question that in case we put the space programme at the bottom of our agenda, delete the preparation of war from it, what alternate use of the scientific knowledge of our inventor be?

The question has already been answered by the Japanese government. The researches of scientists should be directed to explore the resources hidden in the sea instead of wasting them in space and war strategies .

The sea is within the reach of man as against the nearest planet from the earth. The two-third area of our planet is water and it is a huge treasure of' the unknown resources. It has been estimated that there exists the greatest store of natural resources in the sea which remains yet unexplored.

This is a vast field of research for man and in addition to satisfying the desire for research it may also provide a surety that the population will not die of starvation even if it increases ten-fold of the current population.

A yellow female fish lays one million eggs during its life span, but under ordinary circumstances only three fully grown fish can be produced that would be capable of laying further eggs. But when Japan's "sea-farmers" tried to enhance the ability of these eggs artificially and nurtured the stock of eggs and protected them from other animals it resulted in the production of 100,000 fish from the eggs of one fish.

When Apollo-8 returned after its victorious flight I received a telephone call from across the Atlantic a few hours after it, "Do you think this is a revolutionary incidence in the history of mankind?" My answer was 'NO'.

"My answer could have been 'Yes' if the news of that day had been that humanity has suddenly regained its consciousness and it has formed a universal central state, and their researchers have discovered from the depth of the sea things that can be used by mankind for its collective purposes." We have yet to achieve this revolutionary aim, and for that the first step of the world powers should be to divert their resources towards the collective advancement of human beings instead of wasting them in space adventures and war weapons. If this is achieved the population of the entire world can be brought to the standard of living now enjoyed by 80% of American people.

This will indeed be a 'Revolutionary incidence' but this will not be achieved through technology alone. If one wants to reap fruits through the power of technology the essential condition for it is a spiritual revolution. This spiritual surgery is our dire need and without it all our recently discovered' material resources would be useless. Even if we land on the moon without the spiritual revival the dust and ashes obtained from there will mock at our spiritual bankruptcy from which we could not get rid of in our motherland."

In this article Dr. Tyne Bee has made a wise diagnosis of the disease, and if you give a little thought you will know that the root cause of this disease is that the people tracking the heavenly bodies have no definite aim nor any exalted motto of life. All the ways of their struggle have been lost in their childish desire of surpassing others. The result is that they have not been able to utilise their unlimited capabilities for the conquest of this universe that could lead mankind to the goal of peace and tranquillity. All their energy is being spent in combating with each-other, in surpassing or defeating each other, and in this struggle they have overlooked to note what great harm they have inflicted on themselves.

A race between the two parties, no matter how fast and speedy it is, cannot be of any benefit to humanity if it is not in the right direction. Tyne Bee was right in saying that spiritual surgery was needed to take full advantage of science. But what he does not know is that such a surgical treatment cannot be possible without submission to the greatest benefactor of mankind. Muhammad (Peace of Allah be upon him) had made the return trip to heavenly destination far beyond the moon, Mars, Venus and Plato and which is beyond the scientific imagination. Instead of directing his followers to conquer the moon he asked them to conquer the hearts and souls of the people. Unless the world kneels down to his feet and seeks guidance from Him, it will never be able to acquire peace and tranquillity, though it may launch numerous artificial satellites or plant its rags on the Moon or Mars or any other planet. After the landing on the moon all further advancement of science in this direction will prove more disastrous for mankind and only add to the uneasiness and darken the clouds of suffering and distress over mankind.

Dr. Iqbal, the great philosopher-poet of East has rightly said:

> "The one who is seeking the paths of heavenly bodies, could not travel in the world of his own thoughts. He captured the rays of the sun, but could not turn his night into the dawn of life. He was so much involved in the perplexities of his logic that he remains unable to decide between gain and loss."

The Conquest of the Universe : This is no secret : The Holy Quran has expounded the fact in many places that the entire universe has been created for mankind and every particle has been placed for the service of human beings. It stated:

> He is (Allah) Who created for you all that is in the earth. (2:29)

> And He (Allah) has subjugated to you all that is in the heavens and all that is in the earth, altogether from Him. Surely in that are signs for a people who reflect. (45:13)

In these verses, while describing His bounties, Allah has made subtle indication that since all these things have been created for man, it is man's duty to get knowledge and explore them by applying his logic and wisdom bestowed on him by Allah, for the benefit of mankind. He should put to his use all resources that Allah has stored in the universe. There are two kinds of bounties of Allah created in the universe. The things that are general which man uses in his life, yet there are some bounties which can be acquired by the use of knowledge and wisdom. The Quran said:

> Have you not seen how Allah has subjugated to you whatsoever is in the heavens and whatsoever is in the earth, and He has perfected His blessings on you, (both) open and hidden?

In other words, Allah has indeed subjugated the universe to man yet it does not mean that he shall get all these blessings without striving for them and using physical and mental talents for achieving them.

At another place the Holy Quran said:

> Allah is He, who has subjugated the sea to you that the ships may sail through it by His command, and that you may seek of His bounty and that you may offer thanks. (Q.45:12)

In this verse the cause for subjugation of sea has been described as providing it as a means of seeking Allah's blessings and bounties. In the Quran "seeking Allah's bounty" generally means "striving for earning the livelihood". Hence, one meaning of this verse may be that mankind has been given authority and power of navigation on the sea so that he may trade through it. Some commentators have, however, stated that "seeking Allah's bounty" in this verse does not mean trade but research and exploration of countless other bounties that He has created in the sea. The verse then means: "We have subjugated the sea for you after creating in it innumerable useful things so that you may seek for them and make use of them". Thus, every now and then the discoveries of modern science are making it apparent that the treasures of mineral and botanical products hidden in the sea are far more than those on the earth.

The Quran has explicitly pointed out at various places that even new bounties of this universe will get exposed as often as man would march forward in the way of research and exploration. For example, where the Quran has mentioned horses and mules as means of transport, it has further pointed out that in future there will come out such means of transport which man did not know at that stage.

(Allah has created for you) horses, mules and donkeys that you may ride on them, and (in future) He will create such things which as yet you don't know.

In this manner the Quran has pointed out to all kinds of means of communication to be invented till the Last Day.

At another place it said:

> We shall show them Our signs, in the universe and also in their selves until it is clear to them that this (Quran) is the Truth.

This verse signifies that the exposition of Allah's attribute of creation will never cease to create. The new blessings and productions will keep appearing in every-era of time till the Last Day.

Many more statements from the Quran and prophetic traditions can be produced on this subject, but even if these few verses are positively reflected upon, the reality will be exposed as broad daylight that if access through research, investigation, experiments and discoveries is made to the hidden powers of the universe with rightful intentions and rightful methods, it is not condemnable in the eyes of the Quran. Rather, it is desirable, and not only that Islam has not laid down any restriction on such scientific experiments, it has, in fact, encouraged them: This is the reason why Muslims have left lasting impressions of their scientific endeavours which will continue to serve as guidelines for mankind.

However, it must be remembered that the concept of conquering the universe as presented by Islam is quite different from the materialistic concept of the West. The West has also undertaken the task of conquering it, and indeed in the last few years they have attained extraordinary successes in this field. But the first and fundamental difference of Islam with the West is that their restricted material visualisation of things have deprived them of seeing the vast world beyond matter. Hence whatever new inventions are made by them are regarded as the fruits of their own power, intellect and labour. They do not perceive the active hand of the Creator or Master behind these discoveries. But the vision of Islam sees things beyond the investigations, experiments and discoveries and it observes the supreme power of creation of Allah behind them. Allah has subjugated the entire universe for mankind on one hand, and on the other hand it has bestowed man with intellect, wisdom, power and energy through which he has been able to dominate the forces of this universe. Hence the teaching of Islam is that after the success gained in the process of subjugation of universe he should kneel down before his Creator and Master in humble submission rather than be proud and arrogant. It is Allah who awarded him with the honour of ruling over the entire universe. According to the Quranic teaching the call of a true Muslim on such occasions is:

> "Glorified be He Who has subjugated (all) this to us and we ourselves were not capable to do it, and surely to our Lord we shall return."

The second fundamental difference between Islam and the West with regard to the conquest of the universe is that the ultimate object of the Western efforts in this direction is the conquest of the universe itself According to them the aim of man's life is nothing more than gaining the maximum benefit and pleasure out of the universe, and depart from this world. Contrary to this, subjugation of universe, in the eyes of Islam, is not final aim by itself, but it is a means to achieve the goal, and only a milestone on the path of man's destination. Islamic point of view is that man gets the right to utilize the services of this universe only when he fulfils the purpose of his creation and discharges his duties rightly and sincerely. Almighty Allah has not subjugated this universe to man without purpose and the purpose is that man should perform the duty imposed on him with precision and honesty. This duty is worship and submission to Allah.

Allah said:

> "And I have not created the Jinn and mankind but to worship Me". (51:56)

The third fundamental difference between the West and Islam is that any new force or power which man comes to possess as a result of his struggle for dominating the universe can be applied or used for any purpose that is allowed by human reason. But Islam teaches that the purpose of its use is determined by Almighty Allah, who has bestowed that power upon man, hence these inventions and discoveries can be used only for the objectives permitted by Him. When man determines by himself the purpose without the guidance of Divine Revelations, these bounties of the universe may sometimes lead him to the path of destruction instead of giving any benefit to mankind. This results in the fact that despite hoisting his flag on the Moon and Mars his own life seems to fall into the abyss of darkness. Thus the Islamic concept of subjugation of the universe is more universal and comprehensive than of the West and more beneficial for mankind. May Almighty Allah give us the ability to recognise its true values and to practise them in the right directions. (Amen)

Bibliography

Adair and Yazbeck Haddad : *Islamic Values in the United States,* Oxford, New York, 1997.

Ahmad, Aziz: *Studies in Islamic Culture in the Indian Environment,* Oxford, New York, 1964.

Ahmed, Hasanuddin : *Principles of Islamic .Culture,* Goodword Books Pvt. Ltd., New Delhi, 1989.

—— : *Islamic Business Ethics,* Goodword Books Pvt. Ltd., New Delhi, 1998.

Ahmad, Khurshid : *Islam : its Meaning and Message,* Islamic Council of Europe, London, 1976.

Akhtar, Hakeem M. : *Remedies to Spiritual Maladies,* Idara Ishaat-e-Diniyat Pvt. Ltd, New Delhi, 1991.

Ali, Adil : *Presidential Addresses on Arab Islamic Studies,* Kitab Bhavan, New Delhi, 2002.

Ali, S. Ameer : *Muhammadan Law,* Kitab Bhavan, New Delhi, 1986.

Amini, Mualana Taqi : *Fundamentals of Ijtihad,* Idaara-I-Adabiyat, Delhi, 1986.

Arnold and Guillaume : *The Legacy of Islam,* Oxford University Press, London, 1949.

Arnold, T. W. : *Preaching of Islam*, Luzac & Co., London, 1913.

Asborn, Eide : *Human Rights in World Society,* New Millennium Pub., Oslo, 1977.

Aurobindo, Sri : *The Foundations of Islamic Culture*, New York, 1973.

Berkes, N. : *Turkish Nationalism and Western Civilization,* Allen & Unwin, London, 1959.

Bevan, E. R. : *House of Seleucus*, Allen & Unwin, London, 2001.

Brett, M. : *Northern Africa : Islam and Modernization,* Allen & Unwin, London, 1973.

Briffault, Robert : *The Making of Humanity,* Islamic Book Foundation, Lahore, 1980.

Brow, John R. : *Islam, Law, and Equality in Indonesia : an Anthropology of Public,* Cambridge University Press, New Delhi, 1997.

Browne, E. G. : *History of Arabian Polity,* Cambridge, New Delhi, 1922.

Carl, Bockleman : *History of Islamic Peoples,* Oxford, New York, 2003.

Chaghatai, M. A. : *Muslim Monuments of Ahmadabad through their Inscriptions,* Deccan College Research Institute, Pune, 1942.

Crone, Patricia : *Themes in Islamic History,* Cambridge University Press, New Delhi, 2000.

Dawud, Rahbar : *God of Justice,* Mac & Jac Pub., Leiden, 1960.

Dorothy, Vaugham : *Europe and the Turks,* Oxford, New York, 2004.

Engineer, Asghar Ali : *Islam : Challenge in Twenty-first Century,* Gyan Books Pvt. Ltd., New Delhi, 2004.

——: *The Islamic State,* Vikas Publishing House, New Delhi, 1987.

Fatima, T. : *Islamic Law and Judiciary,* Deep & Deep Publications, New Delhi, 2001.

Gaborieau, M. : *The Cult of Saints among Muslims in Nepal and North India,* Cambridge University, Press, Cambridge, 1983.

Gerges : *American and Political Islam : Clash of Cultures or Claush of Interest?,* New Academic Publishers, New Delhi, 1992.

Gibb, H.A.R : *Modern Trends in Islam,* University Press, Chicago, 1950.

Gillispie, Charles Coulston : *Dictionary of Scientific Biography,* Charles Scribner's Sons, New York, 1981.

Gins Berg, M. : *Evolution and Progress,* William Heinemann Ltd., London, 1982.

Grunebaum, Gustave Edmund Von : *Modern Islam,* University Press, Los Angeles, 1952.

Gustav, E. Von Grunebaum : *Unity and Variety in Muslim World,* Oxford, New York, 2003.

Haq, M. Anwarul : *The Faith Movement of Mawlana Muhammad Ilyas*, Country Pub., London, 1972.

Harrison : *India and Pakistan : the First Fifty Years,* New Academic Publishers, New Delhi, 1992.

Hasan, Ehteshamul : *Fundamentals of Islam,* Idara Ishaat-e-Diniyat Pvt. Ltd, New Delhi, 1990.

Haykel, Bewnard : *Revival and Reform in Islam : the Legacy of Muhammad al-Shawkani,* Cambridge University Press, New Delhi, 1963.

Heyworth-Dunne : *Religious and Political Trends in Modern Egypt,* Washington,1950.

Holt, P.M. Lambton : *The Cambridge History of Islam*, Cambridge, New York, 1970.

Houtsma, T. and Others : *Encyclopaedia of Islam*, Macmillan, London, 1934.

Husaini, Waqar : *Islamic Thought,* Goodword Books Pvt. Ltd., New Delhi, 1999.

Husaini, S.A.Q : *The Pantheistic Monism of Ibn al-Arabi*, Feroz Pub., Lahore, 1970.

Ibn, Jubair : *Rihlat Ibn Jubair,* University Press, Cairo, 1955.

Inge, R. : *Philosophy of Plotinus*, MacMillan, London, 1918.

Iqbal, Muhammad : *The Development of Metaphysics in Persia*, Royal Pub., Lahore, 1964.

Irfan, Habib : *The Agrarian System of Mughal India*, Popular Prakashan, Bombay, 1963.

Jamil, Jalbi and Qazi A. Qadir : *The Changing World of Islam,* Royal Pub., Lahore, 1992.

Jotwani, Motilal : *Sufis of Sindh,* Publications Division, New Delhi, 1991.

Karnal, A. Faruqui : *Islam : Today and Tomorrow,* Deep & Deep Pub., New Delhi, 1989.

Khaduri, M. : *War and Peace in the Law of Islam,* Hopkins Press, Baltimore, 1955.

Khalifa, Abdul Hakim : *The Prophet (PBUH) and His Message,* Islamic Pub., Lahore, 1996.

Khan, Wahiduddin : *Islam Activism,* Goodword Books Pvt. Ltd., New Delhi, 1994.

Khan, Mumtaz Ali : *Planning Process and Muslims Responses to Rural Development in India,* Uppal Publishing House, New Delhi, 1996.

Khan, Qamaruddin : *The Methodology of Islamic Research,* Institute of Islamic Studies, Karachi, 1973.

Lewis, Bernard : *The Middle East and the West,* Century Pub., London, 1964.

Lyde, L.W. : *The Continent of Asia*, New Century Pub., London, 1923.

MacDonald, D.B. : *The Religious Attitude and Life in Islam*, Modern Pub., Beirut, 1965.

Malik, Jamal : *Colonization of Islam : Dissolution of Traditional Institutions in Pakistan,* Manohar Publication, New Delhi, 2000.

Mardin, Serif : *The Genesis of Young Ottoman Thought,* Princeton, New York, 1962.

McIver, R.M. and Oage, Charles H. : *The Society,* Macmillan & Co., London, 1959.

McIlwain, Charles Howard : *The Constitutionalism,* Great Seal Books, New York, 1947.

Montgomery, Watt : *The Majesty that was Islam,* Oxford, New York, 1973.

Muhammad, Asad : *Islam at the Crossroads,* Kitab Bhavan, New Delhi, 2003.

Muir, Sir William : *The Caliphate : its Rise, Decline and Fall,* Oxford, Edinburgh, 1915.

Murata, S. and Others : *The Vision of Islam,* Ashish Publishing House, New Delhi, 1991.

Nicholson, R.A. : *A Literary History of the Arabs*, Cambridge, New York, 1930.

——: *Studies in Islamic Mysticism*, Cambridge, New York, 1967.

——: *The Mysteries of Islam*, MacMillan & Co., London, 1914.

Palamer, E.H. : *Oriental Mysticism: a Treatise on the Sufistic and Unitian Theosophy of the Persians,* Lozac & Co., London, 1969.

Pickthall, M. M. : *Cultural Side of Islam,* Idara Ishaat-e-Diniyat Pvt. Ltd, New Delhi, 1999.

Poole, Lane, S. : *The Mohammedan Dynasties*, MacMillan & Co., London, 1895.

Qureshi, W. : *Selections from the Iqbal Review*, Iqbal Academy Pakistan, Lahore, 1983.

Riazul, Islam : *Indo-Persian Relations,* University of Tehran, Tehran, 1970.

Rizvi, Hasan Askari : *Islami Reassertion : a Socio Political Study,* Progressive Publishers, Lahore, 1981.

Rizvi, S.A.A. : *Religious and Intellectual History of the Muslims in Akbar's Reign*, Deep & Deep Pub., Delhi, 1975.

Rodinson, Maxime : *Islam and Capitalism,* Penguin, London,1974.

Rosenthal, E.I.J. : *Political Thought in Medieval Islam,* University Press, Cambridge, 1958.

Sabiruddin : *Muslim Husband and Wife : Right and Duties,* Kitab Bhavan, New Delhi, 2000.

Said, Edward W. : *Orientalism,* Pantheon Books, New York, 1978.

Saran, P. : *Mystical Dimensions of Islam*, Chape Hill, New York, 1975.

——: *The Religious Policy of the Mughal Emperors*, MacMillan & Co., London, 1962.

Sarton, George : *Introduction to the History of Science,* Carnegie Institute, Washington, 1950

Scarman, Leslie : *Law : the New Dimensions,* Stevens and Sons, London, 1974.

Sergeant : *Constitution of Madina,* Feroz Pub., Lahore, 1992.

Shad, Abdur Rehman : *Duties of an Imam,* Idara Ishaat-e-Diniyat Pvt. Ltd, New Delhi, 1990.

Shaheed, A. Q. A. : *Islamic System of Justice,* Kitab Bhavan, New Delhi, 1994.

Sharif, M. Raihan : *Islamic Social Framework,* Islamic Book Foundation, Dacca, 1980.

Sherwani, H.K. : *Cultural Trends in Medieval India*, Popular Prakashan, Bombay, 1968.

Shibli, Numani : *Al-Mamun,* University of Agra, Agra, 1894.

Smith, M.: *Al-Ghazzali: the Mystic*, MacMillan & Co., London, 1944.

Smith, W. Cantwell : *Islam in Modern History,* Princeton University Press, New Jersey, 1957.

Stobart, J.W. H.: *Islam and its Founders,* Uppal Publishing House, New Dlehi, 1974.

Suhrawardi, Umar : *Awarif al Maarif bin Muhammad,* Sheikh Ghulam Shahabuddin Ali & Sons, Lahore, 1964.

Syed, M. H.: *Islam and the Modern Age,* Anmol Publications, New Delhi, 2003.

Syed, Nageeb al-Attas : *Raniri and the Wajudiyyah of 17th Century Acheh,* Century Books, Singapore, 1966.

Tarachand : *Society and State in the Mughal Period,* S. Chand, & Co., Delhi, 1961.

Temple, R.C. : *The Administration of the Mughal Empire,* Feroz Pub., Karachi, 1966.

Thomas, W.F. : *Mutual Influence of Muhammedans and Hindus in India,* Cambridge, London, 1892.

Tutsch, Hans E. : *Facets of Arab Nationalism,* Wayne State University Press, Detroit, 1965.

Umaruddin, M. : *The Ethical Philosophy of al-Ghazzali,* Adam Publishers, New Delhi, 1996

Usmani, Taqi Muhammad : *An Introduction to Islamic Finance,* Idara Ishaat-e-Diniyat Pvt. Ltd., New Delhi, 1999.

Watt, M. : *Muslim Intellectual : a Study of al-Ghazzali,* Edinburgh University Press, Edinburgh, 1959.

Weeramanthy, G. G.: *Islamic Jurisprudence—an International Perspective,* Vishwa Lekha, Culcutta, 1980.

Wilfred, Seamen Blunt : *The Future of Islam,* Macmillan, London, 1991.

Yousuf, Abbas Hashmi : *Rasul (PBUH),* Adam Pub., New Delhi, 2001.

Zaehner, R.C.: *Hindu and Muslim Mysticism,* Oxford, London, 1960.

Zartman, I.W. : *Man, State and Society in the Contemporary Muslim World,* Lozac & Co., London, 1973.

Ziadah, N.A. : *Sanusiyah : a Study of a Revivalist Movement in Islam,* Poul & Co., Leiden, 1958.